Derrida and Hospitality

DERRIDA AND HOSPITALITY
THEORY AND PRACTICE

Judith Still

EDINBURGH
University Press

© Judith Still, 2010, 2013

First published in hardback by Edinburgh University Press 2010

Edinburgh University Press Ltd
22 George Square, Edinburgh EH8 9LF

www.euppublishing.com

Typeset in Sabon
by Servis Filmsetting Ltd, Stockport, Cheshire, and
printed and bound in the United States of America

A CIP record for this book is available from the British Library

ISBN 978 0 7486 4027 0 (hardback)
ISBN 978 0 7486 6963 9 (paperback)

The text for this paperback edition contains corrections
and amendments to the hardback text.

Contents

Acknowledgements

This book has been a long time in the writing and I have incurred many debts along the way. A wonderful treasure was the Leverhulme Major Research Fellowship – three years when it was almost like being a PhD student again, except a little richer and with more baggage. The generous, open-minded spirit of the Leverhulme Trust is a model for funders. It gives time to think and reflect, time to spend in libraries, and thus enabled not only this volume, but also a companion, *Enlightenment Hospitality*, to be published by the Voltaire Foundation in 2011. Over and around the time of the Leverhulme Fellowship, I spent a number of weeks in Paris libraries – which brings me to a dear friend, Elizabeth Fallaize, in whose flat I usually stayed, sometimes with other good friends or family. There are so many happy memories of fine meals and wine, good conversation, and outings to the local shops, in Paris above all, but also Oxford, London, Florida. . . wherever conferences or other work happened to take us. Elizabeth died on 6 December 2009, but her hospitality, in so many senses of the word, will not be forgotten.

Earlier versions of sections of chapters have appeared in *Contemporary French Civilisation*, *Paragraph*, *Third Text*, and *Rewriting Difference: Luce Irigaray and 'the Greeks'* (SUNY Press). I should like to thank the editors for permission to reprint. I have also given many papers based on this work over the years and would like to thank those who invited me, who attended and discussed ideas – often going on over food and drink, making academic life a pleasure. My gratitude also to an anonymous reviewer who spent some time making careful and attentive comments that were much appreciated. Thanks finally to Claire Rutherford, who gave much patient and thoughtful assistance with the preparation of the manuscript.

This book is dedicated to the Fairless family: Keith, Michael, Lily and Ruby.

Abbreviations

The following abbreviations are used throughout the book. All works are by Jacques Derrida unless otherwise indicated. Other works not listed below are referred to in the text by short titles which should, I hope, be easily recognisable, e.g. *Adieu* for Derrida's *Adieu à Emmanuel Lévinas* (Paris: Galilée, 1997), and for *Adieu to Emmanuel Levinas*, translated by Pascal-Anne Brault and Michael Naas (Stanford: Stanford University Press, 1999). All translations from the French are my own where no English edition is specified.

BEW   Luce Irigaray, *Between East and West: From Singularity to Community*, translated by Stephen Pluháček (New York: Columbia University Press, 2002)

DH   *De l'hospitalité. Anne Dufourmantelle invite Jacques Derrida à répondre* (Paris: Calmann-Lévy, 1997)

EOO   Luce Irigaray, *Entre Orient et Occident: De la singularité à la communauté* (Paris: Grasset, 1999)

HJR   'Hospitality, Justice and Responsibility: a Dialogue with Jacques Derrida', in *Questioning Ethics: Contemporary Debates in Philosophy*, edited by Richard Kearney and Mark Dooley (London and New York: Routledge, 1999).

MA   *Le monolinguisme de l'autre* (Paris: Galilée, 1996)

MO   *Monolingualism of the Other; or, The Prosthesis of the Origin*, translated by Patrick Mensah (Stanford: Stanford University Press, 1998)

OH   *Of Hospitality. Anne Dufourmantelle Invites Jacques Derrida to Respond*, translated by Rachel Bowlby (Stanford: Stanford University Press, 2000)

PA   *Politiques de l'amitié* (Paris: Galilée, 1994)

PF   *Politics of Friendship*, translated by George Collins (London and New York: Verso, 1997)

PTT   *Philosophy in a Time of Terror: Dialogues with Jürgen Habermas and Jacques Derrida*, edited by Giovanna Borradori (Chicago and London: Chicago University Press, 2003)

Introduction to the question of hospitality: ethics and politics

Once again, here as elsewhere, wherever deconstruction is at stake, it would be a matter of linking an *affirmation* (in particular a political one), *if there is any*, to the experience of the impossible, which can only be a radical experience of the *perhaps*.

(Une fois de plus, ici comme ailleurs, partout où il y va de la déconstruction, il s'agirait de lier une *affirmation* (en particulier politique), s'il y en a, à l'expérience de l'impossible, qui ne peut être qu'une expérience radicale du *peut-être*.)[1]

We all think that we know something about hospitality – it's an everyday experience. Yet it has also been a burning topic of philosophical and political debate over the last couple of decades, and my epigraph indicates the complexity of the hinge or *brisure* between politics and philosophy here. Why has hospitality recently enjoyed a renaissance? This could be related to at least three factors. The first would be recent movements of population towards, and within, an expanded Europe: what is conceived as economic immigration and also, notably, the arrival of asylum seekers and refugees. The political reaction in the nation states of the pre-expansion European community to these newcomers is often phrased in the language of (the limits of) hospitality. In France in particular there has subsequently been a significant response, not only by political scientists or sociologists, but also from the arts and philosophy, in the face of the increasing inhospitality of the French state.[2] The second factor is the existence of a growing body of powerful philosophical writing, some of which pre-dates the current wave of post-colonial xenophobia, and most of which draws on the experiences of colonialism and of the Second World War as well as the stimulus of more recent events. The third factor, which is perhaps more powerful in the US and the UK than in France, but is important throughout the world, is commercial globalisation, tourism and travel – the 'hospitality business',

1

often perceived as destroying traditional hospitality in its last known habitats.

At first glance then, hospitality may seem to be a matter of inviting friends or relatives into your home, but it is critical also to consider the traditional question of the stranger-guest, and then, beyond moral and social relations between individuals, to recognise that hospitality can be, and *is*, evoked with respect to relations between different nations or between nations and individuals of a different nationality. In this book I shall also draw attention to a textual or linguistic dimension of hospitality, a question of reading and writing, speaking and listening, calling by name and sometimes remaining silent.

The current interest in theoretical writing on hospitality relates particularly to the work of the philosopher Jacques Derrida, the main focus of this book, and beyond and through him, to another philosopher, Emmanuel Levinas.[3] Less attention has been paid to women's work in this area. This book will, however, repeatedly refer to Hélène Cixous, in explicit amicable dialogue with Derrida on hospitality (and much more besides). It will also draw on the work of Luce Irigaray – perhaps a less cosy choice in this context – but an important one if the question of sexual difference is critical to hospitality, as I believe it to be. Sexual difference features less often in discussions around hospitality than do questions of race and nationality. It is more obvious in the political debates at the turn of this century that the complex question of belonging, or being a foreigner, relates importantly to hospitality in a number of ways.

Both Cixous (born in Algeria) and Irigaray (born in Belgium) have been named French feminists by the Anglophone world, just as Derrida (born in Algeria) and Levinas (born in Lithuania) have been branded French theorists. (It is true that all enjoy, or enjoyed, French nationality.) Cixous, Derrida and Levinas are also Jewish, and all, to a greater or lesser degree, explore what that might mean in their works. What would the word 'French' signify (leaving aside the designations 'feminist' and 'theorist' for the present)? From a British or American point of view, of course, it signifies foreign, and probably strange. From a Jewish or Algerian point of view it might also suggest foreign and strange, but in a different sense. Nationality and what it means, citizenship and what it entails, national identity and what it implies – all are woven together in a complex and contested question for a Jewish thinker, such as Derrida, born in Algeria, living there throughout the Second World War (and thus temporarily deprived of French nationality), and then moving to

France to be deemed irredeemably French – at least in the Anglo-Saxon world where his work receives so much attention.[4] Cixous, like the French and Moroccan writer Tahar Ben Jelloun, writes of the hospitality of the French language (and thus brings in the complex question of 'Francophonie'), as well as of the privilege of 'passporosity', not offered to everyone. Ben Jelloun speculates that Derrida is thinking of (South) 'Mediterranean' hospitality when he writes about giving more than you know you have, since his own experience of Moroccan (Arab, Berber, Muslim, Jewish) hospitality is that the poorest peasant would borrow heavily, if need be, in order to offer a feast to his guests.[5] I should note that it is possible to be French *and* Moroccan or Tunisian (i.e. to have dual nationality), but not to be French and Algerian. The colonial histories with respect to Morocco or Tunisia (formerly Protectorates) are less embittered than the history of French relations with Algeria, a colony (or group of French 'departments') to which many French citizens emigrated. In this book the crossings between France and the Maghreb, but especially Algeria, will be a particular focus. This is one history of (in)hospitality (although already a multiple one as I have implied), but there are other French histories intertwined with other parts of Africa, with the Caribbean, the Pacific, Canada . . . And all of these could be sharply differentiated from the colonial histories of England or Spain, never mind the United States. Levinas loved the hospitality of France ('this hospitable France' ['cette France hospitalière'], as Derrida puts it in *Adieu to Emmanuel Levinas*),[6] from a different angle. However, my decision to emphasise this one (plural) element of Algeria more than others is of course because it informs so much of Derrida's and Cixous's work – and because it is one of the most significant stories (some would say the most significant) of (in)hospitality for France and for French writing.

I shall be using the terms 'colonial' and 'post-colonial', without scare quotes, in a conventional way to designate different historical periods in respect of particular nations. This is in spite of the many problems with this vocabulary that have been raised by critics, such as the more or less recognised continuation of colonisation and colonial practices in the so-called post-colonial era. I shall also sometimes use 'Francophone' as a synonym for French-speaking, or 'Anglophone' as a synonym for English-speaking, in spite of the ideological uses and misuses of these terms. My use of 'post-colonial' is not intended to suggest that an absolute break with colonialism has occurred, but rather the opposite. It is hard to find a lexis that is not imbued with history, and which has not been abused; I shall attempt to indicate intermittently some of the issues at stake in the words I deploy, and hope that my reader will fill in some of the gaps. Derrida points out that 'all culture is originarily colonial', and 'institutes itself through the unilateral imposition of some "politics" of language' – (French) revolutionary culture at least as much as monarchical culture (*MO*, 39) ('toute culture est originairement colonial [. . .et] s'institue par l'imposition unilateral de quelque "politique" de la langue' (*MA*, 68)). Nevertheless he does not wish that recognition to efface our sense of specific historical brutalities, particular military conquests, such as that of Algeria from 1830, and nor do I.

Hospitality is my subject for personal reasons, subjective, but also objective, and peculiarly appropriate to Derrida. This is the case not only because he wrote on, and spoke about, hospitality, but because his writing on hospitality is symptomatic of his work.[7] Anne Dufourmantelle's contribution to *Of Hospitality* returns repeatedly to the theme of Derrida's own 'poetic hospitality', and he himself remarks in a seminar: 'Hospitality – this is a name or an example of deconstruction'.[8] Hospitality in theory and practice relates to crossing boundaries ('Come in, come in') or thresholds (even *seuils de tolérance*[9] sometimes), including those between self and other, private and public, inside and outside, individual and collective, personal and political, emotional and rational, generous and economic – these couples that overlap each other's territory without any one exactly mapping another. For those who attack a cartoon deconstruction on the grounds that it denies material reality or promotes some kind of endless free-play, perhaps I should say again that this question of hospitality does entail paying serious attention to the question of political frontiers where admittance or refusal may even be a matter of life or death.[10] It also inevitably touches on that fundamental ethical question (since it is itself an ethical foundation) of the boundaries of the human, and how we set these up.

What is hospitality? Some definitions

> Hospitality . . . The reception or entertainment of guests or strangers with liberality and goodwill. (*Oxford English Dictionary*)

I shall keep returning throughout this book to different definitions of hospitality, host, guest, stranger, or friend; in Chapter 5, for example, I shall turn to French and bilingual dictionaries. There are two fault lines which will run throughout the discussion: (1) the fundamental nature of hospitality – whether this be the weaker claim that it is widely found or very important, or the strong claim that hospitality is foundational (of ethics, humanity, language); (2) the crucial issue of (sexual) difference and of the violence attendant upon hospitality – whether this be the weak claim that hospitality in the many source texts is constantly beset by violence, or the stronger claim that this is structural to hospitality. Hospitality, for Derrida, will be both (or neither, in a strict philosophical sense) the absolute Law of hospitality – which has caught his readers' imagination, and which I shall gloss a little in the next section – and the laws of hospitality. It is the absolute or infinite Law of hospitality which owes most to Derrida's readings of Levinas and of Levinas's tendency to make what can seem like gnomic utterances, such as: 'Le sujet est un hôte' (translated decisively, as indicated by the context, as 'The subject is a host', although the phrase could equally mean 'The subject is a guest') or 'The subject is hostage' ('Le sujet est ôtage').[11]

I shall be paying more attention than most readers of Derrida to the *laws* of hospitality, and will briefly explain here that this sense of 'laws' denotes both the political domain of laws and rights, and also a socially situated moral code. Even in his book on Levinas, largely focused on philosophical (quasi-)absolutes, Derrida writes of the relevance of hospitality to the plight of refugees today, and, for instance, to the situation in the 'Israel' of biblical times and at the time of writing (Egypt being relevant to both). Alongside, and interrupting as well as being interrupted by, these politics of hospitality, there is the moral social code which covers a physical (embodied) practice made up of a series of gestures, and of the labour these entail. These will vary in details and in stringency between cultures and times though with many common elements (bed, board, entertainment, bathing). The code will also explicitly or implicitly refer to an affective structure – if the gestures are made without the heart then there is a transgression of the code of hospitality. Finally, the code regulates the economy of hospitality – any requirement for giving without any return, *or* for reciprocity, *or* for rights and duties. It has been argued that close attention to the (unwritten) code governing the social practice between individuals can, and should, inform the formulation of laws and practices at national or international level. For Ben Jelloun, the laws of hospitality imply both rights and duties (*French Hospitality*, 37; *Hospitalité française*, 57); the problem is that immigrants are often treated as if they are guests who have only duties (43; 65) – to work hard, be polite and so on. He urges that the spirit of welcome should be enshrined in a legal framework for the reception of immigrants, in particular those from the former colonies.

The level and focus of analysis

The term 'hospitality' will be used flexibly in this book, as in Derrida's writing, to cover a wide range of relations, both macro and micro. The same will be true of associated terms such as host, guest, stranger, friend or foreigner.[12] Criticism is sometimes directed (sometimes from a materialist standpoint, sometimes with a self-righteous or politically outraged tone) at the use of any term to cover a range of positions or situations: Marxism's use of class and feminism's use of gender have surely been sufficiently (rightly) chastised for their blindnesses, such that we can now respect their areas of illumination. In this instance, 'stranger' is obviously a very general expression which could refer to wealthy American tourists in the Caribbean, to impoverished state-less refugees in New York, to a Parisian arriving in a small village in Brittany, to Roma travellers in rural Ireland, and so on. All are in very different positions, and yet all have something in common by virtue of being strangers. All could call the host community into question in some way (linguistically, economically, culturally, sexually, for instance) which might be perceived as positive or as threatening by their hosts. The host community may be welcoming or may respond violently to the interlopers, neither response excluding the other; the host (or guest) need neither be considered as homogeneous nor as free from contradiction. Thus *at one macro-level of analysis* it might be valid to consider all strangers together even though the differences between them (race, class, sex or nationality) might ultimately be more significant than the similarities. The same applies to the use of the term 'women' and its cognates (or 'men' in the sense of males). Although this term bundles together half the population of the world with vast differences cutting across it, I shall consider it an acceptable level and focus of analysis where appropriate. At *a different level of analysis* it might be more appropriate to consider only 'British working mothers' or to slice populations differently, for example considering specifically 'British workers of Afro-Caribbean origin'.[13]

Becoming a stranger can unsettle many of our class certainties or privileges and reduce us to the visible signs of sex or race; a woman or a black man who has a secure economic, social and political status 'at home' may be stripped of this when removed from their familiar context into one which is (potentially) hostile – even just trying to hail a taxi in the wrong part of town. A visibly (white) or audibly (upper-class) privileged person may also become a stranger – even King Odysseus might look like just another beggar when he most needs hospitality. In my view, no one level of analysis or one focus (sex, race, class or citizenship, for example), from the most global to the most specific, will ever be adequate on its own. Ultimately each needs to inform the other and there needs to be a degree of oscillation between levels and foci. I shall therefore assume a degree of patience on the part of my reader, so that, for example, where the terms 'stranger' or 'woman' are used I shall hope that the reader does not have an allergic reaction to the effect that: 'but not all strangers/ women are the same' (even though that is self-evidently true).

The ethics and politics of hospitality

In so far as we conventionally divide up experience between, amongst other categories, the psychic, the social and the political, the question arises as to which is the domain of hospitality. The obvious first answer is the social: the area of inter-individual relations governed by ethical or moral concerns. However, the psychic field – intra-individual or the play of the Unconscious – is also relevant to hospitality, as is the political field of relations with the State (or between States). As well as spelling out the question of hospitality within each different domain, we also need to ask what the relations are between the domains. How does the ethics of hospitality relate to the politics of hospitality for instance? Hospitality is always about crossing thresholds – perhaps between the public and private. Hospitality can begin to seem a catch-all word, and indeed the way in which it is currently evoked does give it enormous purchase: Derrida suggests that hospitality is ethics, is the condition of humanity – for *ethos* is place:

> Hospitality is culture itself and not simply one ethic amongst others. Insofar as it has to do with the *ethos*, that is, the residence, one's home, the familiar place of dwelling, inasmuch as it is a manner of being there, the manner in which we relate to ourselves and to others, to others as our own or as foreigners, *ethics is hospitality*; ethics is so thoroughly coextensive with the experience of hospitality.
>
> (L'hospitalité, c'est la culture même et ce n'est pas une éthique parmi d'autres. En tant qu'elle touche à l'*éthos*, à savoir à la demeure, au chez

soi, au lieu du séjour familier autant qu'à la manière de se rapporter à soi et aux autres, aux autres comme aux siens ou comme à des étrangers, *l'éthique est hospitalité*, elle est de part en part co-extensive à l'expérience de l'hospitalité, de quelque façon qu'on l'ouvre ou la limite.)[14]

'The ethics of hospitality' is, therefore, an odd turn of phrase, albeit a necessary one, since Levinas (*par excellence* the thinker of hospitality as ethics) argues precisely that hospitality *is* ethics. As Derrida summarises it in *Adieu*: 'For hospitality is not simply some region of ethics, let alone . . . the name of a problem in law or politics: it is ethicity itself, the whole and the principle of ethics' (50) ('Car l'hospitalité n'est pas davantage une région de l'éthique, voire . . . le nom d'un problème de droit ou de politique, elle est l'éthicité même, le tout et le principe de l'éthique' (94)). Derrida's work on Levinas (who has a tendency to define one noun by another) and hospitality suggests the *complicated* force of that copula 'is'.

Derrida is concerned that the question of the *relationship* between 'an ethics *as* hospitality' (*Adieu*, 19) ('une éthique *comme* hospitalité' (45)) and a politics of hospitality or a right to hospitality (as in Kant's cosmopolitical law) is already *canonical*. To avoid jumping to conclusions and making the easy assumption that the one will found the other (ethics will ground politics), Derrida wants a suspension, a pause for analysis in any given situation (and he mentions in *Adieu* the very different situations of Israel, the former Yugoslavia, Zaire, Rwanda, and the siege of those who took refuge in St Bernard's church in Paris). The distinction between ethics and politics (or law or rights) can be made in at least two ways: first, ethics is the domain of relations between individuals while politics is the domain of relations between States or between the individual and the State. More dramatically, ethics can be seen as the realm of metaphysical absolutes (transcendentals, or, in the case of Derrida and perhaps Levinas, 'quasi-transcendentals') while politics is the realm of pragmatic compromise and of negotiated rules (see *OH*, 135, 137; *DH*, 121), both a necessity and a perversion. Hospitality *as* ethics is unconditional and unconditioned hospitality, so immediate that nothing of the guest can be known and no invitation can be made. Instead the guest arrives, a visitation, and the host is totally open. The host, in any case, being a guest of the house, of the land. This Law of absolute welcoming, in which the other is received beyond the capacity of the self (*Adieu*, 25; 55), evoked in numerous texts by Levinas, is impossible for any nation state or any individual subject. Derrida suggests that it is perverted by (and perverts) the laws of hospitality which make hospitality possible – even as it is necessary for them, even as they are necessary for it. In my view, one of the problems with the reception of Levinas's work on hospitality is that it can encourage a self-flattering (since we readers perceive ourselves as hosts), even if guilty, focus on the host. Yet hospitality could be argued to be constructed between *hôtes* (host and guest) – you cannot have a host alone. Ben Jelloun suggests that we consider the cultural formulation that the guest fills the house; it is empty when the guest leaves. The guest satisfies the host's hunger as well as the inverse – even when the host gives unconditionally (*French Hospitality*, 2–4; *Hospitalité française*, 10–13). This need not be seen as an ethical failing on the part of the host even if it means that absolute hospitality, like any gift, as Derrida argues in *Given Time* (*Donner le temps*), is impossible on a philosophical level.[15] Equally, I shall suggest in Chapter 3 that it is hard to escape the double binds either of Aristotelian magnanimity or of the fusion implied by Montaigne's ideal of friendship.

While Levinas was deeply concerned by the political realities of life, his thinking of hospitality remains silent about the way in which the ethical promise it makes can be translated into politics. It can seem as if, for him, hospitality is infinite and unconditional or does not exist at all (*Adieu*, 48; 91). Close to the end of his moving and patient analysis of Levinas's work, written soon after Levinas's death, Derrida suggests that finally that silence or hiatus gives *us* the responsibility for a response. He writes:

> *This relation is necessary*, it must exist, it is necessary to deduce a politics and law from ethics. This deduction is necessary in order to determine the 'better' or the 'less bad,' with all the requisite quotation marks: democracy is 'better' than tyranny. Even in its 'hypocritical' nature, 'political civilization' remains 'better' than barbarism. (*Adieu*, 115)

> (*Il faut ce rapport*, il doit exister, il faut déduire une politique et un droit de l'éthique. Il faut cette déduction pour déterminer le 'meilleur' ou le 'moins mauvais', avec tous les guillemets qui s'imposent: la démocratie est 'meilleure' que la tyrannie. Jusque dans sa nature *'hypocrite'*, la *'civilisation politique'* reste 'meilleure' que la barbarie. (198))

We cannot, should not, ascribe an answer to Levinas, but we ourselves should take responsibility for analysing any particular situation and deciding what the political 'better' would be:

Ethics enjoins a politics and a law: this dependence and the direction of this conditional derivation are as irreversible as they are unconditional. But the political or juridical *content* that is thus assigned remains undetermined, still to be determined beyond knowledge, beyond all presentation, all concepts, all possible intuition, in a singular way, in the speech and the responsibility *taken* by each person, in each situation, and on the basis of an analysis that is each time unique – unique and infinite, unique but *a priori* exposed to substitution, unique and yet general, interminable in spite of the urgency of the decision. For the analysis of a context and of political motivations can have no end as soon as it includes in its calculations a limitless past and future. As always, the decision remains heterogeneous to the calculations, knowledge, science, and consciousness that nonetheless condition it. (*Adieu*, 115–16)

(L'éthique enjoint une politique et un droit; cette dépendance et la direction de cette dérivation conditionnelle sont aussi irréversibles qu'inconditionnelles. Mais le *contenu* politique ou juridique ainsi assigné demeure en revanche indéterminé, toujours à déterminer au-delà du savoir et de toute présentation, de tout concept et de toute intuition possibles, singulièrement, dans la parole et la responsabilité *prises* par chacun, dans chaque situation, et depuis une analyse chaque fois unique – unique et infinie, unique mais *a priori* exposée à la substitution, unique et pourtant générale, interminable malgré l'urgence de la décision. Car l'analyse d'un contexte et des motivations politiques n'a jamais de fin dès lors qu'elle inclut dans son calcul un passé et un avenir sans limite. Comme toujours la décision reste hétérogène au calcul, au savoir, à la science et à la conscience qui pourtant la conditionnent. (198–200))

Unfortunately, many of those who cite Derrida on hospitality focus largely on the Law of hospitality – even if they begin with a brief summary of his 'opposition' between the Law and the laws. This can lead to two problems. Some critics attempt to 'apply' the Law to a specific pragmatic situation whether in fiction or real life – since the Law is an impossible structure this is rarely successful, and to show its failure tends simply to return us to its definition since it is defined as impossible. Other critics, with or without an attempt at practical application, criticise Derrida's work for its inadequacy when faced with the political problems of today, and yet if they consider the complex interpenetration of the Law with the laws it may seem less inadequate. For instance Sara Ahmed argues that Derridean hospitality is a 'forgetting of names' and yet we need to remember.[16] Richard Kearney uses selective quotation to suggest that Derrida 'seems to preclude our need to differentiate between good and evil aliens, between benign and malign strangers, between saints and psychopaths . . . If hospitality is to remain absolutely just, all incoming others must, it seems, remain unidentifiable and undecidable'.[17] In this article unde-cidability is a problem, and Kearney seems to suggest that it would entail paralysis in decision making. However, Derrida has replied to his critics specifically on this question on a number of occasions; one example is the interview 'Hospitality, Justice and Responsibility' in *Questioning Ethics: Contemporary Debates in Philosophy*. He says:

> Far from opposing undecidability to decision, I would argue that there would be no decision, in the strong sense of the word, in ethics, in politics, no decision, and thus no responsibility, without the experience of some undecidability. If you don't experience some undecidability, then the deci-sion would simply be the application of a programme, the consequence of a premiss or of a matrix.[18]

A decision in this strong sense is indeed a form of hospitality since Derrida does not propose that it can simply emanate from a sov-ereign subject, any more than from a programme, rather it is the other within the self which interrupts the self.[19] He says of the self welcoming the other, and thus interrupting itself: 'This division is the condition of hospitality' (*HJR*, 81). But any of these criticisms of the impossible Law should also return us to the *laws* of hospitality.

The structure of hospitality

Hospitality is by definition a *structure* that regulates relations between inside and outside, and, in that sense, between private and public. Someone or ones, categorised as 'outside', as not necessarily, *by right* or legal contract, part of the 'inside', is temporarily brought within. Thus, for example, my starting point would be to say that it does not make sense to suggest that a spouse offers hospitality to his/her spouse in the home they share, or that they offer hospital-ity to their dependent children, or to an employee paid to live in. Again, as a starting point, it does not make sense to say that the State offers hospitality to its citizens, that the collectivity offers hospital-ity to itself. It is importantly *recognised* as a structure with no fixed content – this recognition did not require structuralist analysis, it is intuitively understood by practitioners. Thus, offering someone a glass of water, or a bed for the night, is *or is not* hospitality depend-ing entirely on the *relation* between the one offering and the other accepting or refusing.[20]

There are many 'grey areas', vestigial forms of hospitality.

Hospitality is a material structure but overlaid with crucial affective elements: the emotional relations associated with hospitality such as heartfelt generosity or sincere gratitude. These can spill over into situations technically not ones of hospitality. The psychology of hospitality and the rules of hospitality can be used as an analytic framework by which to judge situations that are not strictly speaking those of hospitality. For example, the relation between employer and employee is not to be judged by the laws of hospitality or of the gift in so far as each keeps strictly to the terms of their contract. (Of course the individuals concerned may also be old friends and offer hospitality to each other outside these terms.) But there are grey areas (say, if I, as Head of Department, invite a new colleague to dinner or to stay the night), in which an act *may* be regarded as somehow part of an unwritten contract or *may* be regarded as 'over and above' the necessary – as somehow spilling over (and excess is important here) into a gift relation such as hospitality.

Derrida has picked up Levinas's maxim that 'the essence of language is friendship and hospitality', which relates to the latter's claim that the relation to the exterior is not *secondary* but rather *integral* to self-consciousness:

> To posit being as Desire and as goodness is not to first isolate an I which would then tend toward a beyond. It is to affirm that to apprehend oneself from within – to produce oneself as I – is to apprehend oneself with the same gesture that already turns toward the exterior to extra-vert and to manifest – to respond for what it apprehends – to express; it is to affirm that the becoming-conscious is already language, that the essence of language is goodness, or again, that the essence of language is friendship and hospitality. (Levinas, *Totality and Infinity*, 305).

> (Poser l'être comme Désir et comme bonté, ce n'est pas isoler au préalable un moi qui tendrait ensuite vers un au-delà. C'est affirmer que se saisir de l'intérieur – se produire comme moi – c'est se saisir par le même geste qui se tourne déjà vers l'extérieur pour l'extra-verser et manifester – pour répondre de ce qu'il saisit – pour exprimer; que la prise de conscience est déjà langage; que l'essence du langage est bonté, ou encore, que l'essence du langage est amitié et hospitalité. (*Totalité et infini*, 282))

But Derrida has also posed the question whether the Law of hospitality, or unconditional hospitality, does not consist in suspending language and even the address to the other.[21] Hospitality is also a way of theorising the relation between the same and the other, the self and the stranger. Language, in the broadest sense of the term (including

12

silence), and naming in particular, is thus a critical element in hospitality. Naming concerns names given by the state, the community and individual others as well as by the self; this will be analysed in detail in Chapter 4.

Hospitality implies letting the other in to oneself, to one's own space – it is invasive of the integrity of the self, or the domain of the self. This is why it may be seen as both foundational (to be fully human is to be able to alter, to be altered – as Rousseau suggests) and dangerous. It is also perceived as potentially dangerous in economic terms because it implies sharing scarce resources, although in fact guests may be productive and may bring their gifts to the economy. The response to the potential for violence is often to impose restrictions or conditions, to limit hospitality. But limitations themselves can provoke transgression – if they are a gesture of mastery, reinforcing the imbalance of power that creates the need for hospitality in the first place. This is a key issue with (illegal) immigration. There is a historical tendency for the language and practice of hospitality to 'turn' against the guest – the focus on the generosity of the host becomes a focus on the duties of the guest, and notably the construction of the figure of the guest who not only fails to fulfil his duties (the parasite) but even betrays the host (the terrorist). Because ethics *is* hospitality:

> For this very reason, and because being at home with one oneself (*l'être-soi chez soi* – *l'ipséité même* – the other within oneself) supposes a reception or inclusion of the other which one seeks to appropriate, control, and master according to different modalities of violence, there is a history of hospitality, an always possible perversion of the law of hospitality (which can appear unconditional), and of the laws which come to limit and condition it in its inscription as a law. (Derrida, 'On Cosmopolitanism', 17)

> (Mais pour cette raison même, et parce que l'être-soi chez soi (l'ipséité même) suppose un accueil ou une inclusion de l'autre qu'on cherche à s'approprier, contrôler, maîtriser, selon différentes modalités de la violence, il y a une histoire de l'hospitalité, une perversion toujours possible de *La* loi de l'hospitalité (qui peut paraître inconditionnelle) et des lois qui viennent la limiter, la conditionner en l'inscrivant dans un droit. (*Cosmopolites*, 43))

What kind of violence are we talking about? It may take many forms. In some cases it may be metaphorical – cultural alteration experienced as violence – things will never be the same again once the barbarians are allowed in. Hospitality obviously carries the risk of creating the

13

conditions of possibility for theft, assault or murder; sometimes the violence is figured, or enacted, as rape, the most invasive of crimes. While these examples may seem to be contingent, violence stemming from a failure of hospitality or falling upon it from outside, Levinas suggests that the ethical 'face to face' or the welcoming of the other, which I (with Derrida) am calling hospitality, requires a mediating *third* party for justice to be possible (see *Adieu*, 33; 66).

Hospitality is a particular form of the gift that involves *temporary* sharing of space, and sometimes also time, bodies, food and other consumables. The issue of temporality is critical. It may be possible to imagine a permanent guest, but it is also a kind of contradiction in terms, as Kant points out. Of course Kant is writing in the eighteenth century when one of the obvious cases of guests outstaying their welcome was what we now recognise as colonialism. Diderot too was exercised by the fact that Europeans were welcomed in the New World when, he argues, they should have been turned away swiftly before they destroyed their hosts.[22] Now the heirs of Diderot's anti-colonialism may be more exercised by the tendency of former colonial powers to use 'guest' status, whether literally or metaphorically, as a means of making immigrants from former colonies feel insecure. Guest status in this context then has a complex temporality: definitionally short-term (like fish, a guest goes off after three days, as the saying goes), and yet maintained over such long periods of time that children can inherit the precarious position. A rather different issue of temporality is that of the time of hospitality; truly warm (ethical) hospitality should surely be immediate rather than pondered, and yet where political decisions are difficult the host and guest may need time for reflection and analysis.

Like the gift, hospitality is, strictly speaking (if we follow Derrida's logic), impossible in a pure form (remembering that it is importantly, inevitably, a breaking down of purity . . .), and Derrida refers to this necessary and impossible welcoming of the other – with absolutely no conditions attached – as the Law of hospitality. As an ontology that gives way to alterity in Levinas, it might evade the political pitfalls mentioned in that all subjects are *hôtes*. Yet the Law, even if perverted by the moral code which governs a political and social practice, *must* be translated in this way, translated into a version of what is one of the most common and crucial forms of generosity across a range of cultures. These rules of conduct of hospitality admit of two divergent possibilities in two critical respects: the first is that of reciprocity, on the one hand, or non-reciprocity, on the other. The second presents the divergent possibilities of the relation with your peer (between friends or *within* a community), on the one hand, or with the other (the stranger in the broadest sense: the other sex, the one who does not speak or look as you do . . .), on the other hand.

Reciprocity and non-reciprocity

Derrida's hyperbolical Law of hospitality lies beyond debt, exchange or economy and thus even reciprocity, yet its relation to the laws is simultaneously one of mutual perversion and one of mutual need. As Derrida writes: 'It wouldn't be effectively unconditional, the law, if it didn't *have to become* effective, concrete, determined, if that were not its being as having-to-be' (*OH*, 79) ('Elle ne serait pas effective-ment inconditionnelle, la loi, si elle ne devait pas devenir effective, concrète, déterminée, si tel n'était pas son être comme devoir-être' (*DH*, 75)). The distinction between this unconditional hospitality and the laws of hospitality is too easily assumed as an absolute fixed opposition with insufficient attention paid to the *ways in which* each interrupts the other. We read quickly, and we cut bits out. Quotations are taken like keepsakes or trophies – even fetishes which we endow with, or which assume, a life of their own. Rousseau's earlier take on this relationship between a Law and laws (drawing on classi-cal codes of beneficence) is the magical element in the benefaction when a benefactor momentarily believes that s/he will get no return, perhaps not even *reconnaissance*. This *enables* the beneficiary to rec-ognise the benefactor as a benefactor, rather than, say, an employer or a merchant who has tricked him/her into a contractual exchange, and thus to feel gratitude, and hence be on the way to reciprocating. There is thus reciprocity of intention (or sentiment) if not material reciprocity. So in one sense non-reciprocity enables reciprocity even as, in another sense, it perverts it.

Hospitality between individuals (governed by the code) is often theorised (and experienced), on the one hand, as a structure of *reciprocity* and, on the other, as an exchange *between peers*, although *non-reciprocity* and *inequality* are at least as important. (I should note that the pairings are not inevitable.) The linguist Emile Benveniste, in his great work on the vocabulary of Indo-European institutions, claims that reciprocity is inscribed at the very origin of hospitality. He divides the base word (*hospes*) into *hostis* and *potis*. *Potis* takes us in the direction of the power exercised by the master of the house.[23] *Hostis* means the stranger who has equal rights *before* it

15

means enemy (and the two senses lead to different analyses of hospitality). Hospitality towards a stranger who has equal rights would be an attenuated form of *potlatch*, based on the idea that a man is linked to another by the obligation to return any gift. The code of hospitality prescribes gratitude and at least the desire to reciprocate on the part of the guest. The magic of the gift for the ethnographer Marcel Mauss lies in the intimate bond between prestation and counter-prestation. Nevertheless, we should not be too hasty in contenting ourselves with the assertion that the laws of hospitality (operative in everyday or commonplace hospitality) are economic. The old chestnut of the economic versus altruism is too familiar. *If* we recognise an economic element throughout, it is nonetheless important to maintain differentiation within the economic (rather than flattening out). Each of the following categories has many gradations within it:

1. *Simple commerce* could be understood as the exchange of what is agreed to be equal with no temporal lag. You eat dinner in a restaurant and pay immediately after the meal. The penalties of not swiftly returning the agreed equivalent are legally enforced.

2. *More complex commerce* such as a loan structure (where penalties are legally enforced) might mean that you eat a meal in a commercial setting where there is an agreed time lag before payment (for instance, eating dinner in the hotel in which you are staying). Loss leaders are a feature of more complicated commerce without explicitly agreed equivalents, say, you eat 'free' snacks in a shop, or dinner in a casino, where it is anticipated you will spend, or 'lose', considerable sums of money – here there is no legal penalty if you do not return an equivalent for what was offered as complimentary. Commerce can mimic non-commercial structures; even in (1) above, mints may arrive with the bill, you may be offered a free 'digestif'. Why? Is it because it is good business in the sense that I (the vendor) make more money because of the positive affective charge for you, the customer, and/or for my workers in the hospitality industry who therefore work better for their wages? And/or it is a preferred, more civilised way of doing business: there is a positive affective charge for the vendor, who feels more human. A typically ambiguous example would be the 2006 advertisement put out by the Cyprus Tourist Office, showing a buxom woman with outstretched arms offering bread, with a bowl of fruit on the table in front of her. Under the headline 'Love Cyprus', it has the following rubric 'I invite you to an

16

island where people's hospitality shines all year long, day and night. Experience the warmth of "kaplaste", the local invitation for a delicious meal, a drink, a simple conversation.' I shall argue that it is far from irrelevant to the question of hospitality that the invitation is proffered, or rather *mediated*, by an attractive woman, one who is as maternal as she is sensual. (Youthful sex selling holidays involves a different structure, a different appeal.)

3. *Direct social exchange.* I invite you to dinner – you will probably invite me back after an appropriate time lag. There are many differences: are we colleagues, friends or kin? Are we roughly equals or is there, say, a significant age or professional seniority gap? What are the penalties for not reciprocating? (And what is the relationship between the 'I' who invites and those who perform the material and emotional labour of hospitality? To whom should you reciprocate? The host 'I', the host couple, the host family . . . If 'you' are plural then who is responsible for reciprocating?)

4. *Indirect social exchange.* I invite you to dinner – you eventually invite someone else equivalent to dinner and/or someone else in a similar situation eventually invites me to dinner (for example, in a modern academic context, as opposed to traditions amongst nomads, guest speakers or external examiners may be invited to dine in my home rather than in a restaurant). Here there is a kind of circle, but with significant possible disjunctions over time, space, and the individuals concerned. Are there any penalties for the guest who does not reciprocate; what are the benefits for the host?

5. *Invitation without reciprocity.* You are perceived as 'without' means (home, money, contacts) and I invite you to dinner without the expectation that you will eventually do the equivalent either for me or someone else or that I will ever be in your situation where someone could do the same for me. Here there could still be different kinds of payback: whether on the religious or charity model (reward in heaven), or in terms of affective or psychological reward (I feel good). One key element of differentiation: is there an imaginative recognition of similarity (as in some Enlightenment theories of pity)? I *could* be in your position even if it is not likely; if I ever were in your situation then I would want to be treated thus. Hence the possibility of common 'humanity' as similarity alongside difference. Or is the structure rather one of assertion/affirmation of fixed hierarchical difference: I am defined

by my means (I would not be 'I' if I were without), and you are without means, not (quite) a man?

6. *Hospitality to animals.* (This will form the meat of Chapter 6.) I give dinner to my dog. I put seed out for wild birds. Affective payback and services rendered are both possibilities, but does that sum it up? What is the structure in terms of recognition of similarity and difference on the part of host and guest? What are the boundaries?

7. *Absolute hospitality?* The door is open – even, there is no door, but rather perfect openness. Anything, however alien, can come in and take what it likes, do as it likes. Who and what is at risk?

Derrida has coined the portmanteau term 'hostipitality'. Sometimes (*contra* Levinas) social commentators take hostility to be a relationship *prior* to hospitality (a relationship that hospitality perhaps seeks to mitigate, but may work to exacerbate), for instance in the notion that traditional hospitality, the offer of salt, holds enmity in suspense. However, the delicate confusion of economic and what we may want to believe are non-economic relationships can breed hostility where none previously existed, and Derrida's intermingling of enmity and generosity in his *mot-valise* points up that complexity or con-fusion.

Cultural difference

Hospitality can (and does) cement the bond between those who are broadly culturally similar – the homosocial structure (containing difference, thus violence and desire) – but may also be used, where *hostes* becomes enemy rather than equal, to ward off the danger of violence (and desire) between those who are different. Cultural difference is here taken to include differences of class, race, nationality, sexuality, generation . . . The French term *l'étranger* (as in Camus's novel of the same name) denotes a stranger *and* a foreigner, a problem for translators, as Rachel Bowlby points out in her Translator's Note to *Of Hospitality* (*OH*, ix). We should remember the French Republican tendency to universalism, and against identity politics or *communautarismes*; there is resistance even to the keeping of statistics on ethnicity. This is a different paradigm to the one fostered by 'equal opportunities' in the UK or the melting pot of the USA, which still allow hyphenated identities more happily than France does. If we ask 'Who is the stranger?' Julia Kristeva responds in terms of nationality.[24] Here I prefer Derrida's broad definition:

In the broad sense, the language in which the foreigner is addressed or in which he is heard, if he is, is the ensemble of culture, it is the values, the norms, the meanings that inhabit the language . . . A passing remark: without speaking the same national language, someone can be less 'foreign' to me if he shares a culture with me, for instance, a way of life linked to a degree of wealth, etc., than some fellow citizen or compatriot who belongs to what used to be called (but this language shouldn't be abandoned too quickly, even if it does demand critical vigilance) another 'social class'. As Levinas says from another point of view, language *is* hospitality. Nevertheless, we have come to wonder whether absolute, hyperbolical, unconditional hospitality doesn't consist in suspending language, a particular determinate language, and even the address to the other. (*OH*, 133, 135)

(Au sens large, la langue, celle dans laquelle on s'adresse à l'étranger ou dans laquelle on l'entend, si on l'entend, c'est l'ensemble de la culture, ce sont les valeurs, les normes, les significations qui habitent la langue. . . . Soit dit au passage: sans parler la même langue nationale, quelqu'un peut m'être moins 'étranger' s'il partage avec moi une culture, par exemple un mode de vie lié à une certaine richesse, etc., que tel concitoyen ou com-patriote apppartenant à ce qu'on appelait hier (mais il ne faut pas aban-donner trop vite ce langage, même s'il appelle une vigilance critique) une autre 'classe sociale'. . . . Comme le dit d'un autre point de vue Lévinas, le langage *est* hospitalité. Il nous est toutefois arrivé de nous demander si l'hospitalité absolue, hyperbolique, inconditionnelle, ne consiste pas à suspendre le langage, un certain langage déterminé, et même l'adresse à l'autre. (*DH*, 117, 119))

The question of language is critical – forcing the other to speak my language even as they ask for asylum is hardly hospitable. The reader may see immediately how the question of hospitality to *étrangers* (foreigners) relates to language. It also impinges on the question of education – do we offer education only to those who speak the same language that we do? Education is of course a *route* to learning to speak the same language, yet a route that some systems bar to those who are not already insiders via a range of direct and indirect forms of selection. This differentiation through language also impacts on justice in a narrower sense, as many have demonstrated – from Socrates on trial, who declares himself like a foreigner with respect to the language but without the rights of a foreigner (*xenos*) (see *OH*, 15; *DH*, 21), to Barthes's account of the notorious trial of Gaston Dominici in 1950s France.[25] Dominici was a peasant farmer convicted of triple murder in a case where there was little material evidence and so the prosecution relied heavily on psychology. There were numerous misunderstandings, written up in the press reports, between the old farmer and the representatives of the legal apparatus because their languages were mutually impenetrable. Barthes comments:

> Naturally, everyone pretends to believe that it is the official language which is common sense, that of Dominici being only one of its ethnological varieties, picturesque in its poverty. And yet, this language of the president [Presiding Judge of the Assizes] is just as peculiar, laden as it is with unreal clichés; it is a language for school essays . . . These are in actual fact two particular uses of language which confront each other. But one of them has honours, law and force on its side. (*Mythologies*, 50)

> (Naturellement tout le monde feint de croire que c'est le langage officiel qui est de sens commun, celui de Dominici n'étant qu'une variété ethnologiqe, pittoresque par son indigence. Pourtant ce langage présidentiel est tout aussi particulier, chargé de clichés irréels, langage de rédaction scolaire . . . Ce sont tout simplement deux particularités qui s'affrontent. Mais l'un a les honneurs, la loi, la force pour soi. (*Mythologies*, 52))

The question of the name, and the possible policing of names, is also important in this context, and raises a number of general issues relating to identity, legitimacy, inheritance, signature and indeed plagiarism (see Chapter 4).

Codes of hospitality suggest that the host will entertain the (usually his) guest, and an unwritten contract guards them both from harm. However, the possibility of a breakdown may not be contingent but structural, lying in the relation or non-relation between the Law and the laws as well as in the specificies of personal, sexual and socio-political contingencies such as in the cases cited above. Difference exists in a difficult relationship with inequality. Justice is notoriously fragile between non-equals; generosity is equally vulnerable, and what should be a dynamic, at least temporary, diminishing of inequality may instead work to fossilise if not increase it. The breakdown of hospitality (which is a cementing of human interdependency) can then easily spiral into terror (the rejection of mutual dependency to the point of mass destruction). If we can work through some of these issues – either by closer attention to the code and practice of hospitality and/or by the evocation of the superabundant Law of hospitality – we are still left, I would suggest, with the importance of sexual difference. That remainder may be uncannily important for the whole.

Sexual difference

While Derrida asserts the importance of sexual difference in the structure of hospitality, it is either disembodied Levinasian hospitality, or hospitality in relation to racial, ethnic or cultural difference, that has captured the imagination of most interlocutors. The importance of sexual difference in relation to hospitality includes historical and material questions, and also requires consideration of an *imaginary* of the female body (and Luce Irigaray's works will help in analysing this). Via Cixous, as well as Derrida, I shall also be considering more or less hospitable writing economies which are named masculine or feminine.

While much will be made of the reversibility of the French term *hôte* in this book, the reader should bear in mind that it is not so true for women as for men since *hôte*, as host (but not as guest), splits into two with the feminine form *hôtesse*. Host and guest are traditionally marked as masculine; hostess is a generally denigrated term in both French and English. It has overtones that are commercial, including the commercialisation of sex. In dictionary definitions 'hostess' has a range of professional meanings (such as air-hostess) that tend to take precedence over any equivalence to host – and this is to some extent true of *l'hôtesse*. If not commercial, the hostess implies hospitality offered by the master of the house,[26] the true host, *by means of* his woman, the hostess. Her authority is thus only a delegated one, and she is an intermediary, her body (and mental and emotional faculties) a means for two or more men to communicate and bond.

I shall be arguing in Chapter 3, however, that there is an erotic and maternal quality to hospitality even as it is dispensed by *le maître de céans* (as Derrida calls him, after Pierre Klossowski). The female body is uniquely hospitable, and that erotic, reproductive and nourishing specificity is a potent source of fantasy and acts inspired by it. At the same time that hospitable specificity of the female body (for example, the fact that women carry children) implies male interest in inheritance, both the genetic inheritance and the legitimate (or illegitimate) transmission of names and property. That interest entails policing, and also gives an opportunity for transgression. Policing and transgression come together in the culture and economy of sexual violence. Susan Brownmiller has controversially argued that rape is structurally intrinsic to patriarchy's economy of sexual difference with its virgin-mothers who are taught that they must be protected, and its whores (who may be the same women in a different

21

context).[27] In Chapter 5 in particular, I shall return to the question of the violence attendant upon hospitality in relation to the three great monotheistic religions that Derrida brings together (following a certain tradition) as Abrahamic. All three prize hospitality as fundamental, but all three also stage the control of (women's) bodies as critical to social order. The Old Testament stories of Lot and of the Levite of Ephraim are emblematic in this respect. Greek tales of *rapt* (such as Paris' seizing of Helen) and Roman stories of rape (such as Tarquin's violation of Lucretia), specifically in the context of hospitality, are also retold and reinterpreted in many different ages and contexts to be suffused with the meanings of the day. The masculine economy of hospitality (as opposed to the masculine economy more often known as the market) is a patriarchal one – aristocratic or pastoral. It assumes power even as it may choose temporarily to abdicate it. The body is the first sphere of hospitality, before the home, the city, the nation state or the cosmos, and inhospitality is often narrativised as rape. Without analysing these matters in any detail in the work published so far, Derrida often uses the term *viol*, sometimes translated as 'rape' and sometimes as 'violation', for intrusion into the domestic space of hospitality – for example by the State, which makes the possibility of surveillance and punishment a condition of its protection of the *chez-soi* from other invaders (see *OH*, 65; *DH*, 61).

While Irigaray's comments on hospitality have been little studied, her work is critical to the re-insertion of the question of sexual difference more forcefully into the debate.[28] She takes an uncompromising stand on the distinct nature of men and women, and opposes any apparent solution to the oppression of women that involves embracing sexual sameness (and it is, she argues, precisely an imaginary of sexual sameness that allows oppressive structures of *opposition* between men and women as much as complementarity or identity).[29] This makes her work important to engage with when we consider that men and women have historically had (and, I would argue, continue to have) very different experiences of hospitality both as hosts (more often hostesses) and as guests. There are two other reasons for evoking Irigaray's writing; the first is that I should like to put forward the argument that it is a particular imaginary of the female body and of the feminine that marks our cultural understanding of hospitality in many ways, and that relates both to our desire for the experience of hospitality and to our sometimes violent reaction against it. The second is that when we turn to questions of ethnic,

national or cultural difference, Irigaray's work continues to be interesting as a strong statement in favour of celebrating cultures of difference and encouraging dialogue between differences, yet questioning
the often hierarchical sexed structure of cultural groups and, most of
all, challenging, in affirming, ourselves.[30]

It is unsurprising that, particularly in the current macrocosmic
political situation, we are concerned by issues of ethnicity and migration. However, Irigaray alerts us to the danger that patriarchy sub-
sumes an apparent plurality of 'races' into a kind of uniformity; she
argues that only attention to micro- and macro-cosmic sexual difference can prevent the slide into sameness that is characteristic of our
mono-culture.[31] Paying due care to the real difference that is closest
to us and attempting to build what she terms a culture of two subjects, will, she argues, improve other kinds of relations in difference,
including cultural difference.

> Certain historical factors might seem more important to us than treating
> the difference of the sexes: those tied to the migrations of our age, for
> example. Now these migrations risk carrying us off toward an increas-
> ingly disturbing neutralization and phantomization of the environment
> and of the individual, accompanied by an authoritarian guardianship that
> surrounds or integrates the multiple and the foreigner. The recent pater-
> nalist era claims to be plural, but it is a plural often remaining inside the
> closure of the patriarchal world.
>
> (Certains facteurs historiques peuvent nous sembler plus importants
> que le traitement de la différence des sexes: ceux liés aux migrations de
> notre époque, par exemple. Or celles-ci risquent de nous entraîner vers
> une neutralisation et une fantomatisation de plus en plus inquiétantes de
> l'environnement et de l'individu, s'accompagnant de tutelles autoritaires
> pour encadrer ou intégrer le multiple et l'étranger. La dernière époque
> paternaliste se dit au pluriel, mais un pluriel restant souvent à l'intérieur
> de la clôture du monde patriarcal.)[32]

While Derrida is widely cited in work on hospitality, and reference is often made to Levinas, women writers such as Cixous
or Irigaray are rarely mentioned – they are kept in the ghetto of
feminism or women's studies, more easily to be dismissed. Irigaray
is at least recognised as a *feminist philosopher*, in particular outside
France thanks to the translation of *Speculum* in 1985, although we
should not underestimate the attacks she has suffered from feminists
or the degree to which she has been ignored by mainstream (and
male-dominated) philosophy.[33] Cixous, above all a creative writer,
is a more complicated case, and even less happy to be placed within

what she would understand as feminism. She constantly reminds her reader of sexual difference, but just as constantly unsettles our certainties about it. She first came to the attention of an Anglophone public with 'The Laugh of the Medusa', published in English relatively early (1976), and then *The Newly Born Woman*, not translated until the mid eighties.[34] These texts, perhaps unfortunately, gained her a reputation as a proponent of *écriture féminine*, a term sometimes mistranslated either literally or conceptually as women's writing. Feminists in university departments of literature in the USA and the UK had made it one of their priorities, at least from the 1970s onwards, to retrieve from obscurity a number of women writers who had been consigned by a masculine critical orthodoxy, from the nineteenth century onwards, to the dustbin of history. Feminist academics sought both to reappraise women writers from the earliest periods (and to get them republished) and to make sure that contemporary women writers were treated with the seriousness they deserve. This important and difficult project, swiftly tagged 'political correctness' the better to belittle it, contributed to a certain confusion with regard to Cixous's rather different questioning of established orthodoxies. All the same, I should note that the rediscovery of 'women's writing' could certainly be related to hospitality – of the institution, the canon, the critical orthodoxy, pedagogic practices – even though not the same project as Cixous's.

'Writing the body' is less of a 'mistranslation' of *écriture féminine* although it immediately begs the question 'whose body?' In Chapter 6 I shall consider how the question is posed not only to the opposition between the masculine bodily economy of scarcity and feminine economies of abundance, but also to the boundary between human and animal. But even the sexed opposition (which Cixous's critics seem so sure about) might need to be questioned: a writing economy could be across male and female. When read in this way, Cixous would part company with Irigaray's certainties. Peggy Kamuf carefully (seriously *and* lightly) analyses some famous 'vertiginous' passages in Cixous, showing how her phrase 'writing is woman's' assigns each term's meaning to the other, but then 'advances through *contradiction*' ('To Give Place', 77).[35] Later in the same passage Kamuf refers to, Cixous writes: 'Femininity and bisexuality go together . . . It is much harder for the man to let himself be traversed by some other'; Kamuf's analysis shows how this claim in fact unsettles any identity, or even non-identity, of both the term *femininity* and the term *man*. Yet it never settles into a would-be neutrality or neuter. Cixous's

24

openness is a particular kind of hospitality in Derrida's terms. The body described in Cixous's 'Coming to Writing', with its breath and blood,[36] is a hospitable body, characterised by 'a having without limits, without restrictions, but without any "deposit," a having that doesn't withhold or possess, a having-love that sustains itself with loving, in the blood-rapport' ('Coming to Writing', 4) ('Un avoir sans limites, sans restriction; mais sans aucun "dépôt", un avoir qui ne détient pas, aui ne possède pas, l'avoir-amour, celui qui se soutient d'aimer, dans le sang-rapport.' ('La Venue à l'écriture', 12)).

While Cixous's body is named *feminine* with all the contradictions that supposes, it also has qualities related to ethnicity or to the lack of a national identity, and her work has considerable relevance to hospitality in relation to cultural or national difference. Cixous and Irigaray both experience exile and (in)hospitality in different ways. Cixous names herself Jewoman (*juifemme*); and the reader should note that the word insists on sexual as well as cultural difference in a way that would be read blindly in the normal French gendering of Jew ('juif') as Jewish woman ('juive'). She is 'not at home' (writing) in French; she needed to knock before entering:

> Everything in me joined forces to forbid me to write: History, my story, my origin, my sex. Everything that constituted my social and cultural self. To begin with the necessary, which I lacked, the material that writing is formed of and extracted from: language. You want – to Write? In what language? Property, rights, had always policed me: I learned to speak French in a garden from which I was on the verge of expulsion for being a Jew. I was of the race of Paradise-losers. Write French? With what right? Show us your credentials! What's the pass-word? Cross yourself! Put out your hands, let's see those paws! What kind of nose is that?
>
> I said 'write French.' One writes *in*. Penetration. Door. Knock before entering. Strictly forbidden.
>
> 'You are not from here. You are not at home here. Usurper!'
> 'It's true. No right. Only love.' ('Coming to Writing', 12–13)

(Tout de moi se liguait pour m'interdire l'écriture: l'Histoire, mon histoire, mon origine, mon genre. Tout ce qui constituait mon moi social, culturel. A commencer par le nécessaire, qui me faisait défaut, la matière dans laquelle l'écriture se taille, d'où elle s'arrache: la langue. Tu veux – Ecrire? Dans laquelle langue? La propriété, le droit me gendarmaient depuis toujours: j'ai appris à parler français dans un jardin d'où j'étais sur le point d'être expulsée parce que juive. J'étais de la race des perdeurs de paradis. Ecrire français? De quel droit? Monte-nous tes lettres de créance, dis-nous les mots de passe, signe-toi, fais voir tes mains, montre tes pattes, qu'est-ce que c'est que ce nez-là?

J'ai dit 'écrire français'. On écrit *en*. Pénétration. Porte. Frappez avant d'entrer. Formellement interdit.

  – Tu n'es pas d'ici. Tu n'es pas chez toi ici. Usurpatrice!
  – C'est vrai. Pas de droit. Seulement de l'amour. ('La Venue à l'écriture', 20))

She is in some respects a guest and in other respects treated inhospitably as an usurper, and yet there is also love – if only for/in language. Her love for what she elsewhere calls the *hospitable* French language is as complicated as any other kind of love: some critics would see her writing style as an assault on the spirit and form of this (neither quite maternal nor paternal) tongue.[37] Others would see her (and vision is important here) as replenishing the language, and even, ironically, as defending it against the most invasive cultural threat: 'An infectious homonymy would be the guardian . . . of a French language whose idiom could not be better protected against translation's blood-transfusion than by untranslatable homonymy' ('Une homonymie contagieuse sera la gardienne . . . d'une langue française dont l'idiome ne saurait être mieux protégé contre l'ex-sanguino-transfusion de la traduction que par l'intraduisible homonymie').[38]

Writing the body could be set against two traditional kinds of writing: writing the mind, which might involve the transmission (as clearly and transparently as possible) of ideas; and writing the world, which might involve the recording or analysis of facts. Realist fiction would then be an imitation of the scientific writing the world, where verisimilitude takes the place of falsifiability as a criterion of judgement. Writing the body, on the other hand, would operate at a different level of hospitality – closer to the body crossed by drives or the body of the unconscious where the principle of non-contradiction does not apply. This possibility, of the co-existence of what might seem to a more 'flat-footed' reader to be mutually exclusive meanings, is crucial in Cixous's writing. And the French language lends itself to a generic gender play, for example, *elle* can refer to he/him (say, referring back to *la personne*) or it (say, referring back to *la mer*) as well as she/her as a translator might expect. Derrida comments: 'in her general poetics, each genre remains itself, at home, while offering hospitality generously to the other genre, to the other in any genre that arrives as a parasite, as a ghost or to take its host hostage, always following the same topodynamics of the smallest being bigger than the biggest' ('Dans sa poétique générale, chaque genre reste lui-même, chez lui, tout en offrant une hospitalité généreuse à l'autre genre, à l'autre en tout genre qui vient le parasiter, le hanter ou tenir son hôte en otage, toujours selon la même topody- namique du plus petit plus grand que le plus grand') (*Genèses*, 28). This formulation hints that genre could be understood in more than one sense – and this is quickly made explicit: 'Grafting, hybridisa- tion, migration, genetic mutation multiplies and cancels at once genre and gender differences, literary differences and sexual differ- ences' ('La greffe, l'hybridation, la migration, la mutation génétique multiplie et annule à la fois la difference du genre et du *gender,* les différences littéraires et les différences sexuelles') (*Genèses*, 28–9). The texts signed Derrida also of course work at the border between genres; as he comments on *The Post Card*, which some critics have tried to place *within* literature:

> I think it is an attempt to blur the borders between literature and phi- losophy, and to blur the borders in the name of hospitality – that is what hospitality does, blur the border – by writing some sentences, some undecidable sentences, which put in question the limits of what one calls philosophy, science, literature. I try to do this performatively, so to speak. This gesture, to the extent that it is successful, does not belong to philoso- phy, to literature, nor to any genre. (*HJR*, 73)

Looking back at hospitality

Hospitality is a topic that has consistently been considered important over long periods of time, and over wide tracts of the globe. Our con- viction of its *universality* is indeed critical to our understanding of its structure. Nevertheless, like most other forms of human relationship, its significance varies to some extent over time and space. Different cultures have different modes of hospitality, and, as we look to the future, we should think about constructing new modes suitable to a new historical moment. One of the things that interests me about our formal and informal discussions of hospitality is their *intertextual quality* – how elements from a range of earlier or otherwise distant theories and practices are introduced and transformed in the present. How we are haunted by the past, and how we fashion those ghosts in the present. It is hard to find a starting point where discourse about hospitality does not lament a decline in standards. It may ring true when Ben Jelloun writes:

> Some people are more hospitable than others: generally speaking, they are those who have remained close to the soil and live in the wide open

spaces, even if they are poor. The industrialized countries, obedient to a cold rationality, have had to unlearn hospitality. Time is precious and space limited. There's a shortage of accessibility, or in other words of generosity and freedom, because everything is calculated and measured. Doors are shut, and so are hearts. (*French Hospitality*, 37)

(Certains peuples sont plus hospitaliers que d'autres: généralement ceux restés plus près de la terre et qui vivent dans les grands espaces, même pauvres. Les pays industrialisés, obéissant à une rationalité froide, ont dû désapprendre l'hospitalité. Le temps est précieux; l'espace, limité. Il y règne un manque de disponibilité, c'est-à-dire de générosité et de liberté, car tout est calculé, tout est mesuré. Les portes se ferment. Les coeurs aussi. (*Hospitalité française*, 57))

However, we can find similar words in pre-industrial France; in the *Encyclopédie*, for example, D. J. (the Chevalier de Jaucourt) writes in his entry for 'Hospitality':

We are no longer familiar with that fine bond of *hospitality*, and must admit that time has brought about such great changes amongst different peoples and above all amongst ourselves, that we are much less bound by the respectable and holy laws of that duty than the ancients were. . . . The spirit of commerce, while uniting all nations, has broken the links of beneficence between individuals; it has done much good and much evil; it has produced countless commodities, more extensive knowledge of things and people, easy access to luxury and love of self-interest and financial gain. That love has taken the place of the secret movements of nature, which used to bind men together with tender and touching attachments. Wealthy travellers have gained the enjoyment of all the pleasures of the countries they visit, joined with the polite welcome given to them in proportion to the amount they spend. They are viewed with pleasure, and without attachment, like those rivers which fertilize to some extent the lands through which they pass.

(Nous ne connaissons plus ce beau lien de l'*hospitalité*, et l'on doit convenir que les temps ont produit de si grands changements parmi les peuples et surtout parmi nous, que nous sommes beaucoup moins obligés aux lois saintes et respectables de ce devoir, que ne l'étaient les anciens . . . L'esprit de commerce, en unissant toutes les nations, a rompu les chaînons de bienfaisance des particuliers; il a fait beaucoup de bien et de mal; il a produit des commodités sans nombre, des connaissances plus étendues, un luxe facile, et l'amour de l'intérêt. Cet amour a pris la place des mouvements secrets de la nature, qui liaient autrefois les hommes par des nœuds tendres et touchants. Les gens riches ont gagné dans leurs voyages, la jouissance de tous les agréments du pays où ils se rendent, jointe à l'accueil poli qu'on leur accorde à proportion de leur dépense. On les voit avec plaisir, et sans attachement, comme ces fleuves qui fertilisent plus ou moins les terres par lesquelles ils passent. (316))[39]

The debate on hospitality in France today draws on a multitude of textual strands, including Arab hospitality, the mythical political hospitality of the French Revolution, and pastoral traditions. Of course, travellers' tales of any place perceived as 'simpler' than our own may tell of relatively abundant hospitality; the ethnographer Daphne Patai phrases the anthropologist's dilemma when she tells of the offer of chocolate cake from a Brazilian woman who cannot afford it, but whose offer cannot be refused.[40] But North African traditions of hospitality (sometimes termed Mediterranean traditions) are particularly relevant in the light of French colonial history and consequent patterns of immigration into France. In this book the additional strands on which I shall focus are those of 'Homeric hospitality', biblical hospitality (which feeds into the Islamic tradition of course), and the classical discourse of friendship (Chapters 2 and 3).

I should like to say a little more here about the French context, and why the language of hospitality might be appropriate for the public and political domain in France in a way that is less obvious elsewhere. France can and does (like other nations) draw on many traditions to inform its deployment of the language of hospitality. I am using the term 'tradition' as a 'portmanteau' to cover historical reality, cultural memory, myth and so on. Examples of diverse traditions important for hospitality include tales of the Greeks, Romans, Arabs, and the Hebrews as narrated in the Bible, distant ethnographic reports and local rural practices (including notably Corsica). Any of these will of course be understood and experienced differently by different sections of the community. Here I shall briefly focus on the myth of the Revolution to ask what is at stake in the language of hospitality – if we assume that language is not separable from reality, a veil to be lifted, but rather shapes and is shaped by *ethos*.

Hospitality is a key element of the rhetoric, and sometimes the practice, of the French Revolution; and there is a myth of revolutionary hospitality that still exercises a powerful influence today. In Ben Jelloun's biting critique of 'French hospitality' towards immigrants cited above, he still admires the French reception of political refugees which stands out relative to other European countries and which 'remains true to the principles of the 1789 Revolution' (*French Hospitality*, 38) ('reste fidèle aux principes de la Révolution de 1789' (*Hospitalité française*, 59)). The most influential analysis

29

of this that I have come across is by Sophie Wahnich.[41] Like much of revolutionary culture, there is a will to originality (the trope of the *tabula rasa* evident in 'Year 0' rhetoric) in the discourse of openness to strangers, at the same time as the evident need to select from (the best of) the past. There is a process of self construction through narratives. Hospitality is, in any period at any time, evoked as something that has declined relative to some past moment. However, in the early days of the Revolution there is a political determination to reinvent it as asylum from tyranny and oppression. Thus Condorcet, in December 1791, can produce an Address to be sent to foreign peoples assuring them that 'the principle of hospitality' will not be put in question by war. Revolution is to be universalised, and the right to equality and freedom should be universal; deserters from the armies of those who attack France can become citizens after three years. The tone of this appeal is notably different from the one taken by politicians in 1950s France or England, who encouraged immigration for economic reasons – because foreigners' labour power was *needed*. As Anne Gotman points out in *Le sens de l'hospitalité*, the story in 1791 is that the state has something to *bestow* (rights); of course that could be reinterpreted as revolutionary evangelism, even imperialism, yet perhaps we should not be too hasty to judge it so.[42]

However, *la nation hospitalière* still had to think about 'security', and foreigners in fact quickly became assimilated into the category of spies or counter-revolutionaries. The generous and expansive state, that wishes to extend universal rights not dependent on birthplace, becomes the nation state that defines itself *against* others.[43] Again Wahnich traces this trajectory: she follows the fates of certain famous foreigners in France such as Anacharsis Cloots, who points out what a barbarous expression the very word 'étranger' is. By 6 September 1793 a decree suspends public hospitality and expels foreigners born in those countries at war with France. Foreigners have to be policed so that the State can turn out 'those who betray the hospitable nation that protects them' (cited in Wahnich, *L'Impossible Citoyen*, 31). Even long-term residents have to apply for a *certificat d'hospitalité* (though the plan to make them wear tricolor armbands bearing the legend *hospitalité* was dropped) and give proof of loyalty. This required the testimony of a native French person who thus acquired a degree of power over the 'guest'. These two brief vignettes show the language of hospitality deployed for both hospitable and what might seem quite inhospitable purposes – both to welcome the foreigner in and to protect the purity of the state from undesirable foreigners.

These should have obvious resonance for contemporary debates in France as some on the Left use the language of hospitality to underline solidarity while some on the Right use it to emphasise the gulf between the host and the guest who will never be more than a guest.

Contemporary echoes

I should like to point out the insistence/persistence of the figure of *l'hôte* in contemporary French politics. Although hospitality can be evoked from across the whole political spectrum, with those hostile to immigration or immigrants emphasising the precariousness of the *guests'* position, I argue that it should not be analysed 'out', but rather we should seek to work out the ways in which it can still mobilise a radical interrogation of exclusion and hostility towards strangers. This necessitates recognition of its fragility whether as generosity or as reciprocity, and includes the necessity of demystifying as well as celebrating the Revolution and its inheritance.

Immigration today is commonly thought under three broad headings relating to its motivation: economic (immigration for work); domestic (immigration for family reasons); and political (immigration for asylum). The economic modelling of 'hospitality' follows the distribution of goods and people, while the sphere of politics is concerned with rights and responsibilities in particular as regards the individual or group in relation to the nation state, or between one nation state and another. The (global) economy and nation states are of course interdependent – each impacts upon and relies upon the other. But while economic analysis is often viewed as outside the sphere of morality, politics draws it into the realm of ethics. Human rights are often taken to be innate and certainly supra-national. But we need languages and moral codes in which to formulate ethical relations, and these need to be constantly rethought. There is a long tradition of referring to the code of hospitality in order to negotiate relations with 'visitors' in all senses. (I feel I need to fall back on a very clumsy formulation such as 'being in a country which you, and/or the natives, perceive as not your own' to cover the range of situations in question.) It is of course crucial that we do not accept the notion (used rhetorically, strategically, by those who police immigration) that economics, politics, and ethics (notably hospitality) are watertight categories. Accommodation (and subsistence) of immigrants is a major issue feeding into immigration policies as well as the response of the so-called host-community or nation. This can of course exist

31

in a vicious or virtuous circle with work, but can also be a question of state benefits in kind or cash, and/or within the domestic broadly understood. French law demands an *attestation d'accueil* (an official proof of residence) for visitors on a visa – and there is a proviso for inspecting the quality of the lodging offered to these guests.

Whenever there is a law that appears to attack immigrants or asylum seekers there is a degree of protest in France from the Left, and sometimes even beyond, as suggested by this quote from an editorial in *Le Monde*: 'What good are speeches about defending freedom throughout the world if, at the same time, we refuse hospitality to men and women who, at home, risk death, torture or prison because of their ideas?' ('A quoi bon les discours sur la défense des libertés de par le monde si, parallèlement, l'hospitalité est refusée à des hommes, à des femmes qui, chez eux, risquent, pour leurs idées, la mort, la torture ou la prison?')[44] There was, however, a particularly striking mobilisation of opposition to the *projet de loi* brought to the French parliament by Jean-Louis Debré in December 1996.[45] It has been argued that part of the reason for this was the way in which the restriction of public hospitality inherent in any such bill was combined with an attack on private hospitality that made its inhospitality stand out. On 4 February 1997 Jacqueline Delthombe was found guilty of harbouring a friend and her partner from Zaire who did not have the correct papers.[46] The Bishop of Clermont-Ferrand wrote: 'Hospitality still has something sacred about it. It comes out of those unwritten laws which we know every individual and even the State should obey' ('L'hospitalité a gardé quelque chose de sacré. Elle relève de ces lois non écrites dont nous savons qu'elles s'imposent à toute personne et même à l'Etat').[47] Like the representatives of the Church, Etienne Balibar, again in *Le Monde*, makes an appeal to those higher unwritten laws such as 'respect for the living and the dead, hospitality, the inviolable nature of the human being' ('le respect des vivants et des morts, l'hospitalité, l'inviolabilité de l'être humain') and so on.[48] Hospitality (a higher law) is thus used as a justification for civil disobedience. Hospitality is presented as integral to humanity, just as it was in the eighteenth century.[49] Chevènement's attempt to regularise the situation of some of the *sans-papiers* was seen as too narrow in scope; we should note in passing the difference between 'those without papers' and one possible translation 'illegal immigrants'. An editorial in *Libération* asks for greater generosity inspired by 'the spirit of French hospitality inherited from 1789' ('l'esprit de l'hospitalité française hérité de 1789').[50] In summary, the French clampdown on illegal immigrants mobilised intellectuals, and was debated in terms of hospitality, in a way that is quite foreign to us in the UK.[51]

More recently these debates have inevitably been overshadowed in the press by the aftermath of 9/11, the invasion of Afghanistan and then the Iraq war. However, it is still possible to find passionate articles about the spirit and laws of hospitality occasioned by any attempt on the part of the French State to criminalise hospitable behaviour. I shall take just two examples, the first relating to Corsica. Corsica is a region particularly rich in its tradition and myth of hospitality; the arrest of Frédéric Paoli, shepherd and town councillor, for giving shelter to a Corsican nationalist accused of murder in 2003 gave rise to a series of demonstrations and articles in the press around the theme 'hospitality is not a crime'. The lyrical accounts of Corsican hospitality went back many centuries, paused particularly on the period of the Second World War, but also reported that a number of young Algerians were sheltered at the beginning of the 1990s when they fled from repression in Algeria and sought asylum in Corsica.[52]

My second example relates to Calais, particularly affected by the bulldozing of the Sangatte camp at the end of 2002; this did not prevent the arrival of significant numbers of refugees without any means of support, but it did leave them with nowhere to stay. A number of citizens of Calais distributed food and clothes and offered other kinds of help including short-term accommodation. Before long, two teachers (Jean-Claude Lenoir and Charles Frammezelle) were accused of 'aide au séjour irrégulier d'un étranger en France' (aiding a foreigner to stay in France without the necessary permits), a clause in a law dating from 1945; these do-gooders were then pursued in law as if they were people traffickers. Smaïn Laacher and Laurette Mokrani wrote: 'These two ordinary citizens, like thousands of others in our country, have done no more than obey the laws of hospitality', going on to quote Edmond Jabès on the relationship between responsibility, solidarity and hospitality.[53]

If we were to seek wider political resonance, we could think further about hospitality on an international level, for example the situation of refugees and asylum seekers. Derrida has addressed the theme of hospitality as asylum, notably in the short piece, *Cosmopolites de tous les pays, encore un effort!*, in which he promotes the notion of the city of refuge (*ville-refuge*).[54] This originated as an address to the International Parliament of Writers (IPW) in Strasbourg in 1996, which aimed to set up a network of cities of refuge particularly for writers who seek asylum.[55] Derrida's analysis of the decline in hospitality (in France in particular) towards refugees builds on Kant, Arendt and on Levinas.[56] In Kant's 'Third Definitive Article for a Perpetual Peace: Cosmopolitan right shall be limited to conditions of universal *hospitality*', from *To Perpetual Peace* (1795), the Enlightenment produced a key reference point for cosmopolitan theories of the need for nations to unite together and to offer hospitality to the citizens of other nations (even if Kant elsewhere expresses views that today we would regard as racist).[57] Asylum is dependent on, and controlled by, the law; it is a matter of rights. Asylum here is a relation between the State (or local government) and a certain category of persons (defined by law whether loosely such that anyone who asks for asylum should be granted it, or much more tightly). The progressive narrowing of the understanding of asylum on the part of the nation state – so that France, for example can demand that refugees derive no economic benefit from living in France, an almost impossible demand which denies any possibility of social integration, say, through employment – encourages the turn to the city. The specific term 'city of refuge' comes from the Old Testament; it contains a kind of paradox in that these are cities that offer temporary refuge to those who have accidentally killed someone and are pursued by the victim's family intent on revenge. Derrida returns to this question in his more extended analysis of Levinasian hospitality in which he calls for, or suggests that refugees and homeless people throughout the world call out for: 'another international law, another border politics, another humanitarian politics, indeed a humanitarian commitment that *effectively* operates beyond the interests of Nation-States' (*Adieu*, 101) ('Un autre droit international, une autre politique des frontières, une autre politique de l'humanitaire, voire un engagement humanitaire qui se tienne *effectivement* au-delà de l'intérêt des Etats-nations' (176)). This notion of granting asylum to the one who is considered (elsewhere?) as a criminal resonates rather differently in the case of the most dangerous guest of our contemporary *geist*: the terrorist, a figure both hyperbolically masculine and totally feminised. In the case of the terrorist we are brought back to other Old Testament, or Homeric, precedents for the spectacular revenge taken on the violent guest or those deemed to be his people . . .

Today, with our appropriately guilty focus on immigrants and asylum seekers trying to break into so-called 'Fortress Europe' or knocking on the wall between Mexico and the US, we writers on hospitality tend to emphasise Kant's strictures on the limitations of hospitality as if he were a good model in so far as he urges us to be hosts, but also not so good in that he limits the right of hospitality quite considerably. A guest has no right of residence according to Kant, only a right to visit; the former has to emerge from a treaty between States. He is not proposing philanthropy, but a natural right that should be enshrined in law. At the end of the eighteenth century, however, when Europeans were far more likely to be (abusive) guests abroad than hosts at home, Kant's claim that a guest has no right to outstay their welcome seems rather different, especially if we continue this familiar quotation beyond the point where it is usually cut:

> As in the preceding articles, our concern here is not with philanthropy, but with *right*, and in this context *hospitality* (hospitableness) means the right of an alien not to be treated as an enemy upon his arrival in another's country. If it can be done without destroying him, he can be turned away; but as long as he behaves peaceably he cannot be treated as an enemy. He may request the *right* to be a *permanent visitor* (which would require a special, charitable agreement to make him a fellow inhabitant for a certain period), but the *right to visit*, to associate, belongs to all men by virtue of their common ownership of the earth's surface; for since the earth is a globe they cannot scatter themselves infinitely, but must, finally, tolerate living in close proximity, because originally no one had a greater right to any region of the earth than anyone else . . . [Natural right] extends the right to hospitality, i.e., the privilege of aliens to enter, only so far as makes attempts at commerce with native inhabitants possible. In this way distant parts of the world can establish with one another peaceful relations that will eventually become matters of public law, and the human race can gradually be brought closer and closer to a cosmopolitan constitution.
>
> Compare this with the inhospitable conduct of civilized nations in our part of the world, especially commercial ones: the injustice that they display towards foreign lands and peoples (which is the same as *conquering* them), is terrifying. When discovered, America, the lands occupied by the blacks, the Spice Islands, the Cape etc., were regarded as lands belonging to no one because their inhabitants were counted for nothing. (*Perpetual Peace*, paragraph 358, 118–19)

In *Adieu*, Derrida suggests that Kant's argument is almost the reverse of Levinas's account of hospitality as pre-originary; for Levinas violence supposes, arises from, bears witness to, hospitality; even the torturer supposes hospitality – which is a more frightening thesis than Kant's (*Adieu*, 95–6; 167–8). Kant's universal hospitality is a right because men originally had common ownership of the earth's surface; it is a right, and also a *response* or solution to the hostility and violence that he observes (or reads about) in the world.

While this limited welcome falls far short of the Law of hospitality, I shall argue that it needs just as careful attention in my analysis.[58]

Plan of the book

Chapter 2 includes analyses of the *Odyssey* and of episodes from the Books of Genesis and Judges as ur-texts of hospitality, which bring out the working of sexual difference within it. It also takes up the question of intertextuality more generally. This is important not only because hospitality can be used as a model for the experience of reading and writing, but also because discourses about hospitality (political or personal) often refer to the text of the past. Derrida's readings (and he stands out as a philosopher whose writings are almost always explicitly readings) have sometimes been read as violent and intrusive or sneaky and illegitimate. However, I would argue that, like Cixous and Irigaray, he typically reads others, whom he respects, in order to expand generously on what is always already there. Derrida is quick to point to the presents others bestow: for example Levinas, whose first gift to his host country is to introduce phenomenology (Husserl) and ontology (Heidegger) to France in the 1930s, and whose second gift, causing a second philosophical tremor, is to displace that same axis (*Adieu*, 10 ff; 22 ff). This pedagogical *sharing* or nourishing is a critical form of hospitality for Derrida (as he explains in '"Eating Well", or the Calculation of the Subject', analysed in Chapter 6). Chapter 3 will be devoted to sexual difference and friendship, friendship traditionally being conceived as a relationship between men, just as hospitality has traditionally been conceived as a relationship between men, although supported by women's labour. Analysis of friendship and reciprocity moves us away a little from the focus on the subject-host which can result from a certain reading of Levinas. The final section will turn from fraternal friendship to an alternative maternal model of hospitality. Chapter 4 takes up the specific issue of names, (not) asking for a name, calling by name, or naming as a way of exploring problems within hospitality especially in the colonial context of French Algeria, where Europeans were uninvited visitors who took upon themselves the position of mastery. Chapter 5, on Gods and cultural difference, focuses on a specific area of political intervention in the post-colonial world, which remains inhabited by colonialism in so many senses. It evokes the dream and the dangers of hospitality today. Arrivals, many (although not all) from former colonies, may imagine that they are in some sense invited, or indeed that they are at home – while their status as 'guests' is inhospitably emphasised. Chapter 6 takes up the liminal subject of hospitality to animals in order to ask about the boundaries we place around the human, an ethical and political question with relevance to sexual, ethnic and class differences. It raises the issues of companionship with living beings, of co-habitation in the world, and of 'eating (well)'. The question of the human (of what is human) subtends all ethical (and thus all political) questions. Finally Chapter 7 attempts to bring together 'the rest', the questions that remain.

A final vignette – returning to Algeria

To bring together in a concrete form a number of the points outlined above, I shall turn to a touching two-page spread in *Le Monde*, 'Pieds-noirs Retour à Alger', that describes one of the 'pilgrimages' made by the French who were born in Algeria and lived there before the War of Independence (about 60,000 have travelled in the last two years, and the number is growing).[59] Until recently it would have been very difficult and dangerous for them to return to visit what they perceive as their homeland. Now an association, France-Maghreb, has been set up to rehabilitate Christian cemeteries and also organises these tours to 'retrouver vos racines' (rediscover your roots). According to the article these former colonials are received with the warmest hospitality: '"Welcome, make yourselves at home", they are told at the main Post Office, in Bab El-Oued, in the Casbah and so on' ('"Bienvenue, vous êtes chez vous!", leur dit-on à la Grande Poste, à Bab El-Oued, à la Casbah ou ailleurs'). We might note that the set phrase of hospitality: 'vous êtes chez vous', which literally translates as 'this is your home' (and which I have allowed to slip into an equivalent cliché: 'make yourself at home'), has a particular resonance in this context.

'Why did you leave?' the visitors are asked (presumably a rhetorical question). We need you! In return some French visitors set aside their long-held anger and resentment, wish they had never left and confess that they 'had never cut the umbilical cord with Algeria' ('n'avoir jamais coupé le cordon ombilical avec l'Algérie'). The maternal metaphor slips in unnoticed; Algeria is usually feminine. They explain that they were certainly not welcomed when they had arrived in France forty-four years earlier. '"In Marseilles and Toulon they called us 'repatriates', but that's nonsense! We were immigrants.

Here, today, in Algeria, we are repatriates"' ("'A Marseille et Toulon, on nous appelait 'les rapatriés', mais c'est une ineptie! Nous étions des immigrés. C'est ici, aujourd'hui en Algérie que nous sommes des rapatriés"'). One visitor carries a love letter to Algeria and a lock of hair from her elderly mother, with the mission to leave them behind somewhere in Algiers. Another woman says to Algerians who smile at her: "'Khuya! [my brother]" before adding the aside: "I know them, they're my blood"' ("'Khuya! [mon frère]" avant d'ajouter en aparté: "Je les connais, c'est mon sang!"'). A particularly emotional scene shows Pierre daring to knock on the door of the flat where he used to live, amazed to find so little has changed (the new inhabitants liked the style). Even the beverages offered and accepted have their colonial and post-colonial histories. Over 'a glass of Hamoud Boualem lemonade, the pieds-noirs' favourite drink – alongside Selecto, a kind of local coca-cola' ('un verre de limonade Hamoud Boualem, la boisson favorite des pieds-noirs – avec le Selecto, sorte de Coca-Cola local'), the new friends swap addresses: "'Come back with your family and have a week's holiday in the flat" the master of the place insists when his guests say good-bye' ("'Revenez, en famille, passer une semaine de vacances dans cet appartement", insiste le maître des lieux quand ses hôtes prennent congé'). A neighbour calls out: "'This is your home"' (or 'make yourself at home') ("'Vous êtes chez vous"'). The dispassionate reader may reflect that even the ability of a native Algerian to say to a French-Algerian 'this is your home' contrasts vividly with the realities of a colonial situation in which the French made themselves at home at the expense of native Algerians regardless of the lack of any invitation. But the emotion of the moment leaves Pierre naturally in tears, and Jean-Paul comparing himself to the prodigal son. This harmonious description has only the occasional sour note – the son (a night-club owner from Toulouse) of a Jewish *pied-noir*, who says: "'the Arabs here aren't like the scum we have in France"' ("'les Arabes d'ici, c'est pas comme la racaille qu'on a en France"'), to be told by his father, who is delighted at his welcome: "'These are ours!"' ("'Ici , c'est les nôtres!"'). Even a former OAS member, who now lives in America, and is horrified at how dirty things are these days, confesses: "'I have to admit that I've never seen such hospitable people"' ("'je dois reconnaître que je n'ai jamais vu des gens aussi hospitaliers"').

This raises a whole range of issues including the French conceptualisation of Arab hospitality, of course, and Algerians' self-understanding as hospitable. In *French Hospitality*, Ben Jelloun re-tells a 'true story' of a French television crew who, following an immigrant returning home, were royally entertained in an Algerian village for a week – at huge cost in particular to the father of the subject of the documentary. The old man then makes the mistake of taking literally the return invitation made by the director to visit him in Paris, and simply turning up on his doorstep six months later (*French Hospitality*. 3; *Hospitalité française*, 12) – a kind of error in translation. Mireille Rosello rightly points out that this anecdote of clashing cultural codes could be interpreted in a number of ways, and argues that Ben Jelloun's work has a tendency to universalise hospitality as a value to which some (for example, in the Algerian village) adhere more closely than others (for example, in the Parisian bourgeoisie), rather than investigating the need for negotiation between different understandings of hospitality (*Postcolonial Hospitality*, 170–1). I would argue that Jelloun's account is a little more open than Rosello suggests – the city-dwelling reader is free to identify with the Parisian who is confused by a sudden knock on the door one night, and does not immediately recognise the old man whom he had last seen in such a different context. Ben Jelloun apparently uses the story in an unpublished novella ('The Invitation'), and we do not know how the readers of that novella would be invited to respond. However, it is important to note that in *French Hospitality* Ben Jelloun is, amongst other things, using the tale as an allegory relating to Maghrebian immigrants who hoped that France would welcome them.

The huge question of colonial power and exploitation is not raised in the article in *Le Monde*; it is the elephant in the room. An accompanying interview with the historian Benjamin Stora (a respected expert on the Algerian war) is quite neutral in tone, although it does mention with respect to the 'nostalgie' of the visitors that native Muslims did not have the right to vote under French rule (unlike immigrants to Algeria from, say, Italy or Spain, who were given French citizenship).What is a motherland? What is immigration? *Pieds-noirs* say that they should have been regarded as immigrants, but what does this mean? Does this mean they enviously feel that immigrants are better treated when they come (not *back*) to France, or is it only a point about where their home truly is/was. They were seen as returning home, but they were not welcomed in France. How do they feel about other immigrants in France, notably those from the country they are saying is/was their home too? The only example is the highly tendentious term 'scum' from the nightclub owner, and we might note that the difficulty of gaining admittance to clubs if you are recognisably 'Arab' is a recurrent complaint for young men from the *banlieues*. 'La racaille' was also notoriously used by Nicolas Sarkozy (then the right-wing French Minister of the Interior) to describe the rioters in the North-African dominated *banlieues*.

Nostalgia suffuses the article's suggestion that relations were harmonious before war broke out. There is also a sensual, material quality of nostalgia for the physical environment, imbued with special memories of, say, food and drink that was difficult to get in France. *Nostalgia* (*Heimweh* in German) comes from the Greek and enters both the French (as *nostalgie*) and English languages in the eighteenth century. It combines *nostos*, the return home, and *algos*, pain. Even today, the OED privileges the meaning of 'homesickness': 'A form of melancholia caused by prolonged absence from one's country or home', as does the French Dictionary *Petit Robert*, rather than a later meaning of 'regret for earlier times', as we most often use it today. The French dictionary particularly associates the meaning of the word with émigrés and exiles – those most in need of hospitality.

Is there any lesson to be learnt from the example of Algerian hospitality extended to the visiting *pieds-noirs* and children of *pieds-noirs*, those formerly uninvited guests, returning to what they call their motherland, calling their Algerian hosts 'brothers', using the Arab term? Of course many contradictory lessons could be drawn, including a revisionist one that (Arab) terrorism is evil, that it ought never to be conceived as a fight for freedom, and that the French should never have been forced out of or have agreed to leave mother Algeria, which was, or could have been, a land of brothers, fathered by France. Camus might have subscribed to that, but the history of colonial exploitation is against him. Another reading could insist on the benefits of liberalisation, the free market, commercial hospitality, and the need for Algeria (rich in oil and gas, I note) to be 'opened up' for its own good (and ours, of course). But I shall close on a third double reading: let us be able to welcome with warmth and offers of food and shelter even those who *might* be suspected (on the past record) to be less than well-behaved guests. Yet, the shadowy double to this point is that, in order for the hosts to be able to say 'make yourselves at home', they do need to be masters of their own houses in some sense. I have not emphasised sexual difference, perhaps because it is so often an alibi in Western intrusion in the East. Did we invade Afghanistan to help Afghan women? The numerous images which illustrate the *Le Monde* article focus on one particular male *pied-noir*, and on food as much as palm trees; Algerian women are totally absent. They do appear briefly in the text, making gestures and speeches of welcome, feeling pity for their guests; but interestingly veils are conspicuous by their absence, *unlike* many articles in the press that deal with the 'problem' of Muslims in France, women in the *banlieues* and so on. Perhaps there is a desire not to spoil the picture of commonality and brotherhood. I shall return frequently to the sexing of hospitality in the chapters to come.

Notes

1. Jacques Derrida, *Specters of Marx: The State of the Debt, the Work of Mourning, and the New International*, translated by Peggy Kamuf, with an introduction by Bernd Magnus and Stephen Cullenberg (New York and London: Routledge, 1994), p. 35; Jacques Derrida, *Spectres de Marx: l'état de la dette, le travail du deuil et la nouvelle Internationale* (Paris: Galilée, 1993), p. 65.

2. See Mireille Rosello, *Postcolonial Hospitality: The Immigrant as Guest* (Stanford: Stanford University Press, 2001), in particular the Introduction and Chapter 1; and Anne Gotman, *Le sens de l'hospitalité: Essai sur les fondements sociaux de l'accueil de l'autre* (Paris: PUF, 2001); both cite numerous examples including key texts such as Didier Fassin, Alain Morice, Catherine Quiminal (eds), *Les lois de l'inhospitalité: Les politiques de l'immigration à l'épreuve des sans-papier* (Paris: La Découverte, 1997). See also René Schérer, *Hospitalités* (Paris: Economica, second edition 2004); *L'étranger*, edited by Rosie Pinhas-Delpuech, special issue of *JIM. Journal intime du Massif Central*, 8 (Editions du Bleu autour, 2004); Sonia Dayan-Herzbrun and Etienne Tassin (eds), *Citoyennetés cosmopolitiques*, special issue of *Tumultes*, 24 (Paris: Kimé, 2005).

3. I shall not give an exhaustive list of the work on hospitality inspired by Derrida, but a few examples would include John D. Caputo (ed.), *Deconstruction in a Nutshell: A Conversation with Jacques Derrida* (New York: Fordham University Press, 1997), which includes a section on 'Hospitality' (pp. 109–13); Mustafa Dikeç, 'Pera Peras Poros Longings for Spaces of Hospitality', *Cosmopolis*, special issue of *Theory, Culture and Society*, 19:1–2 (2002), pp. 227–47; Clive Barnett, 'Ways of Relating: Hospitality and the Acknowledgement of Otherness', *Progress in Human Geography*, 29:1 (2005), pp. 5–21. William Tregoning interestingly introduces an aboriginal Australian dimension via the work of Margaret Somerville (Margaret Somerville, *Body/Landscape Journals* [Melbourne: Spinifex Press, 1999]) in 'It

Feels Like Home: Hospitality in a Postcolonial Space', *Text Theory Critique*, 7 (2003), no pagination. Just these few examples show the disciplinary range of the responses to Derrida on hospitality – from philosophy and literature to urban planning and geography. Of course, many more will be cited in the course of the book.

4. For Derrida's own analysis of the complexities of French nationality for those born in Algeria see Jacques Derrida and Anne Dufourmantelle, *Of Hospitality: Anne Dufourmantelle invites Jacques Derrida to Respond*, translated by Rachel Bowlby (Stanford: Stanford University Press, 2000), pp. 141ff; Jacques Derrida and Anne Dufourmantelle, *De l'hospitalité: Anne Dufourmantelle invite Jacques Derrida à répondre* (Paris: Calmann-Lévy, 1997), pp. 125ff. See also Jacques Derrida, *Monolingualism of the Other; or, The Prothesis of the Origin*, translated by Patrick Mensah (Stanford: Stanford University Press, 1998); Jacques Derrida, *Le monolinguisme de l'autre* (Paris: Galilée, 1996). For a French account of Derrida's role in the United States, see François Cusset, *French Theory: Foucault, Derrida, Deleuze & Cie et les mutations de la vie intellectuelle aux Etats-Unis* (Paris: La Découverte, 2003); the term 'French Theory' is in English in the title to show that it is an American invention. I should note that Cusset does not include feminist theory within 'French Theory' to any significant extent.

5. Tahar Ben Jelloun, *French Hospitality: Racism and North African Immigrants*, translated by Barbara Bray (New York: Columbia University Press, [1984, 1987] 1999), p. 3; Tahar Ben Jalloun, *Hospitalité française: Racisme et immigration maghrébine*, second edition (Paris: Seuil, 1997), p. 11. Of course a neo-classical economist might argue that your borrowing capacity is part of 'what you have', but we must not allow economism to flatten things out too quickly. There is a difference between the prudent gift and the risky gift.

6. Jacques Derrida, *Adieu to Emmanuel Levinas*, translated by Pascal-Anne Brault and Michael Naas (Stanford: Stanford University Press, 1999), p. 10; Jacques Derrida, *Adieu à Emmanuel Lévinas* (Paris: Galilée, 1997), p. 23. In emphasising how Levinas loved the hospitality of France, Derrida also places weight on how very, very much France owes to Levinas.

7. As well as Caputo, *Deconstruction in a Nutshell*, cited above, see, for example, Michael Naas, *Taking on the Tradition: Jacques Derrida and the Legacies of Deconstruction* (Stanford: Stanford University Press, 2003), Chapter 9. Naas writes: 'deconstruction is itself a kind of hospitality and hospitality, as an open question, always a kind of deconstruction' (p. 155), which seems right to me although these very general statements out of context can seem rather empty.

8. Jacques Derrida, 'Hostipitality', in Gil Anidjar (ed.), *Jacques Derrida: Acts of Religion* (New York and London: Routledge, 2002), pp. 356–420, p. 364. Not yet published in French.

9. 'Threshold of tolerance' is the expression used by French politicians to express the view that there has to be a limit to immigration.

10. See Geoffrey Bennington, 'Derrida and Politics', in *Interrupting Derrida* (London and New York: Routledge, 2000), pp. 18–33 for a masterly response to the suspicions about deconstruction, as well as the hopes, demands and expectations (particularly in English-speaking countries) that Derrida should state unequivocally his political allegiances.

11. Emmanuel Levinas, *Totality and Infinity: An Essay on Exteriority*, translated by Alphonso Lingis (Pittsburgh: Duquesne University Press, 1969), p. 299; Emmanuel Lévinas, *Totalité et infini: Essai sur l'extériorité* (The Hague: Martinus Nijhoff, [1971] 1980), p. 276. Emmanuel Levinas, *Otherwise than Being or Beyond Essence*, translated by Alphonso Lingis (Pittsburgh: Duquesne University Press, 1998), p. 112; Emmanuel Lévinas, *Autrement qu'être ou au-delà de l'essence* (The Hague: Martinus Nijhoff, 1978), p. 142. The reader has to struggle with the question whether these two phrases contradict each other, inform each other (both relating to the subject's fundamental responsibility for the other), or apply in different circumstances. For Derrida's analysis, see *Adieu* (pp. 55; 102–3).

12. Caren Kaplan, amongst many others whom she cites (many less judicious than herself), attacks contemporary theory and other cultural artefacts that use notions of travel or mobility or the nomad in an ahistorical and universalised fashion, the most famous example being Gilles Deleuze and Felix Guattari's 'deterritorialisation'. See Caren Kaplan, *Questions of Travel: Postmodern Discourses of Displacement* (Durham, NC and London: Duke University Press, 1996). I shall not repeat these arguments; Peter Hallward's recent book, *Out of this World: Deleuze and the Philosophy of Creation* (London: Verso, 2006), already does a fine job of showing the metaphysical underpinning of 'nomad thought'.

13. For more on the question of definition and level of analysis see my 'Can Woman Ever be Defined?', in Andrea Cady (ed.), *Women Teaching French: Five Papers on Language and Theory* (Loughborough: University of Loughborough European Research Centre, Studies in European Culture and Society 5, 1991), pp. 29–37; and 'A Feminine Economy: Some Preliminary Thoughts', in Helen Wilcox, Keith McWaters, Ann Thompson and Linda Williams (eds), *The Body and the Text: Hélène Cixous, Reading and Teaching* (Brighton: Harvester, 1990), pp. 49–60.

14. Jacques Derrida, 'On Cosmopolitanism', in *On Cosmopolitanism and Forgiveness*, translated by Mark Dooley and Michael Hughes (London and New York: Routledge, 2001), pp. 16–17; Jacques Derrida, *Cosmopolites de tous les pays, encore un effort!* (Paris: Galilée, 1997), pp. 42–3.

15. Jacques Derrida, *Given Time. I, Counterfeit Money*, translated by Peggy Kamuf (Chicago: Chicago University Press, 1992); Jacques Derrida, *Donner le temps. I, La fausse monnaie* (Paris: Galilée, 1991).

16. Sara Ahmed, *Strange Encounters: Embodied Others in Post-Coloniality* (London and New York: Routledge, 2000), p. 151. Ahmed argues that: 'The model of hospitality based on "welcoming the stranger" *is* to welcome the unassimilable; it hence conceals how that very act of welcoming already assimilates others into an economy of difference. In order to problematize such a model of hospitality we need a double approach: first, *we need an analysis of the economies of differentiation that already assimilate others as strangers* (which is economic in the precise sense of involving circuits of production, exchange and consumption); second, we need an analysis of how encounters with others who are already differentiated in this way *can move beyond the economic by welcoming, or being open or hospitable to, that which is yet to be assimilated*' (pp. 150–1). Her proposal seems excellent to me – but I do not consider that *Derrida's* texts that refer to 'welcoming the stranger' conceal the inevitable assimilation that the act of welcome entails – surely he makes this point on many occasions even if he does not repeat it every time that he uses the term. Her critique is, however, quite valid in reference to a number of other writers on hospitality.

17. Richard Kearney, 'Aliens and Others: Between Girard and Derrida', *Cultural Values*, 3:3 (1999), pp. 251–62, p. 260.

18. Jacques Derrida, 'Hospitality, Justice and Responsibility: a Dialogue with Jacques Derrida', in Richard Kearney and Mark Dooley (eds), *Questioning Ethics: Contemporary Debates in Philosophy* (London and New York: Routledge, 1999), pp. 63–83, p. 66.

19. This point about the decision is clear in the interview cited, and is related to the structure of the very term most associated with Derrida, *différance* (*HJR*, p. 77); it is analysed in some detail in Bennington, *Interrupting Derrida*, for instance pp. 24ff. Derrida also tackles in the discussion the strange claim that 'undecidability' would be a synonym for 'indeterminacy', which it is not (*HJR*, p. 78).

20. Although it is important to relate this to the sense of *home*. Home too is a structure or construction of dwelling. Is it having a sense of being at home that permits the offer of hospitality to the other or in some sense vice versa? This is a question of the psychoanalytical, philosophical *and* socio-cultural sense of self and home – whether this is *definitionally* about me feeling at home or me feeling I can invite the other in.

21. Derrida quotes Levinas's point about language in *Adieu* (p. 10; pp. 22–3) in relation to his love of France. His question is posed in *Of Hospitality* (p. 135; *DH*, p. 119).

22. See, for example, Abbé de Raynal's collaborative work, *Histoire philosophique et politique des deux Indes*, edited by Yves Benot (Paris:

La Découverte, [1981] 2001). In the article 'Les Hottentots' Diderot exhorts the peoples of South Africa not to welcome the 'Barbares Européens' (a reversal of 'barbarian' that is typical of critics of colonialism since at least Montaigne), but to fight (*Histoire philosophique*, p. 49). The fact that it is unwise to welcome Europeans is reinforced in the section on 'Les Natchez'. When the French first arrived in Louisiana 'they were warmly welcomed by the savages and supported in the establishment of the plantations they wanted to set up' ('ils furent accueillis favorablement et soulagés par les sauvages dans l'établissement des plantations qu'ils voulaient former') (p. 292). The friendship between the two nations seemed sincere, Diderot tells his reader, until the greed of the French colonists got the better of them. See my *Enlightenment Hospitality: Cannibals, Harems and Adoption* (Oxford: Voltaire Foundation, 2011), especially Chapters 2–3.

23. When Benveniste ponders how *potis*, one of the base elements of hospitality, can incarnate mastery and self-identity, he elaborates as follows: 'For an adjective meaning "himself" to develop into the meaning "master" there is one necessary condition: there must be a circle of persons subordinated to a central personage who assumes the personality and complete identity of the group to such an extent that he is its summation: in his own person he is its incarnation' (Emile Benveniste, *Indo-European Language and Society*, translated by Elizabeth Palmer [London: Faber and Faber, 1973], p. 74) ('Pour qu'un adjectif signifiant "soi-même" s'amplifie jusqu'au sens de "maître" une condition est nécessaire: un cercle fermé de personnes, subordonné à un personnage central qui assume la personnalité, l'identité complète du groupe au point de la résumer en lui-même; à lui seul, il l'incarne' (Emile Benveniste, *Le Vocabulaire des institutions indo-européennes*, I [Paris: Minuit, 1969], p. 91.)) His example is the master of the house.

24. Julia Kristeva, *Strangers to Ourselves*, translated by Leon S. Roudiez (New York: Columbia University Press, 1991); Julia Kristeva, *Etrangers à nous-mêmes* (Paris: Fayard, 1988).

25. See Roland Barthes, 'Dominici or the Triumph of Literature', in *Mythologies*, translated by Annette Lavers (London: Paladin, 1973), pp. 48–52; Roland Barthes, 'Dominici ou le triomphe de la Littérature', in *Mythologies* (Paris: Seuil, [1957] 1970), pp. 50–3.

26. In her major study of hospitality, Gotman suggests getting over the ambiguity of the term *hôte* in French by using the term *maître de maison* (*Le sens de l'hospitalité*, pp. 9–10) – this tells us something about the ingrained nature of the gender issues here. Derrida frequently uses the term but in a rather more pointed fashion.

27. See Susan Brownmiller, *Against Our Will: Men, Women, and Rape* (London: Secker and Warburg, 1975) for the thesis that both the

practice and the threat of rape are integral to the functioning of patriarchy, providing the need for 'protection' and the possibility of punishment.

28. It is important to note Irigaray's engagement with Levinas (Luce Irigaray, 'Questions to Emmanuel Levinas: On the Divinity of Love', in *The Irigaray Reader*, edited and with an introduction by Margaret Whitford [Oxford: Basil Blackwell, 1991], pp. 178–89) as well as Derrida's (dating from Jacques Derrida, *Writing and Difference*, translated with introduction and additional notes by Alan Bass [London: Routledge, 1990]; Jacques Derrida, *L'Écriture et la différence* [Paris: Seuil, 1967]); both point out the problem of sexual difference. There have been a number of critics who have analysed this encounter including Tina Chanter, *Ethics of Eros: Irigaray's Rewriting of the Philosophers* (London and New York: Routledge, 1995). For Levinas sexuality is secondary to a transcendental humanity; the human paradigm is neutrality 'in all its masculinity' as Cathryn Vasseleu nicely puts it in *Textures of Light: Vision and Touch in Irigaray, Levinas and Merleau-Ponty* (London and New York: Routledge, 1998), p. 111. Self-realisation is ultimately a relationship of proximity between father and son, while he does not allow for the possibility of an ethical relationship between, say, mother and daughter as sexed beings . . . It is hard to say to what extent the legacy of Levinas has encouraged a certain would-be ethical focus on the Law of hospitality that is (to me, perversely) absolutely disembodied.

29. For a clear explanation of this, and other aspects of Irigaray's work, see Elizabeth Grosz, *Sexual Subversions: Three French Feminists* (Sydney: Allen and Unwin, 1989). For the meaning of 'sexual sameness', see pp. 105–10.

30. See Penelope Deutscher, *A Politics of Impossible Difference: The Later Work of Luce Irigaray* (New York: Cornell University Press, 2002), for interesting analysis of the advantages and problems of developing Irigarayan theory with respect to cultural difference. Deutscher raises some particular material cases such as that of the struggle of aboriginal peoples in Australia (which she approaches via Fanon), and discusses the key issue of the temporality of difference (past, present or future); see in particular Chapter 3.

31. When asked about 'diversity' in an interview with Andrea Wheeler (Andrea Wheeler, 'About Being-two in an Architectural Perspective: An Interview with Luce Irigaray', *Journal of Romance Studies*, 4:2 (2004), pp. 91–107), Luce Irigaray replies: 'To promote only diversity, as is often the case in our times, runs the risk of remaining in an unchanged horizon with regard to the relations with the other(s). We then entrust this problem to customs, moral rules or religious feeling without questioning our culture about its capability of meeting with

the other as such. Furthermore we are unable to open ourselves all the time to others different from us. We need to return to ourselves, to keep and save our totality or integrity, and this is possible only in sexuate difference. Why? Because it is the most basic difference, this one which secures for each bridge(s) both between nature and culture and between us. It is starting from this difference that the other sorts of otherness have been elaborated. And if someone would raise here the problem of races or generations, it could be answered that races and generations do not prevent sexual attraction and that the behaviours with respect to them result from an elaboration, or non-elaboration, of sexual attraction. This attraction is stronger than the difference between the bodies. And it is more spiritual in a way. It also arises firstly between the two. It is more initial and fundamental than diversity and can explain it, while the contrary is not true. Diversity is a means today to escape the question of sexuate difference and to reduce or merge women's liberation in a past world in which woman had not yet discovered and affirmed her own cultural values' (p. 93).

32. Luce Irigaray, *Between East and West: From Singularity to Community*, translated by Stephen Pluháček (New York: Columbia University Press, 2002), pp. 16–17; Luce Irigaray, *Entre Orient et Occident: De la singularité à la communauté* (Paris: Grasset, 1999), p. 28.

33. In the English-speaking world, Margaret Whitford's work has made a major contribution to the recognition of Irigaray's work as both feminist and philosophy; see Margaret Whitford, *Luce Irigaray: Philosophy in the Feminine* (London: Routledge, 1991).

34. Hélène Cixous and Catherine Clément, *The Newly Born Woman*, translated by Betsy Wing, foreword by Sandra Gilbert (Minneapolis: University of Minnesota Press; Theory and History of Literature Series, Vol. 24, 1986); Hélène Cixous and Catherine Clément, *La Jeune née* (Paris: 10/18, 1975); Hélène Cixous, 'The Laugh of the Medusa', translated by Keith Cohen and Paula Cohen, *Signs*, 1:4 (1976), pp. 875–93; Hélène Cixous, 'Le rire de la Méduse', *L'Arc*, 61 (1975), pp. 39–54. Peggy Kamuf comments on the slight corpus in translation in the 1970s on which Cixous's reputation amongst non-French speakers was established (Peggy Kamuf, 'To Give Place: Semi-Approaches to Hélène Cixous', in Lynne Huffer (ed.), *Another Look, Another Woman: Retranslations of French Feminism*, special issue of *Yale French Studies*, 87 (1995), pp. 68–89).

35. The quotation is taken from Hélène Cixous, *Entre l'écriture* (Paris: Des Femmes, 1986), p. 85.

36. Hélène Cixous, *'Coming to Writing' and Other Essays*, with an introductory essay by Susan Rubin Suleiman, edited by Deborah Jenson, translated by Sarah Cornell, Deborah Jenson, Ann Liddle and Susan Sellers (Cambridge, MA: Harvard University Press, 1991), p. 10;

Hélène Cixous, 'La Venue à l'écriture', in Hélène Cixous, Madeleine Gagnon and Annie Leclerc, *La Venue à l'écriture* (Paris: 10/18, 1977), p. 18.

37. Cixous calls halt to some complicated play with the words: 'I don't want to ruffle the feathers of those too easily made nervous and hostile by the philosophicomical, philosophical resources of language', my translation; Hélène Cixous, *Dream I Tell You*, translated by Beverley Bie Brahic (Edinburgh: Edinburgh University Press, 2006); ('je ne veux pas hérisser les adversaries trop vite effarouchés des resources philosophiques, philosophicomiques de la langue' (Hélène Cixous, *Rêve je te dis* [Paris: Galilée, 2003], p. 13)).

38. Jacques Derrida, *Genèses, généalogies, genres et le génie: Les secrets de l'archive* (Paris: Galilée, 2003), p. 39, my translation.

39. Denis Diderot and Jean Le Rond d'Alembert (ed.), *Encyclopédie ou Dictionnaire raisonné des sciences, des arts et des métiers*, 35 volumes (Paris: Briasson, David l'Aîné, Le Breton and Durand, 1751–80)

40. Daphne Patai, 'Ethical Problems of Personal Narratives, or Who Should Eat the Last Piece of Cake', *International Journal of Oral History*, 8:1 (1987), pp. 5–27. Patai raises more generally the profit the ethnographer reaps from, or the use she makes of, the subject who has entertained her.

41. See Sophie Wahnich, *L'Impossible Citoyen: L'étranger dans le discours de la Révolution française* (Paris: Albin Michel, 1997).

42. See my *Enlightenment Hospitality*, Chapter 7, for further analysis of Revolutionary hospitality in the light of Enlightenment questioning of hospitality, and for the situation of women and slaves.

43. Ali Behdad has pointed out that in the narrative of nationalism the state of siege tends to be the rule rather than the exception. See Ali Behdad, 'Nationalism and Immigration in the U.S.', *Diaspora*, 6:2 (1997), pp. 55–78.

44. 'Inhospitalité occidentale', an editorial whose title is noteworthy in *Le Monde*, 8 January 1996.

45. Although the notorious Pasqua laws introduced by Charles Pasqua in 1993 had already set the scene. Foreign workers had been 'welcomed' officially (and those without official papers had been 'welcomed' unofficially) when labour was in short supply during the period of post-war reconstruction and throughout the period of economic growth known as the 'trente glorieuses'. In 1974 Giscard d'Estaing was among the first to try to 'close the door' in the face of an economic downturn.

46. See Rosello, *Postcolonial Hospitality*, pp. 36 ff, and Gotman, *Le sens de l'hospitalité*; both give a number of references, a small number of which are reproduced here. This trial coincides with Debré's attempt to introduce a bill with a clause that made it mandatory to declare the departure of a guest on a visa. The uproar that greeted this was

in part a retrospective protest at the *certificats d'hébergement* that had been introduced almost unnoticed in 1982 as a prerequisite for gaining a visa. These had led to intrusive inspections of hosts' accommodation – supposedly in order to ensure decent conditions for guests. In December 1997 these were abolished and replaced by Chevènement with *attestations d'accueil* which did not need verifying in the same way.

47. *La Croix*, 21 February 1997.
48. Etienne Balibar, 'Etat d'urgence démocratique', *Le Monde*, 19 February 1997.
49. Gotman cites Rousseau, *Le sens de l'hospitalité*, p. 44.
50. Joffrin, Editorial in *Libération*, 31 May 1998. This has continued, although not to the same extent; for example: an editorial in *Le Monde* entitled 'Les lois de l'hospitalité', 29 July 2000, is partly economic in inspiration for growth requires immigration – but also contains an appeal to *solidarity between rich and poor nations*.
51. Rosello, in *Postcolonial Hospitality*, emphasises the range as well as extent of intellectual mobilisation including the *Collège des médiateurs* (p. 2) and the manifesto of the 59 film directors (pp. 43–6).
52. Two passionate articles were published in *Le Monde* under the broad titles 'hospitality is not a crime' (*Le Monde*, 10 and 19 July 2003).
53. Smaïn Laacher and Laurette Mokrani, *Le Monde*, 26 June 2004, p. 19. Philippe Lioret's 2009 film *Welcome* tackles this situation.
54. The translation combines this with an essay 'On Forgiveness', which is another example of Derrida's engagement with international political (as well as ethical) problems – in that instance the question of the public or private forgiving of crimes such as those committed recently under Apartheid or in Algeria, or in the Holocaust.
55. This is an organisation, which first met in 1994, co-founded by Pierre Bourdieu, Derrida, Edouard Glissant, Toni Morrison and Salman Rushdie. It was based in Strasbourg, one of the first cities (with Berlin) to declare itself a city of refuge, until 1998 when it moved to Brussels. The network of cities of refuge has been one of its first and most important projects, and a number of important European, and then American, cities have taken up the challenge of acting as host to persecuted writers or artists, including Barcelona, Copenhagen, Salzburg, Valladolid, Venice and Vienna. Others have hesitated, and some have joined then withdrawn, sometimes citing economic grounds. The IPW was disbanded after the European Commission and the French Ministry of Culture amongst others withdrew their support (i.e. funding) following a visit to Palestine by the IPW in 2002. The International Network of Cities-Asylum has taken over much of the work.
56. See Emmanuel Levinas, *Beyond the Verse: Talmudic Readings and Lectures*, translated by Gary D. Mole (London: Athlone, 1994);

Emmanuel Lévinas, *L'au-delà du Verset: Lectures et discours talmud-iques* (Paris: Minuit, 1982), Chapter 3 on cities of refuge.

57. See Paul Gilroy, *Between Camps: Race, Identity and Nationalism at the End of the Colour Line* (Harmondsworth: Allen Lane, 2000), Chapter 2, 'Modernity and Infrahumanity', for Kant on the black 'race' and its inferiority. Gilroy takes off from Ronald A. T. Judy, *(Dis)forming the American Canon: African-Arabic Slave Narratives and the Vernacular* (Minneapolis: University of Minnesota Press, 1993), Chapter 4, section 3, 'Kant and the Critique of Pure Negro'. The Kant text which most notoriously uses a raciological model is 'Of National Characteristics, so far as They Depend upon the Distinct Feeling of the Beautiful and Sublime', section 4 of Immanuel Kant, *Observations on the Feeling of the Beautiful and the Sublime*, translated by John T. Goldthwait (Berkeley and Los Angeles: University of California Press, 1960). Interestingly Kant quotes the 'Swiss' Rousseau on French women as part of his consideration of national characteristics and of feminine hospitality in France (p. 102). Section 3, 'Of the Distinction of the Beautiful and Sublime in the Interrelations of the Two Sexes', would also be relevant to my concerns here. 'To Perpetual Peace' is in Immanuel Kant, *Perpetual Peace and Other Essays*, translated by Ted Humphrey (Indianapolis: Hackett Publishing Company, 1983).

58. I analyse Kant on hospitality at greater length in my *Enlightenment Hospitality*, Chapter 7.

59. 'Pieds-noirs Retour à Alger', *Le Monde*, 16 May 2006, pp. 26–7.

2

Patriarchs and their women, some inaugural intertexts of hospitality: the *Odyssey*, Abraham, Lot and the Levite of Ephraim

> If the readability of a legacy were given, natural, transparent, univocal, if it did not call for and at the same time defy interpretation, we would never have anything to inherit from it. (Derrida, *Specters of Marx*, 17)
>
> (Si la lisibilité d'un legs était donnée, naturelle, transparente, univoque, si elle n'appelait et ne défiait en même temps l'interprétation, on n'aurait jamais à en hériter. (Derrida, *Spectres de Marx*, 40))

This chapter will not attempt to trace the history of the concept or the practice of hospitality, which would require at least a book, better several books, in itself. I have analysed aspects of eighteenth-century hospitality, as a particular pressure point, in *Enlightenment Hospitality*. Here I shall give space to an analysis of some very particular key texts relating to hospitality which seem to haunt the present, or which act as nodal points crossed by the tensions that still beset us today, episodes from the *Odyssey* and from the Books of Genesis and Judges in the Old Testament. I shall go on to discuss briefly the nostalgic relationship of discourses about hospitality in general to the (text of the) past (a form or structure) which means that the past anxiously inhabits the present text. This past can equally be figured as an 'elsewhere', which can be found for instance in praise for (nomadic) Arab hospitality. Finally I shall argue that intertextuality can be understood in terms of textual hospitality, and thus also inhospitality, just as much as discourses about hospitality self-consciously refer to a legacy. What is it to be a reader, to *read*, not just in the simple sense of casting your eye over words and turning the page, but to be *formed* as a reader by a text – to be host and guest with respect to a text? Letting it welcome you in and give you sustenance, warmth and shelter – and welcoming it reciprocally, without prejudice, into your heart. As much as we may write on Derrida, we must also feel that he wrote on us; he marked our work and thus ourselves. Via other texts. In *Politics of Friendship* (Chapter 10), he quotes Kant who suggests

that adopting forms of words, gestures or practices – politeness, good behaviour – may be an illusion, like paper or even counterfeit money. Yet over time these habits of thought and deed become part of us and thus virtuous gold. Education relies upon this, including maternal education. What are 'legitimate' emotions in public and political contexts? And when reading in private, when your best friend is a book? Cixous gives us an extraordinary account of the passions aroused by books in 'Coming to Writing', for instance:

> I beat my books: I caressed them. Page after page, O beloved, licked, lacerated. With nail marks all around the printed body. What pain you cause me! I read you, I adore you, I venerate you, I listen to your work, O burning bush, but you consume yourself! You're going to burn out! Stay! Don't abandon me. ('Coming to Writing', 23)

> (J'ai battu mes livres: je les ai caressés. Page à page ô bien-aime [*sic*], léché, lacéré. A coup d'ongles tout autour du corps imprimé. Quelle douleur tu me fais! Je te lis, je t'adore, je te vénère, j'écoute ta parole, ô buisson ardent, mais tu me consumes! Tu vas t'éteindre! Reste! Ne m'abandonne pas. ('La Venue à l'écriture', 30))

Homer[1]

Homer's *Odyssey* is one of the key intertexts for thinking about hospitality in the Western world; hospitality has always, apparently, declined since the days of Homer. In the *Odyssey*, war is over, there is peace or at least the aftermath of war.[2] Although Odysseus has great physical prowess and bravery, men are not judged first and foremost by those criteria in the *Odyssey*, but rather by hospitality, the virtue of peace-time – particularly necessary in the aftermath of war, a time of travel, perhaps of home-coming. Different episodes in the *Odyssey* can be interpreted along a continuum from a hospitality of excess to bonds of mutual protection for chieftains or heads of household, bearing in mind that these rationally agreed compacts are sealed with feasting and gift exchange that always has the possibility of slipping into sacrificial superabundance. At the same time the details of the Homeric text are sufficiently complex and ambivalent to cover a range of failures of hospitality as well as hospitality itself.[3] In the first book of the *Odyssey*, for example, there are three representations of hospitality. While Telemachus' welcome of Mentes (Athene in disguise) seems to fit the paradigm perfectly, the focus throughout this first book is more on the abuse of hospitality. The background is Odysseus' fate as the unwilling guest of the nymph Calypso, and the foreground is the situation of Penelope and Telemachus as unwilling hosts to the horde of suitors, who are the epitome of badly behaved guests. While the virgin and motherless goddess *disguised as a man* (and peer) receives appropriate treatment from her male host, in both of the other cases we have open sexual difference and desire – and abuse.

The narrative of the home-coming Odysseus or Ulysses has been evoked in a wide range of contexts since Homer first sang of his experiences, and the re-tellings themselves (most obviously Joyce, a favourite for Cixous and Derrida) get re-told, re-analysed. I shall start with a quotation from Cixous's 'Sorties' taken from a passage regarding her identifications, and refusals to identify, with the heroes from both sides of the Trojan War. The context is her memories (a complex genre) of childhood in inhospitable Algeria, a site of conflict even before the 'real war' comes, where it could be hard to know which side you were placed on, and whether you could displace yourself. While the bisexual and brave lover Achilles appeals to her, with his angry outbursts against authority, Odysseus seems to epitomise the typical masculine, circular, nostalgic journey back to the origin:

> 'Silence, exile and cunning' are the tools of the young man-artist with which Stephen Dedalus arms himself to organize his series of tactical retreats while he works out in 'the smithy of his soul the uncreated conscience of his race.' A help to a loner, of course. But I didn't like to catch myself being Ulysses, the artist of flight. The Winner: the one who was saved, the homecoming man! Always returning to himself – in spite of the most fantastic detours. The Loaner: loaning himself to women and never giving himself except to the ideal image of Ulysses, bringing his inalterable resistance home to his hot-shot little phallic rock, where, as the crowning act of the *nostos* – the return, which was so similar, I said to myself, to the Jewish fantasy (next year in Jerusalem) – he produced a remarkable show of force. (Cixous, *The Newly Born Woman*, 74)

> ('Le silence, l'exil, la ruse', *silence, exile and cunning*, instruments de l'artiste jeune homme, dont Stephen Dedalus se munit pour organiser sa série de retraits tactiques, cependant qu'il élabore dans 'la forge de son âme la conscience encore incréée de sa race'. Secours de l'isolé, certes. Mais je n'aimais pas me surprendre à être Ulysse, l'artiste de la fuite. Le 'gagnant', l'épargné, l'homme du retour! Toujours revenant à lui-même –, malgré les plus fantastiques détours. Prêteur: se prêtant aux femmes ne se donnant jamais qu'à l'image idéale d'Ulysse, rapportant son inaltérable résistance à son fameux petit rocher phallique, où couronnement d'un nostos tellement semblable, me disais-je, au fantasme juif (l'an prochain à

Jerusalem), il mettait en scène une démonstration de force singulière. (*La Jeune Née*, 135–6))

For Cixous, Ulysses is a winner, *gagnant*, both economically and militarily – the play on the masculine economy is even clearer in the French. *Le retour* (translated nicely as 'homecoming') also has the sense of repetition, of exchange, of annulling the gift (when the recipient dies, the *droit de retour* returns the donation to the original possessor). Ulysses saves (himself) rather than giving (himself). I would add that this is particularly clear in the case of Nausicaa, the princess whom he allows to believe for a while that he might be a suitor in order that he might secure suitable hospitality. He lends himself, or the dream of a future with himself, to her and gets a significant return. Cixous makes a link between Ulysses' attachment to his ideal home and a Jewish dream of Jerusalem – no longer to wander, a nomad guest of others' hospitality, but to have a fixed place, the self-same. The crowning act of his return is spectacular violence – killing all the guests who have even dared to establish themselves as hosts in his (the master's) place, with a bow which was, appropriately from his perspective, a hospitality gift. This marries with the violent revenge exacted in the Old Testament on those who betray hospitality.

If we go back to the origins of the modern colonial era: in the Early Modern period, the Old World, including Africa or the East, could be defined by the knowledge of Greek and Rome; and the New World, although unknown to classical antiquity, still had to be understood via that optic. Odysseus once again proved his gift for translation/being translated, particularly for sailors with their awareness of the perils of the sea. Adventurers or explorers setting out from Europe to discover new lands often see themselves as Odysseus when they wash up on unknown territory in need of the hospitality of the inhabitants of these foreign lands – whether they are on the journey out or back. Of course in some cases they turn these more or less hospitable environments into new homes, New England, New France – whether they rewrite, edit out or exalt the hospitality of the earlier inhabitants of the 'virgin' soil, making them into cannibals like Polyphemos, lovelorn princesses like Nausicaa or lotus eaters, but usually not industrious farmers husbanding the land.[4]

Aimé Césaire's *Cahier d'un retour au pays natal* (1939) is a new Odyssey of the colonised son returning to his (the colonisers') motherland. However, as Mireille Rosello comments: 'This new Ulysses affirms in fact that Paris is not Ithaca and that the hospitality of the motherland was a lure' ('Ce nouvel Ulysse affirme en effet que Paris n'est pas Ithaque et que l'hospitalité de la mère patrie était un leurre').[5] Paris is not the true destination but a dangerous staging post:

> Césaire suddenly makes us see that Paris is a nymph, a seductive and welcoming Circe, or perhaps even a siren whom you should escape when it becomes clear that her charms are dangerous. The frontiers of France, that welcoming, hospitable land for all individuals ready to embrace the contract envisaged by the Revolution, were thus also defined by what colonialism considered its own, as proper, or indeed as native.

> (Césaire nous fait soudain envisager que Paris est une nymphe, une Circée séduisante et accueillante ou peut-être même une sirène dont il faut s'éloigner lorsqu'il devient clair que l'enchantement n'est pas sans danger. Les frontières de la France, terre d'accueil, hospitalière à tous les individus qui sont prêts à embrasser le contrat imaginé par la Révolution, étaient donc aussi définies par ce que le colonialisme considérait comme sien, comme propre ou bien comme indigène.) (Rosello, 'Frapper aux portes', 61)

Rosello points out the number of other important Francophone writers from the Antilles who have played with these Homeric tropes – one could add Anglophone examples, such as the St Lucian poet Derek Walcott's 1990 epic *Omeros*, named for the Greek Homer, although, like Cixous, Walcott prefers to translate Achilles rather than Odysseus.

Exiles and refugees forced out of their homelands may also relate themselves or be related to Odysseus. David Farr's adaptation *The Odyssey: A Trip Based on Homer's Epic* (produced at the London Hammersmith Lyric in 2005) had the General Odysseus (wanting safe passage back to his kingdom) stuck in a detention centre for would-be asylum seekers alongside a number of homeless Trojans, forced to flee after the Greeks sacked Troy. The spectator has to ask what makes a refugee (something brought home, for example, in the aftermath of the Rwandan genocide) – is the victor or perpetrator as worthy of asylum as the vanquished or the victim? Cixous too makes the link to our present situation: *Le dernier Caravansérail* is subtitled *Odyssées* in the plural. After a reference to the Trojan War and the return journeys chronicled by Homer she writes:

> Today new Wars throw out on to our planet hundreds of thousands, millions of new fugitives, fragments from shattered worlds, trembling shards from ravaged countries whose names no longer signify birthplace

as shelter but rubble or prison: Afghanistan, Iran, Iraq, Kurdistan . . ., the list of poisoned countries is growing longer every year.

But how can we tell the story of these countless odysseys?

(Aujourd'hui, de nouvelles Guerres jettent sur notre planète des centaines de milliers, des millions de nouveaux fugitifs, fragments de mondes disloqués, bribes tremblantes des pays ravagés dont les noms ne signifient plus abri natal mais décombres ou prisons: Afghanistan, Iran, Irak, Kurdistan . . ., la liste des pays empoisonnés augmente chaque année.

Mais comment raconter ces odyssées innombrables?) (*Le dernier Caravansérail*, n.p.)

She is asking how we can remember these important stories, enabling them to be told and recorded. This is only made more difficult by the demand from immigration authorities that asylum seekers sing (the right song) for their supper – as an economic condition of entry, or means of restricting entry.

When we speak of Homeric hospitality, it could be argued that the expression is merely a vague indication, a figural wave of the hand in the direction of an ancient Greek past, any details of which are long forgotten. I shall claim that in fact the details of the Homeric text we read would repay close observation. I shall be focusing on the text we read today, as literary critics often do (for aesthetic purposes), without paying the attention to its origins that a classical scholar might find necessary. Yet it is the representation, and implicit theorisation, of social and economic relations in the text that interest me. Until the middle of the last century, the Homeric text, probably 'composed' at the end of the seventh or beginning of the eighth century BC, was usually considered to represent the Mycenaean civilisation (which collapsed around the end of the thirteenth century BC); this is the period during which the Trojan War is imagined to have taken place. It was the work of Moses Finley, alongside new archaeological discoveries, that convinced the contemporary academic community that the situation was more complex. While many details such as place names or the enumeration of treasures do relate to the 'Mycenaean world', Finley argued on the basis of comparative anthropology and the 'coherence criterion' that the culture and institutions represented by Homer relate to the (early) Dark Ages that followed. He draws on the work of Mauss to analyse the complex system of total gift exchange that created personal bonds in societies less bureaucratic, centralised and fixed in their hierarchies than those that either preceded or succeeded the Greek Dark Ages. This story of the forgetting, and remembering, of archaic gift practices is highly pertinent to the analysis of the representation and theorisation of hospitality.

The *Odyssey* is the classical text of hospitality *par excellence*; it could be argued that hospitality is the major articulation of this text, and that the key form of relationship in the *Odyssey* is the one between guest and host. Hospitality is a prime motor of the text: hosts detain Odysseus and hold him back from returning home as he would wish, while scandalous guests (the suitors) create the narrative interest on the home front. Furthermore the social and moral code of hospitality is the chief means of distinguishing between men in ethical terms. Virtuous and wise men follow the code of hospitality, most particularly as hosts but also as guests, whatever their social status. I should add that following the code is not a simple matter since it prescribes not obedience to a letter, but rather a spirit of generosity that might be understood as simultaneously natural to a good man and cultivated by a virtuous man, but has a fantasmatic relationship to femininity.

While Irigaray has not, to my knowledge, written extensively on Homer, she has insisted in a number of texts on the crucial importance of Greek mythology to our understanding of sexual difference. Margaret Whitford writes with reference to comments in Irigaray's *Le Temps de la différence*, *Je, tu, nous* and *Sexes and Genealogies*: 'Irigaray sees the Greek myths as figurations of a struggle between matriarchy and patriarchy in which patriarchy finally won. There is some suggestion that she sees the struggles as being in some sense still with us . . . Only now instead of a struggle for dominance she sees it more as a struggle for the maternal principle to return to the light of day.'[6]

Although there are many ways in which hospitality can prove devastating, including the case of the murderer-guest (and the suitors do try to kill Telemachus), it is *smothering* hospitality that is critical for father and son in the *Odyssey*. The rational social code of hospitality should prevent excessive hospitality between men – and Menelaus explains to Telemachus how the laws of hospitality dictate moderation, although he seems unable to follow his own dictates. The letter of the laws is never enough – the unbounded spirit is both necessary and dangerous. Menelaus is, of course, of all the men in the *Odyssey*, the closest to the dangerous feminine principle as it is encapsulated in his wife Helen.

In the *Odyssey*, female *hosts*, by which I mean relatively autonomous hosts who are also female, are characteristically amorous and thus liable to hold our hero back – the two examples par excellence are the nymphs Circe and Calypso. None of the human women who engage in hospitality have this degree of autonomy (instead they are hostesses), and the majority of them (Helen, Nausicaa [and her mother Arete], Penelope) are perhaps presented as wiser and more generous than the nymphs – less threatening. At any rate they have less power to detain a guest even if they wish to do so. Nevertheless, in all three cases, though in three completely different ways, amorous passion and deception are significant elements inflecting hospitable relations.[7]

There are many examples of hospitality in the *Odyssey*, about which a great deal could be said. Steve Reece has devoted a book purely to the analysis of hospitality scenes in Homer – although without focusing on questions of sexual difference.[8] I refer/defer to him for a number of thorny issues, for instance, regarding the establishment of the text. One of the particular problems for those professionally concerned with Homer as a poet is that 'conventional' or 'type' scenes may be considered as particularly likely to have had elements or phrases interpolated. As Reece points out, hospitality scenes are normally composites of smaller type-scenes (such as arrival, reception, seating, bathing, feasting, gift-giving) all composed in formulaic diction and in a relatively fixed order. Scribes who left us the many different manuscripts of the *Odyssey* may have been particularly likely to make concordance additions in scenes where convention dictates certain components (for instance, Circe's feast preparation). For the purposes of my particular concerns, issues of attestation are interesting but less vital than for those concerned with Homer the poet and the internal consistency or otherwise of his text. Historical *expectations* of hospitality scenes, and versions of Homer that have been read by and have influenced later generations, are of at least equivalent interest to me.

In the *Odyssey* the hospitality narrative can be divided up into three major strands: Odysseus as guest, Telemachus as guest (and host), and the suitors as guests and hosts. Odysseus as guest is of course the major interest – it is his hosts' desire to detain him that in an important sense provides the rationale for the whole story of his prolonged home-coming. The 'hosts' he encounters run the gamut from Polyphemos who eats his 'guests' and the sirens whose entertainment means destruction, to, say, Alcinous and his family who provide clothes, bath, food, shelter, music, gifts and finally a ship to take him back to Ithaca. In between the two poles there are those nymphs who tend him lovingly and provide for all his sensual needs *but* will not willingly release him to continue his journey as he wishes. It would, however, be over-simplistic to suggest either that the hosts can easily be evaluated according to whether they meet the standards of hospitality – many readers have judged Alcinous and his fellow Phaeacians as distinctly lacking in hospitality in spite of the facts briefly summarised above – or that Odysseus and his men always play the part of good guests.

The 'Telemachy' sub-plot is considered by Reece to be particularly powerful in the way in which it establishes practical and emotional parallels between father and son. In this respect it is homosocial hospitality par excellence. The son has grown up without a father – the story takes place as he reaches manhood and begins to attempt in a rather muddled way to establish some authority over his beleaguered mother. His journey from home to attempt to find (news of) his father reinforces his belief in his paternity – hosts comment on his resemblance to Odysseus and he hears tales of his father's prowess. At the same time he undergoes, in a minor key, experiences that will help him to mature and to understand his father's story. He learns of the ambiguity as well as the value of hospitality, and what it is to be a guest detained. In this respect the sub-plot involves the education of the son, a particular aspect of 'filiation', as discussed by Derrida in *Glas* with respect to Hegel's account of the founding of the family.[9] Both Nestor and his family and Menelaus and Helen are very helpful to Telemachus, but neither set of hosts are straightforwardly so. This complex experience helps to bond him to his father.

The suitors' sub-plot is more obviously integral to the main narrative, creating the tension that makes a difference exactly when Odysseus returns home, and it makes his home-coming excitingly dangerous in a way that spectacularly reveals both his trademark cleverness and his physical strength. What is of particular concern to me is the fact that the unfolding of this sub-plot is entirely bound up with the transgression of hospitality. The suitors' wickedness is established (and this is necessary for listeners to rejoice at their destruction) chiefly by showing them to be overbearing and exploitative guests, and dreadful hosts, rather than by the mere fact that they are courting the unwilling Penelope. Social and economic relations *between men* are thus foregrounded, and even the wise Penelope may simply be sent away by her son.

A great deal can be, and has been, said about all this without particular reference to sexual difference. I shall now try briefly to elaborate on some of the ways in which attention to sexual difference opens up the text. The first, perhaps obvious, point to note is that women do not travel in the *Odyssey* – women are not guests. 'Nomads conquer their territory against the familiarity of the first site, against the sedentary, against the more maternal, more feminine values. They create a culture of between-men, who are enemies or accomplices, for which the divinity is instead patriarchal, God-the-Father' (Irigaray, *BEW*, 13) ('Les nomades conquièrent leur territoire contre la familiarité du premier site, contre les sédentaires, contre les valeurs plus maternelles, plus féminines. Ils créent une culture de l'entre-hommes, ennemis ou complices, dont la divinité est plutôt patriarcale, le Dieu-Père' (*EOO*, 24)). Irigaray's comment here applies equally to the Old Testament and to Homer. When the goddess Athene, the Father-god's virgin daughter, plays the role of a guest in the *Odyssey* she disguises herself as a man. Women are at home, and must be at home, even if, as we shall see, they are not really *at home*. The traditional feminine sphere is the domestic one: women should be inside by (if not actually tending) the hearth. Outside the house in which they live they are particularly vulnerable – and patriarchy might instruct us that they are particularly vulnerable to being shamed, to rape for example. Furthermore women *are* home – they are home for men in a number of ways. 'The family, like woman, moreover, is simultaneously overvalorized and devalorized, colonized' (Irigaray, *BEW*, 14) ('La famille, comme la femme d'ailleurs, est à la fois survalorisée et dévalorisée, colonisée' (*EOO*, 25–6)).

But if we turn to women as hosts or hostesses, then we might note that in some senses women might not be 'at home'; that expression implies a sense of comfort, of feeling at ease in your own environment; it also implies being willing to receive guests. Women might be in someone else's household (their father's or their husband's or even their brother's or son's) and thus their power to act as hostess would be delegated and secondary. They are particularly vulnerable to rape. Susan Brownmiller would argue that patriarchy plays on that vulnerability to keep women in their place and feeling in need of patriarchal protection. Should the master of the house ever be absent (like Odysseus), what might women do to protect themselves from unexpected guests? Freud picks up in a strangely perverse way on the cultural association between women and weaving – he sees this as a technology that protects their modesty, hiding what they do not have.[10] Women can weave clothes, cloth acting as a shield between men and women. Penelope's weaving, and unweaving, is only the most famous example of the very act of weaving being used for apotropaic effect.[11] The apotropaic shield *par excellence*, the Medusa's head (borne by Athena) that petrifies men, reminds us how patriarchy plays on women's vulnerability in part because, as patriarchal mythology shows us, women are not only desired but feared for their sexual power. This imagined power is lethal: the power to be unfaithful to a husband threatens the father's immortality through his descendants who might not be his after all; sexual power is also a power to lure men to their deaths as the sirens do, transform them into beasts as the nymph Circe does, entangle and destroy them like Clytemnestra and her lover. I shall now look briefly at four categorisations of women in the *Odyssey*: the siren or nymph, the prize wife or mother, the servant, and the father's virgin daughter.

Sirens and nymphs suggest to the listener women as sexually entrapping to a greater or lesser extent – bringing men to their doom or simply imprisoning them. This is how women are – in men's dreams. On the human plane this is played out in a vestigial sense with Nausicaa who immediately looks upon Odysseus as a potential husband. More complicated still is the older generation – in particular the figure of the beautiful Helen. In the episode when Menelaus entertains Telemachus, on the one hand Helen is presented, and *presents herself*, as wise, caring, sensitive, helpful beyond her husband. On the other hand, we are reminded of the number of men who lost their lives because of her enchantment by the guest Paris, or by Aphrodite – or was it Helen who was the enchantress? The poet reminds us too of Clytemnestra – a tale of feminine adultery, deception and murder – Agamemnon killed in the bath, the bath which is a key element in so many hospitality scenes. Helen tells Telemachus (and us) a tale of her help to her guest Odysseus, disguised as a beggar, reconnoitring in Troy prior to the building of the horse. Without directly contradicting this story Menelaus counters it with his own story of how Helen, accompanied by her *second* Trojan husband (as if one were not bad enough), sought to make the Greeks hidden in the horse betray themselves by calling to them in the voices of their wives. This tale embodies the layers of deception associated with Helen and the perils of containment or enclosure. One of the ways in which Helen entertains Telemachus and his companion is by giving them an Egyptian drug which makes them forget their sorrows – to the point that they could hear songs of the destruction of members of their families and not weep. It helps them sleep well and could be seen as entirely benign – even if magical – like the sleep that overcomes Penelope thanks to Athene. But it also evokes other episodes such as the visit to the dangerously beguiling land of the Lotus eaters, and Helen's powers, like those of the nymphs who entertain Odysseus, may not be entirely benign.[12]

The woman as prize wife, to be won by the strongest or cleverest as her nearest male kinsman dictates, returns via Penelope (and perhaps lurks underneath the story of Nausicaa and the Phaeacian games). Penelope – usually summarily remembered for her wisdom in keeping the suitors at bay by weaving and unpicking a shroud for Laertes – is treated a little less favourably in the detail of the text. Both Athene and Telemachus treat her with less than perfect respect, seeking to keep her in a woman's place, apart from men. When Athena first appears to Telemachus (disguised as Mentes), s/he tells him:

> as for your mother, if she is set on marrying, let her go back to her father's house. He is a man of consequence, and the family will provide a marriage feast, and see that she has a generous dowry, as is only right for a daughter they value. . . . You are no longer a child: you must put childish thoughts away. Have you not heard what a name Prince Orestes made for himself in the world when he killed the traitor Aegisthus for murdering his noble father? You, my friend – and what a tall and splendid fellow you have grown! – must be as brave as Orestes. Then future generations will sing your praises. (*Odyssey*, 28–9)

Matricide is buried in this speech; Orestes' only crime, here in fact an *exploit*, is killing Aegisthus – his mother is not even mentioned. Similarly the sacrifice of the daughter (Iphigenia) by her father is often 'forgotten' as a motive for Clytemnestra's crime. We modern readers might remember from the *Oresteia* that Orestes (only temporarily mad, unlike his sister and co-conspirator Electra who *remains* mad) is redeemed for his matricide by the motherless and chaste Athena and by Apollo, the lover of men.[13] Here Telemachus is urged to renounce his mother too in order to become the man he already is. This is the particular paradoxical structure of masculinity. Reaching physical manhood with respect to age or biology he is a man naturally (and it is important to cling to this conviction), but also must become a man culturally (striving or struggle is necessary to manhood).[14] Irigaray points out how frequently women are assimilated to nature, and sexual difference treated as analogous to the nature/culture opposition; for her it is urgent that *both* sexes cultivate both their nature and their cultural becoming. While Telemachus will refuse to send Penelope away from 'his' house, shortly afterwards he acts out the expulsion in a lesser form saying to his surprised mother: 'go to your quarters and attend to your own work, the loom and the spindle, and tell the servants to get on with theirs. Talking must be men's concern, and mine in particular; for I am master in this house' (31). Penelope's situation (position and location) is an ambiguous one while her lord and master is away. She is disempowered as hostess in the absence of Odysseus not only vis-à-vis the suitors' wolfish rapacity but also in relation to the series of beggars who exploit her desire to hear news of her husband. Her ways of keeping things going are always suspect; she is imagined at fault and made guilty by the men around her. When Telemachus complains in the public Assembly about the unwelcome guests who are eating him out of house and home, the suitor Antinous replies: 'It is your own mother, that incomparable schemer who is the culprit.' At this Assembly of Ithaca's leaders, Antinous (the least hospitable of the suitors) replies to Telemachus' charge that they are frittering away his wealth by explaining how Penelope deceived them for nearly four years by pretending to be weaving a shroud for Laertes, and advises Telemachus:

> Send your mother away and make her marry the man whom her father chooses and whom she prefers. She must beware of trying our young men's patience much further and counting too much on the matchless gifts that she owes to Athene, her skill in fine handiwork, her excellent brain, and that genius she has for getting her way. In that respect, I grant she has no equal, not even in story. . . . Yet in the present case Penelope has used these wits amiss. For I assure you that so long as she maintains this attitude that she has been misguided enough to adopt, the Suitors will continue to eat you out of house and home. She may be winning a great name for cleverness, but at what expense to you! (36–7)

Telemachus replies:

> It is quite impossible for me to cast out the mother who bore me and who brought me up, with my father somewhere at the world's end and, as likely as not, still alive. Think, first, what I should have to pay Icarius if I took it into my head to send my mother back to him. Again, when that father of hers had done his worst to me, the gods would step in and let loose on me the avenging Furies that my mother's curses would call up as she was driven from home. And finally my fellow-men would cry shame

upon me. . . . If a feeling of shame has any place in your own hearts, then quit my palace and feast yourselves elsewhere, eating your own provisions in each other's houses. But if you think it a sounder scheme to destroy one man's estate and go scot-free yourselves, then eat your fill, while I pray to the immortal gods for a day of reckoning, when *I* can go scot-free, though I destroy you in that house of mine. (37–8).

Naturally everything is the woman Penelope's fault.

The female servants in the master's house often play a key and intimate role in hospitality – for example bathing the guest. Nestor's hospitality is marked as particularly warm and informal by the fact that his daughter, rather than a servant, bathes Telemachus. While Odysseus is away from his house the position of the female servants is a difficult one and many of them have sexual relations with the suitors. This is referred to as rape. Odysseus says to the suitors: 'You ate me out of house and home; you raped my maids; you wooed my wife on the sly though I was alive' (339).[15] However, the women are still deemed unfaithful and disloyal – Odysseus orders that they should be killed by the sword. Telemachus, who has also been obliged to consort with the suitors, does not, however, want the maids to have such a clean death; thus in Book XXII they are given a deliberately degrading punishment, and *hanged* for their crime.[16] Modern readers may recall how women's sexual 'collaboration' in Occupied France was punished in a range of humiliating ways after the Second World War – of course French men who, as prisoners in Germany, had succeeded in forming sexual relationships with German women could be viewed in a more heroic light.

The final category I shall briefly evoke is that of the motherless Athena who sprang fully-formed from Zeus' head, as we know from other sources.[17] Irigaray comments briefly on her appearance in the *Oresteia* in 'The Bodily Encounter with the Mother'; and argues that this mythology underlying patriarchy has not changed:

Here and there, regulation Athenas whose one begetter is the head of the Father-King still burst forth. Completely in his pay, in the pay of the men in power, they bury beneath their sanctuary women in struggle so that they will no longer disturb the new order of the home, the order of the polis, now the only order. You can recognise these regulation Athenas, perfect models of femininity, always veiled and dressed from head to toe, all very respectable, by this token: they are extraordinarily seductive [*séductrices*], which does not necessarily mean enticing [*séduisantes*], but aren't in fact interested in making love. ('The Bodily Encounter with the Mother', 37)

(Encore lieu aussi que surgissent de-ci de-là, les Athénas de service engendrées par le seul cerveau du Père-Roi. Tout à sa solde – soit à celle des hommes au pouvoir – et qui enterrent les femmes en lutte sous leur sanctuaire, pour qu'elles ne troublent pas l'ordre des foyers, l'ordre de la cité, l'ordre tout court. Ces Athénas de service, modèles parfaits de féminité, toujours voilées et parées de la tête aux pieds, très dignes, vous les reconnaitrez à ce signe: elles sont extraordinairement séductrices (ce qui ne veut pas dire forcément séduisantes), extraordinairement séductrices mais que faire l'amour, en fait, ne les intéresse pas. (*Le Corps-à-corps avec la mère*, 17–18))

Athena, like her father Zeus, is a patron of hospitality (*xenia*). René Schérer argues that Zeus is known as 'hospitable' not because he is shown as a host in the various legends, but rather because he might be disguised as a guest and therefore requires human hospitality.[18] The same might be said of Athena, who arrives as an unexpected visitor (Mentes) for Telemachus at the beginning of the *Odyssey*. We might note that the visitation is almost always in masculine form.[19]

It could be argued that the *Odyssey* as we know it tells two stories about women. It presents to us Penelope who is wise, strong and loyal; it also gives us Penelope who is sent to her rooms by Telemachus and ordered not to speak, Penelope about whom Athene warns her son. It introduces Nausicaa as an interesting and clever princess who is a key factor in the hospitality offered to Odysseus by the Phaeacians, and then drops her from the narrative of Odysseus' stay with the Phaeacians altogether. The Nausicaa episode is also the only instance of a (brief glimpse of a) happy mother–daughter relationship. Most striking to the contemporary reader is the representation of Helen. As she plays hostess to Telemachus in a generous and sensitive way she tells him of one of her memories of Odysseus – a memory of her cleverly outwitting the master of disguise in order to play host to him in Troy. But this is set against reminders of Helen's overarching role in the Trojan War – cause of the loss of so many lives thanks to her rapt by the ungrateful and deceitful guest, Paris. Menelaus' tale perhaps shows her lethal siren deceitfulness, her infidelity, *and* her being outwitted by Odysseus. These are two contrasting interpretations of the past (the husband's and the wife's), and the text we have inherited simply allows both to stand. On the other hand, no such doubt is cast over the setting in the present. It reveals a particular sexual inequality when it comes to vertical relations, to descendants. When Telemachus arrives, Helen and Menelaus are 'celebrating' a double wedding – we might note that the son who is marrying is the son of one of Menelaus' mistresses – Helen is now barren we are told. Helen's only child, a daughter, is being married to Achilles' son, the result of a battlefield bargain between the fathers. While sons bring their wives home, the daughter's marriage means her exile to a distant and unknown land. There are echoes here – distantly the echo of Demeter and her daughter Persephone exiled in Hades, more closely that of Iphigenia, lured to her death with the promise of marriage to Achilles, and Clytemnestra who kills Agamemnon in revenge.

I shall briefly sum up some of the points in these episodes. The first concerns horizontal inequality: sexual infidelity, even if involuntary, of women should by rights be punished; it is a kind of magic that makes Menelaus forgive Helen; the serving women get their just desserts. (This magic may cover an issue of land ownership or Menelaus' right to the kingdom that originally came to him through his marriage to Helen.) It is normal for chieftains (Agamemnon, Menelaus and even Odysseus) to have concubines. The second point concerns vertical inequality: the pleasure of a good relationship between mother and daughter, and the pain of losing a daughter for a mother, is present but elided. Men bond through the father's gift of a daughter to her husband. Fathers pass on material and cultural inheritance to their sons. And the father should be able to sacrifice the mother's daughter unpunished; Athene, the daughter who is not born of a mother, but of a father, serves the patriarchal cause. The third point is the structure of enclosure: women are dangerous and should be contained (nymphs on their islands, wives and mothers in their quarters with their beds and their weaving) or even expelled from the text – although the repressed of course returns.

For men, hospitality functions as a test of proper virtuous manliness – some are shown to be good, some bad. Zeus is the god who presides over hospitality while some inhuman male hosts (notably Polyphemos) are the antithesis of hospitality. Hospitality as a test of masculine virtue is a difficult one, and while many perform well they could do better; it is hard to find exactly the right ground between falling short (being insufficiently welcoming) and going beyond (being excessively officious), between the laws and the Law. We might ask whether it is a mythical feminine hysteral economy of abundance that haunts good old Nestor and Menelaus in their retention of guests. Women meanwhile do not have a place of their own. Nymphs and sirens show listeners what can happen when females do have their own place: they enslave their male guests to their senses. It is not that women are portrayed as stupid, passive, purely sensual or emotional creatures in Homer, as they will be in so many later texts. On the contrary they are wise, active and rational as well as sensual beings. The problem lies in their interaction with men, their effect on men being often revealed as a lethal one – bringing men to oblivion, if not to death, singly or indeed in multitudes. Irigaray's point that men project fears and phantasms (in particular castration anxiety) onto women as other of the same – deceivers – is here writ large. The effect of female hosts is sticky – leading to stasis, entropy, the forgetting of the project. That could indeed be (listeners might feel) the effect of hostesses like Helen or Nausicaa or even Penelope were they not more or less successfully disempowered. Women must be contained in the home to be no more than hostesses as handmaidens to the master of the house.

Genesis: Abraham and Lot

Derrida writes of hospitality:

> This is a conjugal model, paternal and phallogocentric. It's the familial despot, the father, the spouse and the boss, the master of the house who lays down the laws of hospitality. He represents them and submits to them to submit the others to them in this violence of the power of hospitality, in this force of ipseity. (*OH*, 149)

> (Il s'agit d'un modèle conjugal, paternel et phallogocentrique. C'est le despote familial, le père, l'époux et le patron, le maître de céans qui fait les lois de l'hospitalité. Il les représente et s'y plie pour y plier les autres dans cette violence du pouvoir d'hospitalité, dans cette puissance de l'ipséité. (*DH*, 131))

He then goes on to discuss two biblical tales of threatened sodomy and the substitution of women: the stories of Lot and of the Levite of Ephraim. In both cases the host is himself a guest in the community rather than a native, and in both tales the host's house is under siege from those who want to rape his guest(s); to save the male guest from sodomy a woman is sacrificed. Hospitality is 'set up' as a relation between men, between the master of the house and his guest, but it is suffused with fantasies of (sexual) vulnerability, and open to many forms of abuse, not only in relation to host and guest, but in relation to third parties, for instance 'womenfolk' (Lot's daughters or the Levite's concubine) – part of the household, if not the goods, of the master or his guest, and sacrificed to consummate the sacred bond of shared consumption between men.

Thus in the final paragraphs of *Of Hospitality* (151–5; *DH*, 131–7), Derrida re-tells two violently shocking stories from the Old Testament, that of Lot (Genesis 19) and that of the Levite of Ephraim (Judges 19–21), as an indication of a tradition we have inherited where the law of hospitality is not only co-extensive with ethics but is placed above a certain ethic (such as family obligations). Lot offers hospitality to 'two angels' at the gates of the city of Sodom (in present-day Jordan), and refuses to give up his two guests to the Sodomites who wish to 'penetrate' them (Derrida uses André Chouraqui's translation *pénétrer*, other translations use 'know'), and instead offers his two virgin daughters. The Sodomites do not accept the substitution of Lot's daughters, and threaten him, an alien, as well as his guests – they are about to force his door when the angels strike them with blindness. When the Lord destroys Sodom with fire only Lot and his two daughters are saved – his (prospective) son-in-laws do not believe that there is any need to flee and his wife is turned into a pillar of salt because she looks back. The second bloody episode is in the Book of Judges in which a Levite and his concubine are forced to seek hospitality with an old man living amongst the Benjamites. He, like Lot, refuses to give up the Levite to the Benjamites' 'unnatural' desires, and offers his virgin daughter as a substitute.[20] The Levite instead offers his beloved concubine who is repeatedly raped throughout the night and expires at dawn. Vengeance is then repeatedly wreaked upon the Benjamites until only six hundred men remain.

Many evocations of hospitality over the centuries have made positive reference to the exhortations to hospitality in the Bible, both Old and New Testaments, and to the hospitable behaviour of the patriarchs – although there has also long been a practice of attacking the 'Jewish Bible' for its inconsistencies and examples of bad behaviour (not least during the French Enlightenment). Derrida is less interested in praising or blaming than in analysing a patriarchal tradition that still inflects behaviour today. I shall begin my own analysis slightly earlier in Genesis with Lot's uncle and patron Abraham – also a key figure for Derrida and for many writers on hospitality (or on sacrifice).[21]

Hospitality in the Old Testament has a great deal in common with the pattern noticed in Homer – the ritual washing of the guest as well as the meal and shelter, the reception of the stranger without demanding his name. I would argue that the (unconditional) offer of hospitality is used as a measure of virtue in the Old Testament as it is in Homer. This is true even for women – when Abraham sends a servant to find a wife for his son Isaac amongst his kinfolk, the test of her suitability is that she gives the servant water from the well, and then offers water to his camels (Genesis 24). Jean Chardin, reflecting on travelling in late seventeenth-century Persia, argues that Abrahamic hospitality functions as a model for Muslims:

> The Persians say in praise of hospitality that *Abraham never ate without a guest*, and that that fortunate encounter with the three angels, of which it is spoken in the Scriptures, happened to him one day when, since no-one had arrived by dinner time, he went out of his tent to see if some acquaintance, or someone worthy of an invitation, would pass by. So, in their homes, everything is eaten, as I have observed, without anything being kept for another time, and the remainder is given to the poor, if there is any.
>
> (Les Persans disent à la louange de l'hospitalité, qu'*Abraham ne mangeait jamais sans hôte*, et que cette heureuse rencontre des trois anges, dont il est parlé dans l'Ecriture, lui arriva un jour que, n'étant encore venu personne à l'heure du dîner, il sortit de son pavillon pour voir s'il ne passerait point quelqu'un de sa connaissance, ou qui fût digne d'être invité. Aussi on mange tout chez eux, comme je l'ai observé, sans garder jamais rien pour une autre fois, et on donne le reste aux pauvres, s'il y en a.)[22]

Here the Protestant Chardin enacts textual hospitality as he praises the generosity of his erstwhile hosts.[23] He subtly links the ethical open-door hospitality of Persians (present-day Iranians), which includes the humble with the great, with an Abrahamic tradition. Abraham goes out to invite in (almost) any stranger, in this instance, angels. This ties together Jews and Christians with Muslims in a potentially positive tradition of hospitality – quite a different tack from that of, say, Voltaire, whose Old Testament examples usually function negatively (Abraham as child-killer rather than host). Religious (in)tolerance is a key aspect of State or collective (in)hospitality. I would also note the consumption of all the food (rather than saving for the morrow) – while this can be ideologically linked to profligacy, here it is associated with generosity and attention to those who have less. It is also positively associated with sobriety, by which Chardin means not eating (or drinking) to excess – something he much admires for health reasons, but also, here, because it means that there is enough for a larger number of people.

Chouraqui, the celebrated scholar of both the Jewish and the Christian Bible and also the Koran, writes in his commentary on Genesis, which he translates from the Hebrew as *Entête*, of 'the generosity proper to Abraham and his passion for hospitality' ('la générosité propre à Abraham et sa passion de l'hospitalité').[24] When Abraham welcomes the angels (Genesis 18, ii–v), Chouraqui notes:

> A typical tableau of the rituals of hospitality; the guests remain at a respectful distance from the opening of the tent. The master of the house demonstrates his great desire to receive them: he *runs . . . Prostrates himself*, he insists and describes in advance all that he is ready to offer them. The guests only accept when the rituals reassure them about the sincerity of the quality of invitation that is being made to them.
>
> (Tableau typique des rites de l'hospitalité; les hôtes se tiennent à distance respectueuse de l'ouverture de la tente. Le maître de maison manifeste son vif désir de les accueillir: il *court . . . Se prosterne*, il insiste et décrit par avance tout ce qu'il est prêt à leur offrir. Les hôtes n'acceptent que lorsque les rites les rassurent sur la sincérité de la qualité de l'invitation qui leur est faite.) (*Entête*, 138)

Abraham instructs Sarah to use three measures of flour to make cakes; Chouraqui remarks that three *séah* is about forty litres: 'Abraham is not skimping on anything. The meal will be prepared, according to nomadic custom, with the best of what there is in the camp' ('Abraham ne lésine sur rien. Le repas va être préparé suivant la coutume des nomades avec ce qu'il y a de meilleur dans le camp' (*Entête*, 138)). Lot, while still exemplary, is a little more cautious – rising to meet his unexpected visitors but not *running* to greet them – perhaps simply because he is not quite Abraham or (Chouraqui speculates) because his hospitality is slightly tarnished thanks to his sojourn amongst the wicked people of Sodom. Chouraqui points out that Lot inverts the order of the typical offer for the guests to wash their feet and then to spend the night – perhaps, he wonders, knowing the Sodomites, Lot would like to be able to point to the dust on his visitors' feet to indicate that they have only just appeared. His attention to the detail of the Biblical text allows both for the allegorical interpretations and for a historical-cultural one; both have considerable purchase on traditions to come.

One twentieth-century example of the association, made in the Enlightenment by Chardin, of Abrahamic hospitality with religious tolerance comes from Louis Massignon (1883–1962), cited by Derrida on a number of occasions including in the closing paragraphs of *Of Hospitality*. Massignon is particularly interested in Abraham's attempt to intercede with God on behalf of the people of Sodom, which occurs between Abraham's entertaining the three angels to which Chardin refers (Genesis 18, i–xv) and Lot's entertaining two of the angels in Sodom. At Christmas in 1956, Massignon is in the Middle East trying to intercede between two terrorisms; he says that his spark of faith is kept alive more by the condemned criminals and Muslims than by those 'bon vivant', 'bien pensant' 'Christians' and 'Jews' who pursue and torture them.[25] Evoking 'our Father Abraham', he writes of his Muslim brothers:

> For these, who are abandoned, there is only one work of misericord, Hospitality; and it is by this alone, not by legal observance, that we cross the threshold of the Sacred: Abraham showed us the way.
>
> Let us seek thus with Abraham, in [the home of] the Muslims whom we are driving into the most atrocious despair, in the Accursed City where we are pushing them – the City of the essential Refusal, of the Denial of Hospitality, asked of Lot, – that final spark of Faith.
>
> (Pour ces délaissés, il n'y a plus qu'une oeuvre de miséricorde, l'Hospitalité; et c'est par elle seule, non par les observances légales, qu'on dépasse le seuil du Sacré: Abraham nous l'a montré.
>
> Cherchons donc avec Abraham, chez les musulmans que nous acculons au désespoir le plus atroce, dans la Cité Maudite òu nous les poussons – Cité du Refus essential, du Reniement de l'Hospitalité, demandé à Lot, – cette ultime étincelle de Foi.) (*Parole donnée*, 285)

Abraham asks God if he will spare the Sodomites if there are fifty good men in the city, and finally barters him down to but ten (Genesis 18, xxiii–xxxiii). Massignon concludes:

> Formerly Abraham, the Friend of God, had objected to Him that there could be ten sparks of Faith still burning, ten believing hosts living in Jordanian Sodom, to save it from the Fire; – no doubt it is from the depths of the spiritual Sodom, from the Hell of 'Il Primor Amore', where Jesus went down to re-kindle the extinguished fire of hospitality that the salvational Indignation of the Judge will spurt forth.
>
> (Abraham, l'Ami de Dieu, Lui avait objecté jadis dix étincelles de Foi encore brûlantes, dix hôtes croyants habitant la Sodome jordanienne, pour la sauver du Feu; – c'est sans doute du fond de la Sodome spirituelle, de l'Enfer d''Il Primor Amore', où Jésus est descendu rallumer le feu de l'hospitalité éteinte que jaillira l'Indignation salvatrice du Juge.) (*Parole donnée*, 285)

A key issue is sexuality – for many readers what is at stake in the story of Lot is the sodomy of the Sodomites, considered as an illicit sexual practice, sometimes translated by mystic or Gnostic readers into 'sterility'.[26] Yet it may be argued that the divine test is not whether or not consensual sodomy is practised, but whether the laws of hospitality (which Abraham has just followed in an exemplary fashion, and his nephew follows too) are observed. The laws of hospitality do not permit raping a guest of either sex – and this is made clearer in the tale of the Levite where the substitution of a woman for a man is accepted by the predators, but does not save them from excessive revenge. One of the aspects that interests Derrida is the question of competing moral codes – does the duty to shelter a guest (stranger) trump everything else including any responsibility for the safety of your own family (and this relates to Kant's argument that the duty to tell the truth takes precedence over the duty of hospitality)?

Alongside homophobic concentration on the sins of Sodom, there is a certain tradition of celebrating the hospitality of the Sodomites as a particular way of embracing the foreigner. Schérer cites Guy Hocqenghem's *La Beauté du métis*[27] (and I could add Jonathan Dollimore's *Sexual Dissidence*[28]) in support of the argument that 'homosexuality' (*avant* or *après la lettre*) is particularly receptive to cultural or class difference; and for Schérer, the reversibility of homosexuality mirrors the reversibility of the *hôte* – he specifically rejects any move into active host and passive invited guest (*invité*) (*Zeus hospitalier*, 148, 206–9). While Schérer's nostalgia for a Golden Age of erotic hospitality does not necessarily exclude women (he criticises Odysseus for his failure to respond to Nausicaa), he is unsympathetic to female figures who exercise caution. He refers to Penelope as: 'Odious shrew, a bourgeoise *avant la lettre*! That bitch Penelope with the locked heart!' ('Odieuse mégère, bourgeoise avant la lettre! Salope Pénélope au coeur fermé!' (170)). This comment pays no attention to any political or economic reading of the suitors' behaviour.

I argued with respect to Homer that (human) women cannot safely act as hosts or guests in their own right – they are deemed to need the protection and authority of the master of the house. Although sometimes that fails, as in the case of Paris' theft of Helen, revenge is then exacted by a band of brothers – and when Menelaus duels with Paris he calls on Zeus to help him avenge the betrayal of hospitality. In the Old Testament it could be argued that the homosocial bond of hospitality goes beyond Homer in its explicit willingness to sacrifice women. The patriarch does not protect his women in the stories to which Derrida draws our attention – he abandons her to sexual predation to save himself or his male guest.

Homer, and his later interpreters, tell us two stories about women

– one that seems more empowering (sometimes helped by the range of goddesses and female demi-deities) and one which shows the abuse of women as daughters, concubines or servants. The Old Testament presents respected wives (Sarah or Rebecca) as well as expendable daughters and concubines, and yet even Sarah and Rebecca are sacrificed by the patriarchs when they find themselves economic refugees in potentially hostile territory. When Abraham flees from famine, he grows very rich in Egypt because he presents the beautiful Sarah as his sister and she is taken as a 'wife' by the Pharaoh.[29] The Lord intervenes, striking the Pharaoh and his household with disease until they send Abraham away with Sarah, and the cattle, silver and gold he has accumulated (Genesis 12). Abraham repeats the trick in Gerar (Genesis 20) – much of his wealth as a migrant is earned by Sarah's body.

Abraham's son Isaac is, in some respects, a product of hospitality – a miraculous birth that occurs more or less a gestation period after Abraham and Sarah have entertained the three strangers. Just as the story of Telemachus is a minor parallel to Odysseus' noble adventures, but shows the son learning of his father in a visceral fashion, so Isaac's tribulations seem less than those of Abraham. Yet Isaac too is a nomad, fleeing from famine and taking refuge with a people who might do him harm, and so, like his father, he insists that his beautiful wife is his sister (in spite of the probable consequences for her) so that he is not killed for her sake (Genesis 26). I shall return to the conception of Isaac in the next chapter.

Judges: the Levite of Ephraim

The story of Lot (never mind the stories of Abraham) has received a great deal of cultural commentary and re-writing over the centuries. This is less true of the later story, in the Book of Judges, although Rousseau turns it into a fascinating prose poem.[30] It has a number of clear similarities with the tale of Lot, but also some important differences. Amongst these is the intriguing element that the story begins with, or is framed by, excessive hospitality. If not as extreme as the sort Odysseus encounters, this does again show anxiety about smothering or sticky hosts – in the context of general praise of hospitality. The Levite's nameless concubine (or wife, depending on the interpretation) has run away from him in a fit of anger, and returned to her father in Bethlehem. After about four months the Levite has come to take her home to Ephraim. He is very well entertained by her father, and the Bible narrative tells convincingly how each successive day they are persuaded first to have something to eat and drink, and then to stay the night because it has got late. On the fifth day they again accept the feasting, but the Levite refuses to stay yet another night. This need to escape the over-generous hospitality of the woman's father means that they are forced to spend a night en route near Jerusalem – and this is the context of the tragedy. Another difference is that while Lot takes in total strangers (the classic divine visitation), the old man who takes in the Levite and his mistress is from the hill county of Ephraim like the Levite. The Levite's general identity has been established, and thus it is not quite unconditional hospitality at the outset as is Lot's or Abraham's for the angels.

The old man is a stranger amongst the Benjamites, but they are all Israelites – the Levite has chosen to stay in Gibeah rather than in a strange town where the people are not Israelites. Thus the violence that occurs is in a sense between cousins, if not brothers, unlike the Sodomites' threatened violence towards Lot. Although it is true that in both cases the reader is presented with a structure in which it seems as if the resident stranger takes in passing strangers, and is effectively punished by the host community for his boldness, the vengeance subsequently wreaked on the Benjamites is experienced rather differently (with belated anxiety) than is the punishment of the Sodomites.

Both stories concern the substitution of one locus which, by the local cultural convention, should not be penetrated (the anus – here doubly sacrosanct since in the case of Lot we are dealing with angels, and in the case of the Levite, a priest) with another locus (the hymen-protected vagina) which may be penetrated only by invitation – by paternal invitation. But in the second story the guest reciprocates his host's generosity, presenting his concubine as substitute for the daughter. A *chain* of substitutions is put in play.

In his grief at his concubine's fate the Levite dismembers her body and sends a piece to each of the tribes of Israel (in what Rousseau presents in his *Essai sur l'origine des langues* as an outstandingly effective example of silent rhetoric[31]). The body becomes the matter of writing, and provokes a war machine. When, after much slaughter, only six hundred men (and no women) remain of the Benjamites it seems clear that the tribe will die out. Faced with this possibility – with the contradiction of a kind of fraternal genocide or auto-immunity – the Israelites decide to wipe out the men of another city (Jabesh-Gilead) who, for fraternal reasons, did not participate in the attack on the Benjamites. They also kill all the women of the city who have had intercourse. The virgin women of Jabesh-Gilead can then be given to the remaining Benjamites as wives. Thus we have passed from target number one (the Benjamites who protected the perpetrators of the atrocity) to target number two (the men of Jabesh who were just not sufficiently on side, and their wives). As the virgins of Jabesh number only four hundred, an old man suggests that the last Benjamites be allowed to ravish the virgins participating in a religious festival. These women are then the third target – and a further sanctioned *rapt*. What is striking is the lack of a female voice or name in the series of deaths and rapes – in a text which is full of proper names. The re-settling of the Benjamites occurs at the very end of the Book of Judges, and the final phrase has a degree of ambiguity: 'and every man did what was right in his own eyes'.

Rousseau's version does not conclude in the same way – the seizing of the anonymous virgins on a pilgrimage to Shiloh is not satisfactory for him. As a degree of mayhem ensues, opening up the possibility of further bloodshed on the part of unhappy fathers, a solution is finally found in the example of one girl (whom he names Axa): the daughter of the old man who proposed the authorised rape responds to her father's and her people's need, and offers herself as willing victim. This *hostia*, the repetition of the female sacrifice, is one of the many interesting motifs in the retold tale. The woman is the sacrificial object par excellence – both dispensable, substitutable and over-valued. Rousseau moves us from the biblical patriarchal sacrifice (Abraham sacrificing Isaac is the best remembered, but I have focused on the more frequent sacrifice of the daughter or wife/concubine) or Homeric sacrifice (Agamemnon offering Iphigenia) to self-sacrifice. Axa's example is imitated by the other young women, and Rousseau's concluding phrase can be 'il est encore des vertus en Israël' (*Oeuvres complètes*, Vol. 2, 1223).

Hospitality has led to terror. And if we look at events prior to the night of horror, it was the excessive hospitality of the concubine's father that has caused a delay leading to the need to spend the night in the Benjamite city. The role of old men or patriarchs as fathers, hosts and political or moral leaders is notable. Rape of the stranger-guest as punishment, control or 'because we can' by the Benjamite barbarians (as Rousseau calls them) provokes a response in the form of collective if not yet 'state' violence which is completely incommensurable with the original crime, horrible as it was. Moral outrage at an individual crime has fuelled the near-extinction of a tribe. In

Rousseau's tale the mass-destruction machine is brought to a halt only by the willing feminine victim – in the original by a sleight of hand which escapes the letter of the covenant made not to give a wife to a Benjamite. Derrida writes: 'One can imagine the desire to efface such an event or, at the very least, to attenuate it, to make up for it, and also to disclaim it. But whether the desire is fulfilled or not, the traumatism will have taken place, with its indefinite consequences, at once destructuring and structuring' (*MO*, 55) ('Le désir d'effacer un tel événement, ou à tout le moins de l'atténuer, de le compenser . . . Mais que ce désir s'accomplisse ou non, le traumatisme aura eu lieu, avec ses effets indéfinis, déstructurants et structurants à la fois' (*MA*, 92)). In this context Derrida is referring to the situation of Jews in colonial Algeria, as a disintegrated community cut off from a mother tongue and history, forced to speak the language of their 'host(s)'.[32] However, the words seem even more appropriate to this foundational tale of hospitality, inhospitality and (self-)mutilation.

The two episodes of hospitality, Lot's and the old man's, raise the question how far you should go for a guest (including betraying other ethical obligations). The duty to a guest can of course bring hospitality into conflict with the law. The aftermath of the two transgressions of hospitality raises the issue of the law again, and of the collective (or divine) punishment for an act that strikes at what is regarded as the heart of civilisation. The tale of the Levite, and of the collective response to an act of brutality which has undermined the possibility of hospitality and thus mobility, inspires reflection on hospitality on an international level: including the situations of refugees, asylum seekers and aeroplane travellers. Not only the host, or the host community (and the Israeli Benjamites and Jordanian Sodomites are certainly figures of Terror), but also the guest can be terrifying. The terrorist is a figure both hyperbolically masculine and totally feminised, the most feared arrival of our day. Terrorist action has been met with spectacular revenge on entire peoples who apparently refuse to give up the perpetrators of a crime.

A sexual dimension to terror should not be forgotten. Rape is still deployed as an instrument of war in modern times, for example in Rwanda or the former Yugoslavia. It is used not only to subdue feminised territory and populations, but also to fertilise the land and, after a partial genocide, to repopulate, mixing the blood and genes of the conquerors with the conquered. The foetus follows the penis as uninvited guest. Abortion and the suicide of rape victims, pregnant or not, are other domains where a woman may not choose to be a host – or where the patriarchs of her community may decide that she is no more than the instrument of their refusal or acceptance of a certain law.

As we have seen, in *Perpetual Peace*, a text which proposes a kind of United Nations *avant l'heure*, Kant includes a section on universal hospitality. This, for Kant, is a right because men originally had common ownership of the earth's surface and 'since the earth is a globe, they cannot scatter themselves infinitely, but must finally tolerate living in close proximity' (358). In this era of globalisation, we have returned to Kant's sense of limited space – we have passed through the false lure of colonialism which re-conceived of the territory of others as virgin land to be husbanded. Post-colonially, hospitality seems all the more necessary – and yet it is not simple and never will be – in particular, where there are extreme imbalances of power and we cannot find Irigaray's solution (even on an Imaginary or Symbolic level) of separate co-existence or creating a new world together. At *best* we offer a grudging invitation to the other to enter our house on our terms. It is not clear that the evil which then befalls host and guest is accidental rather than structural (an allergic reaction). And, post-Marx, we seem to have lost our sense of structure. I have focused on the evil shadowing the good of hospitality as the figure of rape – a real evil but also a figure for the outrage that shames the master of the house even as he invites it. For Levinas, hospitality is (feminine) vulnerability (see Derrida's analysis in *Adieu*, 53–4, and notes; 100). However terrible an outrage is committed against this (very limited) openness, we should beware of spectacular revenge; the Levite's story (and perhaps that of Lot) suggests that a killing machine has its own momentum – once set in motion, in a reversal of cause and effect, it will generate its reasons to kill. On a global rather than local scale we cannot be sure that any 'feminine' act of sacrifice would be grand enough to break the chain.

Reference to the past or to another place – forgetting the violence

Although there has been a recent resurgence of interest in it, hospitality is a topic that has *consistently* been considered important over long periods of time, and over wide tracts of the globe, as these stories show. Our conviction of its *universality* is indeed critical to our understanding of its structure: hospitality is traditionally defined as a universal (even *the* universal) human virtue – as I have suggested in the Introduction, even definitional of humanity for Levinas. While termed (human) virtue in general – hospitality is traditionally offered and accepted by men, and in some contexts is what reveals the virtue, the manliness, the humanity of the man, and thus Abraham deserves to become Father of the chosen nation in the logic of the narrative. Women meanwhile very often perform the labour of hospitality, whether Sarah preparing huge quantities of cakes or Penelope's unfortunate maids who are hanged because of the 'hospitality' forced from them by bad guests.

While we may recognise, and even celebrate in television documentaries, museums or books, a *variety* of exotic hospitable customs, our conclusion tends to draw them together on a continuum of fundamental similarity. In his analysis of an American exhibition of photographs from around the world, 'The Family of Man', shown in Paris as the *great* family of man 'La grande famille des hommes', Barthes suggests how easily we pass from marvelling at the range of human practices of birth, marriage, death rites and so on, in different cultures, to an assertion of essential humanity – the danger in what can be a metaphysical move is that history and economics are evaded (*Mythologies*, 107–10; 173–6).[33] Once the continuum is established, then, according to most rhetorical evocations, it is clear how hospitality is practised 'more faithfully' at certain times or by certain peoples, often peoples who have (or are perceived to have) a stricter division between the sexes.[34] The virtuous Sarah stays in Abraham's tent while the guests are present. The violence attendant on so many ancient tales of hospitality – whether rape, fire and brimstone, or massacre, is 'forgotten'.

René Schérer opens his book in praise of hospitality with the assertion: 'Intolerance towards strangers does not date from yesterday, but from right now. . . . Yes, hospitality has really gone out of fashion! . . . it is only a question, in France and just about everywhere in the world, of restricting it, from the right to asylum to the laws on nationality!' ('L'intolérance à l'étranger ne date pas d'hier, mais d'à présent. . . . L'hospitalité, oui, est bien passée de mode! . . . il n'est question, en France et un peu partout dans le monde, que de la restreindre, depuis le droit d'asile jusqu'au Code de la nationalité!') (*Zeus hospitalier*, 11–12). He implies a former Golden Age when borders and hearts were (relatively) open. Discourse on hospitality frequently refers explicitly or implicitly to a past time period when conduct is deemed closer to the essence of generosity or reciprocity. Sometimes cultures which are spatially and/or culturally distant, for instance the Arab culture of nomadic hospitality, are used as a proxy for temporal distance. Schérer puts it succinctly: hospitality 'reminds the imagination of an other era and an elsewhere' ('rappelle à l'imagination un autrefois et un ailleurs') (19), something he both observes and enacts. One example of a typical anecdote to demonstrate nomadic Arab hospitality runs as follows. Michael Asher, 'desert explorer and author', writes:

> Travelling by camel in the Western Sahara, my wife and I ran out of water. Temperatures were in the fifties Centigrade, and we had seen no one for ten days. We knew we could only last about another twelve hours. Then we spotted a nomad tent in the distance. A boy came running out with a bowl of water, took us to his camp, where the nomads helped unload our camels, and drew us into the shade.
>
> They passed us a huge bowl of fresh camels' milk, and after sunset killed and roasted a goat in our honour. They fed our camels with their own precious grain, and insisted on giving us their rugs to sleep on. In the morning, the boy walked six miles in the blazing sun to show us where we could get water. After helping us to water the camels, he walked another two miles to set us on the right path. These nomads had almost nothing. I have never felt so humbled.[35]

This is typical in its account of superabundant generosity: giving more to a guest than the host can afford. Its elements are classical: the offer of water to a thirsty stranger whose name you do not know; the feast; the giving up of the host's own bed; setting the travellers on their way. However, I should note in passing that almost all these idealised practices from long ago or far away exclude or repress women, and that exclusion/repression echoes with us here and now.

To take what may at first seem a rather different example, in *French Hospitality* Ben Jelloun writes in praise of Moroccan hospitality, as part of *all* Moroccans' tradition and cultural identity; but for Rosello 'the concept of hospitality remains a somewhat monolithic and generalized one' in his work (*Postcolonial Hospitality*, 26). She acknowledges that there may be a certain rhetorical strategy granted the political questions (notably French racism towards North-African immigrants) he is addressing, but of course the case can be made that a less absolute notion of hospitality is more helpful to negotiating the resolution of these tensions. Rosello argues that, rather than allowing for ambiguity, Jelloun tends to idealise Morocco and gloss over any inner tensions – following the pattern of a kind of traditional ethnographic discourse (as in the example I have cited above). I would add that this pattern relates to our sense of what is *natural* – even though hospitality is obviously a social relation. However, it is hard to escape such nostalgia. As Paul de Man remarks:

> The deconstruction of a system of relationships always reveals a more fragmented stage that can be called natural with regard to the system that is being undone. Because it also functions as the negative truth of the deconstructive process, the 'natural' pattern authoritatively substitutes its relational system for the one it helped dissolve. In so doing, it conceals the fact that it is itself one system of relations among others, and it presents itself as the sole and true order of things, as nature and not as structure. But since a deconstruction always has for its target to reveal the existence of hidden articulations and fragmentations within assumedly monadic totalities, nature turns out to be a self-deconstructive term.[36]

The intertexts of other (more natural) locations always function rhetorically in the analysis of hospitality here and now, and, more specifically, of the *failure* of hospitality today (whenever and wherever today is).

One problem which can be related to this is the idealisation of nomadic mobility, the most famous example being Gilles Deleuze and Felix Guattari's 'deterritorialisation' – or the way in which it is taken up by their most enthusiastic readers. The nomad is set against the sedentary just as the rhizomatic is against the arborescent, or the minor against the major literature, as configurations that tend to break up (being out of the world) or consolidate (being in the world). Peter Hallward comments on what he considers to be the metaphysical underpinning of 'nomad thought':

> The relation between the nomadic and the sedentary cannot be understood, according to Deleuze and Guattari, in terms of any sort of historical development. 'The nomads do not precede the sedentaries; rather, nomadism is a movement, a becoming that affects the sedentaries, just as sedentarism is a stoppage that settles the nomads' (TP, 430). No more than the sedentary state-politics that oppresses them, nomads do not evolve or develop but spring immediately into being. The nomad is incompatible with any notion of 'development'. Strictly speaking, then, 'the nomads have no history; they have only a geography' [TP, 393. 'Nomadology is the opposite of a history' (TP, 23)]. As far as history or actuality are concerned, Deleuze and Guattari are quite willing to accept that 'the defeat of the nomads was such, so complete, that history is one with the triumph of States' (TP, 394). But as far as philosophy is concerned, this defeat is of no more consequence than are the actual politics of such states. No more than you might ever see an 'actual' schizo, no more than any process of becoming as such, you will not find these virtual nomads *in* history. (*Out of This World*, 101)[37]

A rather different example of 'Arab' hospitality, one which draws attention to the tensions at play rather than glossing over them, occurs in Cixous's programme notes to the play *The Last Caravanserai* (*Le dernier Caravansérail*, first produced at Le Théâtre du Soleil in 2003) in which a Sufi tale of hospitality is reproduced. It begins by telling how the people of Turkistan are famed for their generosity, pride and love of horses; and ends with the impoverished Anwar Beg feeding his beloved, and extremely valuable, horse to the guest who had wanted to buy it from him, saying: 'hospitality comes before everything else' ('l'hospitalité passe avant tout'). As in Ben Jelloun's work, this citation of absolute hospitality has an obvious meaning in the context of Ariane Mnouchkine's and Cixous's critique of French inhospitality; but it also has a more complex side of violent sacrifice: as in the Old Testament tales of Lot and the Levite of Ephraim the most beloved object is given up (and destroyed) for the *hôte*. The Sufi tale comes close to cannibalism, and, while meeting the physical need for food and psychological need to be welcomed of the guest in general (the guest function), denies the emotional desires of this particular guest (to own the living horse, but also to help the horse's owner) in order to fulfil the position of the host. Derrida reminds us at the close of *Of Hospitality* of the patriarchal structure by which the master of the house makes the laws of hospitality, represents them and bends to them in order to make others bend to them; this is the violence of ipseity in the power of hospitality. The universal absolute of hospitality can clash with the demand to make guests feel at home, which needs to negotiate with particularity – awareness of their difference, and of the differences within hospitality.

The rhetorical triangle of self-critique ('if only we could do as well as they did') I have identified here, between ourselves or our nation as *hosts*, others or strangers who are potential *guests*, and those who were or are *better hosts*, usually safely long ago or far away, is not, however, the only critical triangle. Another relevant structure is the self-*justifying* comparison ('we're not as bad as them') so often drawn between ourselves in our real or potential relation to incomers, immigrants, refugees and other nations, competitor nations, with respect to their relation to subalterns. The British press (or even British sociologists) smugly cite the French Islamic headscarf controversy ('l'affaire du foulard') or disturbances involving young people of North-African descent, as if British institutions have never tried to police clothing which has religious significance and Britain has never known race riots.[38] While this condemnation of others may be sincere and well-meant, it can also serve as exculpation for internal or external border policies at home. Equally there is the liberal rhetorical figure Barthes calls inoculation, introducing criticism of what seem minor contingent problems to ward off radical overthrow of the system: 'One immunizes the contents of the collective imagination by means of a small inoculation of acknowledged evil; one thus protects it against the risk of a generalized subversion' (*Mythologies*, 164) ('On immunise l'imaginaire collectif par une petite inoculation de mal reconnu; on le défend ainsi contre le risque d'une subversion généralisée' (238–9)). Thus a particular incident – the French police chasing after someone to check their papers ending in a horrific accident; Father Christmas refused entry to a British refugee detention centre – can catch the public imagination as a scandal while the principles underlying immigration policy in general remain unchallenged.[39]

Intertextual hosts and guests

The reference to some other place or time, some other text, when hospitality is discussed is rarely simple. Thinking about hospitality after Derrida also involves thinking about reading and writing, about hospitable texts and texts of hospitality. The ethical (and political) imperative of hospitality is double: the immediate and unconditional welcome of the Law of hospitality; the time of reflection and analysis of the laws which are always conditional. I would argue for an openness of reading and writing, along with political openness (at the level of the State) and ethical openness between individuals. Openness of reading (what I, with others, have elsewhere called maternal or feminine reading) brings the self into question as it struggles with the foreign text, and can be immensely pleasurable as well as painful. Openness of writing does not, for me, only concern avant-garde texts (sometimes termed *écriture féminine*) or the experiments and play we find in Cixous, Derrida and Irigaray at their most 'difficult'. The reader can help to open up even a text that may seem already fixed in its meaning, whether on account of style or on account of a canonical interpretation. Derrida has joined in many conversations, including those between Plato, Aristotle, Cicero, and Montaigne on friendship (which I shall turn to in the next chapter), and added to the feast. This example helps to show that welcoming other voices does not mean being overwhelmed or submerged by them – there are always *conditions* on our reading and there is always a need for patient reflection and analysis.

I have suggested that one of the striking features of discussions of (in)hospitality is their particular *intertextual quality* – how elements from a range of earlier or otherwise distant theories and practices are introduced and transformed in the new context. Conversely, hospitality can also be a useful way of thinking about our relationship to texts, in the broadest sense, as opposed to the many other models of reading-writing that have been explicitly or implicitly privileged over the years (scientific or agonistic, to mention but two). Since our readings and narration of ourselves and others are part of our social and political relationships, this is by no means purely a debate within literary criticism. When Derrida was reproached on the grounds that 'if we practise close reading we will never act', he, unsurprisingly, refused the opposition, remarking that 'to read events, to analyse the situation, to criticize the media, to listen to the rhetoric of the demagogues, that's close reading, and it is required more today than ever. So I would urge politicians and citizens to practise close reading' (*HJR*, 67). *Absolute* hospitality to texts is of course impossible (and undesirable, as Derrida's examples show); we consciously (as well as unconsciously) select which elements we will allow into our narratives. Complete openness to the exterior we would probably understand as equivalent to complete insanity. However, respectful and responsible readings are, I would argue, modes of conditional hospitality. Analysis of both Levinas's maxim that *language is hospitality* (a coded relation to the other), and the question of the (impossible) suspension of language, enriches various theorisations of intertextuality whether or not these draw explicitly on the figure of hospitality (and related parasitical tropes). The *tour de force* essay by J. Hillis Miller, 'The Critic as Host',[40] is an impeccable starting point for thinking about intertextuality and hospitality, although it precedes Derrida's major publications on hospitality. Sexual difference also suffuses the representation of intertextual relations.[41] Revisiting intertextuality via hospitality involves threading the questions of passion and of sexual difference (or the phantasm of sexual differentiation) through the various theories – the 'poet's' struggle to be a man (a divine man who gives birth to himself) and his *fear* and *desire* of being 'a woman'.[42] I shall begin the (re)visit by asking some questions about literary hospitality: Is the guest or the host in the position of mastery? Would there be aggressivity on the part of the host (or guest)? Who is the host and who is the guest/parasite in intertextual terms? Is the guest welcome(d)? Would different models of hospitality lead to different understandings of intertextuality? For example:

1) The laws of hospitality which govern the culturally sanctioned role of host as master of the house would fit with the sense of the author as master of his work. As author I would choose to invite in suitable guests who will behave appropriately – not attempt to take over, infiltrate, invade, rob, violate. I would select those who are like me, my peers, who speak my language, and whom I could honour with quotation marks and the use of their proper names. This would fit a theory or figuring of citation or reference as ornamentation: choice jewels or flowers which decorate or embellish the master's house.[43] I would hope not to be *betrayed* by my reference points. On the other hand:

2) There is the singular and absolute Law of hospitality – 'wild' hospitality – where the text would be criss-crossed by the words of others. There would be others' words in my mouth, 'dirty' improper (not *propre*) words, which have already been in the mouths of others (as Bakhtin suggests). Invasions by barbarians, whose names I do not know, whose language I do not speak, who do not obey my rules, my grammar, my code, my law. Possible violence: passion in both senses. Love of books, words. Going to bed with a book (as Cixous suggests) and being ravished by another's tongue. My loss of control might be so great that I do not even know I have been invaded – by secret guests, parasites, even viruses.[44]

Are these models of writing or models of reading – and can we so easily distinguish between the two? I shall briefly return to Harold Bloom's categories and his use of psychoanalysis – the Oedipal agon. This will prove particularly useful for a model of critics' reading. Bloom writes:

> A poetic 'text' . . . is not a gathering of signs on a page, but is a psychic battlefield upon which authentic forces struggle for the only victory worth winning, the divinating triumph over oblivion . . . Few notions are more difficult to dispel than the 'commonsensical' one that a poetic text is self-contained . . . [P]oems are not things but only words that refer to other words, and *those* words refer to still other words, and so on, into the densely overpopulated world of literary language . . . A poem is not writing, but *rewriting*.[45]

And again:

> Any poet (meaning even Homer, if we could know enough about his precursors) is in the position of being 'after the Event', in terms of literary language. His art is necessarily an *aftering*, and so at best he strives for a selection, through repression, out of the traces of the language of

84

poetry; that is he represses some of the traces, and remembers others. This remembering is a misprision, or creative misreading, but no matter how strong a misprision, it cannot achieve an autonomy of meaning, or a meaning *fully* present, that is free from all literary context. . . . The caveman who traced the outline of an animal upon the rock always retraced a precursor's outline. (*Poetry and Repression*, 4)

I should like to juxtapose Bloom's assertion with the case of intellectual property rights and the laws against plagiarism.[46]

In his now classic article, in a collection with Bloom, Derrida et al., Hillis Miller asks:

Is a citation an alien parasite within the body of the main text, or is the interpretive text the parasite which surrounds and strangles the citation which is its host? The host feeds the parasite and makes its life possible, but at the same time is killed by it, as criticism is often said to kill literature. Or can host and parasite live happily together, in the domicile of the same text, feeding each other or sharing the food? ('The Critic as Host', 217)

He points out that deconstructive criticism is said to be parasitical on the 'obvious or univocal' reading.[47] Commenting on images of oak and ivy in Hardy and Thackeray, he explains:

That ivy is somehow feminine, secondary, defective, or dependent. It is a clinging vine, able to live in no other way but by drawing the life sap of its host, cutting off its light and air . . . Such sad love stories of a domestic affection which introduces the parasitical into the closed economy of the home no doubt describe well enough the way some people feel about the relation of a 'deconstructive' interpretation to 'the obvious or univocal reading'. . . . The alien has invaded the house, perhaps to kill the father of the family in an act which does not look like parricide, but is. (218)

Hillis Miller wonders, however: 'Is the "obvious" reading, though, so "obvious" or even so "univocal"? May it not itself be the uncanny alien which is so close that it cannot be seen as strange, host in the sense of enemy rather than host in the sense of open-handed dispenser of hospitality?' (218). Thus he turns back on the critics of deconstruction the charge of being foreign (and so potentially treacherous) bodies. But at least he does not openly call them girls. The polemical feminisation of deconstruction as parasitical on the sturdy masculinity of, not only the strong poet who has fought his predecessors, but even the strong critic, is not surprising. But effeminacy is not a simple insult in these boys' games; it is an important element of the unconscious and conscious agon. Finally, we should remember Hillis Miller's words:

The poem, in my figure, is that ambiguous gift, food, host in the sense of victim, sacrifice. It is broken, divided, passed around, consumed by the critics canny and uncanny who are in that odd relation to one another of host and parasite. Any poem, however, is parasitical in its turn on earlier poems, or it contains earlier poems within itself as enclosed parasites, in another version of the perpetual reversal of parasite and host. If the poem is food and poison for the critics, it must in its turn have eaten. It must have been a cannibal consumer of earlier poems. (225)

Derrida's writing and speaking is peculiarly hospitable, beautiful, sometimes angry, sometimes lyrical, sometimes dense in a way that momentarily collapses the poetic and the philosophical *without* ever collapsing itself or indeed bringing about the chronic collapse of the categories that get stretched to and around their limits. Difficult, yes, often of course – and sometimes a kind of difficulty that makes some readers respond with anger or despair, others with a kind of eager mimicry, a kind of faithful following that maybe in the end resembles betrayal as much as fidelity. Derrida is for me the arche-typical Bloomian strong poet – it is desperately hard to write strong poetry in his wake. Derrida's writing is hospitable in that it gives the reader great sustenance, food for thought. However, readers need to be careful what and how they eat. We could remember the Lotus Eaters in the *Odyssey*; eating their food means becoming soporific, losing your critical faculties and your independence of mind, becom-ing more like (pale imitations of) your hosts. As the reader enters the spaces of Derrida's writing it is possible to become overwhelmed by the riches around her or him, and simply want to have the same. And so many words are spectrally inhabited by Derrida (*différance*, supplement, hymen, grief . . .), his *legs*, our sense of inheritance, his gift.[48] In this context: 'hostipitality'. There's a thin line between love and hate. Derrida gifted us so much. Receiving a gift means being put under an obligation.

When the text, like the *Odyssey* or the stories of Abraham, Lot and the Levite, is 'about' hospitality (and inhospitality) as well as enacting hospitality to its reader then it has a special relationship to the history of practices and discourses of hospitality. The various scenarios are re-worked in a range of historical conjunctures, taking on different significations with the different political or social con-texts.[49] The embedding of sexual differentiation into such a work is inevitable yet also revealing, and certainly creates an opportunity for the reader to analyse the complex knots of sexed hospitality and attempt to refigure these for the future.

Notes

1. An earlier version of this section was given at 'Luce Irigaray and the Greeks', University of Columbia (New York), 2004; see E. Tzelepis and A. Athanasiou (eds), *Rewriting Difference* (New York: SUNY Press, 2010).

2. While hospitality between people of different nations is more associated with peace than war-time, war can provide examples of hospitality overcoming hostility. In the *Illiad* two warriors (the Greek Diomedes and the Lycian Glaucus) recognise each other in the thick of battle: their grandfathers had a compact of guest-friendship, and therefore they throw down their weapons and agree not to fight each other. This is a practical contract more than an emotional tie – after all Diomedes and Glaucus had never met before. This shows the power of such bonds of *xenia* although it is a rare moment in that text. See Arthur W. H. Adkins, '"Friendship" and "Self-Sufficiency" in Homer and Aristotle', *The Classical Quarterly*, 13:1 (1963), pp. 30–45.

3. In *Taking on the Tradition*, Naas evokes the *Odyssey* in a chapter on hospitality; he raises the key questions of threshold and the name, and makes some very interesting points although he does not quite follow the details of the text – for instance he implies that Polyphemos invites Odysseus in as his guest which is not the case (pp. 155–6). He then uses the story of Polyphemos as a parable for states with (fierce) border controls and close inspection of passports, but I am not sure that that works (pp. 156 ff). By the time Odysseus is asked his name the Cyclops has already killed four and eaten two of his crew; it is not clear that the others would have been spared, whatever name/passport had been given, see the *Odyssey*, Book IX. I shall refer to book numbers (in Roman numerals) for ease of comparison between editions. For quotations I shall refer to *The Odyssey*, translated by E. V. Rieu (Harmondsworth: Penguin, 1946).

4. See Peter Hulme, *Colonial Encounters: Europe and the Native Caribbean, 1492–1797* (London and New York: Methuen, 1986) for numerous examples; for instance he quotes George Sandys in Jamestown 1621–25 comparing West Indians to Polyphemos (p. 154). Abandoned princesses or nymphs can be seen in the retold tales of Pocahontas or Yarico. See also my *Enlightenment Hospitality*, especially Chapters 2–3 on the New World.

5. Mireille Rosello, 'Frapper aux portes invisibles avec des mots-valises: la *malgériance* d'Hélène Cixous', in Lise Gauvin, Pierre L'Herault and Alain Montandon (eds), *Le dire de l'hospitalité* (Dijon: Presses Universitaires Blaise Pascal, 2004), pp. 61–74, p. 61.

6. Margaret Whitford, 'Irigaray, Utopia, and the Death Drive', in Carolyn Burke et al. (eds), *Engaging with Irigaray* (New York: Columbia

University Press, 1994), pp. 379–400, p. 388. On Homer, see Luce Irigaray, 'The Return', in Luce Irigaray with Mary Green (eds), *Luce Irigaray: Teaching* (London and New York: Continuum, 2008), pp. 219–30.

7. See Luce Irigaray, *Marine Lover. Of Friedrich Nietzsche*, translated by Gillian C. Gill (New York: Columbia University Press, 1991); Luce Irigaray, *Amante marine* (Paris: Minuit, 1980), e.g. the section 'Veiled Lips' for a number of pertinent remarks on the representation of woman as foreign to truth. See also Derrida, *Spurs: Nietzsche's Styles. Eperons: Les Styles de Nietzsche*, translated by Barbara Harlow (Chicago and London: Chicago University Press, 1979).

8. Steve Reece, *The Stranger's Welcome: Oral Theory and the Aesthetics of the Homeric Hospitality Scene* (Ann Arbor: University of Michigan Press, 1993).

9. Jacques Derrida, *Glas*, translated by John P. Leavey, Jr and Richard Rand (Lincoln and London: University of Nebraska Press, 1986); Jacques Derrida, *Glas* (Paris: Galilée, 1974).

10. Freud's essay 'On Femininity' suggests that weaving is the one art invented by women – and that they invented it out of feminine modesty – to hide their lack of penis. But it is more of an imitation (of natural pubic hair) or an extension of nature than an invention. See Derrida, 'A Silkworm of One's Own. Points of View Stitched on the Other Veil', in Hélène Cixous and Jacques Derrida, *Veils*, translated by Geoffrey Bennington (Stanford: Stanford University Press, 2001); 'Un ver à soie. Points de vue piqués sur l'autre voile', in Hélène Cixous and Jacques Derrida, *Voiles* (Paris: Galilée, 1998).

11. There are of course many analyses of this – I shall just cite one salient one: Peggy Kamuf, *Signature Pieces: On the Institution of Authorship* (Ithaca and London: Cornell University Press, 1988), Chapter XIX, 'Penelope at Work', especially pp. 145–7. Kamuf starts by pointing out that Telemachus twice sends his mother away to weave and spin – leaving men's work such as 'discussion' to him. At the same time metaphorically weaving and spinning is seen as crucial to men's poetic language. Women's work and the domestic interior is veiled to men – imagining Penelope in bed at night when in fact she is undoing her weaving.

12. Helen can be read as the figure of the poet – this is figured most strikingly in the *Illiad*. She is weaving when the reader/listener first encounters her – a story cloth in purple telling of the Trojan War. See Kathryn Sullivan Kruger, *Weaving the Word: The Metaphorics of Weaving and Female Textual Production* (Selingsgrove: Susquehanna University Press/London: Associated University Presses, 2001).

13. I am using a great deal of shorthand here (as Irigaray does in her discussions of Athena and Apollo). Athena is not quite motherless – although

she is born motherless. According to myth, her father, Zeus, swallowed her pregnant mother the Titaness Metis for fear that she would eventually give birth to a son who would kill him as he killed his own father (Cronus) who had killed his grandfather (Uranus).

14. See Judith Still and Michael Worton, 'Introduction' in *Textuality and Sexuality: Reading Theories and Practices* (Manchester: Manchester University Press, 1990).

15. An alternative translation is equally clear: 'You wasted my house, and lay with the maidservants by force, and while I was still alive covertly courted my wife' (Homer, *The Odyssey*, translated by A. T. Murray, revised by George E. Dimmock [Cambridge, MA: Harvard University Press, 1998], p. 347).

16. One of the most interesting of recent rewritings of *The Odyssey* is Margaret Atwood's *The Penelopiad* (Edinburgh: Canongate, 2005) which has the hanged maids as a chorus.

17. Joanna Hodge points out how 'the motherless Athena and her brother, Apollo, triumph over the chthonic gods and the relation between mother and daughter – between Clytemnestra and Iphigenia – is erased' in her comments on matricide drawing on Irigaray's 'The Bodily Encounter with the Mother', in *The Irigaray Reader*, pp. 34–46; *Le Corps-à-corps avec la mère* (Montreal: Les Editions de la pleine lune, 1981), pp. 11–32. See Joanna Hodge, 'Irigaray Reading Heidegger', in Burke et al. (eds), *Engaging with Irigaray*, pp. 191–209, pp. 192–3.

18. René Schérer, *Zeus hospitalier: éloge de l'hospitalité* (Paris: La Table Ronde, 2005 [1993]), pp. 150–2.

19. There are exceptions, for example an old woman can be perceived as a relatively sex-less form – and Athena visits Arachne as an old woman to engage her as a weaver.

20. It is not clear whether he offers the Levite's concubine too – it is a question of the translation/interpretation of the Hebrew. Derrida (and Kamuf) follow Chouraqui who is closer to the original Hebrew than the standard English versions which take a more logical (in terms of the succession of substitutions) line that has the old man offering 'only' his daughter and the Levite 'only' his concubine.

21. In the confines of this chapter I shall not focus on Abraham as Father of nations or on the sacrifice of Isaac. Derrida writes at length on the Hegelian interpretation of Genesis in *Glas*; see in particular pp. 40–45; pp. 49–55. This includes the figure of Abraham as the chosen one (and thus slave), and circumcision as an apotropaic simulacrum of castration.

22. Jean Chardin, *Voyages du Chevalier Chardin en Perse et aux autres lieux de l'Orient*, ed. L. Langlès (Paris: Le Normant, 1811), Vol. 4, p. 58.

23. For more detail on Chardin's account of Oriental hospitality, see my *Enlightenment Hospitality*, Chapter 4.
24. *La Bible*, translated and edited by André Chouraqui (Paris: Jean-Claude Lattès, 1992), Vol. 1, *Entête*, p. 138. Chouraqui, like Derrida, was born in Algeria and then moved to Paris.
25. Louis Massignon, 'A la limite', in *Parole donnée* (Paris: Seuil, 1983), pp. 284–5.
26. Schérer cites the various interpretations of Abraham and Lot by Philo of Alexandria, which transform women into virtues for example.
27. Guy Hocqenghem, *La Beauté du métis* (Paris: Albin Michel, 1979).
28. Jonathan Dollimore, *Sexual Dissidence: Augustine to Wilde, Freud to Foucault* (Oxford: Clarendon Press, 1991).
29. In *In the Time of Nations* (*A l'heure des nations*), Levinas refers to *Deutronomy* (23, viii): '"thou shalt not abhor an Egyptian, because thou wast a stranger in his land"' ('"n'aie pas l'Egyptien en horreur, car tu as séjourné dans son pays"') as an example of hospitality taking precedence over the imposition of alterity (quoted by Derrida in *Adieu*, p. 69; p. 125). Derrida shows how these kind of discreet allusions to Israel and Egyptian hospitality (even where it also ended up in slavery) have a contemporary resonance in the Middle East (e.g. *Adieu*, pp. 70–84; pp. 131–52).
30. Jean-Jacques Rousseau, *Le Lévite d'Ephraïm*, in his *Oeuvres complètes*, ed. Bernard Gagnebin and Marcel Raymond, 5 vols (Paris: Pléiade, 1959–95), Vol. 2, pp. 1205–23. See my 'Acceptable Hospitality: From Rousseau's Levite to the Strangers in our Midst Today', *Journal of Romance Studies*, 3:2 (2003), pp. 1–14, based on my Inaugural Lecture at the Institute of Romance Studies. Thanks also to audiences in Leeds and Lyons. See also Peggy Kamuf's analysis of Rousseau's text as representation of writing in her *Signature Pieces*; Thomas Kavanagh, *Writing the Truth: Authority and Desire in Rousseau* (Berkeley: University of California Press, 1987); and Jean Starobinski, 'Rousseau's Happy Days', *New Literary History*, 11 (1979), pp. 147–66.
31. Rousseau, *Oeuvres complètes*, Vol. 5, pp. 371–429, p. 377.
32. He cites Franz Rosenzweig – who takes the analysis of the Jewish diaspora back to the immigrant Father (Abraham).
33. See Diana Knight, *Barthes and Utopia: Space, Travel, Writing* (Oxford: Clarendon Press, 1997), pp. 98–100, for some details on how Barthes's analysis is just as relevant to the American packaging of the exhibition. Barthes asks his readers what the parents of Emmett Till (an African-American killed by white Americans) or North-African workers in the poorest areas of Paris think of the great family of man.
34. For example, see Rousseau's praise of hospitality in the Valais area of present-day Switzerland in *La Nouvelle Héloïse*, *Oeuvres complètes*, Vol. 2.

35. Michael Asher, 'Escape', *Observer*, 27 November 2005, p. 4.
36. Paul De Man, *Allegories of Reading: Figural Language in Rousseau, Nietzsche, Rilke and Proust* (New Haven and London: Yale University Press, 1979), p. 249.
37. The abbreviation TP refers to the translation of Deleuze and Guattari's *Mille Plateaux*. See also Jeremy Lane, 'Deleuze In and Out of this World', *Paragraph*, 30:2 (2007), pp. 109–16.
38. Since writing this the French government under Sarkozy has gone further in its attempt to impose Republican universalism, opening up a debate on national identity which has proved a gift to the Front National, and setting up an inquiry into the burkha which is considering banning it from the streets of France – since Western identity apparently involves the visibility of the face.
39. This is not to deny the potential power of the seemingly marginal example, which can sometimes have an effect seemingly disproportionate – at an overdetermined moment perhaps. On a daily basis, however, newspaper readers can consume examples that horrify them, and the criticism of those practices does not lead to a demand for radical change.
40. J. Hillis Miller, 'The Critic as Host', in Harold Bloom, Paul De Man, Jacques Derrida, Geoffrey H. Hartman, J. Hillis Miller, *Deconstruction and Criticism*, (London and Henley: Routledge and Kegan Paul, 1979), pp. 217–53.
41. This would be an addendum to the Introduction to Judith Still and Michael Worton (eds), *Intertextuality: Theories and Practices* (Manchester: Manchester University Press, 1990), pp. 1–44.
42. Poet is used here (as in a number of works on intertextuality, albeit with the notable exception of Bakhtin) to mean writer or creator.
43. Of course any of these figures can be made less comfortable. If we take flowers for example, Hillis Miller analyses the way in which Shelley, in his own precursor texts to the *The Triumph of Life* (such as *Queen Mab*), refers to parasite flowers.
44. The trace of a secret guest might be some kind of catachresis or ungrammaticality, as Michael Riffaterre puts it.
45. Harold Bloom, *Poetry and Repression: Revisionism from Blake to Stevens* (New Haven and London: Yale University Press, 1976), pp. 2–3.
46. The issue of originality obviously relates to property rights: 'any claim of originality seeks to protect its fruits as being (on) private property. If no one else has thought quite the same thought, nor written it down in the same way, then the thought and its fruit, the text, must be protected – so, at least, runs the logic. The trouble (one of many) is that an idea cannot be owned since it partakes of human thought and language, which belongs to everyone' (Françoise Meltzer, *Hot Property:*

The Stakes and Claims of Literary Originality [Chicago and London: University of Chicago Press, 1994], p. 1). My thanks to Ziva Ben Porat for pointing out this work which has a number of thought-provoking analyses relating to questions of plagiarism.

47. One of his examples is M. H. Abrams citing Wayne Booth ('Critic as Host', p. 217).

48. See Marian Hobson, *Jacques Derrida: Opening Lines* (London and New York: Routledge, 1998), for a very strong reading of Derrida and language that goes beyond these lexemes (as she calls them) to look at other distinctive features and repeated patterns of articulation of his text. This critical refusal to divorce style and substance in philosophical writing is exemplary both in helping us to read Derrida but also in understanding some of the reading responses to his writing. It also helps us to phrase the tension between respecting the precise context in which these 'thematizable terms' (p. 3) are first produced, and dealing with their necessary afterlife.

49. Ian Donaldson, *The Rapes of Lucretia: A Myth and its Transformations* (Oxford: Clarendon Press, 1982), is a model of the historical tracking of the re-working of an ur-text in different historical contexts.

3

Friendship and sexual difference: hospitality from brotherhood to motherhood and beyond

Why introduce friendship into hospitality?

Critical work on hospitality in the wake of Derrida has usually focused – befitting certain political exigencies of our unequal globalised world – on the other 'stranger', the guest who arrives and who is unknown. Yet this other, however foreign, is welcomed according to the laws of hospitality as *mon prochain* ('my neighbour' as it is sometimes rendered in English), and the model of the one who is close to me (*mon prochain*) is the brother-friend. In this chapter I shall begin by focusing on friendship, most often understood as a spiritual fraternity, and the tensions even *within* friendship between the difference or strangeness of any other (even a friend) and the sameness and proximity of the friend. I shall then unsettle this a little by introducing women, sexual difference, into that masculine bond.

Both Levinas and Derrida often refer to friendship (*amitié*) alongside hospitality, each mutually reinforcing the other. While the arrival of the stranger is recognised as a critical limit situation, our everyday experience of hospitality is most often with kin or friends. In *Eloge de l'amitié*, Ben Jelloun evokes friendship and hospitality intertwined in his friend Edmond:

> His friends are his patrimony; his friendship for them is a complete gift. Everything takes place around the table. Sharing meals is essential; especially as Edmond is a very good cook. Eating good food, drinking good wines under the tutelage of good humour and laughter, that is how Edmond cooks his friendship. It is flavoured with rare and sought-after spices, washed down with vintage wines and simply presented: his affection is visceral. We only need to see each other, talk to each other and tell our stories to each other as often as possible. . . . This is typically Moroccan friendship, greedy and possessive. 'If you don't eat up this food I've made for you then you can't be that fond of me. If you're not hungry then you don't care for me anymore.' That is a little schematic,

but Edmond's relationships with his friends do go through the ritual of meal sharing in that way.

(Ses amis sont son patrimoine; son amitié pour eux est un don entier. Tout se passe autour de la table. Le partage des repas est essentiel; d'autant qu'Edmond est très bon cuisinier. Manger de bons plats, boire de bons vins sous le règne de l'humour et de rire, c'est ainsi qu'Edmond cuisine son amitié. Elle est relevée d'épices recherchées et rares, arrosée de vins millésimés et présentée simplement: l'affection est à fleur de peau. Il n'est besoin que de se voir, se parler, se raconter le plus souvent possible. . . . C'est une amitié très marocaine, c'est-à-dire gourmande et possessive. 'Si tu ne finis pas le plat que j'ai préparé pour toi, c'est que tu m'aimes moins. Si tu n'as pas faim, c'est que tu ne m'aimes plus.' C'est un peu schématique mais les relations d'Edmond et de ses amis passent ainsi par le rituel de la table.)[1]

Ben Jelloun, Moroccan himself, is in favour of this combination of hospitality and friendship even as he delicately shows up the host-friend's anxious desire that his guest-friend show his appreciation of the tender care lavished on him, lest lack of appetite be metaphorical as much as physical. Ben Jelloun's book on friendship is, he asserts, based on stories about his own friendships rather than a search through libraries, although his friends include authors or film-makers he knows only through their works, and quotations from some of the key authorities on friendship, notably Cicero and Montaigne, are interspersed with his anecdotes. Hospitality, in many senses, real and virtual, gives shape to most of the relationships described.

The ritual of hospitality includes sustenance or nourishment – not only of the body but of the mind. When guests are refreshed they should be entertained – but here is an element of reciprocity. While it may not be acceptable to *demand* that guests be entertaining in their turn, guests may demand it of themselves, and the act of telling may bring relief, satisfaction or other pleasures to the narrating guest. As Ben Jelloun has it, of typically Moroccan hospitality around the table: 'We need only to see each other, talk to each other and tell our stories to each other as often as possible' ('Il n'est besoin que de se voir, se parler, se raconter le plus souvent possible') (*Eloge de l'amitié*, 35). Traditionally guests who are strangers tell their story; but guests who are friends also converse with appropriately useful and amusing exchanges.

Even the closest of friends is strictly *other* to the self, yet our traditional philosophical understanding of friendship emphasises the drawing of friends into the same, friends as twin souls. On the

94

corporeal or material level, two friends are physically distinct enti-
ties; but on a psychic or spiritual level the friend is often interiorised,
especially when absent, and most especially in that extreme situation
of absence which is death – but perhaps always already when here.
Thus while friendship is built on hospitality, and quotidian or exceptional acts of welcoming build friendship, at the same time, the very
structure of true friendship is hospitality, or the other within the self.
In other words, friendship is constructed as hospitality, and equally
both the laws and the Law of hospitality require the structure of
friendship. However, just as hospitality is, *strictly speaking*, impossible, so the model of *perfect* friendship introduces the impossible
in the tension between identity and union, on the one hand, and the
need for separateness and distinction, on the other. Commenting on
Levinas, Derrida observes: 'Hospitality assumes "radical separation"
as experience of the alterity of the other, as relation to the other'
(*Adieu*, 46) ('L'hospitalité suppose la "*séparation radicale*" comme
expérience de l'altérité de l'autre, comme relation à l'autre' (88)). Yet
hospitality precisely *brings* alterity into proximity.

The *impossibility* of friendship is conjured up in 'O mes amis, il
n'y a nul amy' (O my friends, there is no friend), what Montaigne
termed 'Aristotle's habitual phrase' ('le mot qu'Aristote avoit très-
familier') in his essay on friendship ('De l'amitié').[2] This echoes
through the centuries, reverberating throughout Derrida's *Politics
of Friendship*. But the quotation does not have an original 'home',
at least not in the shocking form of the apostrophe that Montaigne
repeats in order to distinguish between the perfect friend and the
kind of 'friends' whom you need to treat as if they will one day be
enemies. The form is shocking because the friends addressed must
recognise that absolute friendship leaves us with no friends, just
as absolute hospitality would mean that hospitality is impossible.
Friendships are the perversion of true friendship just as the laws of
hospitality are the perversion of the Law of hospitality. Where does
the nomad phrase come from? And why does it parasitically take up
lodging in so many famous discourses on friendship?

With regard to the 'quotation' from Aristotle, in fact Derrida
refers, with his usual care, to 'the quotation of a saying attributed,
only attributed, by a sort of rumour or public opinion. "O my
friends, there is no friend" is, then, a declaration *referred* to Aristotle'
('la citation d'un mot attribué, seulement attribué, par une sorte de
rumeur ou d'opinion publique. "O mes amis, il n'y a nul amy", c'est
une déclaration *prêtée* à Aristote'). As Derrida points out, this is not

an anonymous proverb, it is *loaned* to Aristotle, but nevertheless 'Like a renowned filiation, an origin thus nicknamed seems, in truth, to lose itself in the infinite anonymity of the mists of time' ('Comme une filiation renommée, une origine ainsi surnommée semble se perdre en vérité dans l'anonymat infini d'une nuit des temps').[3] Yet Derrida's care, and openness, is not sufficient to prevent critics questioning. The saying is commonly referred to Diogenes Laertius' *Life of Aristotle* (V, 21).[4] However, in her book on Aristotle and friendship, Lorraine Smith Pangle claims that Diogenes Laertius in fact attributes to Aristotle 'he for whom there are friends has no friend' (meaning that you can only have one true friend), but that there are no grounds in the *Ethics* even for this version.[5] In a footnote, she suggests that it is a corruption of the *Nicomachean Ethics* 1171a 15–16, and goes on: 'Much less is there warrant for attributing to Aristotle, as Montaigne and Derrida do, the saying that must be a corruption, in turn, of this one, "O my friends, there is no friend"' (*Aristotle and the Philosophy of Friendship*, 240, n. 24). While she is quite right that the quotation from Diogenes Laertius seems to be a misquotation – involving the shift of a diacritical mark in the Greek – it is interestingly far more widespread than she suggests, and there is a German as well as a French tradition of adopting the apostrophic form. Equally, one should add for completeness that when Diogenes Laertius refers to Book 7 of 'the Ethics' he presumably means the *Eudemian Ethics* (VII, 1245b 20–1) rather than, or at least as much as, the *Nicomachean Ethics* (IX, 1171a 15–17), since that would be 'Book 9'. This critical overlooking on the part of the critic is symptomatic of the warfare over the text and the persistent downgrading of the *Eudemian Ethics* (particularly, though certainly not exclusively, in Anglophone classical studies) – the more egalitarian version of Aristotle which Derrida by preference chooses to consult (a mark of his wilful eccentricity in the eyes of some classicists).

The form of *apostrophe* is important. Derrida of course uses this in lectures as is traditional – and we should not forget that Aristotle's *Ethics* are lecture notes. This is an address to an audience, and creates a certain relationship with them. Two sets of Derrida's seminars on hospitality have been published, and in both cases the editors have explicitly chosen not to alter the text designed to be spoken (even more obvious to the reader of 'Hostipitality' than of *Of Hospitality*) because of 'the intimate agreement of thought and speech – their rhythmic agreement . . . you hear that singular rhythm of Derrida's spoken reflecting' as Dufourmantelle puts it (*OH*, 8, 10); ('l'accord intime de la pensée et de la parole – leur rythme accordé . . . On y entend ce rythme singulier de la réflexion de Derrida quand elle s'énonce' (*DH*, 16)).[6] The original audience may have been students, or fellow scholars, or those with an interest in the politics at stake; while we can trace this in the case of Derrida, critics still argue over the make-up of the audience of Aristotle's Ethics lectures and the relevance of this to the texts' arguments and form of argumentation. When spoken lectures are written down and published, as they so often are, then the trace of the earlier circumstances may thus be both present and, to some extent, lost.[7] In some cases the context is one of mourning – and this is relevant I think, for instance to *Adieu*, the first part delivered at the grave of a friend and the second at a memorial event for him. The trembling voice saying 'Farewell' becomes a play on words as we read them in a cold light and from a distant place. The 'Prière d'insérer' (inserted leaf, lost in translation) inserted into *Monolingualism of the Other* begins by quoting the opening paragraphs of the book and then comments:

> This is how this book begins: at once intimate, between one and oneself, and yet 'beside/outside oneself', it is a kind of chatting, the murmur of an animated confession, but also the acting out of an apostrophe, the fiction of a dramatic conversation, finally a political debate – in a language on the subject of that language. (My translation)

> (Ainsi commence ce livre: à la fois intime, entre soi et soi, et pourtant 'hors de soi', c'est une sorte de causerie, le murmure d'une confession animée, mais aussi une apostrophe jouée, la fiction d'un entretien dramatique, un débat politique enfin – dans une langue au sujet de ladite langue.)

One of the questions to be asked, when one considers the relationship between speaker and audience, or the relationship between a text and its implied or real reader, is whether the addressee is assumed to be a *semblable*, someone like the speaker or writer, perhaps a friend if only virtually, so close that the writer-reader could be talking to himself. 'Entre soi et soi' ('between oneself and oneself') does not say 'him', but perhaps this structure of 'within the same' is closer to a masculine economy – especially when it is enacted in public. Is there an identification, an appeal to fellows, or a distinction? If a distinction, then is it similar to that between master and disciple – the gifted pupil will one day be (like) the teacher. And then what *is* the place of women in this conversation?

In *Politics of Friendship* Derrida follows the track that moves between interpersonal relations (friendship) and civic relations (notably democracy). Aristotle (384–322 BC), Cicero (106–43 BC), and many of the modern great source texts on friendship see it as crucial to virtuous politics. Feminism might applaud the interlinking of the political and the personal (the same standard of virtue and equality applied to both),[8] but this is an androcentric script. Apart from the relationship of personal relations to political relations which follows the pattern of micro and macrocosm as a kind of necessary reflection, we might note that the interfaces between personal and political are many and various and it is often at these cross-over points that we become acutely aware of political injustice. Thus in France the recognition that it might be illegal to offer a bed to a friend or relation if you had not checked they had the correct documentation, or that your facilities had to be scrutinised by officials before you were allowed to receive a friend or relation from abroad in certain situations, brought *home* certain injustices and indignities in immigration policy. In *French Hospitality* Ben Jelloun republishes the text of an article which first appeared in *Le Monde*, entitled 'Ma Mère ne viendra pas en France' ('My Mother won't be coming to France'), in which he explains how insultingly difficult it can be for a Moroccan grandmother to come to visit her French grandchildren even *if* she is granted a visa – which is not easily granted since a woman in her seventies is quite likely to be a terrorist or at least be about to steal someone's job. The article earned him a postbag of racist hate-mail amongst other things.

The category of hospitality between friends is often subsumed into the categories of, on the one hand, hospitality between peers, and, on the other, of reciprocity – although these three categories (friendship, equality and reciprocity) are by no means identical even if there are considerable degrees of overlap. Different writers on friendship have different takes on these issues; for example, the calculation of reciprocity would be seen as inimical to friendship by Aristotle or Cicero, and reciprocity even begins to seem irrelevant when true friends hold everything in common as Montaigne explains (see Derrida, *Politics of Friendship*, Chapter 7). While hospitality between friends in the quotidian sense would be governed by the social code of hospitality (the 'laws'), writing on true friendship soon returns us to the impossible absolute Law.

I should like to question the assumptions of writers on (the philosophy of) friendship who typically note major shifts in the importance attached to friendship at different historical periods. I would argue that friendship is consistently important, even though of course its shape changes in different historical contexts, and that the *fraternal* understanding of friendship has also proved remarkably tenacious through the rise of monotheisms and the increase in importance of romantic and/or companionate marriage. For Derrida there is no great break between the classical model of friendship and the Judaeo-Christian (or indeed Islamic) model.[9] Pangle, in common with other recent Anglophone philosophers of friendship, claims:

> The Greek word φιλία [*philia*] can cover all bonds of affection, from the closest erotic and familial ties to political loyalties, humanitarian sympathies, business partnerships, and even love for inanimate things. But φιλία means first and foremost friendship, and it is the contention of Aristotle and all of the classical authors who follow him that precisely in the friendships of mature and virtuous individuals do we see human love not only at its most revealing but also at its richest and highest.
> With the coming of the Christian world, however, friendship fell into eclipse. (*Aristotle and the Philosophy of Friendship*, 2)

Pangle contends that, first, love of God, and, second, love of all men as brothers, meant 'regarding with particular suspicion the fierce, proudly republican, and sometimes homosexual attachments to individual human beings'. For her, this entailed the elevation of the family and the relative elevation of women. She notes a certain revival of philosophic interest in friendship in the Renaissance – Montaigne and Bacon are the favourite examples but one could add, for example, the translations of Plutarch's *Lives* by Jacques Amyot and Sir Thomas North – but asserts that since then 'friendship has virtually disappeared as a theme of philosophical interest'.[10] For her, Rousseau,

> fearing that the modern liberal project was resulting in the impoverish-ment and isolation of the individual soul, sought to counterbalance liber-alism's spirit of cold calculation with a new emphasis on erotic love, now broadened to comprise a freely chosen friendship of two kindred spirits and pointed firmly towards the family as its natural fulfillment. Taking their lifeblood from this root, the great modern stories have almost invari-ably been love stories. The brittleness of the modern family may give us cause to suspect that Rousseau rested his own project too heavily on a slender and intractably wild reed in the human spirit. But the family's fragility has done little to discourage the ubiquitous hope of finding in one lifelong lover the chief companion of one's heart and mind. (3)

Neera Kapur Badhwar, while agreeing with respect to the decline in interest in friendship caused by Christianity, claims that 'the years

since 1970 have seen a remarkable resurgence of philosophical interest in friendship' (*Friendship*, 'Preface', ix); perhaps the fragility
of the nuclear family, increased acceptance of alternative forms of
sexuality, and new modes of urban living have contributed to this
resurgence of interest in friendship.[11]

I should caution that I consider these historical overviews to be
overly simplistic in their narrative of the decline and fall of (philosophical) interest in friendship – it is in part the result of an unduly
restrictive definition of friendship (and perhaps of philosophy!).
Taking only Pangle's example of Rousseau, there are three key
points to make. The first is that he explicitly embraces, along with
a number of his contemporaries, the Plutarchan model of perfect
friendship between men – he discusses this in his *Confessions*, and in
La Nouvelle Héloïse gives us Saint-Preux and Edouard, a model of
classical friendship. *Du contrat social* could be regarded as a fraternal model in the political sphere. The second point is that, unusually
for fiction over a long historical period, Rousseau presents a portrait
of a vitally important and happy friendship between women (Julie
and Claire). This is one respect in which his depiction of friendship is original and seems strikingly modern, although study of the
eighteenth century reveals many other real and fictional examples
of individuals who do not find their sole fulfilment in the family.
Rousseau's great modern love story, *La Nouvelle Héloïse*, begins
with the dysfunctional traditional Etange family and ends with a dis-
solved 'family' to be composed of Claire, Saint-Preux and Edouard,
alongside Julie's widow Wolmar, a friend and host to all of them,
and his children.[12] The relationship between Wolmar and the children is the only one to be based on blood or law, and to result from
desire, and Wolmar asks Saint-Preux, as a friend, to raise them.
While there are many ways of interpreting the trajectory between the
beginning and the end, and the erotic love between Julie and Saint-
Preux certainly captures the reader's imagination, it seems strange to
suggest that *philia* is not of significant importance. My third response
to Pangle's reference to Rousseau's influence in establishing the need
for 'one lifelong lover [as] the chief companion of one's heart and
mind' is that amorous passion is a powerful force for Rousseau but
one that cannot be virtuous unless *philia* takes priority – *philia* found
in particular between men, but also between women and between
men and women (who may or may not be lovers). Derrida's extensive study of Rousseau in *De la grammatologie* shows how dangerous *eros* is in Rousseau's writing, requiring an economy of spacing.

While proximity is desirable for friends, erotic relations require an element of distance (figured in Book 5 of *Emile* by the advice given to Sophie not to have sexual relations with her husband too often). What Rousseau proposes is complex and much misinterpreted, but even misreadings of Rousseau do not always lead away from friendship. One fed into the nineteenth-century version of separate spheres and the angel in the house (one side of the coin of domestic slavery). This precisely assumed that men found their major source of friendship amongst men rather more than in, say, eighteenth-century aristocratic circles where inter-sex friendship featured significantly (though not normally between husband and wife). I would contend that the spouse as lover-friend is a much later phenomenon, and thus not particularly tied to Christianity.

The model of perfect friendship between men and the question of mourning

Politics of Friendship contains wide-ranging analyses of key writers on friendship from Aristotle himself up to Maurice Blanchot, the novelist, philosopher and great friend of Levinas. In this chapter I shall approach the canon largely via the Greek and Roman texts (Plato, Aristotle and Cicero) and Montaigne – leaving Nietzsche, Michelet, Schmitt and others aside for the obvious reasons of space.[13] Derrida also reflects on friendship in many other of his works, not only *Politics of Friendship*. One series of texts that deserves to be introduced in this context is collected together by Pascale-Anne Brault and Michael Naas in *The Work of Mourning*, subsequently published in expanded form as *Chaque fois unique la fin du monde*, pieces written on the occasion of the death of a number of his friends between 1981 (Barthes) and, in the French version, 2003 (Blanchot).[14] For Derrida, friendship always entails imagining that one will die before the other; death is already in the structure (or law) of the name – the name allows us to refer to the person who is absent, even dead. Writing in memory of Paul de Man, about how the (dead) friend lives only in us, Derrida claims that he could have said 'all of this *before* his death. It suffices that I know him to be mortal, that he knows me to be mortal – there is no friendship without this knowledge of finitude' ('dire ce que je dis *avant* sa mort. Il suffit que je le sache mortel – et il n'est pas d'amitié sans ce savoir de la finitude').[15] This relationship *in absentia* is particularly clear in Montaigne's essay on friendship (see Derrida's analysis *PF*, 291 ff.; *PA*, 324 ff.). Montaigne knew La Boétie and

101

was his friend before he had met him: in a lovely phrase he writes: 'nous nous embrassions par noz noms' ('De l'amitié', 187, translated as 'we embraced each other by repute', 'On Friendship', 292). La Boétie's literary reputation or *renommé* (importantly not just fame, but reputation in a positive moral sense), and reading his writing, made Montaigne love him (and the same applied for La Boétie with Montaigne) before their bodies met. After his death, Montaigne is his literary executor, charged with making his name live on in an appropriate way. Friendship involves an interiorisation of the other – incorporation or introjection when the other is dead and we mourn them. Cicero writes in Laelius' voice: 'Although Scipio was suddenly snatched away from us, for me he still lives and always will live. It was his fine qualities that I loved, and those are not dead. Not only are they constantly before my own eyes (since I always had them close at hand), but they will always be famous and eminent among future generations' (*De Amicitia*, 73 [¶ 103]). However, speaking or writing of the friend who has died is very difficult, as well as necessary, and Derrida's texts display that difficulty; the French 'à peine' between the proper translation 'hardly' and the improper sense 'painful', in English, is one of the figures he deploys.[16] Furthermore the anthologised *in memoriam* can seem like inscribing names on tombstones in the cemetery: one kind of perpetual peace – as Levinas hints, after Kant. The latter makes reference to a Dutch inn's ironic name and sign: the words 'To Perpetual Peace' may seem hospitable and inviting, while the image of a cemetery less so (see Derrida, *Adieu*, 99–101; 173–6, for analysis of this). Friendship should be singular, yet, by virtue of this *collection*, the reader is brought up against repetition, the *genre* of the funeral oration for example. The classical genre normally entails a man speaking of his dead friend/ brother, and, while the singular-personal is at the heart, quite often something political is also at stake.

Perhaps I should also be talking about ghosts or spectral visitors, not only the ghost of the friend but also of oneself (the two so close); one issue in classical discourses on friendship is that of survival beyond the grave.[17] Without any need for a woman's fidelity, and biological reproduction, the man can live on through his friend(s) if they are faithful. In *Au-delà des apparences* Derrida responds to a question about the theme of loyalty or fidelity to friends in his work, and replies: 'In one sense, unconditional fidelity is shown when the friend is dead or radically absent, when the other cannot any longer answer for himself, nor in front of us, even less exchange, show some gratitude, reciprocate' ('D'une part, la fidélité inconditionnelle se marque à la mort, ou à l'absence radicale de l'ami, là où l'autre ne peut plus répondre de lui, ni devant nous, et encore moins échanger, marquer quelque reconnaissance, faire retour').[18] In *Politics of Friendship* he writes (apparently on Cicero):

> In this possibility of a *post-mortem* discourse, a possibility that is a force as well, in this *virtue* of the funeral eulogy, everything seems, then, to have a part to play: epitaph or oration, citation of the dead person, the renown of the name after the death of what it names. A memory is engaged in advance, from the moment of what is called life, in this strange temporality opened by the anticipated citation of some funeral oration. I live in the present speaking of myself in the mouths of my friends, I already hear them speaking on the edge of my tomb. The Ciceronian variety of friendship would be the possibility of quoting myself in exemplary fashion, by signing the funeral oration in advance – the best of them, perhaps, but it is never certain that the friend will deliver it standing over my tomb when I am no longer living. . . . Who never dreams of such a thing? But who does not abhor this theatre? Who would not see therein the repetition of a disdainful and ridiculous staging, the putting to death of friendship itself? (*PF*, 5)

> (Tout semble donc concourir dans cette possibilité du discours *post mortem*, qui est aussi une force, dans cette *vertu* de l'éloge funèbre: épitaphe ou oraison, citation du mort, renommée du nom après la mort de ce qu'il nomme. Une mémoire s'engage d'avance, dès ce qu'on appelle encore la vie, dans cette étrange temporalité ouverte par la citation anticipée de quelque oraison funèbre. Je vis au présent en parlant de moi par la bouche de mes amis, déjà je les entends parler au bord de ma tombe. L'amitié, la cicéronienne, ce serait la possibilité de me citer moi-même exemplairement, en signant d'avance l'oraison funèbre, la meilleure peut-être, mais ce n'est jamais sûr, que l'ami prononcera debout quand je ne serai plus. . . . Qui n'en rêve pas? Mais qui ne déteste ce théâtre? Qui n'y verrait se répéter une méprisable et dérisoire mise en scène, la mise à mort de l'amitié même? (*PA*, 21))

For us readers of course, the author is always dead, and his name, his renown, is a text. Derrida's confession in *Monolingualism of the Other* of 'unworthy thoughts', the Jewish-French-Algerian product of a mid-century colonial education system believing (perhaps correctly) that you are taken more seriously without a regional accent, has attracted some hostile commentary.[19] The quotation above is in fact another example of Derrida's willingness to strip bare and voice ignominious thoughts even in political, philosophical writing – he is in any case convinced that 'd'une certaine manière tout texte est autobiographique'.[20] Perhaps it requires the 'je' to assume on my behalf the *méprisable* (which I would translate as 'despicable' rather than 'disdainful') dream about the positive things that a true friend will say on my death.[21] True friendship (twin brotherhood unifying the two) would allow one to know, to co-sign the funeral oration (a synecdoche for all those post-mortem texts) before it can occur.

Friendship thus structured is by definition between men. Taking friendship (from Cicero, Montaigne and the many other poets of male–male friendship) to its logical extreme, friends are the same, the two are one. Derrida has, and wrote about, many male friends (the only exceptional female in *The Work of Mourning* is Sarah Kofman), but I have deliberately chosen to focus in this book on his textual and public friendship with a woman (Cixous). Sexual difference is critical, and yet keeps escaping us; for that very reason we must keep returning to it.[22] Alex Thomson refers to 'the question of the sister which contributes a dominant undercurrent to *Politics of Friendship*' (*Deconstruction and Democracy*, 20):

> The problem Derrida poses through his insistence on this exclusion is whether politics itself, all the concepts and models we have of politics, might not be founded on the absence of women, or at least on the neutralisation of sexual difference. In which case it would be impossible to address inequality between the sexes *within* politics, except at the cost of reducing the sister to a brother.
>
> What future for democracy if it has always been rhetorically organised around a model which excludes the woman, or the sister, if, as Derrida says, 'a political phallogocentrism has, *up to this point*, determined *its* cosmopolitical democracy, *a* democracy, *qua* cosmo-phratocentrism' [PoF 263/294]? This problem may not be just any problem among those of the text. Derrida registers the importance of this question as one of 'the two major questions of "deconstruction"': the question of the history of concepts and (trivially) so-called "textual" hegemony, history *tout court*; and the question of phallogocentrism. Here *qua* phratrocentrism' [PoF 278/309]. The possibility seems to be left open here, as so often in Derrida's work, that, in the form of the question set out by Paola Marrati, sexual difference might not be merely one difference among others; this question must at least remain open. (21)[23]

Derrida proposes two solutions to the problem that political virtue has always been virile virtue in its androcentric manifestation – and both are necessary. The first is to replace politics as such, to invent a new concept; the second is to keep the old name, 'politics', while analysing the logic and topic of the concept differently (*PF*, 158; *PA*, 183). These solutions seem, however, to enable commentators – without, I am sure, a deliberate sleight of hand – to shift this to a general question about 'the political' without really developing the question of gender. Thomson, although his work is a careful reading of Derrida, tends to lose sight of sexual difference as the crux of the problem, even while he occasionally returns to it (for instance, on Derrida on Heidegger on *Geschlecht* [75–8], and on Levinas [131–2]).

I should like briefly to mention Brutus' speech on the suicide of Lucretia (a story that begins with a breach of hospitality) as a variation to the rule that has fascinated writers over the centuries, that it is a virtuous *man* that is the subject of the oration. It could be argued that he is addressing men, and that his subject is a man (the rapist who is also a tyrant and thus should be killed); Lucretia's body is simply his matter and pretext, like that of the Levite's concubine. However, Lucretia is an agent in this – her suicide was not only an act of shame (of the kind St Augustine effectively recommends to rape victims) but an act of denunciation which programmes her funeral oration and the toppling of the personal and political tyrant, Sextus Tarquin. While many feminists would agree that women have historically and bodily been associated with the welcoming (hard) labour of birth and life, do women have a role in our Western cult of death, sometimes associated with masculine philosophy?[24] In the face of the death of the other, in fact in many traditions it is women who do the work of mourning, who bear the rituals of mourning, as well as grieving for the lost one(s). Where women have been 'at home' while men were away (sometimes at war), the imagined death of the other may indeed be held within.

It might also be worth introducing another account of mourning which Derrida likens to hospitality. This love is famously across the sexes, although it has also been *interpreted* not as erotic love between a man and a woman, but as, for example, the love between Christ and the Church – a certain reading tradition that disembodies in favour of the figural. I do not have access to Derrida's original French, but a tantalising parenthesis – '*seul(e)*' – leaves many possibilities open across sexual difference. I shall quote at length; he says:

> I was thinking about the lovesickness . . . in the fervent echo or the melancholy wake of the *Song of Songs*, the *Poem of Poems*, as if the poetical of the poetical [*le poétique du poétique*] of all declarations of love had to do

with this sickness of the other, if not of the foreigner in me, of another in me, outside of me, of the other who angers me and puts me out of myself [*qui me met hors de moi*], the other who puts me outside of myself in me, of the other always more ancient and more to come than me, whom I thus mourn [*dont je porte ainsi le deuil*] as a mourning of me [*comme le deuil de moi*], as if I carried the mourning of me carried by the other, where there would thus begin an ageless hospitality, or a hospitality of all ages, a hospitality which could only survive itself before its time, and of which the poem would say, in sum, from one to the other in me: I love you, I am sick of love from you, sick of love for you, for while wholly wanting, with all my desire, to die before you so that I don't see you die, for you know that one of us will see the other die, well then, while wholly wanting, with all my hopeless desire, to die first, I would also want to survive you, to have at least the time to be there to console you at the time of my death, to assist you and so that you would not be alone [*seul(e)*] at the time of my death: I would want to survive you just enough to help you, the time that it will take to bear my death. 'I love you' would thus signify this impossible grammar, a grammar that one can find at once tragic and comic, as time itself: I would want to survive you at my death, to survive me in you, to guard in me your mourning of me, etc. And this 'I love you, and therefore I guard you/keep you in surviving you' is unforgivable, therefore I ask you for forgiveness there where it is possible to ask for and to grant forgiveness, there where only, you recall, it is unforgivable. ('Hostipitality', 407–8)

This expresses the complex psychic topography of inside and outside, of holding an outsider within, the outsider who (in love-friendship) already holds you within. There is an equally complex temporality – as we might expect since Derrida's most famous *différance* has accustomed his readers to seek time as well as space in his 'impossible grammar'. I will hold you within me when you hold me within you, when I will have died. Any narcissism is irrelevant where the unity of friends or lovers is assumed; instead there is honesty in mourning your lover's mourning of you.

Friendship and writing: past texts as friends

Across the ages there can be conversation, sharing and nourishment – and many writers begin (and end) as great readers, lovers of books. In this section I shall turn to the conversation across the centuries, and across countries, about the nature of friendship. In 'On Three Kinds of Relationships' ('De trois commerces') (*Essays*, III: 3), Montaigne talks of his friends. Some of the greatest friends of that lyric poet of (fraternal) friendship are (male) writers he will never meet in person for they are long dead and gone; but he loves them: they are true friends and give him great pleasure. Seneca makes the same point, and, much later, Ben Jelloun writes of film-makers and writers such as Fellini or Nietzsche who are his friends without them knowing it (*Eloge de l'amitié*, 84). He reads Joyce's *Ulysses* when incarcerated in a disciplinary camp as a young man: 'He authorized my writing. Doesn't someone who gives you that kind of gift deserve your friendship?' ('Il m'a autorisé à écrire. Celui qui vous fait un tel don ne mérite-t-il pas votre amitié?' (85)). The conversation about friendship between writers/readers over the centuries has largely been a homosocial one, as Derrida points out. Women have had to write themselves into this plot as uninvited guests, joining in the dialogue with the philosophers against the grain, as Irigaray persistently does. Cixous figures herself young and lonely in colonial Algeria, searching for *semblables* – like-minded spirits revolting against injustice – and finding a kind of home in Homer ('people who are like me', *The Newly-Born Woman*, 72; *La Jeune Née*, 132), and yet the masculine home-coming plot is one she finds profoundly uncongenial as seen in Chapter 2. And when she becomes aware of the battle between the sexes, Theseus, Ariadne and Medea via Euripides and Plutarch, Dido via Virgil, give much food for thought – though not always comfort.

Derrida draws attention to the position of the speaker or writer, and the question of the *apostrophe* that I have already raised. The speaker who welcomes the audience, in what can become a kind of familiar ritual for us, risks (if we assume that this is not what is desired) appropriating a position for 'himself', a violent, or, at least, masterful, hospitality (*Adieu*, 15; 39 ff.). Derrida writes about the responsibility of a speaker for his words (or his decision to quote others), and the responsibility of the listener to respond if only virtually – which means, however, that whatever challenges to canons and traditional structures we all want to make, we are already implicated in a dominant structure. 'Suppose I am invited to speak to you (but exactly how and by whom, finally? And who invites you to read a book, that is, to invite the word of another into your home, and to put you in charge of it [à vous en charger], at this very moment?)' (*PF*, 229) ('Supposez que je sois invité à vous parler (mais comment et par qui, au juste, finalement? Et qui vous invite à lire un livre, c'est-à-dire à inviter la parole d'un autre chez vous, à vous en charger en ce moment même?)' (*PA*, 256)). When you listen to a speaker (saying in this context 'O my friends, there is no friend'):

You have already marked [Vous m'avez *déjà* marqué, you have already shown me] this minimal friendship, this preliminary consent without which you would not hear me [vous ne m'entendriez pas, you would not understand me]. Otherwise you would not listen to my call, you would not be sensitive to the element of hope in my complaint. Without this absolute past, I would not have been able, for my part, to address you thus. We would not be together in a sort of minimal community – but also incommensurable to all others – speaking the same language or praying for translation against the horizon of a same language, if only to manifest disagreement, if a *sort of friendship* had not already been sealed, before all contracts; if it had not been avowed as the impossible that resists even avowal, but avowed still, avowed as the unavowable of the 'unavowable community': a friendship prior to friendships, an ineffaceable friendship, fundamental and groundless, one that breathes in a shared language (past or to come) and in the being-together that all allocution supposes, up to and including the declaration of war.

Is this incommensurable friendship, this friendship of the incommensurable, indeed the one we are here attempting to separate from its fraternal adherence, from its inclination to take on the economic, genealogical, ethnocentric, androcentric features of fraternity? Or is it still a fraternity, but a fraternity divided in its concept, a fraternity ranging infinitely beyond all literal figures of the brother, a fraternity that would no longer exclude anyone? (*PF*, 236–7)

(Vous m'avez *déjà* marqué cette amitié minimale, ce consentement préliminaire sans lequel vous ne m'entendriez pas. Vous n'écouteriez pas mon appel autrement, vous ne seriez pas sensibles à ce qui entre d'espérance dans ma plainte. Sans ce passé absolu, je n'aurais pu, de mon côté, m'adresser ainsi à vous. Nous ne serions pas ensemble dans une sorte de communauté minimale – mais aussi – incommensurable à toute autre –, parlant la même langue ou priant pour la traduction dans l'horizon d'une même langue, fût-ce pour y manifester un désaccord, si *une sorte* d'amitié n'avait déjà été scellée, avant tout autre contrat, si elle n'avait été avouée, avouée comme l'impossible qui résiste même à l'aveu, mais avouée encore, avouée comme l'inavouable de la 'communauté inavouable': une amitié d'avant les amitiés, une amitié ineffaçable, fondamentale et sans fond, celle qui respire dans le partage de la langue (passée ou à venir) et dans l'être-ensemble que suppose toute allocution, jusque dans la déclaration de guerre.

Cette amitié incommensurable, cette amitié de l'incommensurable, est-ce bien celle que nous tentons ici de détacher de son adhérence fraternelle, de son inclination à prendre les traits économiques, généalogiques, ethnocentriques, androcentriques de la fraternité? Ou bien est-ce *encore* une fraternité, mais une fraternité divisée dans son concept, une fraternité portant à l'infini au-delà de toute figure littérale du frère, une fraternité qui n'exclurait plus quiconque? (*PA*, 264))

In this passage Derrida refers to those who speak the same language, including those who are praying for a translation within the horizon of a same language. He cannot be understood in his mournful plaint 'there is no friend' unless a particular minimal community has been already established ('my friends') who share a common tongue. This is a sort of friendship ('my friends') prior to friendship ('there is no friend') – it must be confessed, but is as impossible to admit to ('there is no friend') as it is essential to acknowledge ('my friends'). Sharing language is necessary for any communication (including a declaration of disagreement, even war), but in this instance this minimal community of friends which is his audience is one, incommensurable, that might challenge the dominant structure of fraternity. Could it break away from fraternity? Or is it still, again, fraternity, but one which is divided, which might be expanded to the point of infinity where no-one would be excluded? Is this utopian? It is time to consider in more detail what androcentric friendship has meant.

What and who is the friend?

The primary text to which Derrida turns for an answer to this question is Aristotle's *Ethics* (not one text, but at least two, as I have indicated). However, the midwife to this child is, typically, Socrates, and the maieutic text (as Derrida puts it, in accordance with a certain tradition) in particular is Plato's *Lysis On Friendship*. This topic of friendship is thereby intimately related to pedagogy,[25] and perhaps, more worryingly, to *paedophilia*, to teaching, or perhaps corrupting, youth. While the dialogue is an oft-cited starting-point for the conversation about friendship, between friends or teachers and pupils, the disturbing origin is equally occluded. Even when Socrates is referenced, we might ask 'what is citation?' for sometimes in the act of referring the reference is kept silent.[26] I shall begin by deviating from the straight path, and turning my gaze to Socrates and his affection for young boys.

Lysis takes place in a wrestling school (*palaestra*). It ends with intoxicated foreign slaves whose Greek is barely comprehensible, Lysis' and his friend's bodyguards, interrupting the discussion of *philia* before any conclusion has been reached, and, refusing to take no for an answer dragging their young charges off because it is getting late. Time for supper? Time for bed? It begins, as so often, with a chance encounter. Socrates, the first-person narrator, is on his way from the Academy *straight* to the Lyceum, but he falls in with a company of young men and one of them, Hippothales, persuades him to deviate from his route – telling him the entertainment will be conversation. Almost immediately Socrates has him blushing by asking him who is his favourite, and we learn that Hippothales (the editor has him as a sixteen-year-old) is in love with the beautiful and noble Lysis (a twelve-year-old our editor guesses from the textual clues).[27] Socrates offers to give Hippothales a demonstration of how he should converse with his beloved in order to make it more likely that he will return his love. Lysis finds the courage to come and listen to his elders' conversation (not knowing that all was in fact for his benefit) when his good friend and peer Menexenus proceeds to join them – but Menexenus is soon called away by his gymnastics teacher. Socrates then uses his typical question and answer technique to show Lysis that he is still deficient in knowledge of many things, and that, he says, 'if you become wise, all men will be your friends and kindred, for you will be useful and good; but if you are not wise, neither father, nor mother, nor kindred, nor anyone else, will be your friends'. In other words, Lysis is persuaded that he is in sore need of a teacher. When Menexenus returns, Lysis begins affectionately whispering in Socrates' ear that he must tell his friend the same thing, or in some way 'put him down'; meanwhile one of the company, a friend of Hippothales, complains that they are talking in secret and 'keeping the feast to ourselves' as Plato has Socrates reporting it. Socrates is happy to share, and, telling Menexenus that he is a great lover of friends, and that he sees he and Lysis are possessed of the treasure of friendship, he asks him: 'when one loves another, is the lover or the beloved the friend; or may either be the friend?' This reference to the possibilities of need in friendship as well as reciprocity sets in motion a series of questions and answers, which lead paradoxically to apparent philosophical dead ends, in which every approach to the question of friendship is stymied.[28]

It is perhaps not surprising then that Aristotle proceeds with a clear and cogent analysis which produces a whole series of assertions about what true friendship is, methodologically the polar opposite of the Platonic dialogue to which he does not overtly refer, but which is everywhere at stake. Socrates uses a set of situations that do not fit the case of friendship in the narrow sense, but which also involve use of the term *philia* (such as the love of men for horses, dogs, cocks or quails; or the desire of the dry for the moist), in order to question and confuse easy assumptions about the definition of friendship. Aristotle, on the other hand, distinguishes carefully between a whole range of

110

possibilities where the same word is commonly used – only one situation is true *philia* for him and he makes this very clear. Plato/Socrates is showing us something; Aristotle tells us what it is. The *Ethics* are a much clearer place to start if one wishes to find a definition of the classical idea of friendship, but perhaps some things get left out.

One of the things that gets left out is youth, or the relationship between youth and maturity; another thing is pleasure or eros. Aristotle distinguishes between true friendship (what some philosophers would now call end friendship, where the friend is an end in himself) and what commonly passes for friendship but is in fact a relationship based on pleasure or profit (a means friendship, where the friend is a means to an end). For Aristotle, friendship between the young is typically based on pleasure and thus is not true friendship; Cicero expands on this, stating that pleasure 'is fit only for animals' (¶ 20). Yet, interestingly, a version of the typical (virtuous) Platonic relationship between an older and younger man occurs in Cicero's *De Amicitia* via (legal) mentoring. The dialogue is between Cicero's old mentor (Quintus Mucius Scaevola) and – the main speaker – Laelius, Scaevola's father-in-law. According to the frame of the dialogue, it is Scaevola who told Cicero of that conversation amongst others. Montaigne, for his part, explicitly refers to 'the Academy' (and thus Plato) to refute any notion that love for a youth (necessarily founded on external beauty) can be compared to true friendship between mature men (founded on like minds) ('On Friendship', 95; 'De l'amitié', 185). However, sometimes it is difficult to disentangle *philia* and *eros* in male–male friendships even, or especially, in those which appear to be based upon heteronormativity. Cicero's Laelius says to his sons-in-law of his relationship with (the married) Scipio: 'We had one home, one common way of life, and shared not only our military service but also our travels and country holidays' (¶ 103). Montaigne's description of his relationship with La Boétie follows many of the conventions of poetic descriptions of erotic love even while he explicitly distinguishes that relationship from something so inferior as physical desire.

Many thinkers on friendship become exercised by a desire for totality, exclusivity or homogeneity – for example: true friendship cannot include any element of need (or it becomes a means friendship). Plato's dialogues, on the other hand, regularly return both to friendship between a lover and beloved where each fulfils the other's needs (typically an older and a younger man), and each is dissimilar to the other (typically the older man wise and the young man beautiful), and *also* to friendship between two similar (similarly wise and virtuous) men which is very close to what Aristotle will develop as his model of perfect friendship. In Plato the first model may, over time, become the second; Montaigne recognises this, but he denies that this is quite equivalent to his own (more Aristotelian or Ciceronian) model because the choice of friend, in that Platonic model, has been made when the mind is not yet mature. La Boétie was older than Montaigne – but we might note that Montaigne first fell in friendship with him via his writing. The text in question was written when La Boétie was sixteen, and Montaigne's first aim in writing his chapter on friendship was to include this piece, *The Voluntary Servitude*, with it; he introduces it with the unexpected words 'But let us listen a little to this boy of sixteen' ('On Friendship', 104) ('Mais oyons un peu parler ce garson de seize ans' ('De l'amitié', 193)). This may well be an attempt to make his friend's achievement seem all the greater, but in the context of a discussion about the inadvisability of falling for youths it rings strangely. Of course at sixteen he might not have been the beloved as 'beardless youth' (disparaged even by Pausanias in *The Symposium*), but he would have been the pubescent boy whom Pausanias praises as the object of male love.

Plato's examples of friendship are all men – but women are not specifically excluded as they are by some thinkers who come later. Perhaps his homosexual homosociality is more open to a development into friendship across sexual difference than the Aristotelian model. In the *Republic*, patriarchal family life and the private sphere are radically questioned; women Guardians are given the same education and opportunities as men since they are like female watch-dogs who should guard the flock and hunt with the males. However, this proposal has been assumed to be a joke by some male commentators, and some feminists (notably Irigaray) have seen it as an attempt to drag women into a masculine economy.[29] Irigaray is more optimistic about the *Symposium* where women are included in other ways. In that dialogue Aristophanes even mentions 'female companions' (lesbians) as one of the amorous possibilities alongside men who love men, men who love women and women who love men. His may be a comic speech, but nevertheless it is a rare moment in philosophy for modern readers. Perhaps more importantly, Socrates presents his account of love as the teaching of the wise woman Diotima – and this, for Irigaray, is the possible point of entry for a dialogue between the sexes. The context of many Platonic dialogues is hospitality; the French 'Le Banquet' of course sounds more inviting than the English academic 'Symposium', but in either tongue we find a play on the role of host and guest, invited or not, and Aristodemus 'found the doors wide open'.[30] Aristotle's format is that of the lecture, and is far more impersonal. His specific remarks on sexual difference (as a hierarchy of activity over passivity or form over substance) have been much critiqued, and I shall not reproduce this here.[31]

Cicero returns us to the dialogue form (though it is far more formulaic than in Plato) and to the context of hospitality. He also returns us to a factional context – like Plato introducing speakers who are historically located even if he invents their speeches. *De Amicitia* has two moving contexts. It is a letter to Cicero's friend Atticus, answering his appeal: 'I have written to a friend in the friendliest spirit on the subject of friendship' 'hoc libro ad amicum amicissimus scripsi de amicitia' (28 [¶ 5]). Within the letter format we have Cicero's memory of conversations with his mentor-friend (Quintus Mucius) about conversations Quintus had with his wise father-in-law Laelius and, in this instance, also with Laelius' other son-in-law (Gaius Fannius); and the one he recounts to us is supposed to have taken place a few days after the death of Laelius' bosom friend Scipio Aemilianus Africanus. The context is thus one of mourning, and Laelius, while claiming that he is coping with the situation, says that, relative to Scipio:

> It is I who have been less fortunate; it would have been fairer for me, who entered this life before he did, also to leave it first. However, that aside, I have the memory of our friendship to enjoy; and this makes me feel that my life has been happy because I have shared it with Scipio. I used to consult him on both public and private matters; I was associated with him both at home and on service abroad; and I had with him that in which the true power of friendship consists – the greatest possible community of interests, wishes and opinions. Hence it is not so much that reputation for wisdom, which Fannius just mentioned, that pleases me, particularly is if is not truly justified, as the hope that the memory of our friendship may be preserved for ever; and this gives me all the more pleasure, inasmuch as in the whole course of history hardly three or four pairs of friends are remembered by name; and I believe there is hope that the friendship of Scipio and Laelius will be known to posterity among these. (35 [¶ 15])

The renowned friendships to which Cicero refers would include Theseus and Pirithous, Orestes and Pylades, Achilles and Patroclus – the most famous classical examples. While I am emphasising the homosocial bias in all this (which hardly needs *emphasising*), I should briefly underline again the importance of traditional, counter-traditional and individual *readings* of these key cultural texts. The love of Achilles and Patroclus, for instance, has often been claimed (in the *Symposium* for example), and reclaimed, as *eros* as well as *philia*. And it must be remembered that, in any case, the Greek term *philia* includes what we would term erotic or romantic love; it is highly flexible and ambiguous, as Plato/Socrates would show us in *Lysis*, far more so than English translations can allow for. The French is more open since *aimer* covers liking and loving, but it still does not achieve the grammatical flexibility or range (the middle voice, for example) that both Derrida and Irigaray admire in the Greek. Some readers find it important to insist that any physical intercourse between Achilles and Patroclus is simply *not there* in Homer, and therefore these heroes did *not* engage in homosexual acts – they were just good friends. It seems clear to me that of course we cannot know exactly what many historical, let alone mythical or literary, characters did (or did not do) in bed, even though in some cases there are parameters of probability! Reading responses in some instances of course tell us as much about readers and their contexts as about the texts.

Problems: fraternity

As I have noted, fraternity is a key trope in discussions of hospitality (as of much else), and Derrida discusses it at length in *Politics of Friendship*. We feminists often used to be pilloried for our inappropriate obsession with language, and taking linguistic forms literally ('chairman' and so on) – what is now demonised as political correctness. Derrida is of course even more obsessional. While acknowledging the value and universalist intention of much of the use of the language of fraternity, which does not intend to refer to blood-lines or to maleness (perish the thought), he is reticent:

> In keeping this word to designate a fraternity beyond fraternity, a fraternity without fraternity (literal, strict, genealogical, masculine, etc.), one never renounces that which one claims to renounce – and which returns in myriad ways, through symptoms and disavowals whose rhetoric we must learn to decipher and whose strategy to outwit. (*PF*, 237)

> (Garder encore ce mot pour désigner une fraternité au-delà de la fraternité, une fraternité sans fraternité (Littérale, stricte, généalogique, masculine, etc.), c'est ne jamais renoncer à ce à quoi l'on prétend renoncer – et qui revient toujours de mille façons, à travers des symptômes et des dénégations dont nous devons apprendre à déchiffrer la rhétorique et à déjouer la stratégie. (*PA*, 265))[32]

In Chapter 4, I shall return to the power of names, and to the dream of fraternity, and the (im)possibility of fraternity in colonial Algeria. Brotherhood is surely better than enmity, and yet maybe the sister is not just an optional addition but critical in the relationship. Certainly women are often blamed for the failure of relationships across a racial divide in the colonies – just as the women of the coloniser are to be 'protected' from any possibility of a sexual relationship with the colonised, and the women of the colonised exploited sexually wherever possible . . .

Where then do we turn first for a definition of *fraternal* friendship? Not so much to Plato's hesitations, as to Aristotle's extensive discussion in two of the Books of the *Nicomachean Ethics*: VIII 'The Kinds of Friendship' and IX 'The Grounds of Friendship'. Derrida in fact largely quotes from the *Eudemian Ethics* rather than from the *Nicomachean*, which is unusual in the Classical tradition.[33] Books 4, 5, and 6 of the *Eudemian Ethics* are supposed to be identical to 5, 6, 7 of the *Nicomachean Ethics*. But the last book of the *Eudemian Ethics* (7) is also on friendship. Anthony Kenney argues (largely on the basis of internal evidence, such as statistical study of features of style, although he also analyses early references to Aristotle's *Ethics*) against the tide of opinion, that the *Eudemian Ethics* are (a) later, (b) undoubtedly by Aristotle, and (c) better. All three of these judgements seem to go together, as does the argument that the three disputed books really belong to the *Eudemian Ethics*.[34] M. Pakaluk claims that the *Eudemian Ethics* are more egalitarian in detail than the *Nicomachean Ethics*.[35] Like most commentators I will, however, give (albeit reluctantly) most of my references to the *Nicomachean Ethics* since it will be much easier for any English-language readers who wish to go back to Aristotle to get hold of the text.

Aristotle begins rhetorically with the fact that some authorities claim that 'birds of a feather flock together' while others maintain that 'opposites attract' (259) – one of the questions raised by Socrates. As his argument advances, unsurprisingly for those familiar with his philosophy, it becomes clear that true friendship for Aristotle is based on equality and similarity (272), to the point that the perfect friend is another self, and thus friendship cannot approximate to self-love (294). He acknowledges that many of what we call friendships, relationships based on profit or pleasure, exist between those who are dissimilar – but these are, strictly speaking, only analogous to friendship (265). They are impermanent by nature and are reliant on contingencies, while perfect friendship, or friendship in the primary and proper sense (265), is enduring, being based on the essential goodness of the friends. Many of the debates over the nature of friendship are resolved by Aristotle by reference to the need to keep the two kinds of relationship distinct. For example, authorities disagree over the question whether a happy man still needs friends. For Aristotle, a good man would be particularly keen to share his good fortune with his true friend – it is only less good men who are more enthusiastic to have 'friends' when they are in need of help themselves (304). Likewise 'womenfolk' (Aristotle uses a pejorative diminutive, as does Cicero who says *mulierculae* seek friendship for protection (51 [¶ 46])) like to see their 'friends' in order to moan about their troubles, whereas a good man tends to be reserved about any problems so as not to distress his friends, even though he rushes to help them as soon as he perceives that they have any kind of problems. This is a rare reference to friendship, even an inferior simulacrum of true friendship, between women.

Equality (267, 269) is important, but this does not mean egalitarianism – it means that we seek out those who are our peers. If a slightly better, or more useful, person is loved more than he loves then a kind of equality may result; it is quantitative equality that is important here rather than equality of merit. However, if there is too great a gap of virtue, wisdom, or affluence then, Aristotle tells us, it is hard to be friends. If love is given in accordance with merit then a relationship is durable (272). Relationships between non-equals are different in kind: for instance, alliances based on utility, a poor man's affection for a rich one (272), father–son, husband–wife or ruler–subjects relations (269). These can never be true friendships for Aristotle.

Cicero takes a more dynamic approach, suggesting that friendship might create equality rather than arising from it. He says that it is very important in friendship to treat inferiors as equals ('parem esse inferiori'), for instance Scipio never put himself before friends of lower rank (¶ 69). If you are of outstanding quality, gifted or wealthy you should share this with your friends (or family including, we might note, adoptive families). The inferior should not reproach the superior but lift himself up.

Aristotle quotes Euripides: 'Two friends, one soul' (*Orestes*, 1046) (301); this issue of similarity – a friend is another self – leads to the question: is self-love good? The answer is clear for Aristotle: yes, in a good man who shows his self-love by fine actions (302), whereas a bad man shows his self-love by, say, greed for money or power. Cicero concurs with the emphasis on virtue, 'friendship cannot exist

116

except in good men' ('nisi in bonis amicitiam esse non posse') (¶ 18), but points out that he does not use the Stoic definition of perfect goodness and wisdom that is so rare that there are almost no examples. He prefers to operate *pingui minerva* – with a fat Minerva, or common sense. His definition of good men is based on examples of

> those who behave and live in such a way that people praise their honesty, integrity, fairness and generosity [*liberalitas*], and have in them nothing of greed [*cupiditas*], intemperance [*libido*] or shamelessness [*audacia*], being also endowed with great strength of character [*constantia*] . . . follow, as far as human beings can, the best guide for living well, that is Nature [*naturam*]. (¶ 18)

Friendship is 'a community of views on all matters human and divine, together with good will and affection' (¶ 20): there is no better gift from the gods, save wisdom. Virtue produces and maintains friendship, and friendship cannot exist without it. Virtue, virile virtue, is commonly understood as something one must actively strive to achieve, rather than an innate quality (like goodness) given by (noble) birth; yet there is always a tension between that *disposition* (is it necessary even if not sufficient?) and the *achievement* of virtue. Derrida deploys a similar tension in characterising the host as naturally generous *and* making an effort ('Hostipitality', 361). Cicero oscillates between a refusal to define virtue so narrowly that no one matches up to it (39) and definitions of friendship where 'I speak now not of the common or incomplete sort, which nevertheless is still both pleasurable and profitable, but about the true and perfect [*de vera et perfecta*] friendship that is found among the few who are remembered for it' (¶ 22). With this kind of friendship: 'he who looks at a true friend sees as it were a reflection of himself' (¶ 23). This notion, from Aristotle, has become a commonplace by the time of Cicero (91).

One of the pressure points in Aristotle arises out of his aristocratic magnanimity, which tends to lead to a competition in giving (even if not for political power or glory) or a desire to confer benefits rather than to receive them – even if it is to confer the benefit of enabling a friend to be a benefactor. This is the man who loves to play the host, but is less comfortable as a guest. The Aristotelian *agathos* is unwilling to tell his friend of his troubles. He cannot show weakness or distress. We might note that dying for a friend (making the gift of your death) may seem the most noble act, but means that you do not endure the friend's death. In French to give death (*donner la mort*) is to kill; *se donner la mort*, giving death to yourself, is to kill yourself.

This trick of language is explored in Derrida's essay 'Donner la mort' which was published in a collection of conference papers on the ethics of the gift.[36] One of Aristotle's few (and disparaging) references to female friendship is the remark that women 'moan' together (309) – is this a point about petty grievances or does it mean his perfect friend cannot show grief? The texts I have chosen for analysis from Cicero and Montaigne both *show* grieving, and, to some extent *deny* it as inappropriate (or self-centred) when the friend has had a good life and a good death.

The paradox of a friend preferring to confer rather than receive benefits is present though less marked as an aporia in the Roman writers who tackle this subject.[37] Cicero insists that friendship is founded on nature not need, on 'Attachment of the mind, accompanied by a sense of affection, [rather] than because of a calculation of the amount of advantage that the association will bring' (¶ 27). But 'strengthening of love does indeed come from the receiving of kindnesses, from the observation of the other's interest, and from the building up of familiarity'; although need is not the origin of the relationship, advantages are a by-product (¶ 28). Like Seneca in *De Beneficiis*, Cicero claims that 'each partner [is] more disposed to do favours than to ask for them in return, and each compet[es] honorably with the other in this matter' (¶ 32). He also insists that it is not utility but the love of the friend which delights when you receive benefits. The flourishing of kindness (¶ 51) is one of the things that demonstrates the value of friendship both for individuals and for the polis in Cicero as in Aristotle.

As Derrida points out, Montaigne takes this further; for him there can be no gift between friends as there is no distinction between them (they are one), and even the hospitality that body offers soul must be complicated by the inherited formula of two bodies sharing one soul. Friends have all things in common – friendship is based on community, friends share everything. Friends are brothers. Indeed while celebrating the fact that he can extend the glorious name of brother to a friend, Montaigne is clear that a friend is *preferable* to a brother (or any other blood relation). First the friend is selected on the basis of similarity while a brother just came out of the same hole, as Plutarch relates. Second, real brothers are likely to compete over property whereas friends wish only to hold everything in common ('On Friendship', 93; 'De l'amitie', 183).

Yet the best a friend can do (as Montaigne, and so many others, tell us) is to let his friend do him a favour; in 'On Friendship' Montaigne tells the story of the poor man (Eudamidas) who had two rich friends and in his will allowed one to take care of his mother till her death and the other to provide a dowry for his daughter (100; 189–90). For Montaigne the only flaw in this exemplary tale is that a man cannot have two friends. (A man cannot have two masters either.) According to this logic, the best legacy is a chance to do service in some way. There is thus a tension between Montaigne's desire to assert that friends are one and hold everything in common (therefore there can be no gift exchanged between them), and his generous desire to show generosity – in this instance by one friend enabling another to serve him.

Montaigne addresses more explicitly than the classical writers the question whether a woman can be a friend in this perfect sense:

> The normal capacity of women is, in fact, unequal to the demands of that communication and intercourse on which the sacred bond [friendship] is fed; their souls do not seem firm enough to bear the strain of so hard and lasting a tie. And truly, if that were not so, if such a free and voluntary relationship could be established in which not only the soul had its perfect enjoyment, but the body took its share in the alliance also, and the whole man was engaged, then certainly it would be a fuller and more complete friendship. But there has never yet been an example of a woman's attaining to this, and the ancient schools are at one in their belief that it is denied to the female sex. ('On Friendship', 95)

> (La suffisance ordinaire des femmes n'est pas pour respondre à cette conference et communication, nourrisse de cette saincte couture ; ny leur ame ne semble assez ferme pour soustenir l'estreinte d'un neud si pressé et si durable. Et certes, sans cela, s'il se pouvoit dresser une telle accointance, libre et volontaire, où, non seulement les ames eussent cette entiere jouyssance, mais encores où les corps eussent part à l'alliance, où l'homme fust engagé tout entier il est certain que l'amitié en seroit plus pleine et plus comble. Mais ce sexe par nul exemple n'y est encore peu arriver, et par le commun consentement des escholes anciennes en est rejetté. ('De l'amitié', 185)

Montaigne is indeed supported in his view by many other authorities as Derrida indicates in *Politics of Friendship*.[38] Cicero mentions parental love (and also the Stoic father of dead sons), but not marital love (and not Irigaray's 'between two'). An editor of *De Amicitia* (Powell) claims that this 'doesn't mean that he doesn't consider it equally important' (88), and affirms that 'the modern reader may naturally jump to the conclusion that [Cicero], and others of his time, could only envisage such an idealized intellectual companionship in an all-male setting. Such a conclusion would, however, be wrong'

(1). It is just that marriage is a separate topic. This seems to stretch the case to me, and as Cicero imagines Laelius talking to his two sons-in-law the omission is all the more striking. The reader might suspect that there is an element of denial on the part of the editor. Montaigne's piling up of reasons why, while women *would be more perfect* friends for men than men are if they *could be perfect* friends, in fact women *cannot be perfect* friends, is also a strangely structured argument. (It is also strangely familiar, as woman's natural failure to meet the imagined heights dreamt up for her by men usually leaves her well beneath the point where men place themselves.) Having shown that perfect friendship is beyond the *normal* capacity of men – indeed over a period of some centuries you might only expect to find one example of true friendship, he suggests that women's 'normal capacity' ('suffisance ordinaire') is inadequate, and that this is a significant problem (whereas such inadequacy is not a problem for men). He writes of a hypothetical friendship between a man and a woman as 'fuller and more complete' ('plus pleine et plus comble'), and yet his singular friendship with Etienne de la Boétie is simply 'perfect' (94; 184), one soul in two bodies (99; 189).

And so Derrida still asks: 'Why would the friend be like a brother? Let us dream of a friendship which goes beyond this proximity of the congeneric double' (*PF*, viii) ('Pourquoi l'ami serait-il *comme* un frère? Rêvons d'une amitié qui se porte au-delà de cette proximité du double congénère' (*PA*, 12)). The brother-friends we have been considering become religious brothers and revolutionary brothers. In 'politics' or friendship, woman can enter as 'sister' if she becomes a brother, in other words if sexual difference is neutralised. When considering mourning in the context of hospitality and friendship above, I could have introduced Antigone (and her sister Ismene) forbidden to mourn at the grave of her father Oedipus and even more famously forbidden to bury their brother.[39] Derrida invites us: 'Let us dream [*rêvons*] of a friendship' – which makes the reader think of Cixous, the dreamer ('elle marche aux rêves'), author of *Rêveries d'une Femme Sauvage* (*Reveries of the Wild Woman*) and *Rêve je te dis* (*Dream I Tell You*), addressed to Derrida. Can we go beyond not only brothers and fathers, but the father's daughter and the brother's sister?

Problems: exclusion and abuse of women

While friendship is modelled as a spiritual and unearthly bond, friendships are nurtured by small everyday acts of hospitality

– invitations to meals or to stay overnight, buying drinks and the like. In general, friendship must develop over time, time spent in the friend's company, doing things together or for each other. This is one of the reasons why perfect friendship is rare. Aristotle suggests that 'you cannot get to know each other until you have eaten the proverbial quantity of salt together' (264) – according to the editor's footnote the proverb refers to one and a half bushels (by my reckoning 12 gallons) – which is an enormous amount! Cicero concurs: 'It is a true saying that, to fulfill the requirement of friendship, one must eat many bags of salt together' (¶ 67). The figure of course invokes hospitality which is implicit in the account of friendship, although it is rarely specified except analogously, for instance in a reference to Hesiod's maxim that you should have neither too many nor too few guests over time – the same is true for friends, Aristotle suggests. This question of quantification (how many friends?) is one of the elements that intrigues Derrida. Aristotle proposes an 'intimate circle', but then points out that all the celebrated friendships seem to be twosomes. Cicero refers to the *natural* bond of associates, which becomes stronger as it is more concentrated, thus fellow-countrymen and relatives are closer than foreigners and strangers. Friendship should be 'aut inter duos aut inter paucos' (¶ 20) – between two or between a few – a puzzling formulation as the editor points out. One might propose that the 'couple' aspect of true friendship is both asserted and shied away from since homosociality in general must repress the homosexual.

Not only does friendship take time, but it involves activity – thus for Aristotle if friends are not spending time together, conferring benefits on each other (and thus growing in virtue) then they are merely in the state or disposition of friendship. The quotation from Ben Jelloun at the beginning of this chapter suggests that today we also consider time spent together as crucial to support and develop friendship. Passive moments (such as sleep) are possible of course, but, for Aristotle, too long an absence induces forgetfulness – *active realisation* is necessary for a perfect friendship to be maintained. Friendship maintained by spending time together and entertaining each other was a feature of Homeric tales or Icelandic sagas (not only for true friends but also for what Aristotle would say were friendships based on utility or alliances) and the same is true today. Homeric or Icelandic hospitality is understood as the warm hospitality a male traveller receives from the master of the house, even if many of these tales provide warning examples of the failure of hospitality. Women, more or less absent from the true friendship of twin souls as *subjects* in themselves, reappear as the *object* of a service done for a friend (as in Montaigne's example of Eudamidas' legacy) or, more often, the *means* by which one man can do his friend a service – they are intermediaries between male friends. Cicero's *De Amicitia*, we may recall, involves a father-in-law and sons-in-law – linked by women's mediation. Women are also the material ground of hospitality: the ones who perform much of the physical labour of hospitality (cooking and serving meals, cleaning houses and so on), and also provide entertainment.[40] Even in apparently all-male environments such as army camps, working-men's clubs or gentlemen's clubs, there are sometimes female servants; and women are at least always discursively available to promote male bonding, for instance, as material for jokes, as Freud suggests. When women are not overlooked (their labour necessary yet unrecognised) they are sometimes abused. However repressed, sexual difference is always at play in the household and in hospitality – even if only one sex is present, the absent other participating in structuring the roles available to our limited imaginations.

The writer and artist Pierre Klossowski notoriously takes this function of the host's woman to its 'logical' or 'perverted' conclusion in his own idiosyncratic 'laws of hospitality', described in *Roberte ce soir*.[41] Schérer considers this text a model, relating it to the utopian Fourier intertext. The 'accidental' rape becomes essential since the ultimate hospitality or sharing is the sharing of the mistress of the house by the master of the house and his guest. If it is by the will of the master of the house, and not by her independent will, then it is indeed akin to rape, the reader might note. In *Of Hospitality*, Derrida analyses Klossowski's, or rather his character Uncle Octave's, 'laws of hospitality', suspended under glass over the bed in the guestroom, returning to them several times. Octave is desperate to be a host, waiting anxiously to spy a stranger whom he might bring into the house as quickly as possible – importantly the guest must *enter*. The guest must come into the interior not just of the house but of his host – and thus must come into the hostess – for one impossible moment thereby achieving union with his host as he possesses her (*OH*, 121–31; *DH*, 109–15). The hostess is both expecting and not expecting this – it is important that she be surprised by the visitor. More classical references (echoed by Rousseau) warn of the danger posed by hospitality to the pudic reserve which must, Rousseau tells us, structure femininity for the sake of both social and biological reproduction.[42] In 'Hostipitality' (and elsewhere) Derrida uses the term *violé* (raped) for the general effect of the surprise visitor whose arrival may be experienced as a violent intrusion by the unprepared host; in the case of absolute hospitality there is simultaneously complete anticipation and total surprise, thus violation (361). The vertiginous exchanges between *hôte* and *hôte*, as in Klossowski where the union must somehow be essential rather than accidental, could be related to perfect friendship where friends hold everything in common. The potential abuse of third parties is usually left unspoken in theories of friendship on the assumption that this would be the action of bad people. Sextus Tarquin is an unexpected guest, arriving at night in the home of the virtuous Lucretia when he knows her husband, his friend, is absent – but as a tyrant he is a classic example of someone who cannot have a true friend. The more interesting examples are less clear-cut, such as the various re-tellings of the exceptional friendship between Gyges and Candaules, which invariably involve violation of a woman's modesty.[43] Stranger-danger is more usually foregrounded: we have to have faith in the virtue of true friends and kinfolk, the only exception being the debate amongst classical authorities over whether true friends are more or less loyal citizens. Montaigne, without mentioning Cicero, responds to the latter's treatment of the conundrum about the friend who asks you to do something wrong by saying that, where true friends are concerned, the other's will is mine. He shifts from Cicero's real political example (of Caius Gracchus, who apparently asks his friend to betray his country) to a hypothetical one that he says is equivalent, that his own will tells him to kill his daughter – in other words it is unthinkable ('On Friendship', 98; 'De l'amitié', 188). Not unthinkable for Agamemnon of course – he sacrifices his daughter on account of the oath sworn by all Helen's suitors that they would support the man who won her against any attempt to seize her from him. Perhaps the unthinkable dead daughter hides something else, such as the sacrifice of women (whether to a husband or worse) on which male bonding is so often grounded. From Greek myths to 'modern' warfare, the rape, sexual humiliation or prostitution of (native) women is often a *shared* experience for comrades or brothers in arms.[44]

If all hospitality, including that between men, traditionally the most common form, harks back to the fear and desire of our first home, what about the position of real women as hosts? What kind of authority do they have over a space such that they can welcome guests; is it always a delegated role, that of the hostess? Or is their lack of the self-same, proper mastery, what makes them more truly hospitable as the Cixous of *The Newly-Born Woman* might argue? Setting aside the host who sacrifices his woman, if they are vulnerable to intruders, should the master of the house ever be absent (like Odysseus or Lucretia's husband, Collatinus), what might women do to protect themselves from unexpected guests? Modest weaving (a trademark of Penelope and Lucretia) of clothes for the living or shrouds for the dead is not always enough to shield from violence – sometimes Athena's aegis is needed too. I should add that modesty is related in a complicated (and sometimes contradictory) way to politeness in welcoming, and this interconnection of sexual difference and hospitality must of course touch upon notions of courtesy. In 'Hostipitality', Derrida evokes Jean de Léry's account of the Tupinamba women in Brazil who weep as a sign of welcome as if the visitors were the dead returning (358–9); nearer home the welcoming smile is conventionally even more necessary for women than for men, yet the hostess must not herself *invite* transgression with 'come hither'. Women in Europe or America today rarely have to absorb themselves modestly in weaving cloth to disguise what they do not have (the phallus), but the domestic labour of hospitality can nevertheless involve a kind of figural weaving together of the display of abundance (flowing wine, conversation, plenty of good food, delightful ambiance created by candles, china, flowers and so on). In 'Hostipitality', Derrida repeats the verbs *se préparer* and *se parer* (361–2); preparation and adornment *are* part of the culture of welcome *even though* according to the Law of hospitality, he notes, the guest cannot be awaited or planned for since there was no prior invitation. This work, I would add, involves also the measuring of the creation of a sense of abundance (not necessarily luxury, but *giving above and beyond*) necessary for true hospitality against the reality of a limited supply of money and time. Where does chore in the construction of hospitableness end and pleasure in hospitality begin, for a woman, and how does this relate to power, to the ownership and control of the domestic means of production, to the extraction of surplus value from the wife's labour, as Delphy would put it?[45]

In what ways can the androcentric tradition of hospitality be reinvented gynocritically? Women's hospitality can cut across the Law and the laws. Feminine hospitalities include the erotic and the maternal but also the domestic or everyday, small services and gifts. Friendship and hospitality between women, a domain where there is something less of a great philosophical or even literary tradition, is concerned with the everyday nourishing (physical and emotional) of the other woman as well as the other man. While a man is a head of household as *pater familias*, he welcomes his guest as a brother-friend. How does a woman welcome a guest? Only as a wife-mother? I shall turn aside now from the fraternal model of friendship and hospitality to investigate the maternal model.

Maternity as hospitality

Hospitality is an ethical structure that wards off the fantasy of the maternal at the same time as it appeals to that fantasy, as I have already suggested in my analysis of the *Odyssey*. John D. Caputo introduces his section on 'Hospitality' in *Deconstruction in a Nutshell* with the phrase a 'mom-and-apple-pie word' (109). In spite of his affection for Derrida's work, Caputo's tone here is somewhat mocking, and he goes on to suggest that 'hospitality' might give some respectable clothing to deconstruction; to me that hint of responding to a demand for modesty again invokes the repressed feminine. The maternal is introduced fleetingly, and only as a rather mawkish element that we sophisticated readers can joke about. The home is homey or homely, the offer of sustenance (apple-pie, Eve's favourite in a safely cooked form) sounds like an advertising slogan for Middle America. Why this defensive debunking? Hospitality involves bringing the other in to the territory of the self for a period of time, and thus can be seen as dangerously, or desirably (say, for Octave), invasive of the domain of the self. Even Octave's desire for union with his male guest must be mediated by his wife. The violable body is particularly at stake, always feminised if only in the cultural imagination. At the same time, from the perspective of the guest, hospitality is again both desirable and perilous. Different societies have different codes laying down sometimes quite specific rights and obligations on the part of both host and guest – warding off the violence that underlies relationships. But typically a reasoned knowledge of these detailed duties of a host in a technical sense falls short of the point; hospitality is an art fuelled by emotion, excess and sensitivity, and thus beyond the rationality of the laws of moderation.

I have suggested that women are always already the intimate ground of hospitality, even where they are expelled from primary social relations of hospitality. How does that relate to Levinas's assertion that 'Woman' ('la Femme' would more usually be translated as 'Woman' rather than 'the Woman') is hospitality *par excellence*? It may seem to be based on a patriarchal notion of the feminine role as absence, discreet self-effacement in the home, even if Levinas presents this as something for a host (in the masculine) to aspire to. He writes:

> The other whose presence is discreetly an absence, with which is accomplished the hospitable welcome par excellence which describes the field of intimacy, is the Woman. The woman is the condition for recollection, the interiority of the Home, and inhabitation. (*Totality and Infinity*, 155)

> (L'Autre dont la présence est discrètement une absence et à partir de laquelle s'accomplit l'accueil hospitalier par excellence qui décrit le champ de l'intimité, est la Femme. La femme est la condition du recueillement, de l'intériorité de la Maison et de l'habitation. (*Totalité et infini*, 128))

As Levinas's account of feminine hospitality develops, it is marked, as Derrida points out, by a series of lacks marked by linguistic negations (*Adieu*, 37; 71–2). While woman is not simply animal (or she could not be truly hospitable for Levinas), and apparently has access to human language, it is a language of silence: 'In human welcome the language that keeps silence remains an essential possibility' (*Totality and Infinity*, 156) ('Accueil humain où le langage qui se tait reste une possibilité essentielle' (*Totalité et infini*, 129)). Derrida worries that this leaves the essentially hospitable woman in a pre-ethical position (*Adieu*, 39; 75). Already in 1947, Levinas insists that woman is *the other* par excellence, and his writings have attracted a great deal of attention from feminists (Irigaray being only the most famous). For Derrida, when Levinas declares that every home presupposes a woman (but not necessarily in empirical terms) 'as the very welcome of the dwelling', he can be read *either* as androcentric hyperbole *or* as a feminist manifesto – indeed perhaps ambiguously *both/and* rather than either/or (*Adieu*, 44; 84). However, if men can learn to epitomise both active presence and discreet absence, then women may not even get to be modestly absent! Derrida also notes that Levinas rather less ambiguously makes a move from the femininity of welcoming to the miracle of paternal fecundity (*Adieu*, 93; 165). Once woman has been dematerialised to *be* welcome for instance, then there is no reason why giving birth (equally removed from base materiality) should not be a masculine prerogative.

As Irigaray points out, biologically women are indeed the first home, *and* represent home for men – who then wish to appropriate generative power:

Western culture is above all masculine, and doubtless we should under-stand the gesture that appropriates the world for oneself as man's attempt to resolve his problems in relating to his origin. It is not easy for man to have been born of someone other to him, to have lived within her for nine months, to have depended on her for his chance of life or death, to have received from her his first dwelling, his first warmth, his first nourish-ment, his first sounds or human words, his first emotions and movements.

([La] culture occidentale est avant toute masculine, et sans doute faut-il comprendre [le] geste d'appropriation du monde à soi comme une tenta-tive pour l'homme de résoudre ses problèmes de rapport à son origine. Il n'est pas facile pour l'homme d'être né d'une autre que lui, d'avoir séjourné en elle neuf mois, d'avoir dépendu d'elle pour sa chance ou non de vivre, d'avoir reçu d'elle sa première demeure, sa première chaleur sa première nourriture, ses premiers sons ou paroles humaines, ses premiers émotions et mouvements.)[46]

In her insistence on the specificity of maternity Irigaray argues that mothers, and women in general, should not be assimilated to the natural element in humanity; motherhood is not a passive condition, which is suffered, but (I would say) a kind of hospitality in an *active* sense:

Rather it is a question of accepting freely to share your life, your flesh, your breath – and thus in a way your soul – with the child to whom you give birth. And not only for a few minutes but for long months, even for long years. That does not mean we should idolise maternity as such, but we should recognise that the woman who engenders the child plays a part on both the human and divine level. We should recognise woman as a fully human subject but different from man, with other tasks to accom-plish, particularly on the spiritual plane. Producing the other as a child within yourself, receiving the other in love within yourself, nourishing it with your own flesh, your own breath – these tasks do not demand the same spiritual attitude as engendering outside oneself, making love outside oneself, nourishing by one's work.

(Il est plutôt question d'accepter librement de partager sa vie, sa chair, son souffle – donc en quelque sorte son âme – avec l'enfant à qui on donne naissance. Et cela non seulement pendant quelques instants mais pendant de longs mois, voire de longues années. Il n'est pas question pour autant d'idolâtrer la maternité comme telle mais de reconnaître la participation humaine et divine qu'elle suppose de la part de la femme qui engendre l'enfant. De reconnaître la femme comme un sujet humain à part entière mais différent de l'homme, avec d'autres tâches, notamment spirituelles, à accomplir. Enfanter l'autre en soi, l'accueillir en soi dans l'amour, le nourrir de sa propre chair, de son propre souffle ne demandent pas la même attitude spirituelle qu'engendrer hors de soi, faire l'amour hors de soi, nourrir de son travail.) ('La Transcendance de l'autre', 47)

Thus motherhood must be a freely assumed choice for Irigaray, and she argues in *Je, tu, nous* that sexuate laws should defend women's autonomous rights over their bodies in this and other respects. Motherhood is a choice to *share* with an other.

When speaking about hospitality, Derrida too sometimes uses a language which refers to pregnancy, for instance:

> We don't know anything about it, of course, but we know enough to say to ourselves that hospitality, what works away in the bosom of hospitality, works away in it like labour, like pregnancy, like a promise as much as a threat, what settles in it, inside it, like a Trojan horse, enemy (*hostis*) as much as future, intestinal hostility, is indeed a contradictory conception, a contraried conception, or a *contraception* of expectation, a contradiction in welcome itself. And something which binds perhaps, as in the pregnancy that produced Isaac, laughter to pregnancy, to the announcement that you are having a child.

> (Nous n'en savons rien, bien sûr, mais nous en savons assez pour nous dire que l'hospitalité, ce qui travaille l'hospitalité en son sein, ce qui la travaille comme un labeur, comme une grossesse, comme une promesse autant qu'une menace, ce qui y installe, en son dedans, comme un cheval de Troie, l'ennemi (*hostis*) aussi bien que l'avenir, l'hostilité intestine, c'est bien une conception contradictoire, une conception contrariée, ou une *contraception* de l'attente, une contradiction dans l'accueil même. Et quelque chose qui lie peut-être, comme dans la grossesse d'Isaac, le rire à la grossesse, à l'annonce de l'enfantement.)[47]

While Irigaray's account is a material one, Derrida uses a simile. Hospitality is 'like' pregnancy, but also as much like contraception as conception – since the guest must both be joyously awaited and yet also unwelcome because unexpected and unknown. Hospitality, or pregnancy, is 'like' the Trojan horse (really a Greek horse) – what seems promising could contain your enemy.[48] This is traditionally a reason for men to keep control of women's sexuality – so that the father brings up his own children and not those fathered by someone else, cuckoos in the nest. Sarah laughs when the visiting angels announce (again) the conception of Isaac because, like her husband, she is so old; she is long past child-bearing and long assumed sterile in any case. Of course the child of a miraculous conception, following the entertaining of a male visitor, like the New Testament version involving the Virgin Mary, can always arouse laughter in cynical readers who cannot help thinking of a material explanation (usually at a woman's expense). At the same time, the metaphor, according to Irigaray, dematerialises and privileges the masculine. The Trojan horse is Odysseus' baby. Elsewhere Derrida critiques philosophers who masquerade as midwives, and in fact produce the self-same (*Adieu*, 17–18; 41–2).

There is, however, an erotic and maternal quality to hospitality even as it is displaced onto the figural. The female body is uniquely hospitable, and that erotic, reproductive and nourishing specificity, experienced by all as 'guests', is a potent source of fantasy and of acts inspired by it; as Irigaray asserts above, it cannot be easy to accept that early disempowerment and obligation. The imagined superabundance, the excessive hospitality of the womb-home, as we figure it, lies beneath the threat of hospitality that contains and retains the guest to the point of imprisonment even as this hostage is lavishly nourished (as Odysseus is nourished by the smothering nymphs). It is an unconditional hospitality, the Law of hospitality that transgresses and is also transgressed by the laws of moderate hospitality even as each is an essential underpinning of the other.

Ginette Michaud insists on the importance of 'maternity as figure of hospitality – Derrida will go as far as saying the absolute figure of hospitality' ('la maternité comme figure de l'hospitalité – Derrida va jusqu'à dire la figure absolue de l'hospitalité' ('Un acte d'hospitalité', 51)). (Although in the quotation she uses Derrida says 'an absolute figure' rather than 'the absolute figure'.) The quotation from *Emile* which we find in *Monolingualism of the Other* is apparently analysed at greater length in Derrida's as yet unpublished seminar: 'Other women, even animals, could give him the milk that she [the mother] refuses to give him; maternal solicitude has no substitute' ('D'autres femmes, des bêtes même, pourront lui donner le lait qu'elle [la mère] lui refuse; la sollicitude maternelle ne se supplée point' ('Hostipitalité', 13 December 1995, cited in 'Un acte d'hospitalité', 52)). Michaud comments that:

> Then Derrida performs an astounding, or inside-out, reading of Rousseau's assertion; more precisely he substitutes for that logic of a mother tongue that cannot be replaced, a logic of substitution which is also that of the host/guest/hostage [*hôte/otage*] of hospitality, that 'host-age' who is always subject to the other, like the child and the mother, in a relationship of reciprocal dependence but without any possible symmetry (besides one should rather evoke a paradoxical reciprocity between mother and child insofar as they are the supreme figures of hospitality).

(Derrida opère alors une lecture renversante, ou retournée, de l'énoncé de Rousseau; plus précisément il substitue à cette logique d'une langue maternelle insuppléable, une logique de la substitution qui est aussi celle de l'hôte/otage de l'hospitalité, cet 'hôtage' toujours soumis à l'autre, comme l'enfant et la mère, dans un rapport de dépendance réciproque mais sans symétrie possible (on devrait d'ailleurs plutôt évoquer, entre la mère et l'enfant en tant que figures par excellence de l'hospitalité, une réciprocité paradoxale). ('Un acte d'hospitalité', 52))

This mention of paradoxical reciprocity, or reciprocal dependence, is reminiscent of Irigaray's discussion of a placental economy in *Je, tu, nous*.[49] Against a certain psychoanalytic tradition, Irigaray does not see the relation between mother and foetus as fusional, but as ordered and mutually respectful, indeed quasi-ethical, with a flow in each direction and the placenta as the mediating threshold, the space inbetween. Michaud goes on to comment on Derrida:

First and last, ultimate *as* first: such is the mother tongue, and that is why it is legitimate, even indispensable, to read, in any scene of hospitality, the acting out of what happens around having children and giving birth, and especially around the mother welcoming into 'herself' – but here more than ever the topology of the enclave finds its full 'conceptual' bearing – or its matrix [womb]! – that guest which she puts up, shelters, or supports . . . just as she puts up with it, subject to expecting passively, both patiently and impatiently, resisting, more or less in spite of herself, without her knowing, its intrusion. For, we know, the child may be wanted and desired, an invited guest only too awaited and longed for, or a visitor who insists on coming, without having been invited . . .

(Première et dernière, ultime *comme* première: voilà la langue maternelle, et pourquoi il est légitime, voire indispensable de lire, dans toute scène d'hospitalité, la mise en acte de ce qui se passe autour de l'enfantement et de la naissance, et tout particulièrement de la mère accueillant en 'elle' – mais ici plus que jamais la topologie de l'enclave trouve toute sa portée 'conceptuelle' . . . ou sa matrice! – cet hôte qu'elle abrite, héberge ou supporte . . ., tout comme elle l'endure, soumise à une attente passive, autant patiente qu'impatiente, résistant plus ou moins malgré elle, à son insu, à son intrusion. Car, on le sait, l'enfant peut être désiré et voulu, un invité (trop bien) attendu et prévu, ou un visiteur, qui demande à venir sans avoir été invité . . . (53))

Derrida asks what is the essence of motherhood if its functions can be separated out as Rousseau indicates (for instance, even if Rousseau certainly does not advocate a substitute, feeding the baby can of course be achieved by means other than the maternal breast).

130

The mother, like woman, Derrida suggests, exists only as a powerful phantasm to ward off the fact that there is no more than 'de la mère' (something of the mother) or 'plus d'une mère' (more than a mother) (Michaud, 'Un acte d'hospitalité', 54). In the unpublished seminar he writes:

> We can replace everything, gestation, fertilization, the breast, food, milk, we can replace all the replaceable parts of maternity but *we will call mother the irreplaceable, as solicitude: there where there is solicitude as irreplaceable, there is a mother*; and that solicitude which therefore is not at all natural in the sense of biological or genetic . . . that solicitude insofar as it is maternal, insofar as it takes care in a disinterested fashion, of the incomer, the new arrival, the child qua the one who needs to be welcomed, fed, sheltered, the one who is in principle, disarmed, infinitely vulnerable and needy, the absolute guest or arrival, well, *that solicitude, the mother, maternal solicitude is undoubtedly an absolute figure of hospitality*; and especially if we define it starting from irreplacability; for the duty to be hospitable enjoins me to welcome in(to) my place whoever arrives but first of all the arrival to whom no one else in my place would give his place: one must offer one's place (I must offer my place) there where no one can offer a place in my place.

> (On peut tout remplacer, la gestation, la fécondation, le sein, la nourriture, le lait, on peut remplacer toutes les parties remplaçables de la maternité, mais *on appellera mère l'irremplaçable, comme sollicitude: là où il y a sollicitude comme irremplaçable, il y a une mère*; et cette sollicitude qui n'a donc rien de naturel au sens du biologique ou du génétique . . ., cette sollicitude, en tant que maternelle, en tant qu'elle prend soin, de façon désintéressée, de qui vient, du nouvel arrivant, de l'enfant comme celui qui a besoin d'être accueilli, nourri, hébergé, celui qui est, en principe, désarmé, infiniment vulnérable et dans le besoin, l'hôte ou l'arrivant absolu, eh bien *cette sollicitude, la mère, la sollicitude maternelle est sans doute une figure absolue de l'hospitalité*; et surtout si on la définit depuis son irremplaçabilité; car le devoir d'hospitalité m'enjoint d'accueillir dans ma place quiconque comme arrivant mais d'abord l'arrivant à qui personne d'autre à ma place ne donnera sa place: il faut offrir sa place (il me faut offrir ma place) là où personne ne peut offrir une place à ma place. ('Hostipitalité', 13 December 1995, cited by Michaud, 'Un acte d'hospitalité', 54))

Michaud argues that anyone then can substitute for the mother if they show this irreplaceable care. Yet, in this logic of substitution, maternal solicitude is irreplaceable. Derrida points out that, unexpectedly, a child is the key instance of substitution; a child stolen from its parents and replaced by another is an example of cruel violence, but equally creates the possibility of a great gift of hospitality towards the adopted child. He finds that the dictionary Littré gives the example of a substituted child first place in its entry for 'substitution' – as if it were substitution par excellence ('Hostipitality', 409–10). Aristotle's chapters on friendship (in common with most of the *Ethics* indeed) focus on the male subject. And yet, strangely, the relationship between mother and child crops up several times – quite unexpectedly. Aristotle proposes that, while the ordinary run of people want to be loved more than to love, perfect friendship consists more in giving than in receiving affection (or benefits). He compares this to mothers' love for their children; he suggests that mothers love their children, and desire their good, *even when they give them away* and therefore the children do not know them and cannot love them in return (271).[50] In other words we are back to maternal solicitude as irreplaceable even when the child has been substituted.

Aside maternity

To summarise: there are real material distinctions between the sexes with regard to hospitality. These are both biological and historical. Biological and historical differences between the sexes also play a role in the relation to the racial or class other (or the other man in general), such as the fear or desire of miscegenation or of sodomy. At the same time, sexual differences, and the fantasies they provoke, powerfully pattern our representations of other differences (including class, race and sexuality). One of the problems for feminists is that mothers, and mother-love, can so easily be accommodated in a virile or androcentric model: the (Spartan) mother of sons, the Virgin Mary. Whether mothers are dematerialised, reappropriated as metaphor, or are only too material, delivering heirs or reproducing the means of production, there are long histories of exploitation. Thus to move hospitality away from the gesture made by the patriarchal master of the house, and away from the union of brotherhood, in order to redefine it as *motherhood*, cannot be an easy solution. But what about what Derrida calls 'heterosexuality' (perhaps we should translate and interpret it as heterosociality to contrast with homosociality), or Irigaray 'the two', the sexuate female subject in herself and in dialogue with the other? Plato is the only classical authority on friendship to allow any productive confusion or association between *philia* and *eros*. What about two women? Can these be friends or lovers? Can they be hosts/guests? Feminism has tried to reclaim the 'sister', just as 'brother' has been reclaimed so many times (we cannot escape our tendency to use vocabulary from the family or so it seems). Can the sister be redefined as friend? Or the lover produced in the feminine as *amante*? While English ignores sexual difference in the case of nouns, French gendering at least has the advantage of allowing a thinker to re-introduce or change genders, as Monique Wittig does. Abdelkebir Khatibi, for his part, introduces the neologism *aimante*, to Derrida's delight. Cixous's solution, I would suggest, is to allow neither the material nor the figural nor the both/and to have precedence in a poetics of hospitality that draws on a feminine economy.

Irigaray has a different take from that of many contemporary thinkers on the question of the 'other'. She insists that we (women) need a space of our own (both in an internal and an external sense) as a first condition of true hospitality. In 'The Path Towards the Other', Irigaray asks what the term 'the other' means today, when it is used in so many different ways. She suggests that what is other to me cannot share the *same* world that I inhabit. If there is difference then there must be a threshold, a 'nothing in common' between us – we cannot quite meet. For her, the primary 'other' is of course the other sex, cultural difference is secondary to that first great divide. The other cannot be a category in my world, my thought, my language (such as 'alterity'). Even if the other is my companion, living literally in the same house, there should be radical strangeness. On the level of our *being* we do, and in a material or sensible sense we should try to, live in separate places within the 'house'. This is the house in many senses, including: the material structure we name house, the patriarchal home and the household organisation that implies, the national or global house, or Heidegger's house of language. Irigaray draws on Heidegger's work on dwelling, and attempts to dialogue with, and re-write, that work in terms of sexual difference or a culture of two subjects. She has commented on our tendency to create an empty space in our homes – a guest room – waiting for someone to come from outside to have a place at our table and rest in the neutral and closed place prepared for them.[51] This could become a prison, and again, this idea should be related to the global scale. She claims that it is useful to make a place for him and a place for her in my house – we tend to forget the other closest to us, we look for someone coming from outside. She argues that this general hospitality, this hospitality on the level of needs, of *having*, is of course better than inhospitality but that what we really need is hospitality on the level of desire, of *being*. Irigarayan hospitality is a response to the call of a particular other, to whom we need to be open, to whom we must listen. This would entail both that we have our own being, and that we are ready for it to be put in question by the other. Like Derrida, Irigaray is questioning the restricted economy of hospitality, but her call to openness is rather different. For her, the particular rather than universal putting in question is what enables the creation of a third world – neither mine nor yours – or what Irigaray calls human *becoming*. Bringing the other into my home reinforces an imbalance of power – instead there should be space for each subject and a space created together.

For men, hospitality and friendship function as a test of manliness – some are shown to be good, some bad, as in the examples from Homer and the Old Testament in Chapter 2. Irigaray, as well as critiquing the patriarchal mythology, suggests a cultivation of sexuate difference (and *not* women as the other of the same). She puts forward hospitality *not* as a fantasised hysteral economy (Nestor, Menelaus and the Levite's father-in-law being male examples of sticky hosts), containing and suffocating as it provides everything in abundance for the other/guest, and not even as a real 'placental' economy, whether we take that either literally or metaphorically. If we take it literally it might seem to suggest a return to the natural pre-Oedipal relation of generation, a purely horizontal relation. If we turn it into nothing more than a metaphor then the material is once again sacrificed to the spiritual. For Irigaray each sexuate subject should rather be an *hôte* in his or her own place with her or his own natural and cultural identity, and both should be involved in creating a third place, a threshold, in-between. This would create a horizontal transcendental between *I* and *you*; you the other would come within while remaining outside and strange.[52] There would be no exclusion yet also no pressure to integrate. And *I* would be a *you* for *you*.

Notes

1. Tahar Ben Jelloun, *Eloge de l'amitié* (Dijon: Libris Editions, [1994] 1999), p. 35.
2. Montaigne, *Essays*, translated by J. M. Cohen (Harmondsworth: Penguin, 1958), I, 28, p. 99; Montaigne, *Oeuvres complètes*, ed. Albert Thibaudet and Maurice Rat (Paris: Pléiade, 1962), pp. 181–93 (p. 189).

3. Jacques Derrida, *Politics of Friendship*, translated by George Collins (London and New York: Verso, 1997), p. 2; Jacques Derrida, *Politiques de l'amitié* (Paris: Galilée, 1994), p. 18.

4. See for example Montaigne, *Oeuvres complètes*, p. 1479. Diogenes Laertius, who wrote in Greek at the beginning of the third century and was first published in the modern era in 1533, was a major source on the lives of ancient philosophers for many centuries.

5. Lorraine Smith Pangle, *Aristotle and the Philosophy of Friendship* (Cambridge: Cambridge University Press, 2003), p. 193. Pangle also mentions, in her only other reference to *Politics of Friendship*, 'Derrida's . . . contention that we should befriend everyone everywhere without restricting ourselves to those whose characters we happen to approve' (p. 192), which seems to suggest that she has not read his work very closely as it is a rather inadequate summary of the book.

6. Derrida's teaching lectures are being published in French (with Galilée) and English translation (with the University of Chicago Press) at the rhythm of one volume per annum since 2008. The editors again choose to give the reader a contact as close as possible with the philosopher's teaching voice.

7. See 'Introduction: Circumstances – of interruption' in Bennington, *Interrupting Derrida*, pp. 1–4, for some thoughts on the circumstantial.

8. Aristotle suggests that in order to be friends the individuals concerned must be equal (and similar) at the outset; Cicero suggests that a process of equalisation could take place within a friendship. See Mary Lyndon Shanley, 'Marital Slavery and Friendship: John Stuart Mill's *The Subjection of Women*', in Neera Kapur Badhwar, *Friendship: A Philosophical Reader* (Ithaca and London: Cornell University Press, 1993), pp. 267–84, for an application of the notion of friendship between equals to marriage.

9. See Alex [or A. J. P.] Thomson, *Deconstruction and Democracy: Derrida's* Politics of Friendship (London and New York: Continuum, 2005), p. 14, for a philosophical argument. In addition, Derrida points out that the revealed religions are also religions of social bond (fraternity and charity for example) – he does not accept the absolute break proposed between the brotherhood of classical friendship and that of Christian orders nor that of the Enlightenment and later radical political forms.

10. A similar case is made by Badhwar in *Friendship: A Philosophical Reader*:

> With the advent of Christianity . . . friendship was replaced by agape – the unconditional love of God and of neighbour – as the chief ethical ideal. When friendship was justified, it was justified by its likeness to agape, or by its usefulness in achieving agape. And with

Luther, friendship lost even this secondary ethical status, and came to be seen, like other 'natural' loves, as a form of self-love. As Søren Kierkegaard was to declare, friendship and erotic love are purely 'natural' phenomena that 'contain no ethical task'. ('Introduction: The Nature and Significance of Friendship', 1)

Philip Blosser and Marshell Carl Bradley observe that 'If friendship was exalted in ancient times and, to a degree, even in medieval times, it has become curiously marginal in the contemporary world.' They do not relate this to Christianity but reference, for example, Eric Fromm to suggest that this marginalisation derives from the alienating nature of industrial-capitalist society, or C. S. Lewis to suggest that it is 'a sort of vegetarian substitute for the more organic loves' or that it runs counter to today's egalitarian or democratic values . . . (Philip Blosser and Marshell Carl Bradley (eds), *Friendship: Philosophic Reflections on a Perennial Concern* [Lanham, New York and Oxford: University Press of America, revised edition 1997], p. viii). None of this seems absolutely convincing to me. Although one can cite vast quantities of examples to illustrate the importance of romantic love today, there are also many examples of the importance of friendship. To take only the case of Hollywood movies (as a finite sample): romance may seem pervasive but if one looks across genres (including Westerns, war movies, horror, action, science fiction, and children's films as well as indeed many romantic comedies) then buddies are crucial too.

11. Marilyn Friedman, 'Feminism and Modern Friendship: Dislocating the Community', in Badhwar (ed.), *Friendship: A Philosophical Reader*, pp. 285–302, argues for the increasing importance of 'chosen', as opposed to 'found', communities. She also points out (unusually, in the context of the philosophy of friendship) the historical importance of friendship for women.

12. Françoise de Graffigny's *Lettres d'une Péruvienne* is a good example of a female-authored eighteenth-century text which closes with the heroine wishing not to marry, but to live with good friends (the man who would have wanted to be her husband, his sister and her husband).

13. The editions will be as follows: Plato, *Lysis*, in *The Dialogues of Plato*, Vol. II, translated by Benjamin Jowett (London: Sphere, 1970); Aristotle, *Nicomachean Ethics*, translated by J. A. K. Thomson (revised by Hugh Tredennick) (Harmondsworth: Penguin, 1976); Aristotle, *Eudemian Ethics*, in *The Complete Works of Aristotle*, The Revised Oxford Translation, ed. Jonathan Barnes, II (Princeton: Princeton University Press, 1984), pp. 1922–81. In common with other English-language editions Books 4, 5, and 6 are omitted (without comment) as these overlap with the *Nicomachean Ethics*. The *Eudemian Ethics* are seen as an earlier version by many (but not all) scholars. Marcus Tullius

Cicero, *Laelius de Amicitia, On Friendship and the Dream of Scipio*, edited and translated by J. G. F. Powell (Warminster: Aris and Phillips Ltd, 1990). I shall give page numbers to these editions plus paragraph numbers for Cicero.

14. Pascale-Anne Brault and Michael Naas (eds), *The Work of Mourning* (Chicago: University of Chicago Press, 2001); expanded edition translated into French as *Chaque fois unique la fin du monde* (Paris: Galilée, 2003); of course the essays were first written and published in French (and had to be translated into English) – it is the Introduction and the 'context' or *mise en livre* which had to be translated into French.

15. Jacques Derrida, *Mémoires for Paul de Man*, translated by Cecile Lindsay, Jonathan Culler and Eduardo Cadava (New York: Columbia University Press: 1986), p. 29; *Mémoires pour Paul de Man* (Paris: Galilée, 1988), p. 49.

16. See *Mémoires*, pp. xiii–xiv; pp. 25–6.

17. Hospitality beyond, or at, the grave is not always between friends. Derrida cites the tradition of a hospitable pre-Islamic poet-knight (Hatim al Tai) from the second half of the sixth century AD ('Hostipitality', in *Acts of Religion*, 405), and the very different case of Don Juan/Don Giovanni who is haunted by the Commendatore, the father of one of the women he tried to rape (as discussed by Anne Dufourmantelle, *OH*, pp. 144–52; *DH*, pp. 128–34). Many accounts of the strange exchange of invitations between the Don and the stone statue or ghost leave aside the female victim. But all these fascinating cases will add to the remainder for another day.

18. See Jacques Derrida and Antoine Spire, *Au-delà des apparences* (Latresne: Le Bord de l'eau, 2002), p. 52. He goes on to point, on the other hand, to an originary *parjure*, a possibility that is not merely accidental to the promise: a third (the possibility of justice according to Levinas) always intervening even in the closest two-some. His third point concerns his emphasis on the 'deconstruction' of Western models and figures of friendship – particularly fraternal models that exclude friendship between a man and a woman, that exclude the sister.

19. See for example Jane Hiddlestone, 'Derrida, Autobiography and Postcoloniality', *French Cultural Studies*, 16:3 (2005), pp. 291–304.

20. Jacques Derrida, *Sur parole: Instantanés philosophiques* (Saint-Etienne: Editions de l'Aube, 1999), p. 10. While this book itself – a collection of live interviews – comes with a health warning about immediacy, Derrida's well-argued point is that his writing is seen as increasingly autobiographical because of his increasing use of the first-person genre, and yet the distinction between those works using academic models and the others is far from clear-cut, or the cut may not come in the place that we expect it.

21. Having just had my first experience of publishing an obituary for a dear friend, I was interested by how many readers commented 'it was just what she would have wanted' – and of course I had indeed wanted to write what my friend would have wanted, as well as what I wanted – and the classical model of friendship assumes that is the same thing. Strangely I am sitting in her seat at her computer in her flat to write this – and she will not have, would not have written these words. The future anterior says it all about the impossibility of such things.

22. Assia Djebar, a great contemporary poet of male–female friendship writes of dead writers and of dead male friends – and the different languages (cultures) in which it is more or less possible for a man and a woman to be friends – in *Le Blanc de l'Algérie* (Paris: Albin Michel, 1995).

23. The article by Paulo Marrati to which he refers is 'Le rêve et le danger: où se perd la différence sexuelle?', in Jean-Michel Rabaté and Michael Wetzel (eds), *L'Ethique du Don: Jacques Derrida et la pensée du don* (Paris: Métailié-Transition, 1992), pp. 194–211.

24. See Annie Leclerc, *Parole de femme* (Paris: Grasset, 1974); she makes a strong case for an obsession with death on the part of male philosophers such as Bataille or Nietzsche and writers such as Freud, Malraux, Miller, or Hollywood cinema (the hero fighting death).

25. One particular modality of time shared within a structure of hospitality is education (in the broadest sense). I should perhaps note that the very term *hospital* once meant not only a university hall or hostel, but also a charitable institution for the education and maintenance of the young. Our own times have seen an enormous expansion of higher education go hand in hand with a gradual erosion of hospitality in favour of the economic, and of the policing that is a necessary part of any economy. Entrance tariffs and entrance barriers combine to narrow participation in some senses even as we must pay lip service to widening access.

26. For example, Cicero, in *Laelius de Amicitia*, alludes to Socrates but does not name him (though many are named in the dialogue), for instance he refers to the one who was 'judged by the oracle of Apollo to be the wisest of all men' (¶ 7, see also p. 79) as a comparison point for Laelius. Laelius replies that it is a compliment (¶ 9) but he prefers Cato whose virtue is in actions (for example, on the death of his son), not merely words. Socrates, suggests Laelius, in many matters said sometimes one thing and sometimes another (¶ 13).

27. Jowett gives his reader this information, but many others pass over the question of the ages of the boys concerned without explanation; for instance Blosser and Bradley (eds), *Friendship: Philosophic Reflections*, include *Lysis* in their selection of key texts on friendship for university students (which runs from *The Epic of Gilgamesh* to an article entitled

'When Harry and Sally Read the *Nicomachean Ethics*') without glossing their term 'youths' for their readers.

28. Though some critics, according to Pangle, read it, against the 'ship-
wreck' view, as presenting a message *either* that friendship should be
based on need (Gregory Vlastos, Laslo Versenyi, David Bolotin) *or*
the opposite (Hans-Georg Gadamer) (*Aristotle and the Philosophy of
Friendship*, p. 20).

29. See my *Feminine Economies: Thinking Against the Market in
the Enlightenment and the Late Twentieth Century* (Manchester:
Manchester University Press, 1997), Chapter 2.

30. 'Symposium', *The Dialogues of Plato*, Vol. II, p. 188.

31. There is a huge bibliography of material; I shall restrain myself to citing
as an example Penelope Deutscher's 'Introduction' to *Yielding Gender:
Feminism, Deconstruction and the History of Philosophy* (London and
New York: Routledge, 1997) where she analyses Genevieve Lloyd's
The Man of Reason (1984) and Karen Green's *The Woman of Reason*
(1993) as exemplary of two of the different approaches to male philosophers seen as phallocentric, including of course Aristotle.

32. This quotation is taken from an analysis of Michelet in a chapter of
Politics of Friendship entitled '"En langue d'*homme*, la fraternité";
the English translation of the quotation in the heading is '"In *human*
language, fraternity . . ."' (my emphases).

33. To give just one very typical example: Amélie Oksenberg Rorty (ed.),
Essays on Aristotle's Ethics (Los Angeles: University of California
Press, 1980) – note the title refers to 'the Ethics' as if there were
only one. Rorty says that the essays are in fact a commentary on the
Nicomachean Ethics, although she acknowledges that there is considerable debate over whether these form a continuous whole, and some
evidence that books 5–7 really belong to the *Eudemian Ethics* (p. 3).

34. Anthony Kenney, *The Aristotelian Ethics: A Study of the Relationship
between the* Eudemian *and* Nicomachean Ethics *of Aristotle* (Oxford:
Oxford University Press, 1978).

35. M. Pakaluk, 'The Egalitarianism of the *Eudemian Ethics*', *The Classical
Quarterly*, New Series, 48:2 (1998), pp. 411–32.

36. Jacques Derrida, 'Donner la mort', in *L'Ethique du don: Jacques
Derrida et la pensée du don* (Paris: Transition, 1992); Derrida's essay is
translated by David Wills as *The Gift of Death* (Chicago and London:
University of Chicago Press, 1995). It begins with an analysis of an
essay by Jan Patočka, one of the spokesmen for the Charta 77 human
rights declaration in Czechoslovakia in 1977 – he died in the same year
after a lengthy police interrogation.

37. See my *Justice and Difference in the Works of Rousseau: Bienfaisance
and Pudeur* (Cambridge: Cambridge University Press, 1993), Chapter
2, 'The Code of Beneficence'.

38. While many in the philosophical canon on friendship (such as Cicero) simply ignore the possibility of the female friend, other writers are more explicit: Michelet declares that women are not yet ready to be friends; Nietzsche, or rather Zarathustra, is more emphatic, repeating this point three times in 'Of the Friend' (*PF*, p. 281; *PA*, p. 313). For Zarathustra woman is incapable of friendship because she knows only love, and thus is tyrant and slave, while friendship is implicitly freedom and equality. However, as Derrida points out (and we notice this kind of structure in Montaigne), man too, thus far, is incapable of sufficient generosity and so he too is unable to be a true man (brother-friend) (*PF*, p. 283; *PA*, p. 315).

39. See Derrida's analysis of the exiled and wandering Oedipus and his daughter, in *Of Hospitality* (*OH*, pp. 35–43, 85–121; *DH*, pp. 37–45, 81–107).

40. These generalisations must not of course be taken as absolute – one could find examples of slippage. For a thought-provoking example from an Icelandic saga, see William Ian Miller, *The Anatomy of Disgust* (Cambridge, MA: Harvard University Press, 1997), Chapter 7, 'Warriors, Saints and Delicacy'. Here the host and master of the house cheats on a guest by offering him a kind of yoghurt to drink, claiming to have no ale. The wife and daughter act on behalf of laws of hospitality, rather than of the literal host, in hinting that there is better fare to be had – and thus bringing a disgusting punishment onto the master of the house. Thanks to Naomi Segal for this reference.

41. First published in 1953; Pierre Klossowski, *Roberte Ce Soir and The Revocation of the Edict of Nantes*, translated by Austryn Wainhouse (London: Calder and Boyars, 1971); *Les Lois de l'hospitalité, La Révocation de l'édit de Nantes, Roberte ce soir, Le Souffleur* (Paris: Gallimard, 1970). See Ian James, *Pierre Klossowski: The Persistence of a Name* (Oxford: Legenda, 2000).

42. See Sarah Kofman, *Le Respect des femmes (Kant et Rousseau)* (Paris: Galilée, 1982), and my *Justice and Difference*. I include an analysis of Rousseau's version of the Levite of Ephraim story and of his unfinished play about the rape of Lucretia.

43. See my *Justice and Difference*, pp. 197–205. Two of the most interesting versions are those by André Gide and Friedrich Hebbel where it is explicitly Candaules' wife whose modesty is violated as part of the bond between the friends who must hold everything in common.

44. Of the many examples, one could of course cite Vietnam not only because of the events themselves, but also because of the many representations in films and novels. Often depiction of training shows soldiers being turned (by brutality) into a band of brothers (a title Stephen Spielberg uses for a Second World War series, where it has less ironic force) and the constant linguistic evocation of sexual violence can be

a part of that (as in Stanley Kubrick's 1987 *Full Metal Jacket*). If you don't fuck the enemy, you will get fucked.

45. See Christine Delphy and Diana Leonard, *Familiar Exploitation: A New Analysis of Marriage in Contemporary Western Societies* (Cambridge: Polity Press, 1992), for an analysis of the emotional and social labour which is a key part of domestic labour for women.

46. Luce Irigaray, 'La Transcendance de l'autre', in Bernard van Meenen (ed.), *Autour de l'idolâtrie: Figures actuelles de pouvoir et de domination* (Brussels: Publications des Facultés universitaires Saint Louis, 2003), pp. 43–55, 46.

47. Jacques Derrida, unpublished seminar 'Hostipitalité II' (1996–7, 8 January 1997), cited in Ginette Michaud, 'Un acte d'hospitalité ne peut être que poétique Seuils et délimitations de l'hospitalité derridienne', in Lise Gauvin, Pierre L'Hérault and Alain Montandon (eds), *Le dire de l'hospitalité* (Clermont-Ferrand: Presses Universitaires Blaise Pascal, 2004), pp. 33–60, p. 39; see 'Hostipitality', pp. 359–60. In general I shall provide my own translation where Michaud cites an unpublished section of the seminars, and otherwise cite Anidjar and give a page reference. In this case I have provided my own translation after consulting Anidjar as it is a particularly tricky couple of sentences.

48. Stories always seem particularly bitter when they involve the killing of parents by children or vice versa. Camus's play *Le Malentendu* tells of a mother and daughter who own a guest-house and make money through killing solitary and well-off guests. Their last murder is of their long-lost son/brother, who was waiting for the right moment to announce his identity. When they discover their mistake the mother hangs herself and then the daughter/sister throws herself into a well. The play was written in 1943 (though the definitive version dates from 1958), and Camus regarded it as the product of exile in France – not a Mediterranean work – and certainly a dark example of inhospitality!

49. Luce Irigaray, *Je, tu, nous. Toward a Culture of Difference*, translated by Alison Martin (New York and London: Routledge, 1993), pp. 37–44; Luce Irigaray, *Je, tu, nous. Pour une culture de la difference* (Paris: Grasset, 1990), pp. 41–9. This is a dialogue with the biologist Hélène Rouch, who explains, for example, that the placenta is 'the mediating space between mother and fetus, which means that there's never a fusion of maternal and embryonic tissues' (p. 39) ('un espace médian entre mère et fœtus, ce qui veut dire qu'il n'y a jamais fusion entre tissus maternels et tissus embryonnaires' (p. 43)). It allows the foetus to grow without exhausting (using up) the mother.

50. Mothers also occur in *Nicomachean Ethics*, pp. 279, 291, 293 and 300. Aristotle argues that mothers love their children more than fathers do because they spend longer with their children, go through more pains to produce them, and know better that the child is their own. I visit the

negative historical side of adoption and hospitality in *Enlightenment Hospitality*, chapter 6.

51. These remarks relate to a paper given in Nottingham in December 2002; it has been published in a revised form in Luce Irigaray, *Sharing the World* (London: Continuum, 2008).

52. See 'Approaching the Other as Other' (*BEW*, p. 123); 'S'approcher de l'autre en tant qu'autre' (*EOO*, p. 162).

4

Frenchalgeria[1] – (not) asking for a name, naming, calling by name in tales of Algerians

Thus he speaks to her in an intimate manner, in the second person singular, using a multitude of given names that he had transformed over the years. The desire to baptize her every time he was overcome with tenderness. Was he trying in some obscure way to make her lose her own first name? Why was he so determined to keep the privilege of naming her in this definite, casual, and terrible way?

In the long run, his violence, speaking in the name of love, would frighten him, would affect him more profoundly than he guessed in a destructive cycle. . . . As long as he was giving her names, she always said: either Yes.[2] As soon as she was unnamed, she became a child again and surprisingly began to stammer.

(Ainsi, il la tutoyait, avec une multitude de prénoms qu'il avait transformés au cours des années. Désir de la baptiser chaque fois qu'il débordait de tendresse. Cherchait-il obscurément à lui faire perdre son prénom? Pourquoi, avec un tel entêtement, maintenait-il cette liberté de la nommer, à coup sûr, désinvolte et terrible?

A la longue, cette violence, qui parlait au nom de l'amour, allait l'effrayer lui-même, pour l'atteindre plus loin qu'il ne devinait, en un cercle destructeur. . . . Tant qu'il la nommait, elle disait infiniment: Oui. Sitôt innommée, elle retombait dans l'enfance et un étonnant bégaiement.)[3]

This chapter will raise the question of names in a range of different contexts of (in)hospitality, but in order to focus the topic (potentially enormous) I shall keep returning to Algeria and to the French (uninvited guests). I want to discuss the power of names – proper names, of course, with their special link to the individual subject or to a place, but also common nouns and even adjectives by which we designate people and places. I shall consider the designations 'guest', 'host' and 'hospitality' further in the next chapter. I begin here with some introductory comments about naming and about hospitality, then turn to the reception (hospitable or otherwise) of two French-Algerians (first Cixous and then Derrida) by their Anglophone readers, and ask how we tend to designate these two writers who set so much store by the question of naming. My example of one particular response to Derrida will focus on *Monolingualism of the Other*, as it is particularly pertinent in this context. My fourth section will analyse three issues around naming in Cixous's writing on Algeria: the name she gave her Algerian maid as a child, the importance of the use of adjectives to qualify people, and the name 'brother'. Finally, I shall turn to Albert Camus. Camus's famous short story 'L'Hôte', usually translated as 'The Guest', was written as the Algerian War of Independence was approaching, and is set in Algeria almost at the time of writing.[4] It features a 'Frenchman' who feels that Algeria, which he loves, is his country, his mother-land. But this is already perhaps a 'nostalgeria', as Derrida will put it – it is what it will become. Although Camus is not noted for his representation of the perspective of native Algerians (views of or view from), a post-colonial reading is not hard to construct from the details of the text. Indeed, within the story the Empire does write back – in chalk on the school-master's blackboard where colonial geography is laid out.

Can there be a hospitality without a name? Can there be hospitality without (exchange of) names? In *Of Hospitality* Derrida once again points out the untranslatability of the proper name (an argument made in many of his texts), and suggests that it is necessary both to speak and to efface it in hospitality (*OH*, 137; *DH*, 121). Absolute hospitality and openness cannot call *by name*, for naming would condition the otherwise infinite range of possibilities. However, this impossible self-denial, which in the abstract can seem like a mystical paradox, also relates to more everyday issues of hospitality and identity such as those on which this chapter will focus. For example, when is it inhospitable to name a guest because that excludes other potential guests whose names you do not know, and when is it inhospitable to name a guest because that entails giving them a name which is not their own? Identities are deeply personal and broadly situational. We want to be who we feel we are – if only knowing and feeling were so simple. How others see us, and how they refer to us, impacts on our lives in so many ways, big and little. This issue can be peculiarly acute in a situation of extreme inequality (typically the case in a colonised territory) where economic, military and political power are underpinned by ideological structures determining that individuals recognise themselves as they are interpellated – as subordinate 'Arabs' or as 'French' in a Manichean society. Cixous

144

and Derrida bring a third ethnicity or culture into play as both are Jewish (-French-Algerians). Analysis of national (and sexual) identity inevitably raises the questions of boundaries and of naming as well as those of perception. Post-colonial identitarian knots such as accompany being French-Algerian (never mind Jewish) raise the spectre of hospitality. Hospitality is always already at stake where a boundary is set up – dividing what I call my territory from what I call yours – but the history/legacy of colonialism's fluctuating divisions raises the question of hospitality in the sharpest way for our times. In the next chapter I shall discuss the situation of 'guests' in France who arrive from former colonies or who have been indirectly affected by colonial history – for example by the fact that their skin colour or attire is taken as a marker that they hail from formerly colonised territories, understood very loosely.

Naming and identities

What is it: to name? It is obvious that there is an Adamic naming that is related to power and authority. Giving a name can be a form of appropriation and enable giving an order.[5] To quote Derrida: 'Mastery begins, as we know, through the power of naming, of imposing and legitimating appellations' (*MO*, 39) ('La maîtrise, on le sait, commence par le pouvoir de nommer, d'imposer et de légitimer les appellations' (*MA*, 68)). Classifying is one aspect of the power of knowledge – 'discovering' new subjects and 'producing' them as objects of knowledge – with, of course, the possibility of these 'objects' re-appropriating their names with pride and establishing counter discourses, whether gay liberation, queer theory, or niggaz with attitude. Naming, or re-naming, is one weapon in territorial disputes;[6] naming can be a way of taking possession. Cixous writes:

> Never treat the power of the name the power of name-words lightly, that was my instinct and my law from the time when I lived the tyranny of denomination in Algeria, the way in which racist insulting names flew about, when any designation was an insult Arab *bicot* Jew French all of them. When France had painted so many places and neighbourhoods with French names, imagine a little Algerian town called Michelet or my neighbourhood which was 99% Arab called Clos-Salembier, but all of this in a kind of arbitrary mixture which could have if there'd been peace instead of war, given birth to births but given the state of apartheid kept engendering alienation.

(Ne jamais traiter légèrement de la force du nom de la force des mots-noms, ce fut mon instinct et ma loi dès que j'ai vécu en Algérie la tyrannie de la dénomination, la façon dont volaient les noms injurieux racistes, où tout mot désignant était insulte arabe bicot juif français tout. Où la France avait peint tant de localités et de quartiers en noms français, imaginez une petite ville algérienne appelée Michelet ou mon quartier à 99% arabe appelé Clos-Salembier, mais ceci dans un mélange arbitraire qui aurait pu s'il y avait eu paix au lieu de guerre, donner naissance à des naissances mais étant donné l'état d'apartheid engendrait de l'aliénation.)[7]

She goes on to point out the martial victories and military heroes celebrated on the French map of Oran. With this passage we are moving from designation with a common noun, as, say, a 'guest', or an ethnic descriptor, as, say, an 'Arab', to the related politics of proper names. While naming can be done with love (as we give a name to our child or our house), if the individual or place is 'ours' only in our opinion, and not at all in the eyes and ears of those we name and those who live in the places we name, then it is a proprietary gesture that could be received as a kind of act of war. Far better, one may think, to ask politely 'what is your name?' However, when it comes to hospitality, perhaps a purer kind of hospitality does not even need a name.

These remarks about one kind of politics of the name could *also* easily be made specific, for example, with respect to relations between the sexes. Patronyms have been the mark of a woman passing from one master (of the house) to another. A husband and father can give his name not only to his wife and children but also to other members of his household, including sometimes servants or slaves. Our thoughts may also turn to other colonial and post-colonial situations. A variation on this Adamic mode is name-calling – what we might call the poetics of abuse – for instance, deliberate misnaming of, or inventing new names for, the other in order to mock and wound. However, naming is not always so – and not-naming can be equally offensive, an indicator that that other is less of a person than a thing – or the other may be given a common name such as 'boy', '*garçon*', '*Madame/Mademoiselle*', or 'love' (any of which could be analysed at length in terms of race, sex, class relations and so on) but not a proper name such as Albert Camus, Hélène Cixous or Jacques Derrida.[8] Calling men or women boys or girls is obviously infantilising but that gesture can bear a range of connotations from the most pejorative and patronising to the most amorous and affectionate with much in between. The *effect* of naming will depend on the context and the power relations between those naming and those named. 'Girls' talk' is definitionally trivial and may well concern love; boys' games can, in spite of the name (which recalls the British TV serial *A Very Peculiar Practice* to me) be deadly. (A war by any other name . . .[9]) Naming *can* be an act of love, and the poetics of playing with names can be amorous or affectionate. This is one thing Cixous evokes. One interesting question, however, is that of the *confusion* between naming with love and naming with power.

In trying to disentangle different kinds of calling by name, does it matter what space there is for the other to respond? With the response 'yes, yes', 'oui, oui, je viens', I am, I do, for instance. The relation between femininity and affirmation in Derrida has often been noted – including in Geoffrey Bennington's 'Derridabase'.[10] The first sentence of Derrida's 'Nombre de oui' ('Numbers of Yes') is 'Oui, à l'étranger.'[11] This could be analysed at considerable length.[12] One famous example analysed in terms of this yes-saying (and one to which Bennington refers) is Molly Bloom's so-called monologue at the end of *Ulysses* – not a monologue because 'yes' has to imply an interlocutor if only an internal one.[13] Does it matter whether the naming inaugurates a dialogue or indeed inaugurates hospitality?

So how does the question of hospitality to *étrangers* (foreigners) relate to language? Does hospitality require a name? Derrida makes the point, quoting Benveniste: 'the foreigner, the *xenos*, is not simply the absolute other, the barbarian, the savage absolutely excluded and heterogeneous . . . "*xenos* indicates relations . . . between men linked by a pact which implies precise obligations also extending to their descendants"' (*OH*, 21) ('Que l'étranger, le *xenos*, ne soit pas simplement l'autre absolu, le barbare, le sauvage absolument exclu et hétérogène . . . "*xenos* indique des relations du même type entre hommes liés par un pacte qui implique des obligations précises s'étendant aussi aux descendants"' (*DH*, 25)). He goes on to argue:

> This right to hospitality offered to a foreigner 'as a family', represented and protected by his or her family name, is at once what makes hospitality possible, or the hospitable relationship to the foreigner possible, but by the same token what limits and prohibits it. Because hospitality, in this situation, is not offered to an anonymous new arrival and someone who has neither name, nor patronym, nor family, nor social status, and who is therefore treated not as foreigner but as another barbarian. . . . [T]he difference, one of the subtle and sometimes ungraspable differences between the foreigner and the absolute other is that the latter cannot have a name or a family name; the absolute or unconditional hospitality I would like to offer her or him presupposes a break with hospitality in the ordinary

sense, with conditional hospitality, with the right to or pact of hospitality
... [A]bsolute hospitality requires that I open up my home and that I give
not only to the foreigner (provided with a family name, with the social
status of being a foreigner, etc.), but to the absolute, unknown, anonymous other, and that I *give place* to them, that I let them come, that I let
them arrive, and take place in the place I offer them, without asking of
them either reciprocity (entering into a pact) or even their names. (*OH*,
23, 25)

(Ce droit à l'hospitalité offert à un étranger 'en famille', représenté
et protégé par son nom de famille, c'est à la fois ce qui rend possible
l'hospitalité ou le rapport d'hospitalité à l'étranger mais du même coup
le limite et l'interdit. Car on n'offre pas l'hospitalité, dans ces conditions,
à un arrivant anonyme et à quelqu'un qui n'a ni nom ni patronyme, ni
famille, ni statut social, et qui dès lors est traité non pas comme un étranger
mais comme un autre barbare. . . . La différence, une des différences sub-
tiles, parfois insaisissables entre l'étranger et l'autre absolu, c'est que ce
dernier peut n'avoir pas de nom et de nom de famille; l'hospitalité absolue
ou inconditionnelle que je voudrais lui offrir suppose une rupture avec
l'hospitalité au sens courant, avec l'hospitalité conditionnelle, avec le
droit ou le pacte d'hospitalité. . . . L'hospitalité absolue exige que j'ouvre
mon chez-moi et que je donne non seulement à l'étranger (pourvu d'un
nom de famille, d'un statut social d'étranger, etc.) mais à l'autre absolu,
inconnu, anonyme, et que je lui *donne lieu*, que je le laisse venir, que je le
laisse arriver, et avoir lieu, sans lui demander ni réciprocité (l'entrée dans
un pacte) ni même son nom. (*DH*, 27, 29))

Thus absolute hospitality implies opening yourself to the unknown,
to those without names – who may be angels or gods but may also be
enemies – while social hospitality involves knowing people's names
(and thus their families, their legitimate genealogies, where they
come from). In passing, I shall recollect that one of Western culture's
inaugural texts of hospitality – the 'Nausicaa' episode in the *Odyssey*
– is quite complicated in this respect. As suggested in Chapter 2, in
Homer in general sexual difference and desire are critical in situations
of hospitality, but often create interference: for example, Paris fails
in his duty as a guest because of his desire for Helen, and he commits
rape as *rapt*; Odysseus is forced to stay on (imprisoned) as a guest
because nymph-hostesses fall in love with him. Here, in the Nausicaa
episode unusually, desire between the sexes works in conjunction
with the law of hospitality. Odysseus is a surprise, an unexpected
guest, who first shows himself to Nausicaa as a naked barbarian,
with only a stick to cover his manhood. His identity is revealed little
by little – this unveiling being largely a striptease in reverse in that

it is a covering with social trappings, starting with the appropriately princely clothes (woven by her mother[14]) that the generous princess offers to him. He reveals his name, and thus his genealogy and home, very late – more as a return for hospitality; these details are not demanded as pre-conditions. This is typical of the Greek code of hospitality as analysed in Chapter 2, which seems to demand a kind of benign fiction that hospitality would be accorded equally to any stranger (who might be a god in disguise) even while relationships of *xenia* or guest-friendship between noble families were more or less morally contractual, as Telemachus discovers when he reveals his identity and is welcomed as a son of Odysseus.

In 'Foreigner question' ('Question d'étranger: venue de l'étranger'), Derrida suggests that the question(ing) of and from the foreigner puts me in question. One of the first questions we ask of people we do not know is often: 'What is your name?' (Famously, the first question we ask of a baby is 'is it a boy or a girl?') Derrida asks us: 'Is it more just and more loving to question or not to question?' (*OH*, 29) ('Est-il plus juste et plus aimant de questionner ou de ne pas questionner?' (*DH*, 31)), and then in 'Pas d'hospitalité': 'In what language can the foreigner address his or her questions? Receive ours? In what language can he or she be interrogated?' (*OH*, 131) ('Dans quelle langue l'étranger peut-il adresser sa question? Recevoir les nôtres? Dans quelle langue peut-on l'interroger?' (*DH*, 117)). Language here is understood not purely linguistically, but as *ethos*. It includes social class or background, and culture; it includes the factors that made Rousseau so ill at ease in Parisian high society when the price of hospitality was to entertain (to be entertaining) – even though French was apparently his mother tongue. And, when Rousseau is asked his name, sometimes he wavers and invents – replying 'Dudding' for example and claiming to be a foreigner, claiming that his mother tongue is a language that he does not speak.[15] This masquerade facilitates seduction.

The author's name

The reception of writers by their reading public can be either welcoming or hostile, or a little of both, as with any stranger who we allow into our interiority and who becomes more or less familiar to us. How we designate an author is of course partly conditioned by their choices (Olympe de Gouges baptised herself), but sometimes shaped by those particular readers who go on to write about those they have read. The decision subtly to emphasise the class position of a writer (de Beauvoir instead of Beauvoir) or class *and* marital position *and* antiquity (Mme de Graffigny or Lady Mary Wortley Montagu instead of Graffigny or Montagu) cannot always be justified by reference to practice by, or at the time of, the writer. Male eighteenth-century writers who were named by their contemporaries with a title rarely keep this in modern critical parlance (Montesquieu, for instance) whereas women writers frequently do – especially in French. Luce Irigaray has a strong preference to be called by both her names simultaneously 'Luce' given by her parents and 'Irigarary' that she chose to adopt on marriage and keep after marriage – yet few critics are willing to depart from standard practice in her case.

In some cultures it is more common than it is in the Anglophone world to refer to writers by their first names: Cixous's 'Clarice' (Lispector) feels to an Anglophone reader like a special intimate – and she is – but her original and continuing Lusophone readership might well name her 'Clarice' in any case. Sometimes use of a first name can have an almost spiritual connotation (as with nuns or saints for example), and those biographers or critics who call Simone Weil 'Simone' surely make that allusion. However, cultural specificity, intimacy or spirituality apart, it can certainly also be patronising or mocking to refer to a writer by her or his first name alone. I shall go on to refer to Derrida's names, but also to evoke the peculiarly famous name Jean-Jacques Rousseau. I call Rousseau peculiarly famous in part because he is in that rare category of celebrities known equally by their first names (a Christian name in his case) and their patronyms. The use of the first name is usually a mark of a particular and intimate relationship with 'readers' (in the widest sense, including even those who have barely read the work, who barely 'know' the person in question). The intimacy of the relationship is not, far from it, only or always loving. Jean-Jacques is bound to many from his earliest entry onto the public stage by passionate hatred.[16] I shall start, however, with Cixous – a writer whose fascination with the signifier leads her to play continuously with her own names and those of others.

How do we designate H.C.?

Each one of the authors in question here has an 'image' and an image problem. Their writing styles generate endless commentary as does their 'style' and its relationship to sex and nationality. Cixous's love of elegant shoes (as much as her fur coats) has no doubt always already been an issue. Cixous first came to prominence in translation as a 'French feminist' thanks to 'The Laugh of the Medusa' and *The Newly-Born Woman*. Her vast fictional output and her work for the theatre, though far more discussed today, have still not eclipsed her reputation as a 'feminist' in the English-speaking world. Granted what could be said about Cixous and identity, it is perhaps ironically fitting that that qualifying adjective and noun are not ones she has particularly welcomed to say the least. These two pieces were very enthusiastically received – but controversial, in part because of fundamental misunderstandings (or wilful misreadings?). A lot of the enthusiasm and controversy occurred outside France – in particular in the UK and the US – and that in itself is significant. One of the questions this raises concerns the role of translation, including translation within and between cultures.

The use of the term 'French' in the reception of Cixous as a French feminist could be commented on at length. That adjective has a range of particular connotations for an 'Anglo-Saxon' audience (notable also in the British press coverage of Derrida's death) including fashionable, sexy and frivolous.[17] One could also relate the adjective to France's own specific brand of Republican universalism and the effects that has on its own 'metropolitan' population and on its former or present colonies – in part via its education system. These are paths we could follow in relation to the ethnic origins of so many of the theorists to whom the term French is applied. Nicholas Harrison points out the mistranslation of *algérifrançaise* in *The Newly-Born Woman* (*La Jeune Née*) as 'Algerian French girl' instead of French Algeria – which has blunted Cixous's point about colonialism and its experiential priority in her understanding of power relations (class and sex came a little later for her).[18] Thus the Anglophone reception of French theorists at once confidently ascribes nationality and overlooks the politics of nationalities in its enthusiasm for, in this case, sex.

By now there has been much commentary on the use of the term 'feminist' – what it means or has meant in a British or American context and what it means or has meant in France, including the importance of 'women's writing' *chez nous*, and hence the misunderstandings surrounding Cixous's term *écriture féminine* – and the slight sense of puzzlement that almost all Cixous's examples of *écriture féminine* seem to be men. The very title of *La Jeune Née* takes us to Genet as much as to Woman, although that does get lost in translation. Her preference for avant-garde writing and faith in the disruptive force of the disrupted signifier does not particularly match either materialist or liberal humanist feminists' preference for realism, authenticity, role models and so on.[19] The debate over essentialism – the suspicion that Cixous is biologistic, that her references to *voice* implies that she is still stuck in the metaphysics of presence – means that she cannot win. Like, of course, other 'white middle-class feminists' she pays no attention to class or race (or so some commentators told us) *and* she (allegedly) homogenises and universalises sex.[20] In fact, even an earlier work such as 'Coming To Writing' has numerous references to colonial Algeria, for instance to the education system or to the changing divisions between Jews and Arabs in terms of nationality and the complications of culpability: 'Nationality? "French." Not my fault! *They* put me in the position of imposture' (15–16) (Nationalité? "Française." C'est pas ma faute! *On* me faisait prendre la place de l'imposture' (23)).

The more recent reception of Cixous's *Les Rêveries de la femme sauvage* (2000) and associated texts focusing on her childhood in Algeria perhaps make it harder to caricature her as a middle-class white feminist in furs and no more than that. These texts show her before she was 'translated'. A poor Jewish girl in Algeria – poor Jewish to the French that is, but French and relatively rich to the native Algerians or 'Arabs' – has an identity split that cannot even be 'solved' with a hyphenated label (such as Franco-Algerian, not quite like African-American). Its pain is conjured up in the tale she tells and re-tells of the young boy smearing red polish on her white sandal: a second-hand shoe from a literal French perspective, a sparkling new affront to the famished littleshoeshine (all one word), a fairy-tale slipper brutally transformed into a bleeding foot for the guilty little girl. She may have believed she was Cinna the poet, and so a friend, but the mob that would tear her apart know she is Cinna the politician, and thus an enemy – both are right. Identities were simple, pre-given and (thus) false:

> We always lived in the episodes of a brutal Algeriad, thrown from birth into one of the camps crudely fashioned by the demon of Coloniality. One said: 'the Arabs'; 'the French.' And one was forcibly played in the play, with a false identity. Caricature-camps. The masks hold forth with the archetypal discourses that accompany the determined oppositions like battle drums.
>
> The Chorus of the French hurled out with a single voice that the Arabs were: dirty-lazy-incapable-thieves.
>
> It was the reign of the insult and the *apostrophe*. ('My Algeriance', 156)

(Nous vécûmes toujours dans les épisodes d'une Algériade brutale, jetés dès la naissance dans un des camps grossièrement façonnés par le démon de la Colonialité. On disait 'les Arabes'; 'les Français'. Et on était joués de force dans la pièce, sous une fausse identité. Des camps-caricatures. Les masques tiennent les discours archétypiques qui accompagnent, comme les tambours de batailles, les oppositions décidées.

Le Choeur des Français lançait d'une voix que les Arabes étaient: sales-paresseux-voleurs-incapables.

C'est le règne de l'injure et de l'apostrophe. ('Mon Algériance', 72))

One of the impossible identities at the time was 'Berber'. It thus seems all the more appropriate that the very name of Cixous, 'My wild bristling sexual name unclean improper cutting like a Barbary fig, vulnerable, attacked, barbarian' ('My Algeriance', 157) (Mon nom sauvage hérissé sexuel pas propre coupant comme une figue de barbarie, vulnérable, attaqué, barbare' ('Mon Algeriance', 72)), a name she thinks of dropping in favour of something less bizarre, turns out, it is suggested, to derive from the name of a Berber tribe (158; 73). That suggestion comes almost like a reward for resisting the temptation of disavowal, for staying faithful.

Jacques Derrida, Jackie and the Monolingualism of the Other

Derrida's national and professional designations are far from straightforward; Marian Hobson has suggested that to call Derrida a 'Theorist' rather than a 'Philosopher' is often a demotion.[21] The former appellation may seem particularly strange in light of the fact that Derrida was strongly associated with a number of projects involving the discipline and pedagogy of philosophy. Beyond nationality and professional identity even, we have the question of the proper name. In an interview collected in *Points*, Derrida tells us that his own first name was Jackie, and makes an aside referring to the possible analysis of the practice in the Jewish community in Algeria in the 1930s of adopting American names, including those of Hollywood stars.[22] When he began to publish, entering 'the space of literary or philosophical legitimation' (l'espace, en somme, de la légitimation littéraire ou philosophique') as he puts it, he adopted the name Jacques partly out of 'good manners' ('"bienséances"') he says, choosing something which was 'very French, Christian, simple' (*Points*, 344) ('très français, chrétien, simple' (*Points*, 354)). In a footnote to *Monolingualism of the Other* (number 9), Derrida discusses, via an analysis of Franz Rosenzweig (so often his point of reference in these matters), the thesis that the Jews have a tendency to adopt the language of their hosts.[23] This dispossession from a maternal tongue is even more true, he tells us, of the Jews of French Algeria who do not even have the recourses Rosenzweig suggests for other Jews, such as some understanding of the sacred tongue.

In *Monolingualism of the Other*, Derrida raises the question of the 'foreigner' who apparently speaks the hosts' language, for example the colonised subject, for example Jacques Derrida. Willy Maley comments: '*Monolingualism of the Other* is a book about autobiography, and the obstacles in its path when one's origins are multiple and mutilated. It is also about the illusions of authenticity, the anxiety of influence and the haunting effects of hybridity.'[24] The question of how an exceptional situation, such as Derrida's, relates to the universal experience of language is also a question to be posed of any poetic text and is a peculiarly autobiographical trope. Derrida tells us:

> This experience of monolingual solipsism is never one of belonging, property, power of mastery, pure 'ipseity' (hospitality or hostility) of whichever kind. Though the 'non-mastery . . . of an appropriated language' of which Glissant speaks qualifies, above all, more literally and more sensitively, some situations of 'colonial' alienation or historical servitude, this definition, so long as it is imprinted with the requisite inflections, *also carries well beyond these determinate conditions*. It also holds for what would be called the language of the master, the *hospes*, or the colonist. (*MO*, 22–3, my emphasis)

> (Cette expérience de solipsisme monolingue n'est jamais d'appartenance, propriété, de pouvoir de maîtrise, de pure 'ipséité' (hospitalité ou hostilité) de quelque type que ce soit. Si la 'non-maîtrise d'un langage approprié' dont parle Edouard Glissant qualifie en premier lieu, plus littéralement, plus sensiblement, des situations d'aliénation 'coloniale' ou d'asservissement historique, cette définition porte aussi, pourvu qu'on y imprime les inflexions requises, *bien au-delà de ces conditions déterminées*. Elle vaut aussi pour ce qu'on appellerait la langue du maître, de l'*hospes* ou du colon. (*MA*, 44))

In the colonial situation, the 'first trick' is that of the coloniser who imposes a language as 'his own' – which of course it is not, but: 'That is his belief; he wishes to make others share it through the use of force or cunning; he wants to make others believe it, as they do a miracle, through rhetoric, the school, or the army' (*MO*, 23) ('C'est la sa croyance, il veut la faire partager par la force ou par la ruse, il veut y faire croire, comme au miracle, par la rhétorique, l'école ou l'armée'

(*MA*, 45)). The second trick, however, is liberation, emancipation and revolution (24; 46) – the impossible attempt by the former colonised people to reappropriate language. Language here is jealousy unleashed – as law and as madness. In this text, Derrida writes autobiographically, as a hyphenated person, a Franco-Maghrebian: my language is the language of the other. He writes explicitly to distinguish himself from Abdelkebir Khatibi, author of *Amour bilingue*, who has a mother tongue (*MO*, 35; *MA*, 63) even if he speaks about it in French. It is Derrida's exceptional situation that is universalised: 'I only speak one language, (and, but, yet) it is not mine' becomes 'we only ever speak one language' (or idiom) and 'we never speak only one language' phrases in quotation marks which, rewritten, echo throughout the text (for example, *MO*, 27; *MA*, 50).

The 'monolingualism of the other' is an expression which can be understood in a number of senses; one of them is 'the monolingualism imposed by the other' (*MO*, 39) ('le monolinguisme imposé par l'autre' (*MA*, 69)). It is particularly clear that the law can impose monolingualism in a colonial situation, but Derrida argues that it is generally true of all culture. He cites the French Revolution as an example of this hegemony of the homogeneous (39; 69).[25] The law is other to the subject – heteronomous – France, the metropole, the master who is particularly incarnated in the figure of the school teacher (42; 73).[26] However, it encourages self-policing – autoheteronomy as Derrida puts it (39; 69).

Monolingualism of the Other makes a confession reminding the reader (me, at least) of Rousseau's shameful secrets (45 ff; 77 ff).[27] The confession is both that Derrida has made a personal effort to speak and write without his Algerian 'pied-noir' accent (and volume), and that he is unable to take intellectuals seriously if they have accents – in particular Southern accents – and he gives the example of listening to the poet René Char. Were we to need any evidence of how shocking this revelation is today (relative to, say, Rousseau's stolen ribbon if not his abandoning his children), we need only read Maley's review (126–7). This review may not (to the uneducated ear) actually be written in Scottish dialect but rather in the postmodern academic style – but it is proudly signed *Willy* Maley as an assertion of proletarian origins, so the author tells us. He refers to Derrida as 'Jackie' throughout – perhaps to remind us how even in his adoption of a professional name Derrida betrays a certain snobbishness or desire to fit in. Maley relates Derrida's confession to the more general question of the policing of language in universities (129). For

Maley (convincingly) the key intertext for this post-colonial autobiographical text, and for the policing of language in particular, is James
Joyce's *A Portrait of the Artist as a Young Man* (125). (At least Joyce
escapes being called Jimmy by Willy – I guess we should be grateful
for small mercies.) This example confirms, for Maley, the sin of snobbishness. Derrida confesses that his perverse taste for purity in the
French language (particularly perverse for the critical opponent of
purity) was contracted, like a disease, at school (*MO*, 48 ff; *MA*, 81
ff). It might also be remarked that women from subaltern communities tend to lose their accents faster and more completely than men.
Socio-linguists try to explain this with a number of hypotheses about
sexed characteristics such as women's desire to fit in, their politeness
(as befitting subordinates), their role as mothers, or their greater
docility in relation to authority, say at school.[28]

For me Derrida's confessional mode is crucially intertwined with
Rousseau's *Confessions*: I am exceptional and universal (*MO*, 20;
MA, 40); I expose myself – as Cixous lovingly points out in her
Portrait de Jacques Derrida en Jeune Saint Juif 'Portrait of Jacques
Derrida as a Young Jewish Saint'.[29] Her title confirms of course
the link to Joyce, but the work refers incessantly to the intertext of
Rousseau's *Confessions* – and also to Montaigne and St Augustine,
which would be another story for another time.[30] Returning to
Derrida's shameful confession of his cutting himself off from his
accent, we should note that accent is critical of course in Rousseau's
theory of the origin of languages in song, brilliantly analysed in *Of
Grammatology*. For Rousseau, the South is associated with love and
passion (interestingly Derrida tells us that he does keep a trace of
his accent in private – which comes out particularly when he is emotional), while the North is associated with work.

As teachers and critics we are bound to the economy of policing –
whether it is the hunt for plagiarism or the enforcement of linguistic
and scholarly standards at every level of education. We also have
passionate responses to texts: love, fear, anger, jealousy to name but
a few. The policing of Derrida is often fuelled by a hostile emotional
response to his words – received as rude and alien to our ears. And
(the double bind) he may be all the more dangerous when domesticated, when not so obviously foreign – amnesiac assimilating Jews
have sometimes been figured as particularly threatening precisely
because they appear to blend in. Derrida's Hebrew name Elie (Elijah)
is the most hidden one; his obscurely feminine name Jackie (at least
feminine to Cixous, or compared to Willy) belonged, relatively

speaking, to the domestic sphere until interviews and autobiography brought it out of that closet.[31] Plain Jacques, the public and professional *nom de plume*, can be seen as just too eager to please and follow the rules. Jacques is so polite that the name is a little like a veil over his true (truly dangerous) identity – and veils of course connote difference to 'us', but in a way that can displease the metropolitan, both conservative and revolutionary, particularly in an educational context. Yet instead of damning him if he is and damning him if he isn't, we could be hospitable, if not maternal, whether we ask 'what is your name?' or not. Radical hospitality – not asking (a name) is perhaps as impossible as abandoning any sense of plagiarism (the signature). The laws of hospitality demand that the guest has a name and behaves appropriately. Derrida, the Jew without a mother tongue, exposes himself to us (for me, like Jean-Jacques) as the man who has cultivated a lack of accent and changed his first name to a Christian name Jacques (although Jackie was no less Christian[32] we might note, and it is the paternal name which is most often changed in order to 'fit in'). The intertext of Joyce, though hardly one to be ashamed of, may lead us (or at least Maley) in the direction of snobbery. The intertext of Rousseau is not only a written text but a phantasmatic figure who arouses great passions of love and loathing. Derrida exposes himself as someone we want to be radical but who actually in some respects not only followed but also internalised the linguistic rules of his hosts. Exceptional and everyman – of course the classic autobiographical trope.

Calling Derrida 'Jackie' is a complex gesture – and of course could be endlessly justified by the liberties he himself takes with (proper) names – his own and other people's. It is not only, however, a feminisation, but in other ways a reminder of issues of cultural difference. Aping vulgar Americans is not always 'the thing' amongst European cultural elites, and intellectual Paris has an uncomfortable relationship to Hollywood and to the American empire in general. Jews are often 'seen' in racist discourse both as simian, apes (those who ape) and as vulgar show-offs, displaying wealth to which they have no title, rather like Americans . . . I should like to turn now to another complex story of (mis)naming.

H.C. and calling others by name

Calling by name is very important to Cixous – we learn that both from her own words and from those of Derrida.[33] Cixous's writing of the body is not only her own or the feminine body, narrowly understood – she expands the parameters of the personal and of sex by affirming, by opening to the other – even as she shows how in practical terms, including political terms the other may say no. One of the 'light' ways of affirming and opening to the other is calling (by name). This calling by name is not quite the same as naming. Cixous is noted for the absence of names in her fictive (fictively autobiographical) writing – a *pudeur* that conserves secrets and opens up the text to manifold interpretations – as much as for her play on certain key names and the letters and syllables therein (Eve, Georges, Hélène, Jacques to name but four).

There are some complex and difficult descriptions of calling by name in Cixous's autobiographical writing. Two of the matters at stake here are: the possibility, or impossibility, of a hospitable opening to the other in the poisonous context of colonialism; the possibility, or impossibility, of a hospitable writing when reflecting back on this from a post-colonial position (in other words, a position that has inherited colonialism and thus has to bear that 'gift' even in rejecting it). The big three inequalities that have shaped so much of the last couple of centuries, class, sex and race, each raises issues related to Modernity in different ways: class having an intimate relationship to capitalism; race inequality violently exacerbated by the colonial project; sexual inequality having a less straightforward relationship to Modernity since patriarchy is far from limited to that historical time-frame yet nevertheless critical to it. 'My Algeriance' in a few words brings all these issues together. It is a *petit récit*, an altobiography perhaps, but (like most postmodern singularities) it is crossed, and in this case it is explicitly crossed by the *grands récits* of modernity. I shall be approaching this through naming – not only literally by proper nouns, but also through the use of qualifying adjectives. Algerian is an adjective long before it is a noun ('My Algeriance', 156) ('Le substantif "Algérien" est né tout récemment. *Avant "algérien" n'était qu'un adjectif* ('Mon Algériance', 72)).

How to read: both, and, or

When we read texts we make a series of choices consciously or otherwise: reading literally and/or figurally, on one level, on many levels and so on. This is not only true of our relationship to the conventional written text but also of our response to the (social, political, emotional) context in which we find ourselves. A strong reading may not be the most faithful – it depends a little on how we understand fidelity and strength. Strength is sometimes allied with forcefulness and clarity – the reading that makes a strong writer of the reader (and perhaps ultimately defeats the writer s/he was reading, reading as a Bloomian agon). But the agony of absolute fidelity, were such a thing possible, would not necessarily serve the writer any better – there is always a need for translation.

Cixous's share of *Veils*, the book she co-authors with Derrida, entitled 'Savoir', recounts her passage from extreme short-sightedness (almost blind like the poet Homer) to sight, thanks to laser surgery. We might understand much of this text, as is so often the case with Cixous's writings, as *also* a meditation on reading and interpretation. Even the title *Voiles*, floating between two genders (masculine veil [*le voile*] and feminine sail [*la voile*] disguised in the plural form), pleads for interpretation. I have said 'between *two* genders', but the 'Prière d'insérer' (the loose sheet inserted into many French publications), so easily lost in translation as is indeed the case here, says of the title (which it enfolds and unmasters, calling it a sub-title to the two texts within): '*Voiles* in *all* genres, that is what is first at stake in the title' ('*Voiles* en tous genres, voilà d'abord l'enjeu du titre'), but lest we take *genres* not to mean sexual difference but literary form, the text immediately refers to the gift of the French language (two genders making two meanings for *voile*) which is the point of departure. I shall cite one typical passage from 'Savoir':

> Limbo: the reign of the myopic, purgatory and promise, dubious environs, the sojourn of the just before redemption. And now she was losing her limbo, which was the water in which she swam. She was being brutally saved. Redemption without delay! But is one saved by a coup de grâce? Or else hit, thrown, struck down!?
> - By going, my poor fairy, my myopia, you are withdrawing from me the ambiguous gifts that filled me with anguish and granted me states that those who see do not know, she murmured.
> - Do not forget me. Keep forever the world suspended, desirable, refused, that enchanted thing I had given you, murmured myopia.
> - If I forget thee, oh Jerusalem, may my right eye, etc.
> - Ah! I see coming in place of my diffuse reign a reign without hesitation.
> - I shall always hesitate. I shall not leave my people. I belong to the people of those who do not see. (*Veils*, 13)

(Limbes: la région des myopes, purgatoire et promesse, lisière douteuse, séjour des âmes des justes avant la rédemption. Et maintenant elle perdait ses limbes, qui étaient les eaux dans lesquelles elle surnageait. Elle était en train d'être brutalement sauvée. Rédemption sans délai! Mais est-on sauvé par un coup de grâce? Ou bien frappé, jeté, foudroyé!?

> – En t'en allant, ma pauvre fée, ma myope, tu me retires les dons ambigus qui m'angoissaient et m'accordaient des états que les voyants ne connaissent pas, murmurait-elle.
> – Ne m'oublie pas. Garde à jamais le monde suspendu, désirable, refusé, cet enchanté que je t'avais donné, murmurait la myopie.
> – Si je t'oublie ô Jérusalem, que mon oeil droit, etc.
> – Ah! Je vois s'annoncer à la place de mon règne diffus un règne sans hésitation.
> – J'hésiterai toujours. Je ne quitterai pas mon peuple. Je suis du peuple des non-voyants. (*Voiles*, 18–19))

Is it clear that this text can be read on a number of different levels? The reference to the people of 'non-seers' might be lightly brushed against other kinds of sexual or cultural identities, even without the casual citation of Jerusalem, or, earlier in the text, the evocation of the girl never quite sure if she has recognised her mother (6; 14). In this text Cixous presents herself as 'entre deux mondes' (18) 'between two worlds' (12) – a resonant expression even for those who have not read her autobiographical texts which tell of her aunt's shop in Oran *Aux Deux Mondes*. She writes in 'My Algeriance': 'So the boutique was dedicated, and I with it, to a universe with two worlds. But I never knew in a clear, explicit or decisive way which the two were. The world was two. All the worlds were two and there were always two to begin with. There were so many two-worlds' ('Ainsi la boutique était-elle dédiée et moi avec à un univers à deux mondes. Mais jamais je ne sus de façon claire, explicite ni décisive, qui étaient les deux. Le monde était deux. Tous les mondes étaient deux, et il y eut toujours deux pour commencer. Il y avait tant de deux-mondes').[34] While the dominant macro-context of this paragraph is the universe of racial tension, Cixous's reminiscences next take her in the direction of sexuality: sailors whose choice of pink reminds her both of Genet and their fiancées, the queer and the compulsively compulsory heterosexual. The context is also commerce in the economic sense – and the sailors' 'choice' to purchase 'pink hearts in the form of Mickey ears' ('My Algeriance', 165) ('des coeurs roses en forme d'oreilles de Mickey' ('Pieds nus', 61)) reminds us of the forces of capitalism and the homogenising power of the US even in the cultural sphere, even in mid-century Algeria.

Not seeing – as not being sure – is lauded here. But a certain colonising blindness is even more hateful than it is enviable:

It was possible to not see, to have never seen anything to not see the misery, to not see the women, to not see the syphilitics and the tubercular patients the puss and the spit.

For me it was the land of the eyes: we sent looks at each other, we saw, we couldn't *not* see, we knew and we knew that we knew we knew, we were nude, we were denounced, threatened, we flung taunts, we received glances. It was the land of the other, not of the fellow human being. The other: foretells me, forewarns me, forecasts me, alerts me, alters me. Impresses me, as Montaigne said, 'I seize hold of the evil that I study and I lay it down in me' (*De la force de l'imagination*, I, 21). As soon as I went into the street I caught Algeria.

I was nearsighted, but I lacked blindness. I would indeed have liked not to see. It was impossible. The anguish of my fellow people pierces me. ('My Algeriance', 164)

(On pouvait ne pas voir, n'avoir jamais rien vu ne pas voir la misère, ne pas voir les femmes, ne pas voir les syphilitiques et les tuberculeux le pus et les crachats.

Pour moi c'était le pays des yeux: on s'envoyait des regards, on voyait, on ne pouvait pas ne pas voir, on savait et on savait que l'on savait qu'on savait, on était nus, on était dénoncés, menacés, on se lançait des traits, on recevait des coups d'oeil. C'était le pays de l'autre, pas le semblable. L'autre: me prédit, me prévient, me prévoit, m'avertit, m'altère. M'impressionne comme disait Montaigne. *'Je saisis le mal que j'étudie et je le couche en moi'* (*De la force de l'imagination*, I, 21). Dès que je descendais dans la rue j'attrapais l'Algérie.

J'étais myope, mais je manquais d'aveuglement. J'aurais bien voulu ne pas voir. C'était impossible. L'angoisse d'autrui me perce. ('Mon Algériance', 73))

Here, in an 'uninhabitable' place, seeing, reading (or Montaigne's *studying*) the other is both essential and dangerous. The naked eye, the undisguisable visibility of the I ('on était nus') is a vulnerability. The other's glance is literally a *coup d'oeil*, a blow from the eye, and 'I' 'get it' (*l'attrappe*), get what is coming to me, whether Algeria is a sickness or a slap for the little Jewish girl. This could be a model of inhospitality in social and political terms. In terms of reading, and feeling, the subject does receive the other in herself – the other enters – but violently, unhappily. Why receive consolation in another's welcome when you should be master of your own house?

While Cixous, the main character in *Reveries*, experiences passionate friendships even in the unpropitious circumstances of colonial Algeria, it is impossible for these to develop along traditional lines including exchange of hospitality. To take the case of her relationship not with an 'Arab', but with a young French girl, whose very name evokes France: 'I cannot enter Françoise's house where Jews are not allowed [literally "admitted"]' ('Je ne peux pas entrer dans la maison de Françoise où les Juifs ne sont pas admis').[35] The strict (social) prohibition on Jews entering French houses is, relatively speaking, more tolerable than the cat and mouse game played over the possibility of her French friend being allowed to be a guest in a Jewish home (*Reveries*, 69, 72–3; *Rêveries*, 121, 127–8). Occasionally an invitation would be accepted, but frequently permission would be withdrawn at the very last moment, leaving the anxious hostess looking out with eager anticipation for her absent guest who never arrives. Outside the chained-up gate of the Cixous family home in Algeria it is madness and violence, and so typically the young girl takes refuge in books: 'I used to read in the Clos-Salembier because it was impossible to survive without books . . . without books I'd have been sunk' (*Reveries*, 47) ('Je lisais au Clos-Salembier parce qu'il était absolument impossible de survivre sans livre . . . sans livres j'aurais sombré' (*Rêveries*, 82)). Books become friends.

Aïcha

In 'My Algeriance' as well as in *Les Rêveries de la femme sauvage*, Cixous refers to her family's maid Aïcha.[36] I shall quote at length:

> In Algiers [families] had Moorish maids. *La Mauresque* was even a synonym for maid.[37] At the Clos Salembier, we had a complex relationship with Aïcha and all her family.
>
> Aïcha was an attractive woman, gentle and strong, femininity itself always pregnant and smiling. Ripe and big. The husband, whom I never saw, was eighty. Later on I learned that she had been Ouled Naïl.[38] Aïcha was replaced, at each pregnancy, by one of her daughters. There was Bahia who limped and whom my father treated. Zouina who was ugly, black, alarmed. All the children different, blond ones, brown ones, black ones, Aïcha entered the garden, like a vine laden with bunches of children in her arms, at her skirts, at her breast.
>
> Her gentle and caressing name.
>
> Whereas all maids in Algeria were called Fatma.[39] But not us. Aïcha was unique. Until the day, very late, after independence, when I discovered: Aïcha was named Messaouda. What? And for twenty years we had kept calling her Aïcha? That's right. There had been I know not what initial error, a parapraxis and Messaouda had docilely let herself be expropriated and reappropriated. She had not dared. We who had wronged her and Fatmaized her for twenty years. We want to avoid causing damage,

it catches up with us. When Rosa entered the service of Freud's sister, she had to renounce her name and be called Dora. Freud was greatly saddened by this. 'Those poor people, they are not even allowed to keep their names . . .' he thought. ('My Algeriance', 157)

(A Alger, [les familles] avaient des mauresques. Nous eûmes, au Clos Salembier, une relation complexe avec Aïcha et toute sa famille.
Aïcha était une belle femme douce forte, la féminité même toujours enceinte et souriante. Mûre et grosse. Le mari, que je ne vis jamais, avait 80 ans. Plus tard je sus qu'elle avait été Ouled Naïl. Aïcha était remplacée, à chaque grossesse, par une de ses filles. Il y eut Bahia qui boitait et que mon père soignait, Zouina qui était laide, noire, effarée. Des enfants tous différents, des blonds, des bruns, des noirs. Aïcha entrait dans le jardin, comme une vigne chargée de grappes d'enfants dans les bras, aux jupes, au sein.
Son nom doux et caressant.
Alors qu'en Algérie toutes les bonnes étaient appelées Fatma. Mais nous non. Aïcha était unique. Jusqu'au jour, très tard, après l'Indépendance où je découvris: Aïcha s'appelait Messaouda. Quoi? Et pendant vingt ans et toujours nous l'appelions Aïcha? Eh oui. Il y avait eu je ne sais quelle erreur initiale, un acte manqué, et docilement Messaouda s'était laissé exproprier et réapproprier. Elle n'avait pas osé. Nous qui pendant vingt ans l'avions lésée et fatmatisée. Nous voulons éviter le dommage, nous sommes rattrapés. Lorsque Rosa entra au service de la soeur de Freud, elle dut renoncer à son nom et s'appeler Dora. Freud en fut tout attristé. 'Ces pauvres gens, il ne leur est même permis de conserver leurs noms . . .', pensait-il. ('Mon Algériance', 72))

The story is told a little differently in the later text. There it is even clearer that, on some level, Aïcha stands for Algeria: 'I'd nestle against Aïcha as soon as she'd taken off her veil . . . I would hug Aïcha's body and, laughing, she'd let me hug her country for a brief moment' (*Reveries*, 6, translation modified) ('je me nichais contre Aïcha dès qu'elle avait ôté son voile . . . je me serrais contre le corps d'Aïcha et elle me laissait en riant serrer son pays pendant un mince instant' (*Rêveries*, 14)). And Cixous suggests that it is not clear that calling Messaouda Aïcha was simply wrong or evil:

Something happened, we don't know exactly whether, as usual, it was harm [or evil] that was done, if what happened was harm, as I thought at first when I learnt, from my brother I expect, this story of Aïcha who is Messaouda and whom everybody including my father always called something else, and when I found this out I was afraid, but for the last two or three years I have no longer thought that only harm was done. (*Reveries*, 53, translation modified)

163

(Quelque chose est fait, nous ne savons pas exactement si, comme d'habitude, c'est le mal qui est fait, si ce qui est fait c'est le mal, comme je l'ai d'abord pensé lorsque j'ai appris par mon frère sans doute cette histoire d'Aïcha qui est Messaouda et que tous y compris mon père nous avons toujours appelée autrement, et que sur le moment j'étais effrayée, mais depuis deux ou trois ans je ne pense plus que seul le mal est fait. (*Rêveries*, 93))

Typically in Cixous, words were and are sensual: 'I loved the feel [touch] of the name Aïcha, nothing sentimental, all sensuous and child-like' (53, translation modified) ('J'aimais le toucher du nom Aïcha, rien de sentimental, tout sensuel et infantile' (93)). This is both the perspective of the young child and that of the writer. However, the reader has no sense of dialogue, of response from Messaouda – and Cixous tells us how, in spite of her childish yearning, she was never invited into Messaouda's home. Her attempts to nestle, to make a nest (*se nicher*) in/on the body of Algeria are perhaps seen as the attempts of the hungry cuckoo – Messaouda already has her own brood and clearly this is part of her motherly charm. The context to this is that Cixous's own mother is not like a woman but a young girl, also represented as masculine – and this paradoxically allows her to nest unworried in Algeria. Her maternal grandmother is also not a woman, but a lady. Cixous's mother is protected by a kind of innocence, a lack of care about what others think and faith in her own freedom that Cixous designates as German. She is never ill or mad. She marches about Algiers and as a midwife is eager (unlike the doctors in the French hospital) to keep women mobile and thus healthy (33–4; 59–60). Even in prison she is like a fish (32; 57).

Qualifying adjectives

I quoted the passages concerning Aïcha in a conference paper, and some of the audience felt that Cixous's use of the adjective black in relation to Zouina ('ugly, black, alarmed') betrayed the author's own casual racism as it might well do in an American context. This moved me to consider the question of adjectives, and particularly adjectives of colour in 'My Algeriance'. What kinds of adjectives does Cixous use in this short piece? It is notable that adjectives of colour are by my count quite rare – notable because the essay is quite poetic and sensual. The only colours to have wholly positive connotations are brown (for instance, 'handsome little brown man' (171); 'un beau petit homme brun' ('Mon Algériance', 74)) and the light green eyes of the father (166; 'Pieds nus', 63). Pink occurs three times, twice (165; 'Pieds nus', 61) in relation to French sailors and their sweethearts (glazed pink postcards and pink hearts), golden twice in relation to chrysanthemums (154; 'Mon Algériance', 71) – in both cases the commercial overlays the sentimental. The most shameful commerce being the selling of flowers, golden flowers grown by the dead father, to the Catholic flower sellers who flog them on at a huge profit to the women come to mourn their dead. Gold is peculiarly appropriate as a colour here; by inverse alchemy it is turned to dust and ashes. The dead father's gift of living pleasure is turned to *geld* – and not enough of it. Navy blue is ruined by its association with Catholic youth and Pétain (163, a passage in neither 'Mon Algériance' nor 'Pieds nus'). *Bleu-blanc-rouge* speaks for itself – and the white and red also occur in the guilty, violent episode with the shoe-shine (166–7; 'Pieds nus', 63–6), one of several examples of the discomfort of relative privilege and wealth. Blond seems positive in its association with native Algerians (157, 161; 'Mon Algériance', 72, second example in neither text), but the tall blond Corsican is hateful and the epitome of casual racism. Black is used as follows elsewhere in the essay: 'black skies of the north' (153) ('la nue noire du Nord' ('Mon Algériance', 71)), 'black little Spanish Catholic merchant women' (154) ('les noires petites marchandes espagnoles' ('Mon Algériance', 71)), 'widows veiled in black' at the Catholic cemetery (154) (no colour reference in the French, 'veuves catholiques' ('Mon Algériance', 71)) and black muzzles of two bullets (156; not in either French text) – 'little black heads' (157; not in either French text) – these are bullets fired by Americans 'liberating' Algeria, and thus welcome in some respects. It is true, then, that black could be said to have some negative connotations in Cixous's text – and that this is insensitive and might be particularly so in a US context. However, the negative content comes from association with the Nazi north and from Catholicism – both markers of racial exclusion for the Jewish Cixous family.

Odour and heat are conjured up in the piece less than one would imagine. The reader comes to French (and British) writing about North Africa with certain expectations – of local colour. Gide offers one important paradigm of the appreciative visitor: the beauty of the desert, the oasis and the colourful, desirable people. Camus provides us with a *pied noir* model – someone who is sure he is at home in this land, but occasionally encounters inexplicable behaviour from shadowy Arabs. Perfumed soil marks *not* belonging for Cixous (153; 'Mon Algériance', 71), the 'arid and perfumed theatre, salt, jasmine, orange blossoms' is a theatre of war (155) ('théâtre aride et parfumé, sel, jasmin, fleurs d'oranger' ('Mon Algériance', 72)). The 'narrow urinated street' again marks not belonging (164) ('rue étroite urinée' ('Pieds nus', 60)). While in Camus's 'The Guest', the failure, even (surely unjustifiable, we must think) rejection, of Daru's good and hospitable intentions is a puzzle for the reader, Cixous does not leave us so puzzled; she translates for us as she writes:

> The bitter taste of my snack that the little Arab demanded of me and to eat outside without sharing was impossible.
>
> But the truth is that I did not share: I was constantly paying the interest on an enormous and interminable debt, there was no gift, only the loathsome impotence of the child who has a house and a school bag. (164)

> (Le goût amer de mon goûter que le petit Arabe me réclamait et manger dehors sans partager était impossible.
>
> Mais la vérité c'est que je ne partageais pas: je versais sans arrêt les intérêts d'une dette énorme et interminable, il n'y avait pas de don, seulement l'infâme impuissance de l'enfant qui a une maison et un cartable. ('Mon Algériance', 73))

Only when the soles of the child's bare feet meet the hot trails, imagining the welcoming palms of the dead – in that sensible transcendental exchange – is there a moment of imagined acceptance from the dust. Against the North African tourist's trope of heat we usually set cool water, and Cixous relishes that refreshing taste in her memory of the water carriers (165; 'Pieds nus', 61). But in this text we more often have abundant and expressive, ex-pulsive, spittle including the child covered in spit (161; not in the French). And it is the 'strong odor of racism' (170; not in the French) that hangs about the colonial exclusions marking beaches and swimming pools (163; not in the French) and the like.

The adjectives that predominate in this text (just over 9,000 words long in the English translation) are overwhelmingly markers of national, linguistic or ethnic identity: by my count French occurs about 60 times (and France 25), words including Algeria occur 60 times – that includes 21 uses of Algerian. Jewish occurs 19 times (Jew an additional 6) and Arab(s) 28. It is man-made political relations that predominate in this text not the beauty or expansiveness of the natural world.

When Algerian Jews were excluded from French citizenship in 1940, and thus expelled from French schools, they set up their own schools:

It was in the un-Frenchified Jewish dining-room-school that I had my first francolinguistic ecstacies. . . . From the back of the room I intercepted the magic that awaited me when I would be in the first row. I heard these prophetic words: '*adjectif qualificatif*' (qualifying adjective). Ah my God is this what you announced to me? One day I will have the keys to the qualifying adjective! ('My Algeriance', 168)

(C'est dans l'école-salle à manger juive dé-francisée que j'eus mes premières extases franco-linguistiques. . . . Du fond de la salle je surprenais la magie qui m'attendait quand j'arriverais au premier rang. J'entendis ces mots mystérieux: 'adjectif qualificatif'. Ah mon Dieu c'est donc cela que tu m'annonçais? Un jour j'aurais les clés d'adjectif qualificatif! ('Mon Algériance', 73))

The qualifying adjective signifies scholastic success and mastery of the tongue. There are five meanings given for 'qualify' in the Oxford English Dictionary:

Qualify 1. *v.t.* Attribute some quality to, describe *as* (*qualify documents as heretical, person as a scoundrel, proposal as iniquitous; adjectives qualify nouns*). 2. Invest or provide with the necessary qualities, make competent, fit, or legally entitled, (*for* be*ing* or do*ing, to* be or do, *for* post or sphere, or abs.); (qualifying examination, round . . .). 3. Modify (statement, opinion), make less absolute or sweeping, subject to reservations or limitation. 4. Moderate, mitigate, make less complete or pleasing or unpleasing; alter strength or flavour or (spirit etc. with water, or vice versa). 5. *v.i.* Fulfil a condition, esp. pass test or take oath, to make oneself eligible (*for* post, competition, etc., or abs.)

To the question: what is '"l'adjectif qualificatif" or what adjective *qualifies* you?' the answer, for Cixous, has to be 'French'. Along with other privileges, the French passport means you have the right to travel, to cross borders. And Cixous consents to a lie, to a masquerade of identity in spite of herself. In Algeria 'we were never invited' (171) ('jamais nous ne fûmes invités' (74)), and colonial Manicheism placed Cixous, unwelcomed, in the bad camp of the French, the enemy, however much she wanted to be a friend. But as she leaves Algeria in 1954, French (pass)porosity (155; 'la *passeporosité* française' ('Mon Algériance', 72)) becomes more hospitable (she speaks of the stormy intermittent hospitality of State and Nation) – and it seems ungrateful to say 'I am not French.'

Fraternity: naming the other 'brother'

Republican France refuses to name race, and also refuses to name sex, however much it acts them out or its citizens hurl abuse. Here I should like to keep introducing sexual difference even where it is not obvious – we might note above how the father and the brother have a certain status in relation to naming or knowing the name (of Aïcha) but it is Cixous who infuses the names with love for us. (Rightly or wrongly? Is it foolish girls' talk?) I'll now turn to a different vignette from Cixous's *Rêveries* – an autofictional text with a title which provides much food for reflection.[40] Cixous and Derrida both started writing 'about' hospitality and 'about' Algeria towards the end of the last century. These are over-determined moves, but one convincing suggestion by Ronnie Scharfman is that the civil war in Algeria in the 1980s and the arrival of a number of Algerian refugees in Paris was a major motivation.[41] It sharpened the need to think through the history of Algeria and their own *algériance* (Cixous) or *nostalgérie* (Derrida). During her childhood in Algeria, Cixous and her brother feel that their destiny is to be with 'those we called "littlarabs"' (*Reveries*, 24, my translation) ('ceux que nous appelions "les petizarabes"' (*Rêveries*, 45)), but the feeling is not reciprocated. At the time she compares her brother and herself to fairytale ugly ducklings (or *cygnes malpropres*) separated from their true siblings, and apparently one incident in 1948 is seen as a sign (*signe*) of future reconciliation. This is just before her father's death, when he stops – absolutely exceptionally, she says – their unreliable (and not guaranteed to start again) Citroën to pick up two Arab hitchhikers.[42]

> In the Citroën it was unforgettable rejoicing, the two passengers joyfully thanking for the unexpected hospitality, they were right to believe and hope for what you cannot rationally count on, the world is not so bad as we believe, look a Frenchman stopped which is wrong I thought my father is not French although maybe he believes he is, my father is a false step in the history of this country, it is as a reject spat out cast out by the French on the one hand and on the other as my ideal doctor living like a madman in Clos-Salembier where no normal doctor in other words with normal medical financial and professional ambitions would choose to live, in that neighbourhood with no French people unsuitable for success unsuitable for socialising, so it must be said, it is as a peculiar kind of Arab that my father an arabizarre stopped and did it knowing that our Citroën stopped in mid flight was always difficult to get going again, and also that was a dozen days before his death which he did or didn't have

a presentiment of, but we'll never know, but we mustn't tell our two passengers – that my father is really an Arab beneath the disguise of a young and handsome French doctor, being Jewish besides, which could come down on either side of the scales – for it would be taking away from our two enchanted guests the marvellous feeling that in this sick country cursed by hatred and totally impossible, despite everything, everything was possible. Arriving at the corner of the Boulevard Laurent-Pichat my father had stopped the car at the top of the hill and our two humans transfigured at the same time as my father my brother and myself, had got out hearts wide open, the door, the door, saying thank you you are a brother thank you my brother god bless you brother in French and in exchange my father said that they were his brothers in Arabic. . . . Ever since we have told each other every year the story of when the doors of heaven opened before us at the corner of the boulevard, my father having been named brother we were the brother's children for a few days. Naturally the sky was incredibly blue, our smiling teeth were extremely white, our companions biblical, and then god died and the book of doors closed in our face. (*Reveries*, 24–5, my translation)

(Dans la Citroën c'est la fête inoubliable les deux passagers remercient avec joie pour l'hospitalité inattendue, ils ont eu raison de croire et d'espérer ce sur quoi l'on ne peut raisonnablement pas compter, le monde n'est pas si mauvais qu'on le croit, voilà qu'un Français s'est arrêté ce qui est une erreur pensé-je mon père n'est pas français quoiqu'il le croie lui-même peut-être, mon père est un faux mouvement de l'histoire de ce pays, c'est en tant que déchet craché destitué des Français d'une part et d'autre part en tant qu'idéal du moi médecin logé comme un fou au Clos-Salembier où aucun médecin normal c'est-à-dire doté des ambitions médicales financières et professionnelles normales ne se serait logé, dans ce quartier sans Français impropre à la réussite impropre à la vie mondaine, c'est donc il faut se le dire, en tant que genre particulier d'Arabe que mon père un arabizarre s'est arrêté et cela en sachant que la Citroën arrêtée dans son élan était toujours difficile à relancer, et cela aussi une dizaine de jours avant sa mort dont il avait ou pas le pressentiment, mais cela nous ne le saurons jamais, mais il ne faut pas le dire à nos deux passagers – que mon père est un véritable arabe sous les fausses apparences d'un jeune et beau médecin français, étant d'ailleurs juif, ce qui pouvait peser sur un plateau ou l'autre de la balance – car ce serait ôter aux deux hôtes enchantés le sentiment merveilleux que dans ce pays malade et maudit de haine et totalement impossible, malgré tout, tout était possible. En arrivant au tournant du boulevard Laurent-Pichat mon père avait arrêté l'auto en haut de la pente et nos deux humains transfigurés en même temps que nous mon père mon frère et moi, étaient descendus le coeur grand ouvert, la porte, la porte, disant merci tu es un frère merci mon frère dieu te bénisse frère en français et en échange mon père dit que ce sont ses frères en arabe. . . . Depuis nous nous racontons chaque année l'histoire de quand les portes du ciel s'étaient ouvertes devant nous au tournant du boulevard, mon père ayant été nommé frère nous fûmes enfants de frère pour quelques jours. Le ciel était naturellement puissamment bleu, nos dents de sourire étaient extrêmement blanches, nos compagnons bibliques, et là-dessus dieu est mort et le livre des portes s'est refermé sur notre nez. (*Rêveries*, 46–7))

This heavily laden scene (with many affectionate ironic touches) of the glory and transfiguration of the host, or rather the *hôte*, is followed by a certain textual unpicking of the web Cixous has woven. This is a memory. Her brother remembers it differently. The men were not hitching, her father simply stopped of his own accord to give them a lift as he was prone to do, 'and they were going down my brother said, into Algiers, they were not even going up' (*Reveries*, 26), ('ils descendaient dit mon frère, sur Alger, ils ne montaient même pas' (*Rêveries*, 48)). For many readers this is an ambiguous assertion – does it means that they did not even get into the car: *monter* frequently has that meaning? Or is it a question of the direction they were going in, as the imperfect tense might indicate? The translator of course would have to decide, the reader in French can be hospitable to both meanings.

But if we stay, however, with the golden scene for a moment, we allow it to be a benign fiction like the benign fiction it contains – something typical of the religious underpinning of political utopias (Plato or Rousseau, who hovers over the text) and of the affective structure of the gift. Cixous tells us that nationality or ethnicity must be obscured, for 'it would be taking away from our two enchanted guests (ôter aux deux hôtes enchantés) the marvellous feeling that in this sick country cursed by hatred and totally impossible, despite everything, everything was possible' ('ce serait ôter aux deux hôtes enchantés le sentiment merveilleux que dans ce pays malade et maudit de haine et totalement impossible, malgré tout, tout était possible'). I should like to suggest here that *hôte* is a particularly appropriate term because of its reversibility. I, as translator, have replaced it by 'guest' – but it could also have the sense of 'host'. In a microcosmic sense, within his archetypically French Citroën, the two Algerians are the guests of Georges Cixous. But in the macrocosmic sense so often used in the book, the Cixous family are the guests of the Algerian people – usually uninvited guests – but here perhaps for a moment there is an invitation. Doors and hearts are opened wide – whereas elsewhere in the book of memory doors are always closed however much young Hélène beats upon them. In this scene there is an exchange of tongues – and in both languages brotherhood is spoken and performed. Brotherhood is a very loaded term of course, and one that can return us oppressively to French Republican exclusions,[43] but here it is a 'possibility'.

The father guarantees the possibility of hospitality – although that possibility is fragile and precarious since he is in fact a Jewish father however much he may wish to be 'international'.[44] The father can be a brother – and thus let his children into the family. Once he is dead the mother becomes a widow, and is removed from the possibility of being offered hospitality. Biblically, widows and orphans are tied to hospitality, but in this sick and *im*possible colonial society divided, by sex and race, Jewish widows are beyond the pale. In this context Cixous uses the term *invitée* over and over again – not the reciprocal *hôte*. The mother can invite but cannot be invited.

This is perhaps a false memory of a primal scene of brotherhood, but acknowledged as fragile, acknowledged as perhaps a girlish fantasy, unlike the collective false memory of the French Revolution as universal fraternity and thus hospitality. Do utopic remembered or imagined moments of *reciprocity* function as powerfully as the superabundant Law of hospitality? The Law does not permit exchange – but I would suggest that this hyperbolic example derives its power from its sense of the mutual, its reversibility, and not from Georges Cixous's generosity. However, where the racial, colonial divide, a gulf like the *ravin* hidden in the title, is temporarily bridged, it is at a moment seemingly free of *sexual* difference. The brother of the brother is reversible in a way the sister of the brother is not. The innocent mother thinks optimistically that by buying a girl's bicycle she can overcome the inevitable masculine bias, and the bike will be shared between brother and sister. But while outraging her son with this poisoned gift, she still does not succeed in freeing her daughter and releasing her into physical mobility. The daughter remains all the more a reader and a dreamer – only the son explores and discovers Algeria in the conventional sense. My argument in short is that, even if we can find moments of hospitality in the most inhospitable environments, sexual difference would interrupt. And so our analysis of the *possibilities* of hospitality must also allow for that particular interruption.

Camus's 'The Guest' or boys' talk?

Someone who expresses himself in his nakedness – the face – is in fact one to the extent that he calls upon me, to the extent that he places himself under my responsibility: I must already answer for him, be responsible for him. Every gesture of the Other was a sign addressed to me. . . . The Other who expresses himself is entrusted to me (and there is no debt with regard to the Other – for what is due cannot be paid; one will never be even). [Further on it will be a question of a 'duty beyond all debt' for the I who is what it is, singular and identifiable, only through the impossibility of being replaced, even though it is precisely here that the 'responsibility of the Other,' the 'responsibility of the hostage,' is an experience of substitution and sacrifice.] The Other individuates me in my responsibility for him. The death of the Other affects me in my very identity as a responsible I . . . made up of unspeakable responsibility. This is how I am affected by the death of the Other, this is my relation to his death, It is, in my relation, my deference toward someone who no longer responds, already a guilt of the survivor.

(Quelqu'un qui s'exprime dans la nudité – le visage – est un au point d'en appeler à moi, de se placer sous ma responsabilité: d'ores et déjà, j'ai à répondre de lui. Tous les gestes d'autrui étaient des signes à moi adressés. . . . Autrui qui s'exprime m'est confié (et il n'y a pas de dette à l'égard d'autrui – car le dû est impayable: on n'est jamais quitte). [Plus loin il sera question d'un 'devoir au-delà de toute dette' pour le moi qui n'est ce qu'il est, singulier et identifiable, que par l'impossibilité de se faire remplacer là où pourtant la 'responsabilité pour autrui', la 'responsabilité d'otage' est une expérience de la substitution et du sacrifice]. Autrui m'individue dans la responsabilité que j'ai de lui. La mort d'autrui qui meurt m'affecte dans mon identité même de moi responsable . . . faite d'indicible responsabilité. C'est cela, mon affection par la mort d'autrui, ma relation avec sa mort. Elle est, dans ma relation, ma déférence à quelqu'un qui ne répond plus, déjà une culpabilité – une culpabilité de survivant.)[45]

'The Guest' is a short story in a late collection by Camus, *Exile and the Kingdom*, first published in 1957. In his unpublished seminar 'Hostipitalité', Derrida chooses it as one of those literary texts in which 'the actual or latent story . . . the poetic or dramatic knot, stages a law of hospitality [and] acts out, *as its own writing* what we might call "hospitality"' ('le récit actuel ou latent . . . le noeud dramatique ou poétique met en scène une loi de l'hospitalité [et] déploie en acte, *comme sa propre écriture* ce que nous pouvons appeler '"hospitalité"') (cited in Michaud, 'Un acte d'hospitalité', 37). Michaud continues: 'if, according to Derrida, we must turn towards literature, this is because hospitality finds resources there, because literature gives, if you like, asylum to hospitality in deploying tropes and turns which give place to hospitality in the very idiom' ('s'il faut selon Derrida se tourner vers la littérature, c'est parce que l'hospitalité y trouve sa ressource, parce que la littérature donne, si l'on veut, asile à l'hospitalité en faisant acte des tropes et tours qui lui donnent lieu dans l'idiome').[46] We might note that the Algerian war of national liberation is now usually considered to have begun in November 1954, three years before the story is published, although the first attacks made by the Front de Libération Nationale (FLN) were downplayed by the French at the time. Derrida discusses the naming of the war (in the context of the United Nations condemnation of 'international terrorism' after 9/11) as follows:

> No one can deny that there was state terrorism during the French repression in Algeria from 1954 to 1962. The terrorism carried out by the Algerian rebellion was long considered a domestic phenomenon insofar as Algeria was supposed to be an integral part of French national territory, and the French terrorism of the time (carried out by the state) was presented as a police operation for internal security. It was only in the 1990s, decades later, that the French parliament retrospectively conferred the status of 'war' (and thus the status of an *international* confrontation) upon the conflict so as to be able to pay the pensions of the 'veterans' who claimed them. What did this law reveal? That it was necessary, and that we were able, to change all the names previously used to qualify what had earlier been so modestly called, in Algeria, precisely the 'events' (the inability, once again, of popular public opinion to name the 'thing' adequately). Armed repression, an internal police operation, and state terrorism thus all of a sudden became a 'war.' On the other side, the terrorists were considered and from now on are considered in much of the world as freedom fighters and heroes of national independence. (*PTT*, 104)

> (Personne ne peut nier qu'il y a eu terrorisme d'État dans la répression française en Algérie, entre 1954 et 1962. Puis le terrorisme pratiqué par la rébellion algérienne fut longtemps considéré comme un phénomène domestique tant que l'Algérie était censée faire partie intégrante du territoire national français, tout comme le terrorisme français d'alors (exercé par l'État) se présentait comme une opération de police et de sécurité intérieure. C'est seulement des décennies plus tard, dans les années 1990, que le Parlement français a conféré rétrospectivement le statut de 'guerre' (donc d'affrontement *international*) à ce conflit, afin de pouvoir assurer des pensions aux 'anciens combattants' qui les réclamaient. Que révélait donc cette loi? Eh bien, il fallait et on pouvait changer tous les noms utilises jusqu'alors pour qualifier ce qu'auparavant on avait pudiquement surnommé, en Algérie, les 'événements', justement (faute encore une fois, pour l'opinion publique populaire, de pouvoir nommer la 'chose' adéquatement). La répression armée, comme opération de police intérieure et terrorisme d'État, redevenait soudain une 'guerre'. De l'autre

côté, les terroristes étaient et sont désormais considérés dans une grande partie du monde comme des combattants de la liberté et des héros de l'indépendance nationale. (*Le 'concept'*, 158–9))

Camus is another writer, and public figure, who inspires devotion and bile in equal parts.[47] Much of the anger relates to his difficulty in doing anything other than condemn 'terrorism' on the part of Algerian nationalists – famously declaring (after his Nobel prize winning speech) that he imagines his mother (who still lived in Algeria) as a possible victim, preferring her to 'justice' in this context.[48] While he had shown courage in his criticism of French colonial abuses, his solution was not an independent Algeria. Albert Memmi puts a strong case against this position in 'Portrait du Colonisateur' showing too how it is almost inevitable granted the material situation of the coloniser.[49] However, many still honour Camus for his fraternal 'bonne volonté'.[50] Djebar includes him in her list of great dead Algerian writers (although the French canon has always seen him as 'French' rather than 'Francophone' of course), telling of his death from the perspective of his adoring, almost-mute mother, so at home in Belcourt (*Le Blanc de l'Algérie*, 103–5). Her next example is the very different case of Frantz Fanon (told via his wife, Josie), making an interesting juxtaposition. It could be suggested that the violent 'events', the terrorism, which took place in Algeria 1990–2000 (as well as the more famous Islamic terrorism against the United States and other Western nations) have created a climate in which Camus's humanist rejection of terrorism has found a renewed audience. President Bush (or his advisors) even, rather daringly, chose *L'Etranger*, with its anti-death-penalty message, for his 2006 holiday reading, as traditionally announced to the public.

'L'Hôte' ('The Guest') takes place in a world of men and/or boys, and the exchanges between characters are couched in very simple sentences with a sparse range of vocabulary – a poor or bare use of language sometimes associated (à la Hemingway) with masculinity. Certainly the use of language is a long way from Cixous and *écriture féminine*. This simplicity can be characterised as useful for clear communication – whether this is seen as an ethical good (real men say what they mean and mean what they say) or a politico-economic tool (the colonial master wishes his commands to be understood and acted upon). In fact, in Camus's story the poverty of the language and of communication entails misunderstanding as much as understanding of self and other – and for today's reader leaves much in suspense.

In the story, Daru, a schoolmaster (if not the very figure of *l'instituteur*) who teaches in a remote area of Algeria – and also distributes grain (*blé*) in times of food shortages, such as the one of the time in which the tale is located – is visited by a local police-man (Balducci) and his prisoner, an Arab who has killed his cousin. Balducci communicates to Daru, whom he calls 'fils' (literally son, translated as 'my boy'), an order: 'you will deliver this fellow to Tinguit' ('The Guest', 69) ('tu livreras le camarade à Tinguit' ('L'Hôte', 86)).[51] Daru refuses: it is not his job. Balducci neverthe-less leaves the prisoner with Daru and returns to his post. With Balducci's consent, Daru unties the prisoner's hands, and offers him mint tea; later he makes him a meal and shares his bedroom with him. The next morning he walks with him to a point where he is two hours walk from Tinguit or can set off in a different direction towards nomads who will welcome him; he gives him food for two days and money, and leaves him. As Daru sets off he sees the prisoner heading in the direction of Tinguit. Back in the school he reads on the blackboard 'among the winding French rivers' ('entre les méandres des fleuves français'), a chalk inscription 'clumsily chalked-up' ('par une main malhabile'), '"You handed over our brother. You will pay for this"' ('"Tu as livré notre frère. Tu paieras"'). The final pathetic sentence of the story reads: 'In this vast landscape he had loved so much, he was alone' (82) ('Dans ce vaste pays qu'il avait tant aimé, il était seul' (101)).

For today's reader, the two evocations of French rivers on the blackboard are of course critical, and not only because of the ques-tion of the education system that imposes a colonial geography on Algerian school children. In addition, the first time they are men-tioned Camus juxtaposes two sentences:

On the blackboard the four rivers of France, drawn with four different coloured chalks, had been flowing towards their estuaries for the past three days. Snow had fallen in mid-October after eight months of drought without the transition of rain, and the twenty pupils, more or less, who lived in the villages scattered over the plateau had stopped coming. (65)

(Sur le tableau noir les quatre fleuves de France, dessinés avec quatre craies de couleurs différents, coulaient vers leur estuaire depuis trois jours. La neige était tombée brutalement à la mi-octobre, après huit mois de sécheresse, sans que la pluie eût apporté une transition et la vingtaine d'élèves qui habitaient dans les villages disséminés sur le plateau ne venai-ent plus. (81–2))

The contrast between fertility and plenty flowing in France, on the one hand, with famine and deprivation in Algeria on the other, is plain. Nature seems inhospitable to Algerians. But Daru appears to see himself as a good man, a decent individual who will not do the work of a policeman, even though the policeman is his friend, and deliver someone to prison.[52] One of the gaps in the story is any precise detail about his reluctance, since there is apparently no doubt that the man committed murder: 'A family squabble, I think. One owed the other grain, it seems. It's not at all clear. In short, he killed his cousin with a billhook. You know, like a sheep, *kreezk!*' (70) ('Des affaires de famille, je crois. L'un devait du grain à l'autre, paraît-il. Ça n'est pas clair. Enfin, bref, il a tué le cousin d'un coup de serpe. Tu sais, comme au mouton, zic!' (87)), as Balducci puts it. Is Daru's reluctance political and specific to the colonial situation? Or aesthetic and related to his own self-fashioning? Balducci does not see the same qualitative difference between their roles. He himself is not an ogre, only doing his job, and they are both part of the state apparatus, both fundamentally on the same side in what Balducci sees is now a war. Daru says he will wait for a declaration of war. Reflecting back on the period we can see why the French State wanted to refer to the situation as 'Troubles' rather than as a war of liberation. As J. M. Coetzee's narrator in *Waiting for the Barbarians* will put it, in words that could apply to Daru: 'I was the lie that Empire tells itself when times are easy, he the truth that Empire tells when harsh winds blow. Two sides of imperial rule, no more, no less' (135). While less enlightened in a humanitarian sense (keeping the prisoner's hands tied, the first thing that shocks Coetzee's Magistrate too), the Corsican Balducci is perhaps more clear-sighted. For it is not so easy for Daru to step out of his role in the eyes of the prisoner *who cannot understand him*. This lack of understanding can itself be read in a number of ways: in terms of the ancient obligations of hospitality, or in terms of carceral conditioning, or in terms of *bêtise*, for example.

Two final points: the first concerns simplicity and poverty. Daru 'chooses' a life stripped bare: very simple food, one room to live in, no family, few words – a pure or puritan aesthetic. He *is* aware that he is rich compared to the starving Arabs around him – famine victims. But is the famine a natural disaster caused by the inhospitality of the land, which the generous paternal French State does its best to alleviate via distribution of grain, as Camus urges in his political writings and as Daru appears to see it? Or, as Azzedine Haddour

argues forcefully in a recent analysis of the text, is the famine political in cause and effect?[53] The French redistributed fertile land to
themselves as colonisers and displaced more indigenous populations
to areas of Algeria which cannot support them – these populations
can then be supported or not by handouts from the French state.
In times of famine, theft of food is close to murder and the Arab's
crime of killing someone who withheld food seems less distasteful
to us than it is presented in the text. It could even be argued that
the original food thief is the French. We do not know – and cannot
know because Camus gives so little human 'thickness' to him – the
Arab's motivation in the crime or in his setting off to colonial prison
rather than escaping when escape is offered to him on a plate. There
are many forms of resistance and many ways in which resistance
can be blunted. My second closing point with regard to this text is
our inability to know the Arab in it – typically for Camus's Arab or
Berber 'characters', who are often barely more than ciphers, we never
know his name. There is certainly no naming with love.[54]

The would-be hospitable French nation, and its language that
Cixous praises for *its* hospitality, have their share of guilty secrets,
Algeria and Jew being names for some of them. If the relationship
to Algeria is different for Camus, or in Camus's writing, than it
is for Cixous, perhaps it is partly a question of gender as well as
time; his style is simply so 'masculine' and hers so 'feminine'. But
Derrida and his silkworms (who feature in *Veils*) complicate any
picture of *biological* sex.[55] No characteristic ascribed to the feminine
by Cixous or Derrida, including complexity, would be foreign to
Derrida's writing. But an easy retreat from the body into style is no
more satisfying than biological essentialism. The situations we are in,
colonisers-colonised, are at least as important as the way we fashion
ourselves. If we are born Cinnas then, born enemies, we should struggle to be heard as friends, but struggling poetically or heroically to be
friends does not mean we are not born enemies . . .

Notes

1. Cixous's term *Algérifrançaise* is the textual concretisation of the forced
   union, showing its strangeness and strained nature. Thanks to audiences in Tallahassee (Florida), the Institute of Romance Studies, UCL
   and SOAS for comments on this material. Three sections have been
   published: 'French (In)Hospitality', *Contemporary French Civilisation*,
   33:2 (2009), pp. 19–41; 'Language as Hospitality', *Paragraph*, 27:1

(2004), pp. 113–27; 'France and the Paradigm of Hospitality', *Third Text*, 20 (2006), pp. 703–10.

2. I am not completely sure why the translator has inserted 'either'. It is also difficult to relate the following sentence to my French edition.

3. Abdelkebir Khatibi, *Love in Two Languages*, translated by Richard Howard (Minneapolis: University of Minnesota Press, 1990), p. 25; Abdelkebir Khatibi, *Amour Bilingue* (Paris: Fata Morgana, 1983), p. 32.

4. Albert Camus, 'L'Hôte', in *L'Exil et le royaume* (Paris: Gallimard, 1957), pp. 79–99; Albert Camus, 'The Guest', in *Exile and the Kingdom*, translated by Justin O'Brien (Harmondsworth: Penguin, 1962), pp. 65–82.

5. See Louis Althusser on interpellation in 'Ideology and Ideological State Apparatuses', in *Lenin and Philosophy and Other Essays*, translated by Ben Brewster (London: New Left Books, 1971), pp. 121–73; Louis Althusser, 'Idéologie et appareils idéologiques d'Etat', in *Positions* (Paris: Editions sociales, 1976), pp. 79–137. First published in 1970.

6. Amongst many other references, one might cite Brian Friel's play *Translations* (London and Boston: Faber and Faber, 1981), first produced in 1980 in the Guildhall, Derry. London/Derry, or 'slash city' is a name laden with signification and revelatory of allegiances – I thank Sabina Rosdarklin for talking with me about that. Thanks also to Joanne Collie who introduced me to Friel's play.

7. Hélène Cixous, 'La Fugitive', *Etudes littérares*, 33:3 (2001), pp. 75–82, p. 79. I have left *bicot* untranslated: it is a pejorative term for a North African. The dictionary offers wog as a translation, a term that has a much more general purchase – indeed for the English 'wogs begin at Calais', or used to . . . The language of ethnic insults necessarily reflects the history of warfare, colonialism and immigration of the country in question.

8. Cixous, like Derrida, has written extensively about and around her own name. See Hélène Cixous, 'Mon Algériance', *Les Inrockuptibles*, 115, 20 August–2 September 1997, pp. 71–4. 'Mon Algériance' was published as one of the contributions from the Parlement international des écrivains; expanded, and translated by Eric Prenowitz, as 'My Algeriance, in other words: to depart not to arrive from Algeria', in Hélène Cixous, *Stigmata: Escaping Texts* (London: Routledge, 1998), pp. 153–72. See 'My Algeriance' (pp. 157–9) for the possibility that Cixous (not French, not Jewish) is the name of a Berber tribe. Bearing out Cixous's point about the barbarity of her name, it is spelt Cixoux on the front cover of *Voiles*.

9. The name of 'war' is contentious – it took time for the Algerian war to be recognised as such (rather than as 'Troubles' or 'the situation'). In other situations (the French Revolution, J. M. Coetzee's Barbarians)

it is crucial to claim that war has effectively been declared and that enemies must be named. Northern Ireland and Iraq are other examples. In *Philosophy in a Time of Terror: Dialogues with Jürgen Habermas and Jacques Derrida*, interviewed by Giovanna Borradori (Chicago and London: University of Chicago Press, 2003); *Le 'concept' du 11 septembre: Dialogues à New York (octobre–décembre 2001) avec Giovanna Borradori* (Paris: Galilée, 2004), Derrida questions 'the war on terror' (e.g. *PTT*, pp. 102–3; *Le 'concept'*, p. 155), both the term 'war' and that of 'terror' do not go without saying. He continues: 'Every terrorist in the world claims to be responding in self-defence to a prior terrorism on the part of the state, one that simply went by other names and covered itself with all sorts of more or less credible justifications' (*PTT*, p. 103) ('Tous les terroristes du monde prétendent répliquer, pour se défendre, à un terrorisme d'État antérieur qui, ne disant pas son nom, se couvre de toutes sortes de justifications plus ou moins crédibles' (*Le 'concept'*, p. 156)).

10. See Geoffrey Bennington, 'Derridabase', in Geoffrey Bennington and Jacques Derrida, *Jacques Derrida*, translated by Geoffrey Bennington (Chicago and London: University of Chicago Press, 1993); Geoffrey Bennington and Jacques Derrida, *Jacques Derrida* (Paris: Seuil, 1991).

11. Jacques Derrida, 'A Number of Yes', translated by Brian Holmes, in *Qui Parle*, 2:2 (1988), pp. 120–33 ; Jacques Derrida, 'Nombre de Oui', in *Psyché: Inventions de l'autre* (Paris: Galilée, 1987), pp. 639–50, p. 639. There is a footnote on p. 643 on femininity and affirmation. See also 'Nietzsche and the Machine', in Elizabeth Rottenberg (ed.), *Negotiations. Interventions and Interviews 1971–2001* (Stanford: Stanford University Press, 2002), pp. 247–8.

12. See *Jacques Derrida* for Bennington's claim that this short essay on Michel de Certeau 'can appear to contain *the whole of Derrida* (if only you have read the rest) in a condensation that would demand hundreds of pages of commentary. This originary "yes", another nickname for what escapes the question "What is . . .?" (AL, p. 296; PS, p. 163), replies to the pre-originary gift (cf. AL, p. 297, where the "yes" replies to the "primal telephonic 'hello'") countersigns it in opening itself to the repetition whose trace is already inscribed in its "first" time' ('Derridabase', p. 202. His references are to *Psyche* and to Jacques Derrida, *Acts of Literature/Jacques Derrida*, ed. Derek Attridge [London and New York: Routledge, 1992]).

13. See Jacques Derrida, 'Ulysses Gramophone: Hear Say Yes in Joyce', translated by Tina Kendall with Shari Benstock, in Derrida, *Acts of Literature/Jacques Derrida*, pp. 253–309; Jacques Derrida, 'Ulysse gramophone ouï-dire de Joyce', in *Ulysse gramophone: Deux mots pour Joyce* (Paris: Galilée, 1987), pp. 57–143. Derrida addresses saying yes (and laughing yes) throughout his work – explicitly, for example, in

writing on Nietzsche or Blanchot (*Parages*) or on the hymen – always relating it to femininity. The possibility of confusion *dire/rire* (particularly on the telephone) amuses him – and it has of course a particular phonological link to (the consonants in) his own name Derrida as he points out in 'Ulysses Gramophone'. Yes translated as *Ja* has a particular link to his three first names – a syllable they all share. Elijah (Derrida's secret name) is a key figure in 'Ulysses Gramophone'.

14. Her wise mother recognises the clothes that she and her maids have made, and thus knows that Odysseus is not quite what he seems or at least is in borrowed trappings – she therefore asks him who he is.

15. See Rousseau's *Confessions*, Book VI, translated by J. M. Cohen (Harmondsworth: Penguin, 1953), p. 237 (*Oeuvres complètes* I, pp. 249–50), for the episode where Rousseau pretends to be an Englishman called Dudding. See Geoffrey Bennington, *Dudding Des Noms de Rousseau* (Paris: Galilée, 1991) for analysis of this and other examples.

16. Bennington's *Dudding* is a tour de force analysis of Rousseau's various adopted names related in his autobiographical writings, and the problematic question of the signature and of fakes and forgeries for Rousseau. This work is not only clearly indebted to Derrida's work on the signature, but is in some ways addressed to Derrida – poignantly as the message must on some level fail to arrive. But it is not only the mode of *pathos* that should mark this – also *ludos*, the game that is also played in *Jacques Derrida*.

17. See Rachel Bowlby, 'Flight Reservations', *Oxford Literary Review*, 10 (1988), pp. 61–72.

18. Nicholas Harrison, 'Learning From Experience: Hélène Cixous's "Pieds nus"', *Paragraph*, 27:1 (2004), pp. 21–32, pp. 21–2.

19. For Derrida, however, it is her gift in both senses. 'Her avowal of avowal gives us food for reading. Food for thought, suddenly, or for dreaming something that's obvious' (*Veils*, p. 37) ('Son aveu d'aveu donne à lire. Il donne à penser, tout à coup, ou à rêver une évidence', (*Voiles*, p. 39)). He comments elsewhere that it is all the more a gift because it gives him nothing. In *Veils* he moves between an analysis of Cixous's tale of her (literal) laser operation to the operation she performs on language (as he does): 'The instance of this irreplaceable operation, hers, this time, the poetic one, will in return have cut into language with a laser. That instance will have moved, burned, wetted, then cut up the old-new French language, the well-beloved language whose inheritors we are, but also the thieves, the usurpers, the spies, the secret agents, the colonized-colonizers, the artisans, the obscure weavers, deep in their shop, for it owes everything to us, does French language, she to whom we owe even more at the moment we get into it, that is [*à savoir*] . . .' (pp. 36–7) ('L'instant de cette irremplaçable opération, la sienne, cette fois, la poétique, aura en retour incisé la langue au laser.

Il aura attendri, brûlé, mouillé, puis découpé la vieille-neuve langue française, la langue bien aimée dont nous sommes, nous, les héritiers mais aussi les voleurs, les usurpateurs, les espions, les agents secrets, les colonisés colonisateurs, les artisans, les tisserands obscurs, au fond de leur échoppe, car elle nous doit tout, la langue française, elle à qui nous devons encore plus au moment de nous y engager, à savoir . . .' (p. 39)). Of course not all other critics have been hostile; apart from those cited elsewhere in this book, I would mention Morag Shiach, *Hélène Cixous: A Politics of Writing* (London: Routledge, 1991); Susan Sellers, *Hélène Cixous: Authorship. Autobiography and Love* (Cambridge: Polity and Blackwell, 1996); Susan Sellers (ed.), *The Hélène Cixous Reader* (New York: Routledge, 1994); Elizabeth Fallaize, *French Women's Writing: Recent Fiction* (Basingstoke: Macmillan, 1993); Françoise van Rossum Guyon and Myriam Diaz-Diocaretz Eds), *Hélène Cixous, chemins d'une écriture* (Amsterdam: Rodopi, 1990); and Verena Andermatt Conley, *Hélène Cixous: Writing the Feminine* (Lincoln: University of Nebraska Press, 1991) amongst other works.

20. While Cixous continues to do important work as a literary critic (and a teacher), her most significant body of work over the last thirty years lies in her 'fiction' ('fictions fictively said to be autobiographical' ('fictions dites fictivement autobiographiques') as Derrida puts it in *Genèses*, p. 18), and her writing for the theatre. While at first she was criticised by some Anglophone critics for what they diagnosed as an essentialism that precluded consideration of racial or class differences (for example, Ann Rosalind Jones, 'Writing the Body: Towards an Understanding of l'Ecriture féminine', in Elaine Showalter (ed.), *The New Feminist Criticism* [London: Virago, 1986], pp. 369–71), her theatre makes clear what was already the case – that cultural and class differences are crucial to her work. Critics may not like her treatment of colonial and post-colonial issues but there is no longer any denying their centrality if we consider her entire oeuvre. While some of Cixous's plays take world historical events as their subject, her prose writing works with a smaller palette albeit one that is criss-crossed with questions of difference. I referred above to 'fiction' but such a term could be misleading – and even 'prose writing' is only correct in a strict sense since her prose is highly poetic. Important recent publications include a number of hybrid forms that cross generic boundaries and, in particular, the boundary between referential truth and products of the imagination: autofiction or altofiction, texts 'about' close family, friends or animals, the transcription of dreams (*Dream I Tell You*), notebooks (*The Writing Notebooks*).

21. See Marian Hobson, 'Derrida: Hostilities and Hostages (to Fortune)', *Paragraph*, 28:3 (2005), pp. 79–84. See *PTT*, p. 106 (*Le 'concept'*, p. 161), for a definition of the philosopher. In some texts Derrida

has clearly not wanted to be enclosed within philosophy; see *HJR* for example. Rodolphe Gasché's work on Derrida is probably the most strongly philosophical.

22. Jacques Derrida, *Points . . . Interviews, 1974–1994*, ed. Elizabeth Weber, translated by Peggy Kamuf (Stanford: Stanford University Press, 1995), pp. 343–4; Jacques Derrida, 'Une "folie" doit veiller sur la pensée', in *Points de Suspension: Entretiens choisis et présentés par Elisabeth Weber* (Paris: Galilée, 1992), pp. 349–75, p. 354. Derrida may be named after Jackie Coogan ('Koogan' in Cixous, *Portrait de Jacques Derrida en Jeune Saint Juif* [Paris: Galilée, 2001], p. 30), the kid in the Chaplin film *The Kid* (who rose to even greater fame in the 1960s as Uncle Fester in the popular television series *The Addams Family*). I should like to thank Keith Fairless for this reference. He also has a secret Hebrew name, Elie (Elijah) which haunts his circumfessions. Unlike the Hebrew names given to his siblings, Derrida's was not registered.

23. *MO*, p. 79 ff; *MA*, p. 92 ff. The translated title sadly has to lose the proximity of *l'hôte* and *l'autre*.

24. Willy Maley, 'Review of Jacques Derrida, *Monolingualism of the Other; or, The Prosthesis of Origin*', *Textual Practice*, 15:1 (Spring 2001), pp. 123–34.

25. This refers to the imposition of what we know as French and the suppression of the many (then) rich and vibrant regional tongues such as Breton or Occitan.

26. The figure of the school teacher has a different resonance in French and Francophone culture than in, say, British or American culture. The school teacher is often seen as the upholder of Republican virtues of universalism and, in particular, secularism or laicity. Most recently this has brought controversy when young Muslim women have been banned from French classrooms for wearing headscarves – religious symbols and marks of separateness that are seen as intolerable.

27. This certainly leads us to Paul de Man's 'Excuses', in *Allegories of Reading*, pp. 278–30, if not to Derrida's many writings on de Man after his death. De Man is of course a key instance of a deconstructive critic whose life has complicated his work for many readers.

28. See Timothy Pooley, *Chtimi: The Urban Vernaculars of Northern France* (Clevedon: Multilingual Matters, 1996), pp. 214–23, for a number of references to work on gender-preferential differences and why 'given similar social characteristics, women almost always use variants closer to the standard prestige norm for any given variable than men'. He cites Trudgill's claim that this is 'the single most consistent finding to emerge from sociolinguistic studies over the past twenty years' (p. 214). I am grateful to Mikael Jamin for this reference. Pierre Bourdieu (who also may be presumed to have lost his accent)

has written about women's greater docility in relation to the educative process. See, for example, Pierre Bourdieu and Jean-Claude Passeron, *The Inheritors: French Students and their Relation to Culture*, translated by Richard Nice (Chicago and London: Chicago University Press, 1979) (*Héritiers, les étudiants et la culture* [Paris: Minuit, 1964]), Chapter 3. I am grateful to Jeremy Lane for this reference. Of course the relevance of this material to the particular case of Derrida would require a far more extensive and subtle analysis than I have space for in this aside.

29. Cixous refers to the links between Derrida's autobiographical project and Rousseau's in *Portrait*, e.g. pp. 36, 47, 78–9, 104–10; 40, 49, 73, 92, 97–101.

30. St Augustine is the explicit and foregrounded intertext in *Circonfession*. His *Confessions* are the pretext to be 'deep in the history of penitence, from repentence to regret and contrition, from public avowal with expiation to private avowal and confession . . .' (Derrida, 'Circumfession' section 17, in Bennington and Derrida, *Jacques Derrida*, p. 86); ('plongé dans l'histoire de la pénitence, du repentir au regret et à la contrition, de l'aveu public avec expiation à l'aveu privé et à la confession . . .' (Derrida, 'Circonfession', section 17, in Bennington and Derrida, *Jacques Derrida*, p. 84)).

31. The role of interviews in the presentation of 'French' theory and theorists has recently been explored in Christopher Johnson (ed.), *Thinking in Dialogue: The Role of the Interview in Post-War French Thought*, special issue of *Nottingham French Studies*, 42:1 (2003). The letters in Derrida's names are tenderly and poetically set to play not only in *Jacques Derrida* but also in Cixous's *Portrait*: she picks out of course the *e* at the end of Jackie, 'his feminine *silenced*' (p. 23) (son féminin *tu* (p. 30)).

32. Of course many Christian names are equally Jewish names with a source in the Bible – how they are perceived will depend on the place and the moment.

33. He discusses this in, for example, *H.C. pour la vie, c'est à dire* (Paris: Galilée, 2002). I shall return to this in Chapter 6.

34. Cixous, 'My Algeriance', p. 164. The original French text does not include the section on the shop or the episode with the shoeshine. These elements are to be found in Hélène Cixous, 'Pieds nus', in Leila Sebbar (ed.), *Une enfance algérienne* (Paris: Gallimard, 1997), pp. 57–66, p. 60.

35. Hélène Cixous, *Reveries of the Wild Woman Primal Scenes*, translated by Beverley Bie Brahic (Evanston: Northwestern University Press, 2006), p. 72; Hélène Cixous, *Les Rêveries de la femme sauvage Scènes primitives* (Galilée: Paris, 2000), p. 126.

36. 'My Algeriance', p. 157 (Mon Algériance', p. 72); *Reveries*, e.g. pp.

6, 51–5 (*Rêveries*, e.g. pp. 14, 90–6). I first came across this thanks to Mary Stevens, and I am grateful to Gill Rye for the reference.

37. The French invented the term 'Mauresque' to designate North African women; it conjures up a certain erotic exoticism. See, for example, Malek Alloula, *Le Harem colonial, images d'un sous-érotisme* (essai illustré de photographies) (Paris: Séguier, 2001); *The Colonial Harem* translated by Myrna Godzich and Wlad Godzich, Introduction by Barbara Harlow (Manchester: Manchester University Press, 1987); See also Leyla Belkaïd, *Belles Algériennes de Geiser: costumes, parures et bijoux*, Introduction 'L'autre regard' by Malek Alloula (Paris: Marval, 2001), for numerous examples of postcards from colonial Algeria made up of photographs labelled 'Mauresque'.

38. The reference to the Ouled Naïl creates an interesting intertext for the reader familiar with Gide's *Si le grain ne meurt*. In my 'Not Really Prostitution: The Political Economy of Sexual Tourism in Gide's *Si le grain ne meurt*', *French Studies*, LIV (2000), pp. 17–34, I try to bring together some of the debates surrounding 'love' for the exotic other. These are also relevant to readings of Barthes, see my 'Gendered Economies and Aneconomies: the Ambiguous Case of Barthes's "Incidents"', *Iichiko intercultural*, 11 (1999), pp. 43–64.

39. Later in life Cixous has a companion and amanuensis called Fatima, the dedicatee of *Rêve je te dis*.

40. See Alison Rice, 'Rêveries d'Algérie. Une terre originaire à perte de vue dans l'oeuvre d'Hélène Cixous', *Expressions maghrébines*, special issue on Cixous, 2:2 (2003), pp. 93–108, for an analysis of the title and the intertextual links to Rousseau. See also Rosello, 'Frapper aux portes'. She argues that the text, with its obsessive repetition that there was no hospitality in Algeria, undoes the notion of a birthplace which is the first model of hospitality, a place to which (like Odysseus) you can always return. Cixous shows that in her impossible position even asking for an invitation, even *frapper à la porte* (knocking at the door) would be a potential act of violence – and *frapper* can be used in the sense of beating (a person) as well as communicating the idea of a polite tap (on a door).

41. Ronnie Scharfman, 'Narratives of Internal Exile: Cixous, Derrida, and the Vichy Years in Algeria', in Anne Donadey and H. Adlai Murdoch (eds), *Postcolonial Theory and Francophone Literary Studies* (Gainesville: University Press of Florida, 2005), pp. 87–101. I should like to thank Françoise Lionnet for bringing this chapter to my attention.

42. I should like to juxtapose this with a hitch-hiking scene from Barthes's *Incidents*. See my 'Gendered Economies and Aneconomies'.

43. See Derrida, *Politics of Friendship*, throughout, but in terms of the

exclusion of the sister see for some particular examples *PF*, pp. viii, 238, 265, 274, 281 ff (*PA*, pp. 13, 266, 297, 304, 312).

44. Mairéad Hanrahan has commented on this scene in '*Les Rêveries de la femme sauvage* ou le temps de l'hospitalité', *Expressions maghrébines*, special issue on Cixous, 2:2 (2003), pp. 55–70. She points out the father's internationalism (similar to the mother's sense that she is international like a new-born baby). The mother's refusal of hospitality given to her only on account of her Jewish identity by other Jews is matched by the refusal of either Arab or French families to invite her.

45. Emmanuel Lévinas, *Dieu, la mort et le temps* (Paris: Grasset, 1993), p. 21, quoted in Derrida, with his interjection, *Adieu*, p. 7; pp. 18–19

46. Studies include Jeanyves Guérin, 'L'autre comme hôte dans les derniers écrits algériens de Camus', in *Le dire de l'hospitalité*, pp. 145–56, which focuses on *Le Premier Homme* (as well as 'The Guest'), a text in which a few (male) Arabs are actually given names (Tamzal, Kaddour, Abder), and which implicitly pleads for a 'fraternal' solution between the various sons of mother Algeria.

47. J. J. Brochier, *Camus, philosophe pour classes terminales* (Paris: Balland, 1979), analyses with wonderful spleen the adoration of those who, he suggests, do not like their philosophy too challenging. See the monthly magazine *Magazine littéraire*, mai 2006, for a much more enthusiastic evaluation.

48. On a human level this is understandable – but seems particularly odd as a public statement from the writer whose powerful work against the death penalty *L'Etranger* shows a French man condemned to death less because he has killed an Arab than because he does not weep at his mother's funeral. A filmed version of Camus's life tries to make his response sympathetic, showing how he makes an off-the-cuff remark in response to repeated questions shouted by a young Algerian, with whom he would rather see fraternal solidarity.

49. Albert Memmi, *The Coloniser and the Colonised*, translated by Howard Greenfield, introduced by Jean-Paul Sartre, new Introduction by Liam O'Dowd (London: Earthscan, 2003); Albert Memmi, *Portrait du Colonisé* (Paris: Gallimard, [1957] 1985).

50. In his Introduction 'Plaidoyer pour quelques hommes de bonne volonté' to Guy Dugas (ed.), *Algérie: Un rêve de fraternité* (Paris: Omnibus, 1997), Dugas begins by evoking approvingly Camus's speech in Algiers 1956.

51. I should note details in French such as 'camarade', which can mean 'comrade' or 'chum', ironic or patronising, or 'méandres' with its connotations of the geography lesson, or even more importantly 'pays' meaning 'country' as well as 'landscape'.

52. An interesting point of comparison is J. M. Coetzee, *Waiting for the Barbarians* (Harmondsworth: Penguin, [1980] 1982). His Magistrate

who cannot bear the torture of prisoners is obviously a more humanitarian individual than the dehumanised and dehumanising officers of the Third Bureau (Colonel Joll or his subordinate Mandel for example), and acts bravely in attempting to return a prisoner to her home and to speak out against abuses. But he is also part of the Imperial structure. The difference in the later text is the degree of self-awareness on the part of the narrating Magistrate who realises he too dispenses the Law: 'For I was not, as I liked to think, the indulgent pleasure-loving opposite of the cold rigid Colonel' (p. 135); who also muses on the mixture of his motives, and says, for example, towards the end: 'And who am I to jeer at life-giving illusions?' (p. 143).

53. Azzedine Haddour, *Colonial Myths: History and Narrative* (Manchester: Manchester University Press, 2000), e.g. pp. 93–6.

54. See Jeremy Lane, '*La Femme adultère* d'Albert Camus', *Vives Lettres*, 13 (2002), pp. 187–203, for an analysis of another story in *Exile and the Kingdom* drawing attention to the way in which Camus's representation of Algeria and the indigenous inhabitants of Algeria falls into Orientalist stereotypes in spite of his best efforts to escape the colourful clichés of travel writing. This kind of political reading of Camus, while thoroughly acceptable in British or North-American University contexts, imbued with post-colonial theory, can prove highly contentious in France as oblique comments in the introduction to the edition of *Vives Lettres* indicate.

55. See my 'When is a Technology not a Technology? When it's Women's Work' in *The Australian Journal of French Studies* (2011), pp. 129–43, for a brief analysis of Derrida's silkworms.

5

The dangers of hospitality: the French State, cultural difference and gods

The term welcome of the Other expresses a simultaneity of activity and passivity which places the relation with the other outside of the dichotomies valid for things. (Levinas, *Totality and Infinity*, 89)

(Accueil de l'autre – le terme exprime une simultanéité d'activité et de passivité – qui place la relation avec l'autre en dehors des dichotomies valables pour les choses. (Lévinas, *Totalité et Infini*, 62))

The welcoming *of* the other (objective genitive) will already be a response: the *yes to* the other will already be responding to the welcoming *of* the other (subjective genitive), to the *yes* of the other. (Derrida, *Adieu*, 23)

(L'accueil *de* l'autre (génitif subjectif) sera déjà une réponse: le *oui* à l'autre répondra déjà à l'accueil *de* l'autre (génitif objectif), au *oui* de l'autre. (Derrida, *Adieu*, 51))

Traditional stories about hospitality warn of the dangers of not offering hospitality to gods. In ancient Greece, denying hospitality to gods in disguise was not recommended – likewise in the Old Testament, Sodom's inhospitality to the angels disguised as men in the story of Lot is a crime that is severely punished. Derrida and Cixous point out that today (although not for the first time) it is the arrival of migrants 'with their Gods' which seems dangerous and problematic. The previous chapter focused largely on the colonial presence (the uninvited guests) in Algeria, and on those fortunate enough to be more or less welcome to hold French passports: 'Christian' (or secular) Europeans whether they originated from France, or perhaps Spain or Germany; and Jews from the time of the Crémieux decree until Vichy removed their citizenship, and then again after Vichy. Arabs were only allowed to become full French citizens *if they renounced Islam*. How and when does religion enter the story? Does it date back to Medieval propaganda, mendacious representations dating from the crusades and other Christian wars against the infidel? This would not be a comfortable reference point for modern France. Enlightenment secularism, apparently epitomised by the anti-clerical Voltaire, is a more agreeable standpoint, within which reason stands against the benighted forces of prejudice and superstition. Thus attacks on the (Islamic) veil are apparently conducted for the sake of secular universalism (a value intimately related to education) as well as in the name of equality for women.[1]

This chapter will pose the question of those who have arrived in France in the post-colonial era either because they originated in former colonies and were pressed to come to work when labour power was needed, or they felt that France would welcome them for that reason, or because they believed in France as a country that took in refugees. Before their situation is regularised it might seem less controversial to designate these new arrivals as 'guests'. I shall begin with some remarks about naming and about hospitality then move on to this question of the label '*hôte*' (host/guest). When we discuss hospitality towards strangers, as opposed to family or friends, as a political question, we often focus our discussion on the border of the nation state, of the United States or of Europe. However, there are many frontiers *within* the state and within cities, and it is extremely important to consider these too. The precarious status of guest (where that is how an immigrant is perceived) can last, if only in a vestigial form, even after citizenship is granted, and indeed can be a perverse inheritance passed on through the generations. In the final section, I shall return to this question, and ask how this too is related to religion.

Derrida was a key public intellectual speaking up on political questions including Eastern European issues, Nelson Mandela's imprisonment and the apartheid regime more generally, and the imprisonment of African-Americans in the United States (composing an open letter to President and First Lady Clinton about Mumia Abu-Jamal).[2] The title of a collection of some of these interventions, *Negotiations*, reminds the reader of the tension between, on the one hand, the ethical and political imperative and, on the other, the impossibility of, say, hospitality – which cannot be a place to rest but can interrupt what might otherwise petrify into fixed political (op)positions. Against those who would suggest that there is an incommensurability between his philosophical work on undecidability and any political engagement, and that therefore he cannot have his cake and eat it, Derrida argues that:

> It is to the extent that knowledge does not program everything in advance, to the extent that knowledge remains suspended and undecided

as to action, to the extent that a responsible decision as such will never be measured by any form of knowledge, by a clear and distinct certainty or by a theoretical judgement, that there can and must be responsibility or decision, be they ethical or political. I am a citizen too. It happens that I take politico-institutional initiatives, that I 'intervene,' so to speak.[3]

Derrida's analysis of the arbitrary (or cynically opportunistic) and unjust treatment meted out to undocumented immigrants is both part of this acting as a citizen, and more. His 'decision' is a hospitable extension of citizenship beyond legal definitions which exclude 'undocumented aliens' or those of a different race. Hospitality is both the genre and the substance of Derrida's public political commitment and solidarity with immigrants, with or without appropriate documents. I shall turn in the second section of this chapter to a brief analysis of a section of a piece that is part of his public intellectual work, a speech made on 21 December 1996 in the Théâtre des Amandiers at Nanterre. This was an evening organised by the Hauts-de Seine Collective and the National Organisation of Sans-Papiers to mark solidarity with the *sans-papiers*: people who may have been working and living quite openly in France for many years but who do not have the correct documentation and were threatened with expulsion by recent legislation.[4] In the summer of 1996 about 300 African women and men *sans-papiers* occupied the Church of Saint Bernard in Paris, with ten of them going on hunger strike. This was widely reported and helped to alert both intellectuals and the wider public to the consequences of the Pasqua Laws passed in 1993 which turned the *clandestin* (an immigrant without the appropriate documentation, who will be renamed *sans-papiers*) into a criminal, and made hospitality to *clandestins* an offence that could be punished by up to five years in gaol. On 28 August riot police stormed the Church and expelled those who had sought sanctuary there. Both before and after this event *sans-papiers* took refuge in the Théâtre du Soleil, where Ariane Mnouchkine (in collaboration with Cixous) put on a collective creation *Et Soudain des nuits d'éveil*. In December 1996 Jean-Louis Debré put forward a *projet de loi* on immigration which gave mayors powers to police the *certificat d'hébergement* which was required before immigrants could enter the country – it was supposed to check that they had decent places to stay (and was presented as a benign, hospitable intervention), but was generally experienced as harassment.

Derrida's improvised speech in December 1996 was subsequently published in the journal *Plein Droit*, and in a book *Marx en jeu* which marked the performance of a play (at the same theatre) based on Derrida's *Specters of Marx*.[5] He chooses to analyse the position of undocumented immigrants according to the laws of hospitality – in part because that is an existing construction on the part both of the State and of individuals, and in part because, he suggests, the status of 'guest' need not diminish 'l'hôte' but rather allows the analyst to interweave the pragmatic political debate with an absolute that is an essential reinforcement for a strongly ethical position (even as, one might say, it will undermine it, as absolutes have a tendency to do). René Schérer, another intellectual who uses his study of hospitality to analyse the present situation of immigrants, puts it thus:

> And so we shall see, in the language of hospitality that is gaining momentum, a contamination of the political, since the latter is constantly forced to use that vocabulary, even when it makes hospitality undergo a process that limits and disfigures it. For it really is hospitality which is in question when we need to define who will benefit from the right to asylum, the welcome to be accorded to refugees and migrants. It is hospitality that, like a critical ferment, allows the contradictions of political discourse to be exploded, when it forges expressions like 'undesirable guests', or when it places hospitality under the sign of limitation of asylum or of expulsion.
>
> It practices the inverse of hospitality, but it uses the language. Hospitality, constantly following the movement of the word, brings back onto the scene the thing itself which is in flight.
>
> (Nous verrons donc, dans le vocabulaire hospitalier qui court sur son erre, une contamination de politique, puisque celui-ci est perpétuellement contraint de l'utiliser, même quand il impose à l'hospitalité un traitement qui la limite et la défigure. Car c'est bien effectivement d'hospitalité qu'il est question, lorsqu'il s'agit de définir les bénéficiaires du droit d'asile, l'accueil des réfugiés et des émigrés. C'est elle qui, à la manière d'un ferment critique, permet de faire éclater les contradictions du discours politique lorsqu'il forge des expressions comme celle d''hôtes indésirables', ou qu'il place l'hospitalité sous le signe de la limitation de l'asile et de l'expulsion.
>
> Il pratique l'inverse de l'hospitalité, mais il utilise son langage. L'hospitalité, suivant toujours le mouvement du mot, ramène sur la scène la chose qui fuit.) (*Zeus hospitalier*, 22)

True hospitality is figured here as contamination; when politicians use the term 'undesirable guests' they wish to keep hospitality within bounds, and control it through the restriction imposed by the perversely disfiguring category of desirability – but it ferments and causes fermentation. Thus, Schérer argues, hospitality bursts the grammatical binding between this incompatible adjective and noun: 'undesirable' and 'guest', revealing the contradictions of political discourse, and thus bringing the real meaning of guest back into play when politicians have wanted to expel it along with the deportees.

Yet the very business of evoking *hospitality* in certain socio-political and indeed economic contexts is highly contentious. Even in England, where the public rhetoric of hospitality is less striking than in France, it is used to a range of ends. Newspapers reported in February 2005 that 'Home Office sources said abuses of the system had led to a feeling that "the fairness and hospitality of the British people had been tested"'.[6] In France it has of course particular historical resonances. The issue of vocabulary is complex and important – and the question of naming those who are in a position of vulnerability is a sensitive one, as argued in Chapter 4. (Naming the powerful as they wish to be named, as noble for example, tends to be imposed upon us.) 'Illegal immigrants', 'asylum seekers', 'enemy aliens', *clandestins*, *sans-papiers* all have their different resonances. Even 'immigrants', 'Arabs',[7] '*beurs*', 'individuals of Maghrebi origin', or 'second-generation' can be loaded terms for reasons that could be unpacked at length – particularly in the context of a State discourse of Republican universalism according to which all French citizens are simply that. They can be terms that stigmatise or they can form part of a powerful counter-discourse. Designating individuals as guests or the State as host (as opposed to, say, speaking of workers and their employer) is described by Rosello as 'a metaphor that has forgotten that it is a metaphor' (*Postcolonial Hospitality*, 3). This is an interesting hypothesis, but I am not so sure we can easily presuppose a proper use of the terms that would underpin what we could agree was figural – or that an inter-individual sense and practice of hospitality in any one culture precedes a collective sense and practice of hospitality. Thus I am not sure whether this political use of hospitality is always a metaphor, nor whether it is always forgotten or whether its rhetorical weight is strategically deployed.[8] From one particular (usually right-wing) political position, calling immigrants 'guests' reminds them or 'us' that their status is more precarious than that of others, say, 'citizens'. They might be told to 'go home' if they do not behave themselves. From a different political standpoint, the use of the term guest has a powerful ethical charge. Schérer claims that it leads to 'the indignant start, the more than moral repulsion that is aroused by the refusal to take someone in or the decision to

expel [the guest]' ('le sursaut d'indignation, la répulsion plus que
morale que suscitent le refus de recevoir ou la décision d'expulser
[l'hôte]') (*Zeus hospitalier*, 41). He refers to 'the almost sacred
horror which accompanies extraditions, even when they seem to be
justified by offences or crimes' ('l'horreur presque sacrée qui accom-
pagne les extraditions, même lorsqu'elles peuvent sembler justifiées
par des infractions ou des crimes') (41–2). This may, however, be
more true of France – with its particular experiences of Nazi occupation as well as its tradition of Republican hospitality dating back to
the 1790s – than it is of the United States or the UK.

Naming *l'hôte*

The question of naming a relationship 'hospitality', of defining one
party as a host, another as a guest is not, however, a simple one –
not simple in social or political terms and certainly not simple for
the philosopher, Derrida. His Paris seminar 'Hostipitality' is as
yet unpublished, and so most readers are reliant either on the sections translated by Anidjar or on fragments quoted by others, such
as Michaud. She cites his words: 'We are also implying that we do
not yet know who and what will come, nor, furthermore, what *is
called* "hospitality" and what *is called* in hospitality, that is to say,
first of all hospitality *calls itself* [or *is named*] even if that calling is
not embodied in human language' ('Nous sous-entendons aussi que
nous ne savons pas encore qui et ce qui va venir, ni davantage ce qui
s'appelle 'l'hospitalité' et ce qui *s'appelle* dans l'hospitalité, à savoir
que l'hospitalité, d'abord ça *s'appelle*, même si cet appel ne prend
pas corps dans du langage humain' ('Hostipitalité', 15 November
1995, cited in Michaud, 'Un acte d'hospitalité', 35). Hospitality 'calls
itself /is called' – the French reflexive is normally translated by an
English passive.[9] Michaud makes the point that hospitality cannot
name itself: the act of saying 'this is hospitality' or 'I am hospitable'
annuls itself (35). This is the kind of assertion that certainly emerges
from Derrida's analysis of the Law of hospitality (and also has an
everyday resonance), but need not be understood as a solitary absolute. It co-exists with the spectrum of more or less hospitable words
and gestures governed by the laws of hospitality. Any statement
such as 'I am hospitable' will exist in a context, and could be used
with sophisticated irony, or with such simplicity that it evades the
obvious odious gesture of mastery. At the same time, the words need
not be *spoken* for their meaning to be communicated in almost any

gesture of hospitality. Derrida analyses in detail the polite formula 'Faites comme chez vous', insisting on the role of 'comme' to *remind* the guest that this is a fiction and that s/he cannot be 'at home' as much as the host is. In English we might note that 'Make yourself at home' implies that you are not always already at home as the host is, but must perform being, or 'make yourself' be, at home in the host's house. Thus all these hospitable expressions carry a germ of inhospitality in their reminder of the respective positions of host and guest, just as Schérer shows how inhospitable uses of the language of hospitality can be contaminated by true hospitality.

Anidjar comments:

> But who or what is the subject of hospitality? To one reading of this question, the French language provides a disarmingly and quantitatively simple answer; the *hôte*. In French, the hôte is both the one who gives, *donne*, and the one who receives, *reçoit*, hospitality. As Derrida argues, however, this distinction finds its condition in the aporetic laws of hospitality that, prior to either, give to both hôtes the possibility and impossibility of the gift of hospitality. . . . To translate this hôte as either 'host' or 'guest' would be to erase the demand made by hospitality as well as the violence that is constitutive of it, 'the notion of the *hostis* as host or as enemy.' ('A Note on "Hostipitality"', in Derrida, *Acts of Religion*, 356)

What Anidjar calls 'the aporetic laws of hospitality' is, I think, what I have been calling the Law of hospitality (to differentiate it from the social codes of hospitality or the laws passed by nation states in relation to hospitality). I should add that I do not agree that in practical terms it is always impossible to translate *hôte* by either host or guest (although *sometimes* that translation decision is hard if not impossible), and the example given from the beginning of *Adieu* (of the one who dares to say welcome) seems to me to be legitimately translated as 'host' – in so far as any translation is ever legitimate . . . The translation of *hôte* in a French text into *hôte* in an English text is perhaps as violent as the decision to render it as either 'host' or 'guest' since an everyday French word is thereby translated into a philosophical problem. This is rather different from the defamiliarising effect of *différance* which functions in both languages. As *hôte* is used in every context (as in Anidjar's translation of 'Hostipitality') it can become depoliticised; while philosophically or (pre)ontologically we are all both host and guest, in particular contexts it may be critical that we are regarded as one rather than the other.

In spite of my worries about *consistently* translating *hôte* by *hôte*,

I do want to note the homonyms or near-homonyms of *hôte*, the homophonies or near homophonies and echoes such as *ôte(r)* (to remove), or, of course, *l'autre* (the other). For Cixous the French letter par excellence is J (because of the name of the letter, so different in German, so resonant in its implications for *Juifs* or *Juden* in the middle of the last century), but for an Anglophone it is that R which turns *l'hôte* into *l'autre* when we speak French – the sound that as learners of French we most easily recognise as foreign and, little monkeys, enjoy the thrilling sound in our mouths, the trilling feel on our tongues, or hate its/our awkward unfamiliarity. That combination of visual (reading the difference), oral and aural pleasure is a constant for the constant reader of Derrida, 'l'inventeur de la différance, le poète de la danse de l'écrit avec l'ouïe, ouïe si souvent inouïe' (the inventor of *différance*, the poet of the dance of writing with hearing, hearing so often unheard) as Cixous hymns him.[10] His significant inventiveness with this language, which both is and is not his mother tongue, does not, of course, far from it, make him beloved of all.

Of even more import is the reversibility, the reciprocity, of the French term *hôte*. This reversibility has not existed in English since the sixteenth century. Bilingual dictionaries have a tendency to play to the English sense that *hôte* must means host (a *faux ami* or false friend as language teachers call it, rather appropriately in this context) and invite us to use the term *invité* for guest. But Schérer argues that it is crucial not to confuse the guest with someone who is *passively* invited (*Zeus hospitalier*, 148). Gotman, who has written a major sociological study of hospitality, is a good example of the French *resistance* to this easy solution to the potential confusion between *hôte* and *hôte*. Two other points that interest me about the definitions of the *hôte* are (a) the constant possibility of interference from the economic, and (b) the play of sexual difference.

I should like to cite two examples to reinforce the point.[11] First Gotman makes the following comments about terminology: 'Of course *hôte* in French is used to designate both host and guest. This double meaning is sometimes attributed to the reciprocity of the institution [of hospitality] which requires that *l'hôte* be alternatively in the one and then the other place' ('On le sait, *hôte* en français s'emploie aussi bien pour désigner celui qui reçoit que celui qui est reçu. Ce double sens est attribué par certains à la réciprocité de l'institution qui veut que l'hôte soit alternativement à l'une et l'autre place') (*Le Sens de l'hospitalité*, 9). *L'hôte* would thus be a figure for the practice or institution of hospitality – and this would be more important than which role the individual plays at any given moment since reciprocity would be assured. In the Shorter OED an obsolete sense of the English 'host', given with the latest recorded date of 1559 is 'A guest'. Yet reciprocity is only one model of hospitality – the other one being that of superabundant generosity. Gotman continues:

> Whether this is true or not, the confusion that can come out of this lack of differentiation requires in some situations that you adopt certain conventions. I have therefore chosen the terms *master of the house* and *hôte* [guest] in order to designate whenever necessary the two positions respectively, the latter nevertheless being able to be used to designate host when the context is completely unambiguous.

> (Quoiqu'il en soit, la confusion qui peut résulter de cette indifférenciation oblige, dans certains cas, à adopter des conventions. Pour désigner sans ambiguïté leurs positions respectives, j'ai donc choisi, chaque fois que nécessaire, les termes de *maître de maison* et *hôte*; ce dernier terme pouvant néanmoins être employé pour désigner celui qui reçoit lorsque le contexte ne laisse aucune ambiguïté possible.) (*Le Sens de l'hospitalité*, 9–10)

This seems perverse for Anglophone readers since *hôte* conjures up host for us first, but of course she is writing for a French-speaking audience. Nevertheless to suggest *maître de maison* without comment, as if it were a neutral equivalent for host – bearing in mind that Gotman's politics in general seem to err on the radical side – tells us something about the ingrained nature of the gender issues here. Later in her work (68) there is a brief pejorative reference to the *maîtresse de maison* as a cipher of inhospitality – not wanting dirt to be brought into her nice, clean house – reminiscent of Beauvoir's housewife in *The Second Sex*. To finish the quote from Gotman:

> Likewise, when the situation clearly evokes the co-presence and complementarity of the protagonists of hospitality, as in the expression 'between host and guest', it is the word '*hôtes*' in the plural which is used to designate the whole composed by host and guest.
>   I have resisted as much as possible the very useful neologisms invented by Jean-Michel Belorgey '*hôtants*' and '*hôtés*', except in the fourth section, when the hugely complex exchanges of role made it necessary.

> (De même, lorsque la situation évoque clairement la coprésence et la complémentarité des protagonistes de l'hospitalité, comme dans la formule 'entre les hôtes', c'est le mot *hôtes* au pluriel qui sert à désigner l'ensemble de celui qui reçoit et celui qui est reçu.

J'ai résisté autant que faire se peut aux néologismes fort commodes de Jean-Michel Belorgey 'hôtants' et 'hôtés', sauf dans la quatrième partie, lorsque les échanges de rôles particulièrement complexes l'ont exigé.) (*Le Sens de l'hospitalité*, 10)

Gotman goes on to consider other terms – but never suggests using *invité* for guest and *hôte* for host.

I shall turn from Gotman's difficulties to a bilingual French-English dictionary for my second example. *L'hôte*, a masculine noun, is said to mean host in both the social and the biological sense, and *l'hôte*, a masculine or feminine noun, means guest (both nouns also mean occupant). My Oxford-Hachette French-English dictionary tells me this,[12] and then when I look up *host* I find that masculine noun *l'hôte*. ('Hostess' or '*hôtesse*' meanwhile have a range of sexed *professional* meanings, such as hostess in a night-club.) But when I look up *guest* then I find a host of expressions such as *invité(e)*, *client/-e* or *pension- naire*. Unlike Gotman, the bilingual dictionary runs from *hôte* as the most obvious translation of guest. The only occurrences of *hôte* as a translation for guest are masculine: *hôte payant* (introducing the eco- nomic) and what is termed 'the biological' *hôte* – a very odd expres- sion that I took to mean 'parasite'. I did find 'parasite' as a meaning of guest in the shorter OED, but this struck me as pretty unusual and hence strange in a fairly selective and modern bilingual diction- ary. Starting from the French again: I could not find *hôte* in the *Petit Robert* (or the *Trésor de la langue française*) as meaning biological 'parasite', only biological 'host'. Thus that biological – as opposed to social – reversibility strangely introduced from the English does not seem to exist in French. Again turning to the translations of 'guest' in the bilingual dictionary: two translations are given for guest worker – *travailleur immigré* and *travailleuse immigrée*. I could not find 'guest worker' in an English dictionary, although of course many of us would recognise it as a translation of a German phenomenon (a term invented for a country that needed labour but did not have the colonial reserves to draw on that England and France had). I should like to underline the importance of gender and power – and the prox- imity of economic structures – in these definitions.

Strangers or undocumented aliens

I remember a bad day last year: it was as if the breath was knocked out of me, and I was really going to be sick, when I heard for the first time, barely understanding the term, 'the crime of hospitality'. In fact, I'm not sure I did hear it, I wonder if anyone could really ever have pronounced those words, and had that venomous expression in their mouth, no, I didn't hear it and I can hardly repeat it, I read it silently in an official document.

(L'an dernier, je me rappelle un mauvais jour: j'avais eu comme le souffle coupé, un haut le coeur en vérité, quand j'ai entendu pour la première fois, la comprenant à peine, l'expression '*délit d'hospitalité*'. En fait, je ne suis pas sûr de l'avoir entendue, car je me demande si quelqu'un a jamais pu la prononcer, et la prendre dans sa bouche, cette expression venimeuse, non, je ne l'ai pas entendue, et je peux à peine la répéter, je l'ai lue sans voix, dans un texte officiel.)[13]

First of all I'd like to note 'Je', the personal form, especially personal for J.D.[14] Names, and signatures, are very important here. Also J for Jew (*juif, Jude*). Cixous has often told the story of how her mother in mid-twentieth-century Algeria (a dangerous time and place, although also a refuge, a less dangerous place at that time than Germany or Vichy France for example) carefully took the precaution of only ever using J for Jew – especially on the street (see Cixous, *Portrait*, 3; 11). Appellations have enormous power, at any time and in any place (but specific to a context), to damage or to empower, to dehumanise or to show respect or indeed love ('love' as a designation being a good example of the importance of context), as analysed in Chapter 4. In the violent contexts of colonisation, of war, and of exclusion, appellations can be particularly powerful. The J-word being a case in point. Derrida will go on to talk about the name *sans-papiers*. He takes language extremely seriously. The dizzying effect of some of his writing has led certain readers to emphasise *play*, even free play. A lightness of touch in passing over allusively, elusively a range of references to matters he has discussed extensively elsewhere can be considered lightweight or just modishly obscurantist. For me, in spite of the humorous moments, the work is always also serious, serious in its passion.

Derrida chooses in the speech in the Amandiers theatre to speak personally to his audience, almost speaking autobiographically. He speaks with passion: 'j'avais eu comme le souffle coupé, un haut le coeur en vérité'. The expression 'the crime of hospitality' is something that you don't want to have in your mouth – we can all think of things – that make you feel dirty just to have them pass your lips. The expulsion of the words is like taking in their venomous meaning. You don't want to hear these expressions either – the poison can enter through the ear as well as other orifices. Emotional reactions with physical symptoms – breath knocked out of you, you can't breathe, you feel sick. Derrida thinks aloud that he can't have heard it, no-one would have said it, he must have read it 'sans voix' (we might note the infectious *sans*). Reading writing rather than hearing speaking – what's the difference? To answer this as a grammatical rather than rhetorical question: it is partly a question of context. Even if certain expressions are poisonous in themselves, it would be more contaminating to be in the audience at a National Front rally or to hear a neighbour casually speak as if with your consent.

In *Adieu*, Derrida suggests that Levinas appeals to his reader to consider the plight of many different kinds of 'refugees' and migrants since at least the First World War, aggravated by the crimes *against* hospitality:

> The crimes against hospitality endured by the guests [*hôtes*] and hostages of our time, incarcerated or deported day after day, from concentration camp to detention camp, from border to border, close to us or far away. (Yes, crimes *against* hospitality, to be distinguished from an offense of hospitality [*délit d'hospitalité*],' as today it is once again being called in French law, in the spirit of the decrees and ordinances of 1938 and 1945 that would punish – and even imprison – anyone taking in a foreigner in an illegal situation.) (*Adieu*, 71)

> (Les crimes contre hospitalité qu'endurent les hôtes et les otages de notre temps, jour après jour incarcérés ou expulsés, de camp de concentration en camp de rétention, de frontière en frontière, près de nous ou loin de nous. (Oui, les crimes *contre* l'hospitalité, à distinguer du 'délit d'hospitalité' aujourd'hui réactualisé sous ce nom par le droit français, dans l'esprit des décrets et ordonnances de 1938 et 1945, pour sanctionner, jusqu'à la peine de prison, quiconque héberge un étranger en situation illégale). (132))

But now we come to repetition. We are brought to representation. If something can be said (or written) then it can be repeated – even if 'à peine', barely; we Anglophones might say, painfully. It is the condition of language that we *can* repeat – even if the repetition is never the same as the first (or last) time some thing was said or written, if only because it is a repetition. The repetition may be like a theatrical 'répétition' (and Derrida is speaking in a theatre) where we speak the words of others without taking responsibility for them – acting has some links to academic quotation but of course there is a difference too, a corporeal and passional difference. And in this case at the Amandiers theatre, like the work at the Cartoucherie theatre to which Derrida refers, speaking is also acting, *agir*, and bearing witness. We have a duty to repeat. Theatrical representation can become asylum when parliamentary representatives are closing borders, imposing phobic controls and limits, policing both those who offer hospitality and their guests.

Derrida raises the question in this speech of not only (perhaps not ever) speaking *for* in the sense of 'in the place of' others ('Quand j'ai entendu l'expression', 4) – the deprived, those described or named privatively with *sans*. *Sans-papiers* (illegal immigrants), *sans abri* (homeless), *sans emploi* (unemployed) and so on. Cixous raises the same point with respect to refugees when writing about the play *The Last Caravanserai*, a play that is composed of the words of refugees, their stories in their own words:

> How is it possible not to replace the words in your mouth even with well-intentioned words?
>
> How is it possible not to replace your foreign tongue with our French tongue?
>
> How can we keep your foreign tongue without being impolite and inhospitable to our public, our guests in the theatre?
>
> How is it possible for our hearts to communicate when we don't understand each other's words?
>
> How is it possible not to appropriate others' pain when we turn it into theatre?
>
> (Comment ne pas remplacer la parole de ta bouche par la parole même de bonne volonté?
>
> Comment ne pas remplacer ta langue étrangère par notre langue française?
>
> Comment garder ta langue étrangère sans manquer de politesse et d'hospitalité à l'égard du public, notre hôte dans le théâtre?
>
> Comment, sans se comprendre en mots, se comprendre quand même en coeur?
>
> Comment ne pas s'approprier l'angoisse des autres en en faisant du théâtre?)[15]

In the context of the Théâtre des Amandiers, rather than the Théâtre de la Cartoucherie, Derrida suggests: 'Here speaking means that the *sans-papiers* have a right to speak: we are here to listen to them and to hear them tell us what they have to say to us, to speak with them and so not merely to speak about them or in their place' ('Parler ici, cela veut dire que les sans-papiers ont droit à la parole: nous sommes là pour les entendre et les écouter nous dire ce qu'ils ont à nous dire, pour parler avec eux et non seulement, donc, pour parler d'eux ou à leur place' ('Quand j'ai entendu l'expression', 4)). They are not 'without' the right to speak in this place. Although they are definitionally, by name 'lacking', without something – in particular without papers which give rights – and then seemingly without human dignity or worth *indigne*, unworthy of French hospitality, like those refugees who were, Derrida reminds us, designated as 'unworthy to live on our soil' ('*indignes de vivre sur notre sol*') (4) in similar xenophobic vein in 1938. Political, fraternal bonds – fraternising – these can be bonds of love or hate, even terror. As Mona Ozouf writes with respect to the French Revolution: 'Exclusion . . . constituted a fraternity of combat. As Sartre ably demonstrated, in every revolutionary group closure is indispensable to the sentiment of fraternity, and violence is inseparable from collective action. In the Revolution, that violence was directed not only against external enemies but internal ones' ('On retrouve . . . l'exclusion constitutive d'une fraternité de combat. Pour tout groupe révolutionnaire, Sartre l'a bien mis en lumière, la clôture est indispensable au sentiment de la fraternité, la violence inséparable de l'action collective. Violence dirigée contre les ennemis extérieurs, mais aussi les ennemis intérieurs').[16] Is the nation always modelled somehow on the family? *Politics of Friendship* returns systematically to the friend as brother: 'the figure of the friend . . . seems spontaneously to belong to a *familial, fraternalist* and thus *androcentric* configuration of politics' (*PF*, viii) ('la figure de l'ami semble spontanément appartenir à une configuration *familiale, fraternaliste* et donc *androcentrée* du politique' (*PA*, 12)). Thinking about hospitality to strangers, openness to others in some sense, usually falls into speculation on inhospitality, and that is certainly the case here.

Nevertheless the power is not simply on the part of the host; it is not just an act of generosity to allow those designated as 'foreigners', rather than 'citizens', to speak – even when these are not foreigners as honoured citizens of a respected country with whom we have reciprocal hospitality arrangements (*xenia*), but foreigners defined negatively as non-citizens, perhaps even state-less. For Derrida, following Levinas, there is a structural inevitability that the stranger will always already question. The *question de l'étranger* (as objective genitive: 'the question of the foreigner') makes the foreigner sound like a problem that 'we' legitimate hosts can and should inquire into and debate, or seems to refer to the inhospitable interrogation of the stranger (for example the asylum seeker), asking them for identity papers or at least a convincing narrative (of unspeakable suffering).[17]

In the opening paragraph of *Of Hospitality*, Derrida typically displaces the genitive 'de' so that 'the question of the foreigner' becomes also the subjective genitive, 'the foreigner's question': the question that the outsider poses to the insider, thus calling the insider into question. This is one of the many valuable (albeit not always comfortable) things that the guest brings to the home. The duality of the genitive *de* (which is also made explicit in the epigraph to this chapter concerning *l'accueil de l'autre*) works rather better in French than in English, where we often prefer an apostrophe followed by 's' to show possession. 'The foreigner's question' is relatively unambiguously different from 'the question of the foreigner' in idiomatic English, indeed it would be a mark that a foreigner was speaking if the two were confused. However, we should not assume too quickly that this is facile French word play. It is critical to the fundamental question of hospitality that where we question the foreigner, the foreigner puts us in question, that where the host welcomes the guest, the host has always already been welcomed.

Yet we need to consider the law and the power of the State. The law, and the people's representatives, have the power to create 'délit d'hospitalité', hospitality as a crime. 'Hospitality is not a crime'; it may seem obvious, particularly to those of us who have a different history, for instance those who did not experience occupation during the Second World War, that such an absolute cannot hold (in other words, that there are contexts where hospitality might indeed be a crime). It is not the Kantian model – which makes hospitality secondary, for example, to truth. For Kant (contra Benjamin Constant) it would be wrong to lie to save a guest, a friend, from assassins, and this Kantian ideal of pure transparency opens up the domestic space to the police (see *OH*, 67; *DH*, 63). Yet emotionally the notion that hospitality cannot be a crime does have a hold, a certain tradition casts a spell (see Schérer, *Zeus hospitalier*, 41–2); this is a tradition other than the Kantian conditional one. There were some interesting articles in the French press supporting Corsican demonstrations in support of Frédéric Paoli (a shepherd as well as a local councillor) who gave shelter to the nationalist Yvan Colonna wanted for the assassination of Claude Erignac.[18] The crime of harbouring illegal immigrants or failing to denounce them or notify the police with respect to the departure of temporary residents is punishable by imprisonment – State (in)hospitality. We can guess of course that those most likely to be punished for the crime of hospitality are those who are themselves still perceived as guests in some sense, even if born in France.

The Enlightenment tradition: tolerance or Islamophobia?

We are haunted by the past, and we should be careful how we fashion its ghosts in the present. The debate in France draws of course on the mythical political hospitality of the French Revolution, arising from the notion of the universal rights of man. The reference to the French Republican tradition often echoes the rhetoric of the 1790s, as I have suggested in Chapter 1, whereby the State would welcome those lovers of liberty and equality who suffer under totalitarian regimes (such as late eighteenth-century England). One rationale for speculation on the past is to discover fractures or contradictions in what may be *present*ed as a seamless or utopian narrative (as Wahnich does for the revolutionary discourse of the 1790s).

The Republican tradition dating back to the French Revolution is evoked in France today as a model of universal fraternal hospitality. One of the filtering devices used to control entry into the stories told about the eighteenth century is a sense of 1789 as the culmination of revolutionary political thought and a rejection of the old regime. Both elements are crucial in our analyses of, and rhetoric about, political and personal hospitality today. There were two exhibitions at the national libraries in Paris from March to May 2006 celebrating the Enlightenment; the main one entitled 'Enlightenment! An Inheritance for Tomorrow' ('Lumières! Un héritage pour demain'), emphasising the continuing relevance of a certain Enlightenment. The presuppositions underlying both the exhibitions and the publications associated with them could be analysed at length; in this context I shall simply quote some pertinent assertions from one editorial; first: 'Speaking of our conception of secularity in the face of the return of the religious and the irrational, is thus also a way of remembering the Enlightenment' ('Se souvenir des Lumières, c'est donc aussi parler de notre conception de la laïcité face au retour du religieux et de l'irrationnel').[19] Here the Enlightenment is mobilised in a coded fashion to address one of the major issues with respect to French 'hospitality' towards immigrants today: Islamic fundamentalism (although it should be said that Protestant fundamentalism, with its American resonances may also be targeted). The editorial begins:

> What an era! Voltaire, Rousseau, Montesquieu, Diderot, Condorcet . . . and also Kant, Hume, Goethe, Mozart, and then Benjamin Franklin, Adam Smith, but also Vico, Beccaria. Libertines and puritans, moderates and radicals, the passionate, the wise, the inspired . . . All free men, terribly free. . . . They were called the Enlightenment. They lived in Europe

in the eighteenth century. People say that they invented everything: secularism, democracy, the rights of man, the emancipation of the individual, the citizen, science, progress . . . Yesterday, we celebrated the eighteenth century for its flightiness, its libertine ways, its discovery of pleasure; today, agonising over our famous 'loss of ground rules', we are looking for indisputable principles.

(Quelle époque! Voltaire, Rousseau, Montesquieu, Diderot, Condorcet . . . et encore Kant, Hume, Goethe, Mozart, et puis Benjamin Franklin, Adam Smith, mais aussi Vico, Beccaria. Des libertines et des austères, des modérés et des radicaux, des tempétueux, des sages, des inspirés . . . Tous hommes libres, terriblement libres. . . . On les appelait les Lumières. Ils vivaient au XVIIIe siècle en Europe. On dit qu'ils ont tout inventé: la laïcité, la démocratie, les droits de l'homme, l'émancipation de l'individu, le citoyen, la science, le progrès . . . Hier, on célébrait le XVIIIe siècle pour sa légèreté, son libertinage, sa découverte du plaisir; aujourd'hui, angoissé par notre fameuse 'perte des repères', nous y cherchons des principes indiscutables.)

The argument is then presented that, while the rejection of these ideas is very dangerous, it is also dangerous to apply them as dogma (the shadow of totalitarianism). The list of great men (and no women), with which this publication, like so many others, opens, begins with Voltaire. The editorial ends with an invocation of what is seen as his hallmark, irony, as perhaps the most precious legacy of the Enlightenment: 'Irony mocks false authorities and impostors without wearing itself out by anathematising its opponents' ('L'ironie se rit des fausses autorités et des imposteurs sans s'user à lancer des anathèmes'). But this is not necessarily Socratic irony which gently questions our assumptions. Sometimes it is biting polemic whose violence may be necessary when directed against embedded power, but is hardly so when directed against the vulnerable.

Voltaire tends to be evoked today as a tireless advocate of progress and free speech, for instance by the French newspaper *France-Soir* when it reprinted all twelve of the inflammatory Danish cartoons of Mohammed in February 2006, or by the Mayor of London, Ken Livingstone, when he was reprimanded, at about the same time, for his jibes to a Jewish reporter from the *Evening Standard* (which could be argued to have a history of anti-Semitism) about Jewish concentration camp guards. Voltaire's free speech was often directed against the three great monotheisms; today, we secularists fondly remember his attacks on the powerful Roman Catholic Church, and it is often assumed that his vicious tirades on the subjects of Judaism or the Jews (rather less powerful enemies at the time) are 'really' indirect attacks on the abuses of Catholicism.[20] The same is assumed of his contributions to Islamophobia in works such as his Tragedy *Le Fanatisme ou Mahomet le prophète* (1741) which shows Mohammed as a deceitful murderer whose only motive in setting up a new cult ('new chains' 'de nouveaux fers', II, 5) is personal power (so that he can indulge his passion for women) and military dominance for Arabs.[21] Voltaire shows him boasting of this in private:

> I am ambitious; so is any man;
> But never's King, pontiff, leader, citizen,
> Conceived a project great as mine.
> Each people's had its turn to shine,
> By law, by art, and most of all by war.
> Arabia's turn has come at last
>
> (Je suis ambitieux; tout homme l'est sans doute;
> Mais jamais roi, pontife, ou chef, ou citoyen,
> Ne conçut un projet aussi grand que le mien.
> Chaque peuple à son tour a brillé sur la terre,
> Par les lois, par les arts, et surtout par la guerre.
> Le temps de l'Arabie est à la fin venu.) (II, 5)

Voltaire's writing for the theatre, celebrated in the eighteenth century, has been long neglected and is therefore only available in scholarly editions. *Le Fanatisme ou Mahomet le prophète*, however, has been recently brought out in France in a cheap popular edition (with three other plays) in which the editor calls for these works to be performed on the stage once again. It seems legitimate to ask what Voltaire's 'free speech' and 'irony' would mean in our context today when (French) Muslims feel (and often are) disparaged, despised and discriminated against. Voltaire's polemics against national, organised religion are often read today in the light of *tolerance* towards non-conformism (remembering those Protestant refugees who had to flee from France). This can be presented as an appropriate enlightened openness to different beliefs as well as, importantly, secularism. Yet the proposition that we might campaign for Voltaire's plays to be staged once again in France today needs, I would argue, to be set in the context of hospitality to Muslims, whether guests or fellow citizens, whose experience of Islamophobia might make them less eager than some scholars to understand Voltaire's representation of Mohammed in this generous fashion.

Gods and terror

Hospitality between men is a human virtue that helps to define humanity. Derrida so often points out our recurrent desire to define the human, to settle that frontier with the animal (see Chapter 6). But if we do not offer hospitality to those whom we do not regard as fully human, not sufficiently 'like us', lacking in some human quality or essential qualification, then (as so many classical or Biblical texts warn us) we may fail to offer hospitality to gods or angels in disguise. But the question is now perhaps: what about hospitality to other people's gods? Referring to Derrida's work, Cixous writes:

> The question is posed via religion; today, the question of the right to asylum and the welcome to be offered to the refugee or immigrant is made more difficult by having to welcome god. In fact, strangers arrive with their languages, families maybe, and almost always with their gods. As we know, that is not always straightforward. It even stirs up identity politics and fundamentalisms.
>
> In this way Kantian universal human hospitality leads us to think through the ethnic and political difficulties of actual, concrete hospitality.
>
> (La question se pose à travers la religion; aujourd'hui, la question du droit d'asile et de l'accueil du réfugié ou immigré s'alourdit de l'accueil du dieu. En effet, l'étranger arrive avec sa langue, sa famille peut-être, et son dieu presque toujours. Comme on le sait, cela ne va pas de soi. Cela ranime même les communautarismes et les intégrismes.
>
> C'est ainsi que l'hospitalité universelle humaine Kantienne amène à penser les difficultés politiques et ethniques de l'hospitalité concrète, actuelle.) (programme notes, *Le dernier Caravansérail*)

We should return here to the notion of the *sans*, the *indignes*, the not-human, those to whom we need not offer hospitality?

Cixous tells us in the programme notes to *Le dernier Caravansérail* that the term 'refugees' (from the Latin) is first used for French Protestants fleeing religious persecution with the Revocation of the Edict of Nantes in 1685 – whom we call Huguenots:

> Louis XIV immunized the kingdom against itself: on the pretext of defending religion he seized bodies, goods, businesses, industries, finances, arts, sciences and the rest.
>
> A primal scene for France, emblematic of so many other executions-expulsions up to the present day. The most tragic of the last century being the expulsion of the Jews under Pétain. History repeats itself, barely disguised.

(Louis XIV porte au Royaume un coup auto-immunitaire: sous prétexte de défendre la religion, il s'arrache à lui-même corps et biens, commerce, industrie, finance, arts, sciences et le reste.

Scène primitive pour la France, emblématique de bien d'autres expulsions-exécutions jusqu'à nos jours. La plus tragique du siècle dernier étant celle des juifs sous Pétain. L'histoire se répète, à peine déguisée.)

While one of Cixous's chief targets in these notes is Australia, and Prime Minister Howard, for its recent maltreatment of asylum seekers, she is careful not to allow this to let France off the hook, with its self-image as 'terre d'asile' (land of asylum) barely tarnished (the kind of rhetorical strategy familiar from colonialism – others are always worse colonisers than 'we' are).

Happy days, happy memories for us, when Protestant Europe opened its door to Protestant refugees, bringing, at least in some cases, all sorts of advantages in terms of wealth and technical know-how. Take the case of the Protestant French jeweller and author Jean Chardin, known as The Traveller, ennobled as Sir John by Charles II even before he took British nationality.[22] England did accept Huguenot refugees from Ancien Régime France – but partly for economic reasons including commercial espionage. And Early Modern England may not have been quite as tolerant in matters of religion as it seemed at first sight (to Voltaire, for instance, in his *Letters Concerning the English* of 1733), not least given its treatment of Roman Catholics. Today there is more of a concern to *differentiate* between political (or religious) refugees and economic migrants, even though there is a desire to profit from the skills that incomers have to offer where there is a shortage. In Britain even children (without families) who are asylum seekers are to be deported if it is suspected that they have come for economic reasons.

Today, when Europe or North America considers immigrants, especially post 9/11,[23] our attention is rather drawn to another Abrahamic monotheism, Islam: 'about which even the most ignorant know that it too has always presented itself – perhaps even more than Judaism and Christianity – as a religion, an ethics, and a culture of hospitality' (Derrida, 'Hostipitality', 365).[24] Derrida's use of the term 'Abrahamic' refers to the work of the Orientalist scholar Massignon; for Massignon it is critical that these three religions are descended from a patriarch who was a '"stranger, a hôte, *gêr,*" and a kind of saint of hospitality' ('Hostipitality', 369), according to the Book of Genesis (12: i), where Yahweh orders him to leave his homeland. Derrida raises the intrinsically interesting question of internal and external hospitality in Arabo-Islamic countries or cultures as also a particularly urgent one here and now to be linked to 'the hospitality extended or – most often – refused to Islam in non-Islamic lands, beginning here "at home" ["*chez nous*"]' (366). How does Jewish/ Christian/secular Europe or America act towards those, perceived as guests, who actively adopt and confess Islam, this religion and culture of hospitality?

In *Philosophy in a Time of Terror*, Derrida explains once again the relationship between pure hospitality and the political and juridical hospitality of the nation state. He is brought to this by Giovanna Borradori's question: 'Would you agree with the claim that tolerance is a condition of hospitality?' (*PTT*, 127) ('Est-ce que vous seriez d'accord si l'on vous disait que la tolérance est une condition de l'hospitalité?' (*Le 'concept'*, 186)) To which he replies with striking firmness even if he goes on to nuance the point:

> No. Tolerance is actually the opposite of hospitality. Or at least its limit. If I think I am being hospitable because I am tolerant, it is because I wish to limit my welcome, to retain power and maintain control over the limits of my 'home,' my sovereignty, my 'I can' (my territory, my house, my language, my culture, my religion, and so on). (*PTT*, 127–8)

> (Non, justement. La tolérance est l'inverse de l'hospitalité. En tout cas sa limite. Si je crois être hospitalier parce que je suis tolérant, c'est que je tiens à limiter mon accueil, à garder le pouvoir et à contrôler les limites de mon 'chez moi', de ma souveraineté, de mon 'je peux' (mon territoire, ma maison, ma langue, ma culture, ma religion, etc.). (*Le 'concept'*, 186))

He argues that we have become interested in tolerance again (over two centuries after Voltaire's article in his *Philosophical Dictionary*) because of a hasty assumption that it is the 'return of the religious', and religious intolerance, that is the major problem – whether expressed metonymically by the name 'Bin Laden' or by the name 'Bush'. While it is crucial, he says, for intellectuals (in the broadest sense of the word) to take a stand against violent orthodoxy, what is important for Derrida is to analyse the phenomenon more carefully in order to distinguish the different strands therein, to see what is new as well as what is recurrent, what part is played by culture, tradition or by institutions, for example. While it is obvious that tolerance is better than intolerance, the discourse of tolerance is insufficient, too rooted in religion and too clearly a condescending concession from those who retain power. Derrida also points out the biological or organicist connotations of tolerance, for example in the phrase 'seuil de tolérance' (threshold of tolerance) used by French politicians to suggest that 'beyond a certain number of foreigners or immigrants who do not share our nationality, our language, our culture, and our customs, a quasi-organic and unpreventable – in short, a natural, phenomenon of rejection can be expected' (*PTT*, 128) ('au-delà d'un certain nombre d'étrangers, d'immigrés qui ne partagent pas notre nationalité, notre langue, notre culture et nos moeurs, il fallait s'attendre à des phénomènes de rejet quasi organiques et irrépressibles. Naturels en somme' (*Le 'concept'*, 187)). Rather than tolerance, when Derrida joins in an appeal for civil peace in Algeria in 1994, he argues for 'the real dissociation of the theological and the political'. He says:

> Our idea of democracy implies a separation of state and religious power; that is, a radical secularism and a flawless tolerance that not only provide shelter for religious, cultural, and thus also cultural and linguistic communities against all terror – whether it be state terror or not – but also protect the exercise of faith and, in this case, the freedom of discussion and interpretation within every religion. For example, and in the first place here: in Islam, the different readings of which, both exegetical and political, must be allowed to develop freely, and not only in Algeria. This is, moreover, the best response to the anti-Islamism tainted with racism to which a so-called Islamist violence, or a violence that still dares to claim its roots in Islam, can give rise.[25]

Hospitality of visitation, or absolute hospitality, which allows new arrivals who are non-identifiable and unforeseeable, as opposed to hospitality of invitation ('"I invite you, I welcome you into *my home*, on the condition that you adapt to the laws and norms of my territory, according to my language, tradition, memory, and so on"' (*PTT*, 128)) ('"je t'invite, je t'accueille *chez moi* à la condition que tu t'adaptes aux lois et normes sur mon territoire, selon ma langue, ma tradition, ma mémoire", etc.' (*Le 'concept'*, 187)) is dangerous. It can open 'a wild space of pure violence which would make it lose even its meaning, its appearing, its phenomenality as hospitality . . . We must not ignore this risk, nor therefore despise those who wish to establish legal responses to, or safeguards against, this madness of absolute hospitality' ('un espace sauvage de violence pure qui lui ferait perdre jusqu'à son sens, son apparaître, sa phénoménalité d'hospitalité . . . Nous ne devons pas ignorer ce risque, ni donc mépriser ceux qui veulent établir les contre-feux ou les garde-fous du droit contre cette folie de l'hospitalité absolue') ('Hostipitalité', cited in Michaud, 50). In *Of Hospitality*, Derrida also points out how a restriction of hospitality (a filtering of guests) is necessary for hospitality to exist at all (*OH*, 51, 53, 55; *DH*, 51, 53); there is a collusion between the violence of power and hospitality. As Levinas acknowledges: that which identifies itself outside of the State (such as hospitality) has a framework in the State (see *Adieu*, 99; 173). For example, the State will not guarantee the safety of the private domain without demanding in return the right to control it, and therefore the right to penetrate into it uninvited. Technology (for instance mobile phones, the internet) makes the possibility of surveillance (a range of forms of penetration) ever easier even as it helps those who would escape surveillance. But:

> would a hospitality without risk, a hospitality backed by certain assurances, a hospitality protected by an immune system against the wholly other, be true hospitality? . . . without at least the thought of this pure and unconditional hospitality, of hospitality *itself*, we would have no concept of hospitality in general and would not even be able to determine the rules for conditional hospitality (with its rituals, its legal status, its norms, its national or international conventions). (*PTT*, 129)

> (mais une hospitalité sans risque, une hospitalité garantie par une assurance, une hospitalité protégée par un système d'immunité contre le tout autre, est-ce une vraie hospitalité? . . . sans la pensée, au moins, de cette hospitalité pure et inconditionnelle, de l'hospitalité *elle-même*, on n'aurait aucun concept de la pure hospitalité en général, on ne pourrait même déterminer aucune norme de l'hospitalité conditionnelle (avec ses rites, son statut juridique, ses normes, ses conventions nationales ou internationales). (*Le 'concept'*, 188))

Internal barriers and veils

Political hospitality in the present has at least two broad facets. The first concerns the external frontiers of the nation state, of America or of Europe, and the question of who is allowed in and under what conditions. The second concerns the more porous (but not porous enough) frontiers within the nation between those 'de souche' and those 'issus de l'immigration', the haves and the have-nots, men and women. Those three distinctions are all tangled together, and this brings us to the question of the *banlieues* or *cités* (housing schemes on the outskirts of large French cities) – where the recent disturbances have demonstrated the degree of social exclusion and alienation in France.[26] The words 'ghetto' and even 'apartheid' have been used in the press to indicate the force of the internal frontiers that operate within and around big cities. I could select three texts at random – Mehdi Charef, *Le thé au harem d'Archi Ahmed* with its untranslatable pun on Archimedes' theorem,[27] Fadela Amara's *Ni Putes Ni Soumises*,[28] and the 2005 film *La Blessure* by Nicolas Klotz – to cover different aspects of frontiers within France and the lack of hospitality across these thresholds. The playful title of Charef's novel refers in the pun to the hospitable gesture of offering tea (one of those beverages closely tied to colonial history and to class distinction) in an imagined grand harem.[29] The disenfranchised play at projecting an identity where power would clearly include traditional power over women – and the novel itself describes a number of situations where the socially excluded men who are the protagonists batter and socially degrade the women around them.[30] The title also refers to the failure of the French Republican education system – the boys or young men of the banlieue do not recognise themselves in classical theorems or the universal education they are given.

Amara's autobiographical/sociological study (co-written with a journalist) makes the point that schools should be tackling some of the questions of sexuality, race, poverty and violence that have burning relevance in the *quartiers* (Amara, *Ni putes*, 52, 124–5). She argues that sexual inequality is getting worse. While her generation of women from the banlieues (militants from the 1980s) had it tough – from fathers and brothers – things seemed to be improving for them. They were not *encouraged* to leave home, even to go to university, but after much negotiation were sometimes allowed to do so (45–6). Relations with boys had to be secret, but were possible (59). She argues that lack of government investment (61) and increasing levels of social exclusion for the young men of the *banlieues*, especially those 'issus de l'immigration', has meant that 'brothers' (sometimes a designation referring to all young men of a *quartier*) terrorise their 'sisters' to a greater and increasing degree, regardless whether these brothers have taken refuge in crime or in fundamentalism (34 ff). The young women in their turn may adopt a range of alienated or pathological strategies (43 ff). In a micro-culture where love and tenderness are supposed to be hidden (a respectable girl cannot be seen holding hands with a boy) but pornographic videos and DVDs circulate, where unemployment is high, and where the macro-community withholds marks of respect or affirmation, spoken or actual violence (including sexual violence) is an obvious solution. The problem of sexual repression and violence in the North-African dominated *banlieues* has received a certain amount of media publicity; we can sit comfortably and read with a certain *frisson* about gang rape euphemised with the term 'tournante', or women cruelly punished for transgression (54). The consumer of news or feature articles can feel at a reassuring distance from these shameful practices, apparently expelled to the ghetto, but to what extent is there in fact collective social responsibility? Should we face up to our part in the fate of many migrants ('sans-papiers', undocumented and hence potentially illegal, effectively internally exiled), including the trafficking of women from Eastern Europe? What about our part in the guilty secret of even middle-class women, *bourgeoises*, at home, sometimes confined, sometimes battered, sometimes raped by their husbands albeit *français de souche* (white Frenchmen)? Brothels or red-light areas in European cities today (never mind pornography whether on the net or in other forms) could be seen as the democratisation of the harem – democratisation meaning, as it so often does, an expansion to include larger numbers of men. Until recently, most British prostitutes were British nationals, now it is said that about 80 per cent of sex workers in the UK are foreigners. And swelling supply means prices have fallen. The pride of the Persian and Turkish harems, which have seemed so exotic to the Western imagination for many centuries, were the Circassian girls from the North Caucasus (between Russia and Georgia), famed for the whiteness of their skin; and their descendants, along with many others from 'the East' as well as 'the South', continue to be sex slaves *chez nous* today.[31]

Abdelmalek Sayad has used the term 'doubly absent' for those who exist neither in their country of origin nor in their country of destination, 'terre d'accueil' (country of welcome) as the French has it.[32] That absence, that lack, that *sans* can be inherited – an illegitimate inheritance and an inheritance of illegitimacy. I have used the term 'immigrant' even 'illegal immigrant' but neither of these terms goes without saying or is easy to define. Derrida comments on the importance of considering internal divisions as well as the exclusions that operate at national borders:

> If we drop the term immigration and re-interiorize the question of differences, then we should reconsider the question of thresholds, or see it re-emerge, not in the sense of frontiers where foreigners arrive but in the sense of an alterity which is produced or reproduced within a nation, society or culture. Hospitality does not only concern the foreigner.

> (Le fait de laisser tomber le mot immigration et de réintérioriser la question des différences, devrait conduire à réconsidérer ou à voir réapparaître

la question des seuils, non pas au sens de frontières par où arrivent les
étrangers mais, à l'intérieur d'une nation, d'une société, d'une culture,
celles de l'altérité produite ou reproduite. L'hospitalité ne concerne pas
seulement l'étranger.)[33]

The question of language should also be raised: can we demand that
incomers speak our language? Should we demand that a stranger
shares our culture? (To what extent would this still be hospitality?)
This is a highly topical question for many countries including France,
the UK and the US (where the singing of the national song in Spanish
touched many a raw nerve).

Cixous writes of the French antipathy to the gods of others;
Derrida too:

> What seem to be the most tolerant of discourses are measured accord-
> ing to the principle of secularism. Islam is accepted as one of the most
> important religions in France on the condition that it does not disturb
> this principle which insists that there should be a clear boundary, firmly
> established, between private and public life. This discourse is defended by
> Right and Left equally strongly in the name of Republican principles. But
> what happens when you are dealing with a culture and a tradition where
> that secular principle (with its distinction between private and public) is
> not valid as it is in Republican France? Must the new arrival be obliged to
> conform to the rule of distinguishing between private and public, which is
> the legacy of a long history and in no way derived from a natural state of
> affairs? What should hosts do when the very principle of their hospitable
> generosity is not shared by their guests? Or when the guests act violently?
> Of course I don't have any ready-made answers to these kinds of ques-
> tions. It seems to me that we should evaluate the conditions under which
> this conflict can erupt, and the least repressive, least violent and least
> reductive way in which to deal with it.

> (Les discours apparemment les plus tolérants se mesurent au principe
> de laïcité. L'islam est accepté comme l'une des plus grandes religions
> de France, à la condition qu'il n'interrompe pas le principe de laïcité
> selon lequel existerait une frontière nette et rigoureusement tracée entre
> la vie publique et privée: ce discours est aussi bien défendu à droite
> qu'à gauche, au nom des principes républicains. Mais que se passe-t-il
> lorsque l'on a affaire à une culture et à une tradition où ce principe de
> laïcité (avec sa distinction entre public et privé) n'est pas valide comme
> il l'est dans la France républicaine . . .? Faut-il obliger l'arrivant à se
> plier à la règle de distinction entre privé et public, héritage d'une longue
> histoire qui ne relève aucunement d'un état de choses naturel? Que doit
> faire l'hôte recevant quand le principe même de sa générosité hospital-
> ière n'est pas partagé par l'arrivant? Ou lorsque l'arrivant exerce de la

violence? Je n'ai évidemment pas de réponse toute faite à de telles questions. Il faudrait, me semble-t-il, évaluer les conditions dans lesquelles ce conflit peut surgir, la manière la moins répressive, la moins violente et la moins réductrice de le traiter.) (Derrida, 'Responsabilité et hospitalité', 137–8)

This touches on the real tensions and dangers of hospitality, the practical (as opposed to philosophical) reasons why pure hospitality is impossible. Yet if inviting someone into your home(land) did not carry some danger or some cost to be reckoned, even conditional hospitality would hardly be a virtue.

The advantage of the French *hôte* is its reversibility – its hint in the direction of the Klossowskian guest as host of the host. Or of Levinas, as Derrida reads him:

A hyperbolic transgression brings about a disjunction in the immanence to self. In each case [*sic*], this disjunction has to do with the pre-originary ex-propriety or ex-appropriation that makes of the subject a guest [*hôte*] and a hostage, someone who is, *before* every invitation, elected, invited, *and* visited in his home as in the home of the other, who is *in his own home in the home of the other*, in a given *at home*, an at home that is given or, rather loaned, allotted, advanced before every contract, in the 'anachronism of a debt preceding the loan'. (*Adieu*, 99)

(Une transgression hyperbolique disjoint l'immanence à soi, laquelle disjonction renvoie toujours à cette ex-propriété ou ex-appropriation pré-originaire qui font du sujet un hôte et un otage, quelqu'un qui se trouve, *avant* toute invitation, élu, invité *et* visité chez lui comme chez l'autre, qui *chez lui chez l'autre*, dans un *chez soi* donné – ou plutôt prêté, alloué, avancé avant tout contrat, dans l'"anachronisme d'une dette précédant l'emprunt' ([Levinas,] *Autrement qu'être*, 143). (*Adieu*, 173))

In the translation of this quotation it is interesting to note that *hôte* is rendered by 'guest' when elsewhere it is rendered by 'host'. This is one line to follow when thinking about the real make-up of the nation (rather than fantasising about its purity), and about those 'guests' who might have a right to be here, who, if not doubly present should be at least singly present – should be no more *sans* than the rest of us if truth were to be told. The invocation of Klossowski serves to remind us again, however, that the 'solution' to inhospitality, to inequality, often involves a fraternal, indeed homosocial, bonding – we must not forget to continue asking questions about the place of the sister in all this.

Notes

1. The second decade of the twentieth-first century has begun with a group set up by President Sarkozy to see if the burkha (tagged by politicians as a prison for women) should be banned in public. We feminists are of course divided on this issue – at least it is a mobile prison relative to confining women to the home. We might note that feminist attempts in France last century to argue for controls on advertising that used (what some would call pornographic) images of naked women were laughed out of court. The attack on the full veil coincides with anxiety about terrorism – and the value of such voluminous garments in concealing explosives, identities and so on. Some (such as Raphaël Liogier) would argue that fewer women in France are now forced by husbands to wear the burkha, and more are choosing to wear it – which is what the State finds threatening. However, statistics to support his case may be hard to come by.

2. There are many other instances that I shall not discuss here; see Rottenberg (ed.), *Negotiations*, which includes many examples of Derrida's activities as well as his reflection on the ethical and political importance of speaking out. The tradition of political intervention by intellectuals in France is a strong one: Zola, Gide, Sartre, Beauvoir, Irigaray, Le Doeuff are all good examples.

3. 'Politics and Friendship', interview with Michael Sprinker (1989), translated by Robert Harvey in *Negotiations*, pp. 147–98, p. 178.

4. For more details on these events see Fassin et al. (eds), *Les lois de l'inhospitalité*; Rosello, *Postcolonial Hospitality*, Introduction and Chapter 1; and Gotman, *Le Sens de l'hospitalité*. Part of this chapter was given at an In Memoriam session at the 2005 French Studies conference, published in *Paragraph*, 28:3.

5. Jacques Derrida and Marc Guillaume, *Marx en jeu* (Paris: Descartes et Cie, 1997).

6. *Observer*, 6 February 2005, p. 1.

7. See David Macey, 'The Algerian with the Knife', *Parallax*, 4:2 (1998), pp. 159–67, for an account of the pathological categorisation and characterisation of Algerians (known as 'Arabs' even if they are Kabyles and do not speak Arabic) as dangerous criminals.

8. See Anne Gotman (ed.), *Villes et hospitalité: Les municipalités et leurs 'étrangers'*, (Paris: Editions de la Maison des Sciences de l'homme, 2004). Thanks to Eleonore Kofman for drawing this and other references to my attention. In her Introduction Gotman writes that hospitality is not a metaphor for the public reception of strangers but 'its general schema' (p. 6).

9. Caputo points out that Derrida 'is exploiting the four senses of *heißen* in Heidegger's *What is Called Thinking?*' He comments: 'the aporia is

not conceptually resolved by a bit of intellectual adroitness but strained against performatively, by an *act* of generosity, by a giving which gives beyond itself, which is a little blind and does not see where it is going' (*Deconstruction in a Nutshell*, p. 112).

10. Hélène Cixous, 'Prière d'insérer', in *Portrait de Jacques Derrida*, my translation. Translated as 'the inventor of *différance*, the poet who makes writing and hearing – and what an extraordinary sense of hearing he has – pair up and dance' in 'Author's Note', in *Portrait of Jacques Derrida as a Young Jewish Saint*, translated by Beverley Bie Brahic (New York: Columbia University Press, 2004), p. vii.

11. Derrida comments on the untranslatability of the term in a short analysis of Camus's story 'L'hôte', which I analysed briefly in the previous chapter; the English translation opts for 'The Guest' which immediately impoverishes the range of meanings of this very ambiguous tale, and so is an 'inhospitable' translation in Derrida's terms. See Derrida, 'Responsabilité et hospitalité', in Mohammed Seffahi (ed.), *De l'hospitalité: Autour de Jacques Derrida* (Genouilleux: La Passe du vent, 2001), pp. 131–49, pp. 139–40.

12. Oxford-Hachette French–English dictionary (Oxford, New York, Toronto, 1994). I also consulted my 1979 edition of the Collins Robert (Paris, London, etc.) dictionary. This did give *hôte* as one of the possible translations for guest, and did not include either of the oddities 'biological guest' or 'guest worker'.

13. Jacques Derrida, 'Quand j'ai entendu l'expression "*délit d'hospitalité* . . ."', *Plein droit*, 34 (1997), pp. 3–8, p. 3, my translation throughout. 'Derelictions of the Right to Justice (But What are the "Sans-Papiers" Lacking?)', in *Negotiations*, pp. 133–44.

14. Derrida's interest in the phonemic qualities of his name and those of others is well documented. In *Genèses*, Derrida focuses on the importance of G for Cixous – but less the name of the letter than the sound – sometimes that sound is transliterated with J and sometimes with G which adds to the complexity.

15. Programme notes, *Le dernier Caravansérail (Odyssées)*, unpaginated.

16. Mona Ozouf, 'Fraternity', in François Furet and Mona Ozouf, *A Critical Dictionary of the French Revolution*, translated by Arthur Goldhammer (Cambridge, MA and London: Harvard University Press, 1989), pp. 694–703, p. 698 (*Dictionnaire critique de la révolution française* (Paris: Flammarion, 1988), pp. 731–41, p. 735).

17. Chowra Makaremi writes of the characteristic experience of Ghislaine K., probably a Rwandan asylum-seeker, at Roissy-Charles-de-Gaulle airport. She highlights the trauma of the interrogation for someone who does not understand what is happening to her (lack of information about the process being one of the strategies deployed against those being held). A non-stereotypical, clear and detailed account of great

suffering has to be produced by the new arrival on the spot in about quarter of an hour. See 'Zones d'attente', in *L'Etranger*, special issue of *jim* 8, 2004, pp. 19–27.

18. See, for example *Le Monde*, 10 and 19 July 2003.

19. Catherine Portevin, 'Editorial', in *Les Lumières des idées pour demain*, Télérama hors série, Paris, 2006, p. 2.

20. Voltaire is the master of the casual comic insult – according to the blurb on the cover of my edition of his *Dictionnaire Philosophique* 'Voltaire's laughter has destroyed more than Rousseau's weeping' ('Le rire de Voltaire a détruit davantage que les pleurs de Rousseau') (Alexandre Herzen), Voltaire, *Dictionnaire Philosophique*, ed. René Pomeau (Paris: Garnier-Flammarion, 1964). In his article on cannibalism, he turns to the Jews with their evil habits – here notably human sacrifice, although in a 'catch-all' spirit he adds 'it is true that in the time of Ezekiel the Jews must have been in the habit of eating human flesh . . . And indeed, why would the Jews not have been cannibals? That would have been the only thing lacking in God's chosen people to make them the most abominable people on earth' ('il est vrai que du temps d'Ezéchiel les Juifs devaient être dans l'usage de manger de la chair humaine . . . Et, en effet, pourquoi les Juifs n'auraient-ils pas été anthropophages? C'eût été la seule chose qui eût manqué au peuple de Dieu pour être le plus abominable peuple de la terre') (p. 42). This catch-all attack does slightly weaken his general position in the article (following Montaigne), that cannibal practices are not an abomination – yet he cannot resist it. The back cover blurb praising Voltaire's talent for destruction appears all the more appropriate – especially as his next and final example in the article is of an Irish woman who sold excellent candles made with the fat rendered from English corpses – hardly a crime he suggests. See my *Enlightenment Hospitality*, Chapter 3, for Voltaire on cannibalism in general and Jews in particular.

21. See Voltaire, *Zaïre, Le Fanatisme ou Mahomet le prophète, Nanine ou l'homme sans préjugé, Le Café ou l'écossaise*, ed. Jean Goldzink (Paris: Flammarion, 2004). The other tragedy in the collection (dedicated to Falkener, 'Marchand anglais, depuis ambassadeur à Constantinople', to show how open-minded and commercial-minded the English are relative to the French) is set in the seraglio at Jerusalem and turns on the slave Zaïre's conversion to Christianity.

22. Chardin is best known for his *Voyages en Perse*, which were a major source of reference for many Enlightenment (and later) works concerning Persia, including, notably, Montesquieu's *Persian Letters*. Very little has been published on Chardin; the most comprehensive account of his works as well as his life is Dirk Van der Cruysse, *Chardin Le Persan* (Paris: Fayard, 1998); see my *Enlightenment Hospitality*, Chapter 4.

23. Michaud remarks that Canada invoked the events of 9/11 in May 2002 when it tightened its requirements on asylum seekers – only those already granted that status by the United States would be recognised as such ('Un acte d'hospitalité', p. 40).
24. One interesting example of Islamic hospitality that Derrida quotes from Levinas concerns the Second World War: 'on this very soil Jews, menaced by racial laws, heard the voice of a Muslim prince [Mohammed V, King of Morocco] place them under his royal sovereignty' (Emmanuel Levinas, *Difficult Freedom: Essays on Judaism*, translated by Séan Hand [Baltimore: Johns Hopkins University Press, 1990], p. 12, cited in 'Hostipitality', p. 368).
25. Derrida, 'Taking Sides for Algeria', in *Negotiations*, pp. 117–24, p. 122.
26. While there are regular incidents (such as setting cars alight) in the *banlieues*, the riots that began in October 2005 in Clichy-sous-bois, after Zyed Benna (17) and Bouna Traoré (15) were electrocuted while hiding from the police, were sufficiently large in scale to receive a significant amount of attention from politicians and from the media. More than 10,000 cars were set on fire and about 250 public buildings destroyed or seriously damaged – and of course many young people were imprisoned. The unemployment rate in Clichy is about 20 per cent, but there is no ANPE (Agence nationale pour l'emploi, the national employment agency which helps job-seekers find work) or Assédic (job centre), as an article in *Le Nouvel Observateur* (4 October 2006), looking at Clichy one year on, remarks (p. 17).
27. Mehdi Charef, *Le thé au harem d'Archi Ahmed* (Paris: Mercure de France, 1983).
28. F. Amara with S. Zappi, *Ni Putes Ni Soumises* (Paris: La Découverte, 2004). The book is named after the political movement which Amara co-founded; it has been instrumental in drawing public attention to the plight of women, in particular Muslim women from the banlieues. Unsurprisingly the movement is controversial and has drawn fire from many quarters – including those who feel that it too easily accepts a universalising Republican 'solution' to some difficult issues. However, it continues to draw attention to cases that might fall beneath the media radar, such as that of the young woman set on fire at the time of the 2005 riots who received rather less coverage in the newspapers than the cars set ablaze by the rioters. Thanks to Paul Smith for drawing this case to my attention.
29. See Chardin's *Du bon usage du thé*, written in 1680, for an early account of the tea trade, and how to drink tea (Chardin, *Du bon usage du thé et des épices en Asie: Réponses à Monsieur Cabart de Villarmont*, ed. Ina Baghdiantz McCabe [Briare: L'inventaire, 2002]). The noun first occurs in French dictionaries in 1789 with the wonderful innocent gloss 'they

bring us the leaves' ('on nous en apporte les feuilles') (Dictionnaire de l'Académie française).

30. This is the theme of a number of French films (and indeed this novel has itself been made into a film), including Fabrice Genestal's first feature *La Squale* (2000) in which one woman (Désirée) eventually gets revenge on the perpetrators of gang rape. Thanks to Jeremy Lane for mentioning this film, and Andrew Asibong for lending it to me. See Carrie Tarr, *Reframing Difference:* Beur *and* Banlieue *Film-Making in France* (Manchester and New York: Manchester University Press, 2005) for more information on the 'genre' of banlieue film.

31. The history of Circassian women (once matriarchs in some tribes and proud equals in others) as objects of exchange merits detailed study. Not only, the prime consideration, were they sold into slavery in Turkey and Persia, they also became symbolic pawns in the discourse around enslavement in nineteenth-century America – where 'rescued white slaves' were often displayed in dime museums and circus side-shows.

32. See Abdelmalek Sayad, *La double absence: Des illusions de l'émigré aux souffrances de l'immigré* (Paris: Seuil, 1999). In the Preface, Pierre Bourdieu writes of the doubly absent immigrant 'who forces us to question not only a rejection which, taking the State to be an expression of the Nation, justifies itself by claiming to found citizenship on a community based on language and culture (if not "race"), but also a false assimilationist "generosity" which, believing that the State, armed with the education system, will know how to produce the nation, could disguise a chauvinism based on universalism' ('il nous oblige à mettre en question non seulement les réactions de rejet qui, tenant l'Etat pour une expression de la Nation, se justifient en prétendant fonder la citoyenneté sur la communauté de langue et de culture (sinon de "race"), mais aussi la fausse "générosité" assimilationniste qui, confiante que l'Etat, armé de l'éducation, saura produire la Nation, pourrait dissimuler un chauvinisme de l'universel' (p. 12)).

33. Jacques Derrida and Michel Wieviorka, 'Accueil, éthique, droit et politique', in Seffahi (ed.), *De l'hospitalité: Autour de Jacques Derrida*, pp. 179–95, p. 179.

6

Animals and what is human

Let us say yes *to who or what turns up*, before any determination, before any anticipation, before any *identification*, whether or not it has to do with a foreigner, an immigrant, an invited guest, or an unexpected visitor, whether or not the new arrival is the citizen of another country, a human, animal, or divine creature, a living or dead thing, male or female. (*OH*, 77)

(Disons, oui, *à l'arrivant*, avant toute détermination, avant toute anticipation, avant toute *identification*, qu'il s'agisse ou non d'un étranger, d'un immigré, d'un invité, ou d'un visiteur inopiné, que l'arrivant soit ou non le citoyen d'un autre pays, un être humain, animal ou divin, un vivant ou un mort, masculin ou féminin. (*DH*, 73))

Why animals and hospitality?

In working on this book on hospitality, I have regularly come up against the question of the animal in Derrida, Cixous and Irigaray. This may seem on the face of it a contingent rather than necessary conjuncture. Why introduce animals into the question of hospitality (already a vast enough topic, to put it mildly)? And, from the other perspective, why would it be useful to the understanding of animality vis-à-vis humanity or animal–human relations to use the language of hospitality? Human–animal relations can be discussed very satisfactorily using the language of exploitation or opportunism or many other non-altruistic reference points – or, at the other extreme, say, the language of strange kinship. Donna Haraway discusses, for example, the case of the official website devoted to Satos (street dogs) rescued from Puerto Rico and brought to no-kill animal shelters in the US, then introduced to 'proper homes' and 'forever families' (especially if a dog is the right size).[1] Website stories introduce strange kinship relations (such as, human aunts, cat-brothers or budgie-sisters to the adopted dog), a 'heterospecificity' that pleases Haraway though she certainly does not want dogs to be seen as baby substitutes in general – they are or should be (wanted as) dogs

(*Companion Species*, 95–6). She also finds praise of the 'unconditional love' supposedly offered by dogs to be both perverse and dangerous for the dogs who are dependent on an economy of affection, although she considers 'love' to be an accurate term for the emotion experienced on both sides of what she views as a co-dependency. She does not use the term hospitality.

Here, though, are some of the reasons for choosing to bring together animals (those who are not *xenoi*, but barbarians who do not share our language) and hospitality:

1. To allow for this relationship between humans and other animals as a possibility.
2. To encourage this as an ethical relation between humans and (all) animals.
3. To open up the question of the boundaries within and between species, which particularly haunts philosophy and maybe also fiction as the definition (or 'end') of man.
4. To reflect back on human–human hospitality after this detour via other species.

These four reasons are of course not mutually exclusive, and all the texts to be considered here eventually entail a reflection on the third and fourth issues: the definitions of man and of hospitality. My first text, however, by Derrida, explicitly begins as a response to (an invitation to respond to) the question of the (human) *subject* in philosophy pre- and post-deconstruction.[2] Cixous, on the other hand, allows us to see, sense, imagine, feel *the other*, the animal as uninvited guest – as the one who breaches the human subject, the host as master of self and home (though importantly, perhaps, this is a hostess which is already not quite *the same*). Irigaray suggests via a series of personal stories, showing the philosopher sometimes lonely and in pain, that animals, mysterious even when close to us, are the ones who offer us solace, indeed that they are our hosts.

While hospitality has been an important question in French philosophy at least since Levinas, it has of course a much longer pedigree in fiction, myth, custom, popular discourse and so on. Animals have that same long pedigree; while, in addition, the question of the animal as one of the chief boundaries to man is a long-standing and obvious philosophical figure at least since Plato. But questions concerning animals in themselves (animal rights for instance), or animals in *continuity* with man, are a more (post)modern preoccupation. In this chapter I was planning to talk about hospitality and animals with reference to two genres: first the genre of philosophy, or at least philosophical dialogue, and here I have chosen an interview between Derrida and Jean-Luc Nancy – our postmodern form of the philosophical dialogue.[3] (And even if an interview suggests something ephemeral, the history of this one implies something more durable.) Second, the genre of narrative, *petits récits* which may or may not be true (or autobiographical). But of course this generic distinction I was intending to set up does not quite hold. Irigaray's text was written for the collection *Animal Philosophy*, and so should be philosophical and indeed does contain philosophical statements in her own unique style, though much of it draws on autobiographical anecdotes by way of illustration. In the essay Irigaray is giving thanks for *relational memories*; it is thus a speech-act too. Philosophy may be defined by its general statements, but we know how much even classic philosophy enjoys figures, illustrations and anecdotes or stories, including autobiographical ones.[4] Derrida's 'L'animal que donc je suis' (with its strange homage to Descartes), from *L'animal autobiographique*, is one of several intertexts that will haunt the chapter.[5] The two texts by Cixous, different kinds of narrativisation than the touching fragments in Irigaray's 'Animal Compassion', are *Or: les lettres de mon père* and *Messie, récits*.[6] I shall close with a return to Derrida in pedagogical mode, introducing an element of opening out via a new text: Derrida's words on the poem 'The Snake' by D. H. Lawrence.[7] These words (recorded by his students) occur in the context of a seminar, a teaching situation designed to inspire discussion rather than a written lecture, and thus an example of education and nourishment. There will be then no sting in the tail, no scorpion in our bosom, but rather a golden snake, where Derrida focuses on the other end – the head, mouth or tongue, if not the face.

Derrida and Cixous on boundaries

Derrida and Cixous encourage us to pay attention to the placing of boundaries – including generic boundaries, divisions between genres, genders[8] and genuses;[9] and the border-line around the body (brought to our attention for example when we eat something or when we are pregnant) or around the text. This inevitably touches on that fundamental ethical question of the boundaries of the human, and how we set these up. In this chapter, I shall focus on the boundary between animal and human, with particular reference to cats[10] and the snake. Hospitality between men is a definitionally human virtue: Derrida so often points out our recurrent desire to define the human, to settle that frontier with the animal – speaking, laughing, entertaining, giving hospitality . . . Things we do with each other. But if we (carno-phallogocentrics Derrida calls us) do not offer hospitality to animals . . . we may fail to offer hospitality to gods. Referring to Derrida's work, Cixous writes:

> For Kant, hospitality has to be universal, any man, anything human, has a right to this hospitality. So any human stranger. But the non-human, the animal for example, is excluded. So be it. No cat in my house then?
> And gods?

> (Pour Kant, l'hospitalité doit être universelle, tout ce qui est homme, humain, a droit à cette hospitalité. Donc tout étranger humain. Mais le non-humain, l'animal par exemple, est exclu. Soit. Pas de chat chez moi alors?
> Et les dieux?) (Cixous, programme notes, *Le dernier Caravansérail*)

Of course this relates to the notion of the *sans*, the *indignes*, the not-human, those to whom we need not offer hospitality (see Chapter 5). Hospitality to a snake may seem to stretch a point too far. However, as Dufourmantelle quotes Derrida: 'If you don't do justice to hospitality toward animals, you are also excluding gods' (*OH*, 142) ('Si l'on ne fait pas droit à l'hospitalité envers l'animal, c'est aussi le dieu qu'on exclut' (*DH*, 126)). Hospitality to animals is a limit case, on the borders of the question of hospitality, yet it can be argued that we need to investigate the boundaries we set to the human in order to analyse the foundations of any inequality. This relates to the importance of the proper name, the signature, and to the questioning of the closure of the human (excluding the animal amongst others).[11] The young Derrida's 'hospitality' to the silkworms (which he remembers in *Veils*, 88–90; *Voiles*, 82–4) not only raises questions of the border between animal and human (that inflects so many sexist and racist discourses), but also makes us reflect on the issue of the relationship between employer and employee, boss and worker, master and slave, husband and wife – any relationship where the surplus value produced by the one is appropriated by the other. Can there be hospitality within a structure of exploitation? Can there be love? Anglophone critiques of Cixous, Derrida, Irigaray, and other 'French feminists' or 'Continental Philosophers', sometimes seem to be asking the plaintive or querulous question: 'why can't they be more like us?' (Not all critiques do this of course.) Why don't they tackle issues relating to inequality, including also cultural difference or sexuality or animal rights, as we do – in a way that promotes practical reform? This is the spirit in which Atterton and Calarco introduce *Animal Philosophy*. This kind of politics often demands argued, referential discourse or stirring polemical pieces – and is critically important even though we know how it can be recuperated, and how the (plaintive and querulous but) powerful question lies behind the first: 'why can't a woman/ foreigner be more like a man/"white man"?' Other ways of working, or playing, can of course also be recuperated. The text that is dancing or dreaming, so that we do not know what divides the fictive from the referential from the figural, can be mythologised (in a Barthesian sense) by repetition. But that deadly end which threatens all our work need not define the work in process, and so I shall argue for taking both lightly and seriously the cats and other animals scattered throughout my texts and intertexts here.

Traditional mind–body dualism has been both a contributing cause and an effect of women's historical subordination; feminists have spilled much ink to show women's association with the bodily, and how this has been presented in a negative light. It is played out in literature not only within texts (on the level of representation and even of form) produced by men and women, but also in the constraints at work on both the production and consumption of women's writing. Hence the assertion of the body from the 1970s onwards in the writings of, amongst others, Cixous, Irigaray and Kristeva, in their different ways, had a startling effect and met with a very mixed reception from feminists and non-feminists alike. Two things should be remembered in a discussion of the subordination of the bodily today: the first is the relation of our theories and representations of the body to our changing understanding of animality; the second is the fact that any subordinated term in an opposition will be available for representations of a range of subaltern subjects. Thus the historical downgrading of the material, relative to the spiritual or intellectual, feeds in not only to the traditional understandings of femaleness but also to representations of the working class or of oppressed races and ethnicities. The gendered body in particular, however, is suffused with the maternal and the range of psychic and economic issues that relate to motherhood and to reproduction. The maternal body is important in evocations of writing the body – but it is simultaneously a material biological reference point, *and* a structure that, in Cixous's *Newly-Born Woman*, allows a daughter to suckle her mother, or a lover (male or female), or to give birth to her beloved. If we attempt to dematerialise this writing and let it all drift off into metaphor, then it becomes little more than a poetic, and indeed patriarchal, commonplace: male geniuses have traditionally seen themselves as 'giving birth' to their masterpieces, and this spiritual or intellectual birth is *of course* of far greater value (and harder work) than common childbirth. On the other hand, if we readers ignore the complexities of the writing and attack it as 'biological essentialism', then we are precisely ignoring complexity in order to launch our attack. In a dialogue with Derrida on violence towards animals, Elisabeth Roudinesco comments quite rightly:

> One of the major tropes of racism, sexism and anti-Semitism has always been to make the figure whom you want to exclude from the human inferior and stigmatize them by virtue of physical characteristics that would return them to the world of animality. Hence the idea in fact that the Jew would be more 'feminine' than the non-Jew, that the woman would be more animal than the man, and finally that the Black would be even more 'bestial' than all the rest.

> (L'une des grandes figures du racisme, du sexisme et de l'antisémitisme a toujours été l'infériorisation de celui que l'on veut exclure de l'humain et sa stigmatisation en vertu de traits physiques qui le ramèneraient au monde de l'animalité. D'où, en effet, l'idée que le Juif serait plus 'féminin' que le non-Juif, que la femme serait plus animal que l'homme, et enfin que le Noir serait plus 'bestial' encore que tous les autres.)[12]

However valid this point, it *also* shows the dangers of our passing from material animals to analogical ones, since this is part of a response to Derrida's attempt to suggest that the way we have come to treat animals over the last couple of hundred years is a kind of genocide comparable to the Nazis' treatment of the Jews. This shocking proposition may invite a focus on what is *comparable*. Can the suffering or death of any non-human animal be weighed in a measure with human suffering or death, or is it, as is often assumed, incommensurable? This question is treated variously in different societies; in Hindu India cows are revered, while British culture accepts the slaughter of cattle for gastronomic pleasure (often represented as nutritional need) thus placing those animals in a radically different category to humans. However, what is considered 'gratuitous' causing of pain or death to mammals can be, and occasionally is, prosecuted in a British court of law – implying that there is some common measure even if the torture of non-human animals is a lesser crime than the torture of humans.

Derrida and eating well

Derrida's interview with Jean-Luc Nancy, entitled, '"Eating Well," or the Calculation of the Subject' ('"Il faut bien manger" ou le calcul du sujet') has been much reproduced both in English and in French.[13] In it Derrida comments:

> It is thus not a matter of opposing another discourse on the same 'things' to the enormous multiplicity of traditional discourses on man, animal, plant, or stone, but of ceaselessly analyzing the whole conceptual machinery, and its interestedness, which has allowed us to speak of the 'subject' up to now. And the analysis is always more and something other than an analysis. It transforms; it translates a transformation already in progress. Translation is transformative. (274)

> (Il ne s'agit donc pas d'opposer à cette énorme multiplicité de discours traditionnels sur l'homme, l'animal, la plante ou la pierre, un autre discours sur les mêmes 'choses', mais d'analyser sans fin et dans ses intérêts toute la machinerie conceptuelle qui a permis de parler de 'sujet' jusqu'ici. Et l'analyse est toujours plus et autre chose qu'une analyse. Elle transforme – ou traduit une transformation en cours. La traduction est transformatrice. (288))

Certainly the translation of Derrida's writing on animals (which has received much more attention than either Cixous's or Irigaray's writing on animals) into English entails a certain interesting transformation. National identity is at stake here, as in much else of course, but peculiarly fore-grounded. The intimate real and imaginary relationship between diet and national character has a long history[14] – and meat-eating is more than just a custom, as Derrida will explain. Phallogocentric (or, almost tautologically for Derrida, carno-phallogocentric) discourses, such as Heidegger's when he insists on an abyssal rupture between man and animal, have a sacrificial structure, in the sense that they want to recognise a place for a putting to death that would not be criminal:

> ingestion, incorporation, or introjection of the corpse. An operation as real as it is symbolic when the corpse is 'animal' (and who can be made to believe that our cultures are carnivorous because animal proteins are irreplaceable?), a symbolic operation when the corpse is 'human.' But the 'symbolic' is very difficult, truly impossible to delimit in this case. (278)

> (avec ingestion, incorporation ou introjection du cadavre. Opération réelle, mais aussi symbolique quand le cadavre est 'animal' (et à qui fera-t-on croire que nos cultures sont carnivores parce que les protéines

animales seraient irremplaçables?), opération symbolique quand le cadavre est 'humain'. Mais le 'symbolique' est très difficile, en vérité impossible à délimiter dans ce cas . . . (293))

The symbolism of the Mass, as the body and blood of Jesus sacrificed, can be related to the paternal sacrifices of Isaac, replaced by a ram, and Iphigenia, replaced by a deer. I should like to add two footnotes here – one is that the question of anthropophagy or cannibalism is important for hospitality; the second that the focus on dietetics, on what we put in our mouths and take into ourselves and what that does to us, is as much of an obsession today as it has ever been.

Equally, the tendency to view other nations as barbaric because of the way they treat (women, children or) animals seems to have infiltrated the Anglo-American philosophical prejudice against so-called Continental Philosophy – the strange collection *Animal Philosophy*, which includes Irigaray's 'Animal Compassion', a short extract from Derrida's 'The Animal That Therefore I Am', and Cixous's 'Birds, Women and Writing', amongst others, being an interesting example.[15] In the 'Editors' Introduction' (*Animal Philosophy*, xviii–xix), Peter Atterton and Matthew Calarco wonder whether it is partly Heidegger's nefarious influence that has led Continental Philosophy to its 'general neglect' of the animal question in spite of its stance against humanism. Boasting, by contrast, of the importance of the issue in Anglo-American philosophy they cite only Peter Singer and Tom Regan . . . Hardly canonical or household names relative to the Continental thinkers they have selected, yet here clearly a cause for American and British pride.

Singer argues in the Preface that Anglo-American philosophers writing in the 1970s have had 'a significant impact in changing both popular attitudes and practices regarding the treatment of animals' (*Animal Philosophy*, xii).[16] (He does not cite any names but does refer the reader to the preface of one of his books.) Others of course might suggest that the change has been bottom up rather than top down. In any case, Singer judges that *none* of this philosophical impetus 'came from writers in the philosophical traditions of Continental Europe', and asks 'What does this failure say about the much-vaunted critical stance that these thinkers are said to take to prevailing assumptions and social institutions?' He suggests that we readers ponder the deficiencies of the various thinkers in the collection in order to 'learn more about the possible limitations of our own thinking when we consider beings who are not members of our own species', and does allow that some Continental thinkers may have *'unwittingly* provided a philosophical framework that cannot, while remaining true to itself, be limited to upholding the special moral status of members of our own species' (xiii, my emphasis). Roudinesco (admittedly a champion of the great traditions of French gastronomy against the potential dangers from animal rights activism, in the face of Derrida worrying about veal calves) claims that as animal rights thinkers extend the boundaries of the human to, say, great apes, they (more or less inevitably) restrict the boundaries elsewhere, cutting out of the human, say, the mentally or physically handicapped. While one may well consider that she is over-stating the case (and she has an unsettling conviction that psychic, affective or intellectual economies work on a kind of 'fixed cake' principle), it is true that the animal rights philosophers here seem less generous in terms of gender or nationality/ethnicity than one might wish. Nationalisms or other divisions are asserted even as new kinship claims with animals are made. Yet to me this seems far from inevitable.

Turning finally to 'Il faut bien manger', I shall still prevaricate by pointing out that the situation of the piece is important – the dialogue with a close friend, Nancy, who is particularly implicated in the question which has been posed to make up a special issue of the journal *Topoi*. Derrida has already doubly blotted his copybook in that he has not provided an article for the special issue, unlike all the other contributors, so the interview is second best – and then it is both too late and too long to be transcribed in full for the special issue. In addition he keeps questioning the question 'Who comes after the subject?', or the terms of the letter of invitation, and his good friend and philosophical ally Nancy seems to develop quite a tetchy tone as Derrida insists on talking about animals and apparently not answering the questions. The response to the real Holocaust, metonymically described by Nancy as Auschwitz (a metonymy that Derrida feels should be called into question), seems to be elided while the sacrifice of animals (which Derrida will controversially call genocide) is insisted upon. Nancy appears to want (but Derrida cannot quite believe this) Derrida (quickly before time runs out) both to denounce Auschwitz and to denounce Heidegger for not denouncing Auschwitz. Perhaps Nancy was feeding his old friend lines in ways we readers cannot quite recognise, but to illustrate the fact that readers may indeed be confused I shall quote Sara Guyer who comments that 'Nancy's final interjections refer to Derrida's failure to recognize political abuses and their historical situation, even if Nancy's tack repeats too familiar questions about Heidegger's silence' ('Albeit Eating', 77). Thus 'Heidegger' and 'Hitler' play strange rhetorical roles in these discussions: for animal rights philosophers, Heidegger (with his odour of the fascist) may lurk behind the failure of Continental Philosophy to take animals seriously.[17] For Nancy or Roudinesco (and many others) the importance of a reassuring ritual of once again communally condemning (particularly Nazi) violence towards human beings (by implication on a different *scale* to anything one could do to animals), or the retort 'Hitler was a vegetarian' seem to play an uncanny role in the debate. It is as if the failure to sacrifice animals leads directly to sacrificing humans – Derrida gently points out that empirically there does not appear to be any such relationship, and that his interlocutors need not worry too much as it seems improbable that we will stop sacrificing animals altogether (or indeed human beings) any time soon, if ever.

The question 'Après le sujet qui vient?' seems to suggest that, thanks to Heidegger and co, we have passed into an era (of philosophy? or more?) after the subject. Derrida is very resistant both to the notion that there ever was (one notion of) the subject, and also to the assumption that it has been 'liquidated' (as proposed in the letter of invitation, although this is quite unclear in the English translation which leaves the reader a little bemused as to why Derrida has produced this word he is so unhappy about). For Derrida, while there are a number of common elements between the so-called classic theories of the subject (such as those of Descartes or Kant), they are not identical. Equally the various thinkers such as Heidegger, Lacan, Foucault or Althusser, who have perhaps 'decentred' the subject, have neither all done so in the same way, nor in any case actually done away with the subject for good, however much they have questioned the various classic theories. He is also concerned that the assertion that the subject has been liquidated then allows the *slogan* of a 'return to the subject' which plays into a particular agenda – one which Nancy would presumably not wish to be associated with.

The dialogue keeps returning to Heidegger, a major point of reference both because of the context of the interview and because Heidegger's definition of man *against* animal has long been, and here remains, an issue for Derrida. However, he also turns to Levinas, for whom subjectivity is first of all constituted as that of *hostage* (a term with a complex and important relationship to hospitality for him), and thus delivered to the other:

The subject is responsible for the other before being responsible for himself as 'me.' This responsibility to the other, for the other, comes to him, for example (but this is not just one example among others) in the 'Thou shalt not kill.' Thou shalt not kill thy neighbour. (279)

(Le sujet est responsable de l'autre avant de l'être de lui-même comme 'moi'. Cette responsabilité de l'autre, pour l'autre, lui advient par exemple (mais ce n'est pas un exemple parmi d'autres) dans le 'Tu ne tueras point'. Tu ne tueras point ton prochain. (293))

With all the consequences: do not make him suffer, 'thou shalt not eat him, not even a little bit, and so forth. The other, the neighbor, the friend' ('tu ne le mangeras pas, pas même un petit peu, etc. L'autre, le prochain, l'ami'). Thou shalt not kill is addressed to, and supposes, him. 'It is destined to the very thing that it institutes, the other as man. It is by him that the subject is first of all held hostage' ('Il se destine à cela même qu'il institue, l'autre comme homme. C'est de lui que le sujet est d'abord l'otage'). The Judeo-Christian tradition, including Levinas, never understood this as: '"Thou shalt not put to death the living in general." It has become meaningful in religious cultures for which carnivorous sacrifice is essential, as being-flesh' ('"tu ne mettras pas à mort le vivant en général." Il a pris sens dans des cultures religieuses pour lesquelles le sacrifice carnivore est essentiel, comme l'être-chair' (293)).

Almost ten years later, Derrida returns to this point, making its relevance to hospitality more explicit:

Hospitality – if there is any – must, would have to, open itself to an other that is not mine, my hôte, my other, not even my neighbor or my brother (Levinas always says that the other, the other man, man as the other is *my* neighbor, my universal brother, in humanity. At bottom, this is one of our larger questions: is hospitality reserved, confined to man, to the universal brother? For even if Levinas disjoints the idea of fraternity from the idea of the 'fellow [*semblable*],' and the idea of neighbor [*prochain*] or of proximity from the idea of non-distance, of non-distancing, of fusion and identity, he nonetheless maintains that the hospitality of the hôte as well as that of the hostage must belong to the site of the fraternity of the neighbor). Hospitality, therefore – if there is any – must, would have to, open itself to an other that is not mine, my hôte, my other, not even my neighbor or my brother, perhaps an 'animal' – I do say animal, first of all with regards to Noah who, on God's order and until the day of peace's return, extended hospitality to animals sheltered and saved on the ark, and also with regards to Jonah's whale, and to *Julien l'hospitalier* in Gustave Flaubert's narrative [*The Legend of St Julian Hospitator* (*La légende de Saint Julien l'Hospitalier*)]. ('Hostipitality', 363)

229

So while Heidegger and Levinas upset a certain traditional humanism they are still deeply humanistic because they do not sacrifice sacrifice.[18] 'The subject (in Levinas's sense) and the *Dasein* are "men" in a world where sacrifice is possible and where it is not forbidden to make an attempt on life in general, but only on human life, on the neighbour's life, on the other's life as *Dasein*' ('Eating Well', 279) ('Le sujet (au sens de Lévinas) et le *Dasein* sont des "hommes" dans un monde où le sacrifice est possible et ou il n'est pas interdit d'attenter à la vie en général, seulement à la vie de l'homme, de l'autre prochain, de l'autre comme *Dasein*' ('Il faut bien manger', 294)). Carno-phallogocentrism and carnivorous virility is implied in the dominant *schema* (i.e. what links concept to intuition) of the concept of the subject. The very term *carno-phallogocentrism* is a sort of hetero-tautology: 'it suffices to take seriously the idealizing interiorisation of the phallus and the necessity of its passage through the mouth, whether it's a matter of words or of things, of sentences, of daily bread or wine, of the tongue, the lips or the breast of the other' (280) ('il suffit de prendre au sérieux l'intériorisation idéalisante du phallus et la nécessité de son passage par la bouche, qu'il s'agisse des mots ou des choses, des phrases, du pain ou du vin quotidien, de la langue, des lèvres ou du sein de l'autre' (294)). I should like to add another footnote: there is obviously a great deal more to say about mass or holy communion, with their real and/or symbolic anthropophagy, and I think that these are not unrelated to the colonial construction of native peoples, their hosts in the first instance, as cannibals. Is it by chance, Derrida asks, that women[19] and vegetarians are just beginning to be included in the concept of subject, citizen, etc., at the moment of the deconstruction of the subject? Authority and autonomy are given first to *homo et vir*, the adult male (father, husband, brother [friend]). The leader or *chef* (the Head of State) must be a carnivore,[20] as well as a married man and so on.

Derrida goes on to suggest that, in the real or symbolic experience of what (importantly) he runs together as eating-speaking-interiorising ('"manger-parler-intérioriser"' (296)), the ethical frontier might no longer pass rigorously between the dominant 'thou shalt not kill' (thy neighbour) and what has been unacceptable for our cultures: 'thou shalt not put to death any living being'. Instead it might run between *several* different modes of the conception-appropriation-assimilation of the other 'la conception-appropriation-assimilation de l'autre'). Then the question of the Good (*Bien*) 'will come back to determining the best, most respectful, most grateful, and also most giving way of relating to the other and of relating the other to the self' (281–2) ('reviendra à déterminer la meilleure manière, la plus respectueuse et la plus reconnaissante, la plus donnante aussi de se rapporter à l'autre et de rapporter l'autre à soi' (296)). *Bien manger* for Derrida becomes a metonymy for everything that happens 'au bord des orifices' (all senses). It is not a question of *whether* it is good to 'eat' the other (or *what* it is good to eat) – you eat him/it (a translation problem) anyway *and* get eaten by him ('il faut bien manger', well we have to eat, a sense that sometimes gets lost in English translation as 'eating well'):

> The so-called non-anthropophagic cultures practice symbolic anthropology [*sic*, should be anthropophagy] and even construct their most elevated socius, indeed the sublimity of their morality, their politics, and their right [or law], on this anthropophagy. Vegetarians, too, partake of animals, even of men. They practice a different mode of denegation. (282)

> (Les cultures dites non anthropophagiques pratiquent l'anthropophagie symbolique et construisent même leur socius le plus élevé, voire la sublimité de leur morale, de leur politique et de leur droit, sur cette anthropophagie. Les végétariens eux aussi mangent de l'animal et même de l'homme. Ils pratiquent un autre mode de dénégation. (296))

Since we have to eat, then the question is *how* do we *eat well*? What does eat mean? 'How is this metonymy of introjection to be regulated?' ('Comment régler cette métonymie de l'introjection?') Including: how does a question give you food (for thought)? It must be nourishing and must be *shared* (the hospitality of teaching and learning). '"One must eat well" does not mean above all taking in and grasping in itself [or grasping and taking into oneself], but *learning* and *giving* to eat, learning-to-give-the-other-to-eat. One never eats entirely on one's own: this constitutes the rule underlying the statement, "one must eat well." It is a rule offering infinite hospitality' (282) ('"Il faut bien manger" ne veut pas d'abord dire prendre et comprendre en soi, mais *apprendre* et *donner* à manger, apprendre-à-donner-à-manger-à-l'autre. On ne mange jamais tout seul, voilà la règle du "il faut bien manger". C'est une loi de l'hospitalité infinie' (296–7)).[21] What is to come (the Derridean *à venir*) could be: 'the thinking of a responsibility that does not stop at *this* determination of the neighbor, at the dominant schema of this determination' (284) ('la pensée d'une responsabilité qui ne s'arrête pas encore à *cette* détermination du prochain, au schème dominant de cette détermination' (298)).

Levinas has indicated an ethical path in his writing – and in his teaching at the Collège International de Philosophie – as Derrida points out in a lecture at that same College on the first anniversary of Levinas's death:

> This master never separated his teaching from a strange and difficult thought of teaching – a magisterial teaching in the figure of *welcoming*, a welcoming where ethics interrupts the philosophical tradition of giving birth and foils the ruse of the master who feigns to efface himself behind the figure of the midwife. (*Adieu*, 17)

> (Ce maître ne sépara jamais son enseignement d'une pensée insolite et difficile de l'enseignement – de l'enseignement magistral dans la figure de *l'accueil*, précisément, d'un accueil où l'éthique interrompt la tradition philosophique de l'accouchement et déjoue la ruse du maître quand il feint de s'effacer derrière la figure de la sage-femme. (41))

While Levinas thus seems to avoid a kind of teaching which unveils only what I am already in a position (*à même*) to know *myself* (*moi-même, ipse*), he is still addressing his fellow men. We know who is my neighbour for Heidegger and Levinas, but who is s/he for us? Even though we need to eat, can we eat well, sharing, infinite hospitality, with other living creatures (or even *le vivant* in general)? That is the question.

H.C. and calling by name again

Here I shall pass to a different genre, perhaps easier for the imagining of 'other' relations. I have already made an attempt to analyse the importance of calling by name in Cixous's writing (Chapter 4). Derrida discusses Cixous's work in a number of places and relates it to affirmation. (I should note that the 'yes' in Derrida is one of the many elements regarded with suspicion by those critics who consider that deconstruction is somehow tainted with fascism.[22]) It is important that their dialogue is between a man and a woman, and also that their work disallows that simple gendering of their texts. One example from a male author analysed in terms of this yes-saying is Molly Bloom's so-called monologue at the end of *Ulysses*. Derrida returns to this in *H.C. pour la vie, c'est à dire . . .* in relation to Cixous's reference to her cat (Thessie) in *Or* (*H.C. pour la vie*, 83 ff). He claims that Cixous honed or forged her style in her thesis on James Joyce.[23] He quotes (in two sections):

> But everything begins with proper names. I desire you and keep you and hold you firmly above the void by your name, I pull you from the pit by the braid of a name. There is no minor crime more wounding for me than

for me to forget the name of someone who greets me. And the worst thing is that, if I ask that person, whom I've forgotten, what they're called – then I am executing them before their very eyes. But I didn't want to kill the apparition of that person! Well I suppose I don't have enough blood to give them and before my very eyes they will stay amongst the shades.

Between my cat and myself the pact is in the pronunciation. It is not only that I call her with intensity, but also that between us each time it is a nuptial engagement; in the timbre of my voice lingering on her name there is a question that unites us. She hears 'Will you?' and her body racing means yes I do yes, and each time it's for life. I am well aware of this, I never throw out her name like a piece of fish.

(Tout commence par le nom propre. Je te désire et je te garde et je te tiens solidement au-dessus du néant par ton nom, je te tire de la fosse par la tresse de nom. Il n'y a pas de petit crime plus blessant pour moi-même que de me prendre à oublier le nom d'une personne qui me salue. Et le pire c'est que si je lui demande, à cette personne que je ne retiens pas, comment elle s'appelle alors je l'execute sous ses yeux. Mais je ne voulais pas tuer l'apparition de cette personne! Ah sans doute je n'ai pas assez de mon sang à lui accorder et sous mes yeux elle demeure parmi les ombres.

Entre ma chatte et moi le pacte passe par la prononciation. Ce n'est pas seulement que je l'appelle intensément, c'est qu'entre nous ce sont chaque fois des fiançailles, il y a dans le timbre de ma voix allongée sur son nom une demande qui nous unit, 'Veux-tu?' entend-elle et l'élan de son corps est un oui je veux oui, et chaque fois c'est pour toute la vie. J'en suis bien consciente, jamais je ne lance son nom comme un morceau de poisson.)[24]

To summarise: Cixous tells us that using someone's name keeps them out of the abyss of nothingness, the name is like a woven or plaited thread; she cannot bear to forget someone's name – it is like killing them. When she calls her cat's name and the cat comes running it is like a life-time nuptial bond – expressed in the *timbre* (or tone) of her voice as she pronounces the name and the passionate *movement* of the cat's body as she responds. It is important not to throw a gift, such as a loving summons, like a morsel of fish.[25] While food, material sustenance is important, it is by no means the key element of the bond even to an animal. (Is this girls' talk?) The manner of giving is important as is the manner of receiving. Derrida comments: 'A body moving can pronounce a yes, decide a yes, without saying yes. Thessie the cat can mean yes for life, like Molly, without saying yes like Molly' ('Un mouvement du corps peut prononcer un oui, décider d'un oui, sans dire oui. La chatte Thessie peut signifier oui pour la vie, comme Molly, sans dire oui comme Molly') (*H.C. pour la vie*, 83–4). I should like to draw out two elements of the feminine that

Derrida relates to Cixous – weaving ('la tresse de nom') and affirmation (of life).

Messie

For cat lovers, some of the most beautiful passages in Cixous are to be found in *Messie*, published the year before *Or*. The cat threads through the whole of this difficult/wonderful text, which recounts a difficult/wonderful love affair, but I shall focus on the chapter 'Arrivée du chat', which is roughly in the centre and certainly at the heart of the text. The cat's arrival, the Event, takes place in the woman's house. The woman has always refused the many suggestions made by friends that she should have a cat: 'She'd been aware since the age of five that she should never have a creature under her roof who might be devastating for a tender heart' ('Avertie, elle l'était depuis l'âge de cinq ans. Sous son toit jamais de créature épouvantable à la tendreté du coeur') (53); the author adds: 'I would have been the same, before, I would never have imagined that' ('Moi non plus, avant, je n'aurais jamais imaginé cela'). The author, or the 'je' at any rate, would never have imagined that a cat would enter into one of her stories or one of her lives. The woman's lack of invitation, and lack of hospitality, to any possible cat, however needy, is the context to the arrival of 'a little creature barely formed' ('une petite créature à peine formée') (54). The smallness (and the cat is often referred to as 'la petite') and vulnerability of the cat are like those of a baby: a real (physical) weakness and a real (potential) strength in that they often inspire protective behaviour.[26] The woman takes the cat strictly for two days only as a favour to someone suddenly called abroad; the trip is prolonged first for ten days and then longer. This is the role of chance or fate. Meanwhile: 'fully armed the woman defends herself metre by metre against the animal. The beast does not put one ear into her bedroom. The woman is inside, the cat is outside. "Don't love me," the woman orders, "because I'm certainly not going to love you"' ('toute armée la femme se défend mètre à mètre contre l'animal. La bête ne met pas une oreille dans la chambre. La femme est dedans, le chat est dehors. – Ne m'aime pas commande la femme parce que moi je ne vais pas t'aimer') (54).

This is the image of inhospitality, of the would-be impregnable fortress heart and home. But there are chinks in the logic of the speech. The woman orders: 'do not love me', but that is an order that always has a paradoxical air. It is not always a felicitous speech act;

it presupposes the power to command the emotions but where would that power lie if there is no love? Finally, on the twenty-first day, a Saturday, the woman takes the cat and deposits her at the cousin's house, but:

> On Sunday morning the little one came back, her ear ripped into lace by a passing dog. On Sunday evening the woman forgot to close a door. That is how Thea made her entrance into the heart of this tale. With one ear out of two and an eye up like an egg she came to thank her hostess for having saved her from the hell into which the latter had thrown her.
>
> (Le dimanche matin la petite revint l'oreille tailladée en dentelle par un chien qui passait. Le dimanche soir la femme oublia de fermer une porte. C'est par là que Thea fit son entrée au coeur de ce récit. Avec une oreille sur deux et un oeil comme un oeuf elle s'en vint remercier son hôtesse de l'avoir sauvée de l'enfer dans lequel elle-même l'avait jetée.) (54)

The symbolic ear that had not been allowed into the bedroom is now a real ear tattered and torn to ribbons. But the infant-like vulnerability, and willingness to climb on to a lap without being invited and to take the initiative of a kiss on the lips, is accompanied by a more adult ability to love and act on love.

> The goodness was on the side of the little one who had never suspected the violent thoughts that the woman hid beneath the gestures of hospitality.
>   The cat passed the night on the corner of the bed next to the door. The woman could not harm someone who put her life quite trustingly in the care of her good will. She had lost the power to close the door with confidence. She had lost all taste for power. It was love already, but she wouldn't know that until a little later.
>
> (La bonté était du côté de la petite qui jamais n'avait soupçonné les violentes pensées de la femme cachées sous les gestes de l'hospitalité.
>   La chatte a passé la nuit sur le coin du lit côté porte. La femme ne pouvait pas faire du mal à celle qui mettait sa vie sans méfiance à l'abri de son bon vouloir. Elle avait perdu le pouvoir de fermer la porte avec l'assurance. Elle avait perdu tout goût du pouvoir. Déjà c'était l'amour, mais elle ne le saurait qu'un peu plus tard.) (55)

For weeks she thought that she had finally agreed to take a cat, but: 'It wasn't a cat. It wasn't a take. She wasn't the mistress of a cat. Nothing was what the words said' ('Ce n'était pas un chat. Ce n'était pas un prendre. Elle n'était pas la maîtresse d'un chat. Rien n'était ce que les mots disaient') (55). They would play the game of mistress and cat, but at night the cat was mistress and mother:

The way that the cat would treat her as an equal, join her on the bed and take her in her arm-paws and go down her with her lover's gestures, without worrying herself at all about the difference in size, in features, in kind of lips and nose, the way she would express an infinite tenderness licking the woman as herself, until the woman finally entered into understanding of the mystery.

(La façon dont la chatte la traitait à égalité, la rejoignait sur le lit et la prenait dans ses bras de pattes et descendait sur elle avec les gestes de l'amant, sans se soucier du tout de la différence de taille, de traits, d'espèce de lèvres et de nez, la façon dont elle exprimait une infinie tendresse en léchant la femme comme elle-même, jusqu'à ce que la femme entre enfin dans la compréhension du mystère.) (56)

Words that were familiar up to that point (such as 'I took in a cat' or 'I have a cat') no longer have any meaning. Proper(ty) relations are disturbed. There is a need to find a new vocabulary to describe this new experience, the failure of habitual expression is conveyed by textual stuttering: 'What do you call this that that that this thing? That no one had ever seen? Woman with cat? Or Cat woman? Or Cats? Or Women? Or foreign woman?' ('Comment appeler cette ce ce ce cette chose? Qu'on n'avait jamais vue. Femme au chat? ou Femme à chat? ou Chats? ou Femmes? ou l'étrangère?') (56).[27] There is a radical questioning of the boundaries between species in this text. The possibility of betraying your own kind is phrased here in terms of a radical welcoming of a cat, but the language could be applied to many other situations, for example she imagines her lover's response: 'You don't argue with a heretic' ('On ne discute pas avec une hérétique') (57). Cixous tells us elsewhere that the first refugees to be named refugees were the heretical Huguenots expelled by Louis XIV – who had to rely on hospitality in England or other Protestant lands. And the woman imagines her lover abandoning her because of her sisterly behaviour towards the cat, tipped off by a letter of denunciation – an echo of behaviour in the Second World War, when hospitality to Jews (deemed less than human) and other enemies of the State was a crime. At other times, being suspected of being a witch, of giving hospitality to spirits often in animal form, was a dangerous reputation to have: 'it's a witches' sabbath what would your colleagues say if they knew?' ('c'est un sabbat que diraient tes collègues s'ils étaient au courant?') (57). The cat may be an incarnation:

I sense that she has come to come back. Or indeed that she could only come to me as someone who has come back (from the dead). That is why

I resisted so fiercely, I didn't want her, I didn't want ghosts appearing, it's so difficult to receive them and so difficult not to receive them . . . It's as if you had to adopt your father.

(Je sens qu'elle est venue revenir. Ou bien qu'elle n'a pu m'arriver que revenante. C'est pour cela que j'ai tellement résisté, je ne la voulais pas, je ne voulais pas que les revenants reviennent, c'est si difficile de les recevoir et si difficile de ne pas les recevoir . . . C'est comme si tu devais adopter son père.) (61)

Any guest might be a ghost. The reversal of filiation is both desirable and terrifying.

The inadequacy, or more than adequacy, of words, or the need constantly to re-examine the words we think we know because they do not match the circumstances, can also be related to sexed vocabulary. Cixous's writing makes us think, and undo thinking, notably about personal pronouns ('she', 'he', noting that in French 'it' is always masculine or feminine and 'they' is either completely feminine, or else masculine when any number of feminine creatures are included along with at least one masculine one) and 'la femme', which means both 'the woman' (the protagonist of this text) and 'woman' in general. There is very little naming in the text although the cat is Thea, and the man is sometimes called her Eschyle.

The woman, who did not choose to invite the cat into her house but experienced the mystery of absolute obligation, is torn between her identification with the disapproving Chorus, the voice of public opinion, and her experience of the night. The voice of the Chorus of citizens cries out:

'she is giving way to a cat,
she is losing her mind,
she is bringing down her family home,
the fascination of animals is terrifying
a terrible temptation and challenge to mortals,
who already have so many cares besides.'

('elle cède à un chat,
elle perd la raison
elle ébranle la maison de sa famille,
redoutable est la fascination de l'animal
terrible tentation et défi aux mortels,
qui par ailleurs ont déjà tant de soucis.') (65)

However, walking at night by the ocean: 'she would foreswear her fear and ignorance and she would promise herself not to deny the innocent animal mystery and to respect it in her cat' ('elle abjurait la peur et l'ignorance et elle se promettait de ne pas renier l'innocent mystère animal et de le respecter dans son chat') (65).

Hospitality to a stranger, here the cat, brings discord into the family home. Eschyle's son feels disinherited even as he identifies with the cat. The woman's mother chops onions with an Angry (capital A) hand, and her aunt complains in German. The mother says: '"The world's turned upside down. In this house we do whatever the cat wants. And *I* make the food for everyone"' ('"C'est le monde à l'envers. Dans cette maison on fait tout ce que le chat veut. Et moi je fais à manger pour tout le monde"') (67). While Cixous's text often operates at a confusing level of allegorical abstraction, which can leave the reader feeling at sea, it also constantly gives the reader piercing details, both physical and emotional, which create moments of recognition, landmarks from experience. Both the level of abstraction where normal rules of verisimilitude do not apply, and the moments of recognition, may be comforting or acutely uncomfortable. In the case of the woman's hospitality to the cat we can recognise the way in which long-term or even medium-term guests, such as migrants staying with kin or with friends who have arrived in their new homeland before them, can receive a mixed reception. Sometimes the master of the house may act as host on a symbolic level, and gain symbolic capital from his welcoming of guests, as well as being the recipient of their expressions of gratitude. While he is content, his children may feel (and be) displaced, and his wife and other womenfolk may have to perform the labour of hospitality – and so be acutely aware of the costs of hospitality (both time and money). One guest may displace others: the aunt grumbles that: '"the cat takes precedence over [invited] guests"' ('"le chat passe avant les invités"' (67)). Equally quite different fractures can exist across the space and time of hospitality. Aside from the splits between friends and kin, the arrival of the cat, the passion for the other, has also been the coming of death in life. The cat's love for life[28] opens up the experience of death for the woman, who feels that opening the door for the cat to let her out will one day bring about her death, yet she cannot keep the cat a prisoner. Again Cixous combines the metaphysical question of the subject with the quotidian experience of caring. I have to confess that the Levinasian term *hostage* makes more sense to me here in this almost concrete representation of inter-species sharing than in the theologico-philosophical sententiae of so many exegeses – that is also a point about ingestion or 'eating well', the hospitality of the text.

Luce Irigaray and animal compassion

For Irigaray, our focus on the human host can become a certain arrogance. She is interested in the animal-*hôte* in two other ways, both of which insist on the *difference* between the human (world) and the animal (world). Typically she is sure that we must not (on some level, cannot) deny difference simply (but of course not at all simply) because we find it so difficult to prevent difference becoming hierarchical (which for her means that it has somehow returned to the same, since hierarchies really exist between things that can be measured on the same scale). Her challenge to us is to love difference or love in, or with, difference. In 'Animal Compassion' she insists on difference (even strangeness) between humans and animals – yet also on the possibility of relating, receiving, perceiving, becoming 'delicate friends'.

One kind of animal-*hôte* is the animal as the uninvited guest who brings a gift which is a message, who brings help in times of trouble – this is what I immediately understood from reading her 'Animal Compassion'. However, the second kind of animal-*hôte*, which became clearer to me in dialogue with her, is the animal who offers us hospitality, the hospitality of the world. I had perhaps too quickly seen the animal who wanders into human space (touching your arm, entering your house, your garden, your park, your forest . . .) as a guest. But we need to re-think the question of property and possession and indeed mastery (starting with legal tenure, then physical fact or force, including moral *jouissance* . . .?). Declaring oneself as host is of course a gesture of mastery. In what sense do we own the land or the air vis-à-vis the birds, rabbits, squirrels, butterflies, cat or hornet whom Irigaray evokes. In each case the relation is different, but in each case we need to be wary of our tendency to appropriate or even ingest.

One of the themes of Irigaray's short essay is the relative rarity of compassion in the human world, and the many signs of compassion that we receive from animals when we need them: 'The comfort lavished by animals, especially winged, is as timely as grace.' Human help is different; it can be more or less. Very occasionally it can help us towards the future of human becoming, as she puts it ('Animal Compassion', 201); however, for Irigaray, animals more often show the kind of pity that does not drag us into an economy of obligation but simply *helps*. At the beginning of the essay, she confesses to her desire as an enraptured young girl to capture a butterfly thus

239

ending the wonder of contemplating butterflies (195). A little later she realises that here generosity lies in immobility: 'I stayed immobile the time [the butterfly] wanted to stay [on me], indeed to walk or flutter on me here and there, and I let it go away when it pleased.' As an adult she can appreciate the gift which a butterfly can bring, the seeming friendship of the butterfly alighting on her when engaged in difficult conversation with a human friend (196). I should note that it is important for Irigaray's text that the animals to which she refers are real animals, to whom she is bearing witness, and not philosophical examples.

She also returns to her childhood to remember the critical importance of pet rabbits for an unhappy child, and recalls how, when ill and persecuted as an adult (constantly expelled from human communities), caring for a little rabbit helped restore her to health. Yet domestication is the least attractive kind of relationship with animals for Irigaray – she prefers to watch animals who are more clearly in their own world ('I like animals in their home, living in their territory, and coming from time to time to offer me freely some testimony of friendship' (198)), and to appreciate signs of welcome from a rabbit, birds, squirrels (197), greeting her as she returns to her house in the forest of Fontainebleau.

The animals whom perhaps she appreciates most are birds, whom she calls (literally rather than metaphorically) angels: 'They accompany persons who are alone, comfort them, restoring their health and their courage.' Or again:

> Birds lead one's becoming. The bird's song heals many a useless word, it makes the breath virginal again and helps it rise. The bird's song restores silence, delivers silence. The bird consoles, gives back to life, but not to inertia. The bird animates breath while safeguarding its materiality. It is, more than overly logical speech, the pathway to restore but also transubstantiate the body, the flesh. (197)

In order to gloss my comment above that Irigaray refers to birds as angels – evoking a certain kind of visitation – but not exactly as a figure of speech, I shall turn to the Preface to a collection of her poems. Irigaray writes: 'there are no metaphors, in the strict sense, in the feminine poems presented in this book' ('dans les poèmes féminins présentés dans ce recueil, il n'y a pas de métaphores au sens strict').[29] She goes on to try to exemplify this point:

> So between a beloved lover and a bird, passages are made on behalf of the kinship between them. No creation of images then, but a memory of

continuity between human and bird. A bird is the lover who is able to conserve breath in him and use it to love: through flight, through song and through arms. Arms which do not take or detain the other but which shelter in an aerial and light way, like the wings of a bird, or an angel. A bird and an angel – the two being here also related – is the lover who unites body and soul by a transmutation of breaths: a celestial messenger who weathers heaviness and whose flesh speaks in a manner more divine than words themselves.

(Ainsi, entre l'amant aimé et l'oiseau, les passages existent au nom d'une parenté entre eux. Pas de création d'images donc, mais mémoire d'une continuité entre l'humain et l'animal. Oiseau est l'amant qui sait garder son souffle, l'utiliser pour aimer: de son vol, de son chant, de ses bras. Bras qui ne prennent ni ne retiennent pas mais abritent de manière aérienne et légère, telle des ailes d'oiseau, ou d'ange – les deux étant là aussi apparentés. Oiseau et ange est l'amant qui unit le corps à l'esprit par la transmutation des souffles, messager céleste qui surmonte la pesanteur et dont la chair parle plus divinement parfois que les mots mêmes.) (*Prières quotidiennes*, 25–6)

I have quoted this passage (and would like to quote at greater length) not only because of its rejection of metaphor as a substitution of one thing for another, which privileges the masculine spiritual over the feminine bodily. It is also interesting because in these 'feminine poems' it seems as if the male lover too can cultivate breath in a sensible transcendental – not, we may assume, in the *same* way as the female lover but in communion with her. I shall not dwell now on the divine element in these *hôtes*, but recall in passing the divine quality of Thea, the cat in *Messie*. Bird song is precious, and calling to love by singing, a lesson:

To subdue, to possess, to violate the modesty or intimacy of the other, seems, for them [learned philosophers], a proof of virility, rather than learning to sing to invite, at a distance, the other to come much closer. Western reason has led us to forget song and poetry as words permitting an encounter between us. We pass from submission to a language founded on abstract argumentation to mute comportments where there is a dominator and a dominated. It is always the same logic, alien to the sharing of speech, of love, of desire. Birds seem more advanced than we are in the amorous dialogue, and could serve as our guides at least a part of the way, if we keep still to listen to them. ('Animal Compassion', 198)

The intimate bond here between form and content also relates to the way in which we take things in. Our experience of the poetic (even in Derrida's prose about silkworms in *Veils* or Lispector's about cockroaches, one might add[30]) or of amorous dialogue is a different way of sharing 'food' to that of the transmission of learning by virile (and no doubt carnivorous) philosophers – who are, Irigaray remarks, always etymologically translated as those who love knowledge rather than those who know love.[31]

Irigaray is a vegetarian – as she puts it, she has given up killing to eat. But, like most of us, she confesses, she is still afraid of some animals who might crawl into our living space. She says: 'Let us hope that Buddha will lead me to universal hospitality and that every animal will become, by that fact, a guardian for me' (199). She recounts her best triumph over such fears with the tale of a hornet that flies away in the morning after she has succeeded in leaving it unmolested overnight in her flat. For animals, potential guardians, bring help:

> Capable of perceiving a call where human beings hear nothing, and of providing a comforting presence where more rational arguments would have neither appeased nor healed the suffering or distress. Where a human body or affectionate gesture would not have been able to have the simplicity of an animal presence. (199)

One example is the lordly cat, a friend's pet, who senses the guest's vertigo and silently and elegantly allays her fear. She describes the animal as:

> a living body having at its disposition sense capabilities that we, as humans, have lost. In separating body and mind, matter and thought? In claiming to make of one the dominator of the other, renouncing thereby without knowing or wanting it so all the potentialities resulting from the passage of one to the other, from one into the other. (200)

In the Cartesian tradition animal reaction is distinguished from human response – here the animal response of compassion is not the same as the human one, but certainly not a mere physical reaction, rather a combination of physical and spiritual, perhaps like Irigaray's *sensible transcendental*. Derrida asks in 'Eating Well':

> Does the animal hear the call that originates responsibility? Does it question? Moreover, can the call heard by *Dasein* come originally to or from the animal? Is there an advent of the animal? Can the voice of the friend be that of an animal? Is friendship possible for the animal or between animals? Like Aristotle, Heidegger would say: no. Do we have a responsibility toward the living in general? The answer is still 'no,' and this may be because the question is formed, asked in such a way that the answer must necessarily be 'no' according to the whole canonized or hegemonic

discourse of Western metaphysics or religions, including the most original forms that this discourse might assume today, for example, in Heidegger or Levinas. (278)

(l'animal entend-il cet appel dont nous parlions plus haut, à l'origine de la responsabilité? L'animal répond-il? Questionne-t-il? Et surtout l'appel que le *Dasein* entend peut-il, en son origine, venir à l'animal ou venir de l'animal? Y a-t-il une venue de l'animal? La voix de l'ami peut-elle être celle d'un animal? Y a-t-il de l'amitié possible pour l'animal, entre animaux? Comme Aristote, Heidegger dirait: non. A-t-on une responsabilité à l'égard du vivant en général? La réponse est toujours non, et la question est formée, posée de telle façon que la réponse soit nécessairement 'non' dans tout le discours canonisé ou hégémonique des métaphysiques ou des religions occidentales, y compris dans les formes les plus originales qu'il peut prendre aujourd'hui, par exemple chez Heidegger ou Lévinas. (292))

Irigaray is one example of a yes-saying without uniting the human and the animal on an undifferentiated continuum. In *Messie*, the woman struggles with just these canonical or religious negations, for instance when she imagines the interminable mourning that would follow from the death of the cat: 'she could not even drink her tears for it is said do not weep for the animal your companion and dispose of its corpse, for you are born to bury human bodies' ('elle ne pourrait même pas boire ses larmes car il est dit garde-toi de pleurer l'animal ton compagnon et enfouis sa charogne, car tu es né pour enterrer les cadavres humains') (68–9). Yet together 'elles' (woman and cat) 'had opened up the hell that is love' ('avaient ouvert l'enfer de l'amour') (69).[32] Maybe I should turn to one woman and her dog:

> We have had forbidden conversation; we have had oral intercourse; we are bound in telling story upon story with nothing but the facts. We are training each other in acts of communication we barely understand. We are, constitutively, companion species. We make each other up, in the flesh. Significantly other to each other, in specific difference, we signify in the flesh a nasty developmental infection called love. This love is an historical aberration and a naturalcultural legacy. (Haraway, *The Companion Species Manifesto*, 2–3)

One of the questions that flows for Haraway from thinking about this singular yet connected relationship, and the thought-provoking question with which I should like to end, is: 'how might an ethics and politics committed to the flourishing of significant otherness [which I might call hospitality] be learned from taking dog–human relationships seriously' (3)?

Derrida's snake

While Levinas excludes the animal in general from the ethical relation, when he recalls his lowest moment as a man stripped of his
humanity, a monkey-Jew, it is a real dog, Bobby, ironically 'the last
Kantian in Nazi Germany', who welcomes him as a man.[33] Peter
Atterton's commentary on this piece (and on an even shorter extract
from an interview) puzzles over it as paradoxical, and then concludes
that Levinas 'did not make much of an effort' on the animal question
(*Animal Philosophy*, 61) – rather like a school report! I am not so
sure that it is puzzling – Levinas calls Bobby 'Kantian' (partly as a
despairing commentary on Germany no doubt) but adds 'without the
brain needed to universalize maxims and drives' (49). Bobby knows
the Jewish prisoners are men because he does not have human per-
versity (epitomised in the Nazis) just as he does not have humanity.
A parallel example gives us perfectibility, the freedom to change (to
be either a carnivore or a vegetarian, for instance), seen as particular
to humanity by Rousseau, amongst other philosophers, implying that
men can make progress but equally can degenerate. One may disagree with this position but it is no more paradoxical (perhaps less so)
than any of the other philosophical attempts to delineate humanity.
The men know that Bobby is a dog even though he does act as a kind
of divine conduit like the miraculous non-barking dogs of Biblical
Egypt. Levinas obviously sees dogs as man's best friends and thus
closer to men than, say, snakes – but he does not see them as ethical.
Nevertheless, for those readers who would rather keep the door open
on an ethical relationship with the animal, the unexpected arrival of
(the real dog) Bobby could be an instance of what Irigaray sees as
the power of the animal to extend 'hospitality', to restore humanity
with love.

Levinas famously relates the ethical dimension to the face, that
which sees/is seen, that which speaks, and hears or understands
speech. The problem is how that relates to the boundary of humanity
– and how it relates to veiled women, one might ask. Derrida
reminds his interlocutors, in a 2002 seminar, of Levinas's embar-
rassed response to the question: 'do animals have faces?'[34] With
what could be regarded as a traditionally Jewish (though it might
also be Socratic) strategy he answers with a question: 'would you say
that a snake has a face?' (Derrida, *The Beast*, 237; *La Bête*, 317).
This question reminds the interlocutor, as Derrida often does, of the
potential boundaries within, as well as around, 'the animal'. Derrida

points out that this example does not come about by accident – and not only because of Genesis; the snake has a role to play in many stories and has more than one symbolic role. 'It's to a face that our ethical responsibility is addressed, from a face . . . that I receive the imperative: "Thou shalt not kill"' (237) ('c'est à un visage que notre responsabilité éthique s'adresse, c'est d'un visage . . . que je reçois l'impératif: "Ne tue point"' (317)). Thus, the question about whether a snake has a face is also the question: is it permitted to kill a snake?

The setting of the Lawrence poem 'The Snake' is the speaking subject finding a snake has come before him to drink at his water trough when he arrives with a pitcher to fetch water 'On a hot, hot day'. Providing drinking water is a fundamental act of hospitality, and I am reminded of Rebecca who is drawing water from the well when Abraham's envoy arrives. Rebecca shows her worth by not only giving the servant a drink, but also offering water to his camels. This makes practical sense of course, and is of benefit to the travelling man. However, in the absence of any indication in the Genesis text, we could surmise that she shows hospitality to the animals as well. A snake is of course a different kettle of fish. Lawrence's reference to the way he lifts his head, 'as cattle do', uses a simile to make a link which also reminds us of what is usually perceived as a difference – between peaceful, pacified, domesticated cattle (raised for consumption) included in man's household, permitted to drink his water, and the outsider, possible enemy, snake. Lawrence represents this scene explicitly as one of hospitality, and Derrida points out the importance of allowing the guest to go first, 'after you'. This like so much I have considered has, for Levinas (and for Derrida commenting on his work), a philosophical signification relating to the anteriority and priority of the other. The snake is the first comer, the man second. At the same time there is a quotidian meaning concerning politeness and common courtesy. Derrida comments:

> He is the first comer, and whether or not he wants to or might kill me, I owe him, I ought not to kill him, I ought to respect him. He is therefore a guest: this is a classic scene, a classic biblical scene, a classic Middle Eastern scene: it happens near a source of water, the scene of hospitality takes place near a source of water, in an oasis or near a well, and the question of hospitality is posed as to water, as to the disposition of the water source. (240–1)

> (Il est le premier venu et qu'il veuille ou qu'il risque de me tuer ou non, je lui dois, je dois ne pas le tuer, je dois le respecter. C'est donc un hôte: scène

classique, scène biblique classique, scène moyen-orientale classique. Ça se passe près d'un point d'eau, la scène de l'hospitalité a lieu près d'un point d'eau, dans une oasis ou près d'un puits, et la question de l'hospitalité se pose quant à l'eau, quant à la disposition du point d'eau. (321))

Apart from the question of whether you might want to put a potential enemy to death, drinking water itself can mean the difference between life and death in a desert – and while the biblical context Derrida refers to is ancient history, sadly water shortages and water security are still with us on a global scale. Allowing your guest to go first also means he has the less polluted water.

In terms of the local (Sicilian) knowledge about snakes to which Lawrence refers, black means innocence while gold means dangerous venom – a judgement by appearances that reverses the Western cliché. The golden snake is thus potentially lethal if hostile. The subject speaking the poem is beset by the voice of his education telling him to kill, and then by voices saying that if he were a man he would take a stick to break the snake. Yet the host feels honoured by his guest, like, as if he were, a god or a king.

Derrida has argued that if men offer hospitality only to men then they are like (how we imagine) animals – like La Fontaine's dolphin who realises that the monkey is *(une) bête* (stupid and thus an animal), and therefore does not save his life.[35] Men need to offer hospitality to *others* (not only *semblables*, our like) in order to achieve humanity. However, it is interesting, if hardly surprising, that we read the snake as a guest – to whom does the land and water belong in the eyes of the snake? Irigaray would perhaps claim that the human is the guest in the natural world.

In *Sur Parole*, Derrida reflects on his work on Levinas and summarises:

We set off from thinking about welcome as the primary attitude of the self before the other, from thinking about welcome to thinking about the hostage. I am in a certain way the hostage of the other, and that hostage situation where I am already the other's guest as I welcome the other into my home, where I am the other's guest in my own home, that hostage situation defines my own responsibility.

(on part d'une pensée de l'accueil qui est l'attitude première du moi devant l'autre, d'une pensée de l'accueil à une pensée de l'otage. Je suis d'une certaine manière l'otage de l'autre, et cette situation d'otage où je suis déjà l'invité de l'autre en accueillant l'autre chez moi, où je suis chez moi l'invité de l'autre, cette situation d'otage définit ma propre responsabilité.) (66)

Is it sufficient to say that the host-man is already the hostage of his guest-snake, as is always the case with hospitality? Perhaps the snake-host is the hostage of the man, the unexpected visitor to his watering place?

Derrida ends his introduction to the poem with the following, rather surprising (although literally true) sentence: 'And there is no woman here, no woman, just a man and a snake' (*The Beast*, 246) ('Et il n'y a pas de femme là-dedans, pas de femme, il y a un homme et un serpent' (*La Bête*, 329)). He is making the contrast with the story of the expulsion from Eden in which Eve is so prominently guilty. But while there may be no woman as such, there is certainly the question of virility as a warrior (killing a dangerous animal, a rival for scarce resources) as opposed to host, showing hospitality to an exiled sovereign (as the snake is imagined by Lawrence) – reminding me of Odysseus. The speaking subject does not resort to an act of violence until the snake turns his back and goes into 'that dreadful hole'. At this point the poem's narrator puts down his jug and throws 'a clumsy log'. The banal Freudian symbolism, in a Lawrence text, seems overwhelming. Virility is asserted via a log at the point when the narrator is overcome with 'A sort of horror, a sort of protest against his withdrawing into that horrid black hole.' The recording of Derrida's voice bears the trace of an odd slip – on the two occasions that he refers to the man taking up and throwing a missile instead of using log (*bûche*) he says pitcher or jug (*cruche*) (242–3; 324). A Freudian slip would replace a phallic symbol with concavity. It is when the guest turns his face away, 'now his back was turned', that the host treats him as *hostis*.

The snake then convulses in undignified haste and writhes:

Into the black hole, the earth-lipped fissure in the wall-front,
At which, in the intense still noon, I stared with fascination.

The narrator may have been under the apotropaic spell of Medusa. But the snake gone, he regrets his petty, 'vulgar' meanness.

Freud does enter the seminar, as the theorist who tells us in *Totem and Taboo* that ethics (civilisation) comes into being with the remorse that follows the fraternal crime of patricide (*The Beast*, 245; *La Bête*, 327) – Derrida points out that remorse for the murder in fact pre-supposes the moral law at least in a virtual form. In the poem, attempted murder results from obedience to the social code, inculcated by the education system, of limited conditional hospitality – a welcome extended to those who are safe and useful (cattle) and not to those identified as poisonous snakes. Regret comes from the failure to exercise impossible unconditional hospitality.

At the beginning of the set of seminars on sovereignty and the beast, Derrida evokes the wolf (an image of man against man), but the she-wolf, he reminds us, is figured as an adoptive mother in the founding of Rome. Why is the snake male for Lawrence (if we really need to ask)? Derrida answers that this is a feature of the English language which tends to assign either genders or neutrality for animals so that, for example, the cat (he gives *le chat*) is female in English. Again Freud (or even pop psychology) seem like Banquo at the feast. Derrida resists any vulgar Freudian metaphor, any argument based on similarity (the snake is *like* a penis); here he chooses synecdoche. The snake stands for all snakes, even for all animals, even for all guests. The reader may of course resist both the metaphor and the synecdoche: taking pleasure in the literal, material description of one singular event on a 'hot, hot day'.

In an autofictional moment in *Veils* Derrida remembers his childhood passion for cultivating silkworms – presumably pets separated off from their work function and thus saved from being boiled alive. It is even more difficult to give a face to a silkworm than to a snake, hard to tell one end from the other, sex(ual) organ from head. He writes: '*In the beginning, there was the worm that was and was not a sex, the child could see it clearly, a sex perhaps but which one?*' (90) ('*Au commencement, il y eut le ver qui fut et ne fut pas un sexe, l'enfant le voyait bien, un sexe peut-être mais alors lequel?*' (84)). The word worm (*ver*) takes the French reader or listener to the word of truth, a trick of language not easily translated, a trick of sound, homophony and sight. Lawrence's narrator has the snake as 'he', but does he know the truth? Does it make a difference? Can welcome to the animal undo sexual hierarchy in the scene of hospitality, or do we humans inevitably project sexual opposition? Derrida's worm can be a '*little fantasy of a penis*' ('*petit phantasme de pénis*'), no doubt Lawrence's snake could be fitted in to that mould. The question of hospitality or inhospitality to animals (or the philosophical reflection on 'the animal') can be turned into a heroic boys' own story – whether the philosophical equivalent of one man and his dog or of the tiger-shooting adventurer. Equally narratives of animality can fall back on catty witches and other bestial women – sentimentalised or despised. This is sexual opposition as the same old thing. Yet can we not retain alterity, difference, in Derrida's dream of hospitality to the other? If Lawrence's snake is *no more than* a masculine fantasy of manhood then its interest is historical. As I read it (did read it as a teenager) – it is allowing the reality of one particular beast and an event to *be* welcome.

Can there be love without differentiation? It may seem that all the examples I have offered here are on the margins – not what the woman in the street would recognise as instances of hospitality or of sexual differentiation. However, for me their liminality is useful in trying to analyse not only practices of hospitality and inhospitality but also ways in which the language, code, theorisation and emotions associated with hospitality spill over into our representations of situations that may not seem at first sight self-evidently to be those of hospitality. The framing of humanity with animals means that welcoming or rejecting these border figures feeds back one way or the other.

Notes

1. Donna Haraway, *The Companion Species Manifesto: Dogs, People, and Significant Otherness* (Chicago: Prickly Paradigm Press, 2003), p. 89 – thanks to Michael Sammers for this reference. Another recent work which might be relevant is Alice A. Kuzniar, *Melancholia's Dog* (Chicago and London: University of Chicago Press, 2006) – thanks to Nick Harrison for this one, and to the others at the *Paragraph* event (Dublin, 2006), including Malcolm Bowie for the last time – we 'ate well'.
2. This chronology is something that Derrida sometimes resists on the grounds that deconstruction is not a period. See, for example, 'Hospitality, Justice and Responsibility'.
3. See Johnson (ed.), *Thinking in Dialogue*, for reflections on interviews.
4. This has been a particular theme of Michèle Le Doeuff; see, for example *The Philosophical Imaginary*, translated by Colin Gordon (Stanford: Stanford University Press, 1990); *Recherches sur l'imaginaire philosophique* (Paris: Payot, 1980).
5. Derrida, 'The Animal That Therefore I Am (More to Follow)', translated by David Wills, *Critical Inquiry*, 28 (2002), pp. 369–418; 'L'animal que donc je suis (à suivre)', in Marie-Louise Mallet (ed.), *L'animal autobiographique: Autour de Jacques Derrida* (Paris: Galilée, 1999), pp. 251–301.
6. Luce Irigaray, 'Animal Compassion', in Peter Atterton and Matthew Calarco (eds), *Animal Philosophy* (London and New York: Continuum, 2004), pp. 195–201, not yet published in French. Hélène Cixous, *Or: les lettres de mon père* (Paris: Des Femmes, 1997). Hélène Cixous, *Messie* (Paris: Des Femmes, 1996).

7. Derrida, 'Ninth Session February 27, 2002', in *The Beast and the Sovereign*, Volume 1, translated by Geoffrey Bennington (Chicago and London: Chicago University Press, 2009), pp. 236–49; 'Neuvième séance Le 27 février 2002', in *Séminaire La bête et le souverain Volume I (2002–2002)*, ed. Michel Lisse, Marie-Louis Mallet and Ginette Michaud (Paris: Galilée, 2008), pp. 315–35.

8. In *Messie* (as in many of Cixous's writings) the personal pronouns *je, tu, il, elle* are often ambiguous. The narrator is 'I' but also 'she'. 'She' is also the cat, when it is *la chatte* (a female cat, or slang for pussy). 'You' is both the lover and the cat; 'he' is also both the lover and the cat when it is *le chat* (which stands for cats in general, just as man stands for people in general). For an example, see pp. 72–3. The potential for gender play in the language is exploited to interesting effect in Marguerite Duras's writing as well; one striking example is in *L'Homme assis dans le couloir* (Paris: Minuit, 1980) when the woman giving fellatio is *elle* but so is the man's penis (which could be *la verge*, although this is never specified).

9. A genus comprises one or more species – it has a narrower definition than 'family' for biologists, but is wider than species. It groups together species that are viewed as having something in common.

10. Here I shall focus on Cixous's cat(s), but I should mention that Derrida's cat features in *L'Animal autobiographique*.

11. Derrida explains in a number of places why deconstruction has a responsibility to think in the wake of a reinterpreting, decentring or displacing of the subject (or politics, law, etc.); there is a very pertinent discussion of this question with Jean-Luc Nancy, in what will be the main text for analysis of the chapter, reproduced as Jacques Derrida and Jean-Luc Nancy, '"Eating Well", or the Calculation of the Subject', translated by Peter Connor and Avital Ronell, in Derrida, *Points . . . Interviews 1974–1994*, pp. 255–87; Jacques Derrida and Jean-Luc Nancy, '"Il faut bien manger" ou le calcul du sujet', *Points de suspension: Entretiens*, pp. 269–301. Thanks to Diane Morgan for helping to find the original French version for me. In this dialogue, he suggests again that something like the subject might take shape out of a 'dislocated *affirmation*' (p. 261; '*affirmation* disloquée', p. 276) – 'the "yes, yes" that answers before even being able to formulate a question, that is responsible without autonomy, before and in view of all possible autonomy of the who-subject, etc. The relation to self, in this situation, can only be différance, that is to say alterity, or trace' (p. 261) ('ce "oui, oui" qui répond avant même de pouvoir former une question, qui est responsable sans autonomie, avant et en vue de toute autonomie possible du qui-sujet, etc. Le rapport à soi ne peut être, dans cette situation, que de différance, c'est-à-dire d'altérité ou de trace' (p. 275)). This affirmative answer to the other ('even if I think I am answering "no"'

(p. 261); 'même si je crois y répondre "non"' (p. 276)) is marked feminine. The classical subject is of course man – caught up in the phallic
and sacrificial logic of carnivorous introjection.

12. Jacques Derrida and Elisabeth Roudinesco, 'Violences contre les
    animaux', in Derrida and Roudinesco, *De quoi demain . . . Dialogue*
    (Paris: Fayard and Galilée, 2001), pp. 105–27, p. 117.

13. It was first published in French in *Après le sujet qui vient*, special issue
    of *Cahiers Confrontation*, 20 (1989) almost in its entirety. It was
    already published in English translation in *Topoi*, 7:2 (October 1988),
    and re-edited as a book chapter: Eduardo Cadava, Peter Connor and
    Jean-Luc Nancy (eds), *Who Comes After the Subject* (New York:
    Routledge, 1991). The note in Derrida's *Points de suspension* seems
    to suggest that the Special Issue was entitled 'Who is coming after the
    subject?'(p. 269, where there is no mention of the edited book). Derrida
    was unable to write a text in time for *Topoi* and so proposed an inter-
    view instead – it was too late to be integrally transcribed and translated
    in *Topoi*, and so only about half was published.

14. Nietzsche critiques the German diet: to be virtuous you must ingest
    the right food stuffs including meat; 'Anti-vegetarianism for Nietzsche
    exudes a certain virility in the face of his insistence upon absten-
    tion from alcohol' (Sara Guyer, 'Albeit Eating: Towards an Ethics of
    Cannibalism', *Angelaki*, 2:1 (1995), pp. 63–80, p. 64). We should note
    that he argues that you should not eat simply to be polite to hosts (or
    guests?). See Nietzsche, *Ecce Homo* in *On the Genealogy of Morals
    and Ecce Homo*, edited and translated by W. Kaufmann (New York:
    Random House, 1969), pp. 237–8. The question of national character
    or philosophies or taste is important; it is very common in accounts of
    nations or peoples to focus on food. Rousseau writes on the English
    and their taste for beef that is not well done. Chardin's writing on
    Persia often turns to diet. Modern guidebooks too give guidance on this
    question. Rousseau, Chardin or Nietzsche may indeed seem close to the
    obsessions of our own post-modernity with dietetics.

15. *Animal Philosophy* collects together nine male and two female philoso-
    phers; seven male and three female commentators; no comment is made
    on this gender (im)balance. While the claim is made that these are the
    most original and exemplary studies from those of the highest current
    stature within Continental Philosophy (to show how the Continent
    is lagging behind?), and 'constitute in every case their most sustained
    treatments of the animal topic' (not true), in many cases they are very
    short extracts followed by much longer commentaries from non-
    Continentals (largely Americans and a few Brits?), offering a 'critical
    perspective' 'to guide him or her [i.e. the reader] on the way' (p. xvii)!
    In the case of Derrida the extract is about the same size as the com-
    mentary, but 'The Animal that therefore I am' (pp. 113–28), is much

abridged relative to the version in *Critical Inquiry*. The exception is Irigaray, allegedly because she wrote the piece specially (p. xvii).

16. Peter Singer, 'Preface' to Atterton and Calarco (eds), *Animal Philosophy*, pp. xi–xiii.

17. The fact of Heidegger's engagement with Nazism, highlighted in publications in the 1980s, and the discovery of the young Paul de Man's newspaper articles in Nazi-occupied Belgium, have led to many gross and unfounded accusations against Derrida and deconstruction. For a brief account and references to some of the key publications, see Bennington, *Interrupting Derrida*, pp. 198–9.

18. In Cixous's *Messie* the woman is afraid of the consequences of the arrival of her cat-guest: 'It was her fault if the mother had the knives out. Should she kill the cat on the altar?' ('Si la mère avait des couteaux dans l'air c'était de sa faute. Devrait-elle tuer le chat sur l'autel?'; 'sa' refers to the woman, but could be mother or cat.)

19. According to Derrida, women's condition has deteriorated from the fourteenth to the nineteenth century in Europe, reaching a nadir when the Napoleonic code inscribed this concept of the subject into law ('Eating Well', p. 281; 'Il faut bien manger', p. 295).

20. Derrida gives a footnote to Hitler, who admittedly was a vegetarian, but did not propose his vegetarianism as a model. He suggests that reactive and compulsive vegetarianism is a denial and repression in the history of cannibalism. Compare Roudinesco's comment: 'Especially since from a psychoanalytic point of view, the fear of ingesting animality can be the symptom of a hatred of living beings pushed to the point of murder. Hitler was a vegetarian' ('D'autant que d'un point de vue psychanalytique, la terreur de l'ingestion de l'animalité peut être le symptôme d'une haine du vivant poussée jusqu'au meurtre. Hitler était végétarien' (Derrida and Roudinesco, 'Violences contre les animaux', p. 115). Derrida calls this a gross fallacy.

21. Kant emphasises tasteful party-planning, dinner conversation and 'pleas[ing] the ladies present' in *Anthropology from a Pragmatic Point of View*, translated by M. J. Gregor (The Hague: Martinus Nijhof, 1974), p. 146; for Kant, it is not what we eat but how we eat, comments Guyer ('Albeit Eating', p. 75). Kant focuses not on physical satisfaction which you could have by yourself, 'but companionable enjoyment for which physical satisfaction must seem to be the only instrument' (see Guyer, 'Albeit Eating', p. 144).

22. See Bennington, 'Derridabase', pp. 196 ff; 182 ff.

23. Hélène Cixous, *L'Exil de Joyce ou l'art de remplacement* (Paris: Grasset, 1968).

24. Cixous, *Or*, pp. 21–2. For Cixous's relation to the beloved cat that arrived unwanted, unexpected like a miracle, see her 'Writing Blind: Conversation With the Donkey', translated by Eric Prenowitz, in

Cixous, *Stigmata*, pp. 139–52, pp. 151–2. She does not tell us the name of the cat here but only that she names the cat after the Greek word for miracle – presumably *theourgia*. Coming to Cixous as a non-specialist it would of course be hard to disentangle autobiography from poetic invention – even if such an enterprise is legitimate in this context. Where and when does a real cat (or cats) Thessie, Théa or Messie – all resonant names – become the figure of a cat? Gill Rye put this to me in discussion: I should like to thank her for sharing her thoughts on Cixous on several occasions. The theme of the dog who cannot be invited in because of the cat is also a rich seam to be mined; see, for example, Hélène Cixous, *Le Jour où je n'étais pas là* (Paris: Galilée, 2000). The cat as miracle is also related to the arrival of writing (a novel as guest) and of sight. Cixous's laser operation is recounted in *Messie* and in 'Savoir', in *Voiles*.

25. Compare the scene in Hélène Cixous, *Osnabrück* (Paris: Des Femmes, 1999), p. 89, analysed by Mairéad Hanrahan, 'The Place of the Mother: Hélène Cixous's *Osnabrück*', *Paragraph*, 27:1 (2004), pp. 6–20. The prize morsel of fish must be given up by the mother for the daughter – Cixous gives and betrays as she slips the piece of fish that her mother has given her on to her daughter's plate.

26. While these details could be taken as fiction or autobiography, one could also relate them to the troubling fact (raised in Haraway's comments on Satos mentioned at the beginning of the chapter) that large abandoned dogs are notoriously much more difficult to place in new homes than smaller ones – a limit to our hospitality obviously. Large dogs are more welcome in general as workers than as pets – a line of thought which could lead us towards the cooption of dogs in our more *inhospitable* practices. To take what is perhaps a less obvious practice for example, in the *banlieues* Frenchmen who see themselves as descended from Gauls ('les vrais Gallois') sometimes keep a dog for 'protection', partly on the assumption that 'Arabs' do not like dogs.

27. *L'étrangère* (what Barthes called Kristeva) is more elegant than 'foreign woman' and of course carries the sense (female) 'stranger' as well as foreigner. Cixous is notoriously difficult to translate; while *Messie* is by no means one of her least translatable texts, the ability of French to give a gender to a noun *la petite* or *la chatte*, for example, is both important in the text and very hard to render in English without clumsiness or whimsy.

28. 'From morning to night the cat was busy living! living! living! living! Seeking, sensing, stroking, grazing the limits of the abyss so close, gauging the celestial gulfs, eyes full of clouds of birds, crying with all her soul: living! living! living! living! Hup! Hup! Hup! Flying after her soul, divinity cloistered in the feline finitude. Little ball of fur with a goddess inside' ('Du matin au soir la chatte s'affairait à vivre! vivre!

vivre! vivre! cherche, flaire, flatte, frôle les limites si proches de l'abîme, jauge les gouffres célestes, les yeux pleins d'oiseaux de nuages, criant de toute son âme: Vivre! vivre! Vivre! vivre! Lahaut! Lahaut! Lahaut, volant derrière son âme, divinité cloîtrée dans le fini félin. Petite boule de fourrure avec une déesse à l'intérieur') (Cixous, *Messie*, pp. 69–70).

29. Luce Irigaray, *Prières quotidiennes Everyday Prayers* (Paris/Nottingham: Maisonneuve and Larose/University of Nottingham, 2004), English translation by Luce Irigaray with Timothy Mathews (p. 48).

30. See Clarice Lispector, *The Passion According to G.H.*, translated by Ronald Sousa (Minneapolis: University of Minnesota Press, 1988), pp. 44 ff. See Hélène Cixous, *Reading with Clarice Lispector*, edited and translated by Verena Andermatt Conley (Minneapolis: University of Minnesota Press, 1990), and *Readings: The Poetics of Blanchot, Joyce, Kafka, Kleist, Lispector, and Tsvetayava*, edited and translated by Verena Andermatt Conley (Minneapolis: University of Minnesota Press, 1991).

31. See Luce Irigaray, *The Way of Love*, translated by Heidi Bostic and Stephen Pluháček (London and New York: Continuum, 2002), not yet published in French.

32. Cixous and Haraway both use the word 'love' while Derrida and Irigaray focus on compassion or pity. For Rousseau there is a continuum – pity is our first affective relationship to the other, the extension of *amour de soi* to the other, and the source of love.

33. Emmanuel Levinas, 'The Name of a Dog, Or Natural Rights' (from Levinas, *Difficult Freedom*), in Atterton and Calarco (eds), *Animal Philosophy*, pp. 47–9 – note the shortness of the extract.

34. Derrida also referred to this exchange in *L'animal que donc je suis* – from the 1997 Cerisy colloquium.

35. Derrida comments on this Fable in the 'Tenth Session March 6, 2002' in *The Beast and the Sovereign*.

7

Concluding around hospitality

Concluding

Should there be a conclusion to this book, on this topic? Can it be an opening up and out to the reader even if – in order to do her best to prepare, adorn (*prépare, pare*), provide a feast – the writer has to condition a response. The etymology of *conclusion* is probably well known; in both English and French the term derives from the Latin *concludere, con* plus *claudere* which means 'to shut'. The subject of hospitality would seem to be an open one both in the sense that the living subject should be open (open hearts, doors, frontiers) and also in that the intellectual subject under discussion invites interminable analysis. Yet an end, a close, a finish, or a wind-up of some kind is inevitable, and perhaps it is the preciousness of writers that resists closure, and the drawing (to) a conclusion: the French dictionary *Le Petit Robert* cites that icon of writerliness Flaubert in its entry for *conclure*: 'The obsession with coming to a conclusion is one of the direst manias' ('La rage de vouloir conclure est une des manies les plus funestes'). Readers may feel differently, and the same dictionary provides an anonymous imperative and complaint: 'Conclude! This writer does not know how to finish up' ('Concluez! Cet écrivain ne sait pas conclure'). The issue at stake is of course not only the last word in a literal sense, but also an outcome in the sense of a 'judgement arrived at by reasoning' (OED). I shall do my best.

It is important to note in any case that the laws of hospitality assume an opening *that can be closed*. If visitors enter then they may wish to close the door behind them – especially if they are in flight, whether from the elements or from human pursuit. A shelter or refuge has got to shut out what you are sheltering or taking refuge from. The fact that the primary meaning of 'to conclude' in the *Oxford English Dictionary* is 'I 1.To shut up, enclose, include (*arch.*)' does not rule it out of hospitality. The archaic meaning of 'inclusion' seems very appropriate. The OED also gives, typically, antinomies: 'comprehend and comprise', on the one hand bringing in, and 'restrict', with the other hand shutting out. Both are uncannily pertinent.

Concluding, like hospitality, covers a range of material practices as well as the literary or discursive domain evoked above and in meanings such as 'to overcome in argument, confute, convince'. It has an economic sense, when you conclude a deal (in French, there are expressions such as 'conclure une affaire' or 'marché conclu'); it has a political or diplomatic sense, when you conclude a (peace) treaty – again one of the examples in the *Petit Robert*. You can also conclude a marriage in both languages.

The final illustrative quote in the French dictionary is from Voltaire, a writer who certainly wanted his reader to come to the *right* conclusion rather than leaving matters open, and whose *ends* were felt to justify the means. The citation is from one of his famous short stories, *L'Ingénu* (1767): 'They decided to have the ingénu baptised' ('Ils conclurent à faire baptiser l'ingénu'). (We might note that, translated into English, ingénue only exists in the feminine, but this is a naive young man.) This might seem, and is, a mockery of 'ils' – the religious authorities who are so anxious to convert what they think is a native North American; the Jesuits (a favourite target of Voltaire) notoriously baptised as many of the indigenous peoples of Canada as they could get their hands on. However, the story ultimately argues for the benefits of assimilation – Voltaire has no doubt that the *ingénu*'s life will be improved by exposure to European knowledge, science and culture even if his ingenuous questions of course show up the stupidity of many French prejudices and practices. In fact the transition from Huron[1] to Frenchman is compared by the man himself to the transition from animal to human being. In Early Modern France, the issue of integration or assimilation was raised sharply by 'New France' (which we now know as Canada); there was a worry, on the one side, about settlers involved in the fur trade 'going native' as 'coureurs de bois'. At the same time, whether attempting to convert native peoples to Roman Catholicism or using their warriors in fighting the English, the French constantly had to negotiate between the ideal (to 'civilise' first) and the pragmatic compromise (to be dramatised from an Anglo-Saxon perspective in tales or films such as *Last of the Mohicans*). Today the issue of sovereignty and assimilation is raised most sharply by the engagement between French Republican secularism (implicitly, if not explicitly, seen as more civilised or advanced) and Muslims in France. Perhaps more surprising to Voltaire's reader is the implicit message in his tale that blood will out – the intelligent 'Huron' turns out to be a Breton by birth although he was brought up by 'savages', famously, hospitably, enthusiasts for adoption. Without forgetting that blood-marked shadow to the Enlightenment tale, we should note that this is another aleatory example of child substitution to add to the evidence that this is critical to hospitality.

This book has focused on the writing of Derrida, and also on his dialogues, explicit and implicit, with other thinkers, including Levinas, Kant, Heidegger, Aristotle, Plato, Cicero, Montaigne, Cixous, Irigaray, Camus, Ben Jelloun, Khatibi, and to some extent the thinkers and thinking of the French Revolution, and Enlightenment, which he calls the 'Age of Rousseau' in *Of Grammatology* (Rousseau, the anti-Voltaire in so many, though not all, ways). Derrida oscillates between the Enlightenment Kant and (a more mystical or absolute) Levinas. I have focused on cultural difference and hospitality, largely via the relationship between France and Algeria, France and 'Arabs'. In this 'conclusion', I shall close by returning to ethics, violence and sexual difference, but start the closing with, once again, our relationship to texts.

What do we ask of Derrida? In what language and using what name?

Do we ask Derrida to tell us what to believe or to do, or at least give us a method for being a good host? Derrida is closer to Socrates, in some respects, than many of the other philosophers I have cited – not in respect of the Ideal Platonic forms but in terms of his style, courtesy and charm, along with the mischief and the sting, the maddening uncertainties and the focus on the signifier of *Lysis*. *Lysis* is sometimes read as an instruction in (pedagogical) method even though it does not conclude on the question concerning *philia* (friendship). In 'Eating Well', Derrida tells us that sharing knowledge, wisdom, is a major form of hospitality. Teaching is part of this, whether in lecture form (with the apostrophe to the audience 'O my friends') or seminar form (closer to the Platonic dialogue), and this reminds us of the complicated relation to 'youth' (a relative and variable term) who might be corrupted as much as nourished by a midwife-philosopher. Where no clear answers are given by a controversial philosopher it is often his very practice of philosophy that comes under suspicion. The anxiety that philosophy's questioning might undermine cherished certainties, which in ancient Athens led to Socrates' death, has not entirely disappeared. Without my mentioning honorary doctorates withheld in Cambridge, spoof journal articles, or savaging in the press (even in the obituaries), I am sure my reader will be able to think of her/his own examples of the ill-informed exercise of power intended to save innocent youth from the seduction of the Arche Debunker (or else turn to some of Derrida's more enthusiastic supporters for the detail). Derrida's reading and writing has inspired or provoked some brilliant responses, and the notion of hospitable sharing of thoughts and questions might lead us in the direction of a democratic co-creation of the text between reader and writer. However, we should not ignore the master-apprentice, or, more dangerously, master-disciple effects. These may have a degree of legitimacy: the importance of time taken. They may also be illegitimate effects of power, or of blind admiration with its mimetic (parasitic?) outpourings. For a benefactor-host to be a benefactor or a host there must be a distinction between that function and that of the beneficiary-guest – even as the work of deconstruction shifts our understanding and displaces that distinction, which should in any case be a dynamic one. A suppliant should not be fixed as a suppliant for all time. Mimesis is an important way of learning; nevertheless, the role of difference in repetition is a critical one. Books may be friends, guests or hosts at different stages in our analysis, but that in itself need not lead to genuine confusion over who has signed the work. It would be too boring if the market were flooded with Derrida forgeries; perhaps we should express gratitude for academic policing and the surveillance of plagiarism, even as we question the boundaries.

In the course of this book, I have intermittently focused on intertextuality as well as textuality; I have argued that reference to the past (or another place) is particularly powerful in the discourse and practices of hospitality. This is most often a nostalgia for a traditional form (they did it better in the days of Homer or Abraham), since hospitality is importantly figured as a practice that has a very long history and very wide geographical sweep, particularly important if it is to be definitional of humanity. Sometimes we can detect an assumption that hospitality is best practised in more simple (less economically sophisticated) societies and that this greater simplicity also relates to a clearer division of labour between the sexes. More rarely, this reference to the past, or to elsewhere, is an agonistic assertion that 'we' are more hospitable than they were – the rhetoric of the French Revolution (universal rights of man leading to universal hospitality) obviously needs to assert itself against the exclusions of the Old Regime even when it does so via admiration for the virtue of Rome or Sparta. Post-colonial and feminist critical writing necessitates critique of colonial and patriarchal forms and residues, and of the exclusions that are operational within them. However, when these incisive beams of light are focused on the shadows in earlier texts to condemn their inhospitality to the Other, certain new inequalities can result. Lady Mary Wortley Montagu, for example, who in one light could be deemed as conditionally hospitable to otherness as was possible in her own difficult times, is treated to a harsher interrogation by critics policing the borders of the acceptable than the iconic (slave-profiteering) Voltaire.[2] Montagu brings us neatly to the role of names, as I have argued that what we call writers is sometimes an indication of our respect, affection or distaste. 'Lady Mary Wortley Montagu' is a mouthful which might indicate simply recognition of her period, but might also connote the quaint archaism of the Lady Writer (relative to those included in the 'living' canon whom we know by a single name, such as Montesquieu), or a desire to foreground her rank (and marital status) by those who disapprove of it. The role of language in hospitality, and of names, is of course much more extensive than this – the example of colonial Algeria, where uninvited visitors laid claim to being the masters of the house, alone gives us food for thought when we consider place names, names given or not given to individuals, the teaching of French language and culture in schools. The reception of immigrants and refugees in France would give rise to a second series of reflections on language and naming: the example of the term *sans-papiers* being but one, *Arab* being another.

To stay with Derrida, the author is always already dead, and this sets up a range of responses in the reader: the agonistic reader does battle with the dead Father; the melancholic reader holds the text in a crypt within, and so on. But how does the text attempt to programme mourning for the reader? In *Of Hospitality*, Derrida reminds us of Theseus who is host to Oedipus and becomes hostage to his promise to his (dead) guest not to reveal the site of his grave (to Oedipus's daughters). Does Derrida's text hold its faithful reader hostage to a difficult promise? The site of the ancestors' graves is one definition of home, but a more portable definition for our globalised world is the mother tongue. For the Jewish-French-Algerians Derrida and Cixous in particular there is an acute issue of the hospitality of the (French) language, and of the mother tongue as phantasm. Derrida, like Cixous, is both locked out of and locked into French language (see, for example, *Circumfession*, section 53, especially 284–5, 289; *Circonfession*, 263, 267), and this could relate to their taste for words (even letters), for the level of the signifier. This painstaking attention to detail has not always endeared them to readers – ready sometimes to pass it off as frivolous word-play rather than take the time of active friendship. But is not the faithful reader ethically bound by an implicit textual contract, committed to a certain labour (which, as hospitality, takes time) on and with the language of the other – translating, but not rushing too quickly to translation, into their own mother tongue?

A final point: if we literally read Derrida in (English) translation then we need to pay attention to the effects of the translation, for example the decision which has to be made to translate *hôte* as *either* host *or* guest when, in an example like Camus's short story of this name, that translation decision is far from obvious. But if a word seems to a translator (such as Anidjar) to be untranslatable, like *hôte*, then the thing that the untranslated word becomes in the other language cannot be the same as it was in the original – especially if it is, importantly, an everyday noun that seems clear in its meaning to a French speaker in very many contexts. That everyday familiarity and clarity-effect is an important element in our reading of hospitality. However, if we read Derrida or any other writer in the original tongue there is still a translation process – the transformation that the text performs and the one that the reader performs, willy-nilly. We can never consume a text raw; we always cook it. The culinary metaphor returns us to the hospitable (which we have never left) and to the maternal-feminine; these can be figures of the ethical reading mentioned above (without any denial of the violent elements within this) and of taking time and care.

Ethics and hospitality (again)

This book more or less begins with, and returns frequently to, what could be a very bold claim on the part of Derrida, or at least Levinas, that hospitality *is* ethics. It is what is and also what ought to be; that conventional distinction hardly seems to hold in Levinas's writing. Is the identification of hospitality with ethics, and with our very being (always already inhabited by the other) such a big claim that it ends up as tautology or (con)fusion? There is a problem with defining one noun by another in a way that suggests they are synonyms, and not that one is a particular case of the other – if hospitality were simply being given as one example of ethical behaviour then this would be a very small (because so familiar) claim! In either case (and I shall assume the larger), there are a series of tensions that Derrida phrases as the Law versus the laws of hospitality, for example, a tension between immediacy and analysis: the question of temporality. Hospitality as welcome should be immediate; the move to politics, to responsible decisions, requires time for analysis. In the eighteenth century Rousseau resolves this core ethical issue as a necessary emotional impulse (immediate and partial) which must be moderated by justice which involves rational universal thinking, and comparisons. Derrida does not allow the tension to be resolved, he keeps it working, even though he urges the coming to a decision since social and political structures, communities and the law (rights), and international hospitality require it. Temporality is the deferring that necessitates the 'a' in *différance*.

A second tension lies between the economies of hospitality (such as reciprocity – and guest-friendship status can even be inherited, allowing for reciprocity with a long time-lag) and the would-be aneconomy of the gift. A third tension (but perhaps these are all the same tension) lies in the structure of proximity – which may be a keeping at a distance by keeping close (hostis-enemy, hostage) or the closeness of friendship (the intimacy of companionship, consuming 'salt', and actively spending time together and doing each other benefits). I have argued that it is necessary to consider friendship – and the very structure of subjectivity – in order to understand hospitality to the other-stranger. Friendship secures survival beyond the grave, and it is related to the renown of name. When perfect friends are as one then they can no longer give each other anything or offer hospitality to each other – the things which nourish friendship are impossible. And yet if you hold your friend within yourself (as if the friend were absent, even dead) then that is a kind of hospitality. The structuring of sameness and distinction between two returns us to *différance*.

Finally, the stranger-other is received as neighbour-friend and as fellow man in most philosophical treatments of ethics including those of Heidegger and Levinas. This brings us to the question of the boundaries of the human, and thus of the animal. Not just the figural animal (the woman, the other race), but real animals. Hospitality usually involves eating, and Derrida suggests that meat-eating is neither necessary nor accidental. Thus from companion animals to eating animals, cruelty to animals, the holocaust or sacrifice of animals (the etymology of *host* in communion), we are brought on to the question of violence and how it relates to hospitality.

Violence

Hospitality is often seen as epitomising peace, breaking bread together, sharing salt. Yet it is especially necessary in violent times – for example the hospitality extended to Jews under Nazi occupation. External violence, including the violence of the hostile host-community, can break in upon the hospitable home, forcing violent choices – not only the lie that would shock Kant (the Enlightenment philosopher most associated with hospitality today), but even the sacrifice of some of the household to save the others, as in the case of the Levite or Lot, where the womenfolk are sacrificed to save men from the brutality of the Benjamites or the Sodomites. In both these stories a terrible vengeance is wreaked for the violence done. The tales of Odysseus give us a range of violent hosts, notably the cannibal Polyphemos whom he robs and blinds. Thus equally we have examples of violent or transgressive guests: Paris, Sextus Tarquin – in both cases again the vengeance is terrible. And the destruction of a people brings up the issue of a disproportionate response. Of course each case is different: in the stories of the Levite or of Paris the infraction of hospitality stands alone. In the cases of Lot or of Tarquin there was already a desire to destroy those known for transgression or tyranny, and the infraction of hospitality is of the nature of a last straw. If we desire examples closer to home, then we only need to consider colonial violence, the Holocaust and Israel, post-colonial violence and post-9/11 (in)hospitality to Islam as well as the violence of those who claim to speak in its name. Foreigner-guests who may be temporary guests, refugees, immigrants, or invaders can be objects or subjects of terror, both literal and figural. Foreigner-hosts, including those encountered on voyages of exploration, in colonial situations, or wars of 'liberation' (Vietnam, Iraq, to mention but two) may be, or may be figured as savage – and may be treated with unspeakable savagery.

It could be argued that all this violence, however terrible, is contingent upon hospitality, that true hospitality shines as a peaceful beacon against aggression. Yet any fraternity or inclusion involves exclusion. The laws which are necessary for hospitality to exist must create friction, transgression. The possibility of the hostage or of the sacrifice-*hostie*; the possibility of the host-guest relationship becoming a host-parasite relationship where the guest consumes the host, or of the host being a cannibal who ingests his guest – these possibilities *inhabit* the hospitable relationship if only virtually.

Sexual difference (finally)

In this book there have been two related, interpenetrating, approaches, empirical and textual, to the intersection of hospitality and sexual difference. The mother is always the first home and source of nourishment for both men and women (and Luce Irigaray argues that this has different meanings for each sex), and this has been put in relation to a series of material and discursive matters. On the empirical side I have cited the historical master of the house with his property rights: his land ownership (even on the level of the nation state), his ownership of goods, of people (slaves, servants, women) and finally of his own body. Women in this general model are therefore chattels, objects of dispute between men, and mediation between men. Women are also the ground on which men are built/build themselves, that is again the man as *agathos* and master of house – with his network of relations with other heads of household (also men). Fraternity and homosociality (with its repression of the homosexual) is mediated by women. Women are the means to secure survival beyond the grave for men – a biological inheritance – and hence there is a need to control sexuality. Adoption or substitution can represent hospitality; but the possibility of substitution is a source of great anxiety. If the adopted/substituted child has not been invited, and is not known as such, then s/he is a cuckoo in the nest, a bastard foisted upon the unwitting father. Rape in this context is rapt, theft from another man, before it becomes a source of social and thus personal shame for the woman as well. In a traditional structure women cannot be hosts or guests: in a 'harem' structure they should not receive strangers nor be mobile even where they mediate hospitality and perform the labour of hospitality. The possibility and reality of rape of women is also a form of patriarchal control; on another level the fear of the vulnerability of the body, of male rape, leaves woman as substitute-sacrifice. This is our inheritance in the twenty-first century when much has changed, but not so much as might have been hoped. When we mention refugees today, we should not forget the specificities of sexual violence endured and enduring. The opening of Eastern Europe and the trafficking of sex slaves from the former Eastern bloc alongside women from formerly colonised countries (at least as bad as the Oriental harems which have long fascinated us as the epitome of tyranny) is just one example.

The woman is a key instance of 'the stranger within'. As Beauvoir pointed out in the Introduction to the *Second Sex*, women are scattered amongst men, they do not live in ghettos as those of another class or race may do. Where a woman is also an 'immigrant' resident, or has inherited stranger-ness or acquired stranger-ness, say, by dress, or by displacement even within the city, she may be seen as a fifth column or Trojan horse (as Jews were perceived, and now Muslims) involved in a kind of guerrilla warfare. Of course this kind of feminine masquerade was received positively in the French Resistance to the Nazis. As America is marked by the experience of Vietnam, where one of the many horrors from the point of view of US soldiers was the difficulty in telling the difference between peaceful 'innocent' civilians and enemy combatants (who might even be women) or supporters, so France is marked by the Algerian war. After a much longer and more intimate association than Americans had had with the Vietnamese, veiled Algerian women were comprehended by the French as erotic objects (the harem of colonial postcards) as mothers (like Aïcha) and as subjugated beings. Thus women freedom fighters who wore European dress were perfectly camouflaged as 'not Arabs', they passed checkpoints carrying weapons; and, once that ruse had been understood, women who were instead the very image of passive repression could carry bombs under their veils. The hostility to the veil in France today, with a law passed so that even headscarves (alongside any other striking mark of religious affiliation of course) would be banned in state schools, has many causes, some more well-intentioned than others. For my part, I would say that any item of clothing has meaning relative to a given context – and an enforced veil can most certainly signify repression and be repressive. Without trying to exhaust the range of meanings, I could suggest that a veil can also feel like protection in a situation perceived as hostile, and may feel like a necessary assertion of cultural or religious identity where that is threatened. Christian veils and other regalia have carried all these significations at certain times. Presumably a hospitable response would support women as they wish to be supported rather than trying to bend them to a language which they do not wish to speak, or which they wish to construct in their own idiom. Driving women out of the state education system is hardly hospitable (or even desirable for those who wish to emphasise the duty of guests to accommodate themselves to their hosts). Thus empirically, women's structural role in hospitality has been crucial yet downplayed, threatened, risky, unless within the confines of playing handmaiden to the master of the house.

On the discursive and figural side while the *hôtesse* is not reversible as *hôte* is (the sister of the brother, the daughter of the father are not reversible either), the maternal-feminine is cited as hospitality by Levinas. There is indeed a cultural imaginary of hospitality as maternal even as the invitation may be proffered and accepted between men. The dangers of the guest who becomes a parasite on the host, or the host who holds a guest hostage, are also linked to maternity in our imaginary; the relationship figured as too close, suffocating or smothering. When Derrida, after Levinas, uses the name 'mother' or 'woman', what does he mean? One of his most brilliant and closest interpreters, Bennington, cautions against an empirical reading of what he calls a 'nickname'. He writes: 'the point is not to promote a matriarchal power against a patriarchy, but to show that what has always been understood by "father" (or even by "power") is constituted only on the basis of an anteriority which can be called "mother" solely on condition of not confusing it with the habitual concept of mother' (Bennington, 'Derridabase', 210). Thus, he suggests, the relationship between the Derridean 'mother' and an everyday sense would be similar to the relationship between Derridean arche-writing or trace and the everyday sense of writing. Sexual opposition is masculine, and the 'feminine' shows how the opposition depends on what it devalorises. This does not mean the erasure of sexual difference into neutrality – which, Derrida is well aware, would mean the return of the masculine. Nor does it imply a purely 'strategic' deployment of sexual difference. All these points that Bennington makes are completely convincing. And yet the relationship with Derrida's 'Circumfession' written below Bennington's 'Derridabase' is of course supplementary – each supplements and supplants the other. The Derridean supplement appears to be flesh, liquid, emotion. Derrida's writing is dense and difficult as well as poignant in its descriptions of his dying mother's body with its suppurating lesions.[3] While the very word, the signifier *escarre*, gives rise to a thought construction, the reader's awareness of what is signified, and indeed the thing itself, leaks emotion, a bodily reaction, for some of us at least. His dying mother makes Derrida think of his own death as what she had feared for him – again logos, a conceptual structure, combines with pathos. His own body's vulnerability to pain and assault is accentuated with the intertwining of the ribbon of circumcision throughout 'Circumfession'. The intimate play between analysis and affective charge is reiterated even with the quotations from St Augustine, when Derrida recalls that he began to learn Latin as a result of a decision from Vichy – which a year later expelled him (as a Jew) from the school where he was learning it.

Freud, in *Totem and Taboo*, focuses on the sacrifice of the father by the sons, as, in the Christian story, Christ lays down his life for the brotherhood of man, after a Last Supper that we re-enact in Holy Communion, drinking his blood and eating his flesh. Irigaray points out, however, that it is rather the mother who is sacrificed in our culture, one key myth example being the matricide of Clytemnestra (culminating in Athena's judgement in favour of fathers or sons against mothers or daughters). In the Enlightenment, Rousseau adapts the Biblical tale of the Levite of Ephraim so that the nameless *woman who is sacrificed* to the Benjamites has an ethical counterpart in Axa, the *woman who sacrifices herself* in marriage to a stranger, so that the bloodshed should finally end. This is the classic shift from external compulsion to internalised compulsion. In an unfinished play Rousseau turns to another familiar tale, Lucretia who sacrifices herself after she has been raped; this not only gives the right meaning (ethical and political) to the rape in a patriarchal society, but also enables Brutus to inspire an uprising against tyranny over her dead body. When we align hospitality with maternity or femininity, as Levinas does, then this can entail sacrificing the material body (empirical women) in order to construct a metaphor (like the transcendental Christ) – a manoeuvre Irigaray has pointed out in a number of texts. Bennington's Derrida defines the 'mother' or the 'feminine' as a critical *différance* relating to both sexes. Would this be another sacrifice of the (maternal) flesh? We female and feminist academics can learn to do this too. But Derrida chooses to display a real sexed and wounded body and to confess his trouble, knowing that thereby he could be said to turn it into words, even into literature. The pact with the reader, however, is different than it would be with a philosophical example or illustration – the possible impact on the reader is different. I argue that the woman's body as hospitality has to be recognised as material at least as much as figural. The reality of the revolt against that body in substitution and in sacrifice has to be recognised as well. To avoid the suffocation of the fusional, Irigaray argues for separate domains and thresholds which allows for the hospitality of desire as well as need. Hospitality is everyday pleasure, special-day pleasure, as well as difficult and dangerous in extreme situations. Historically, political hospitality has enriched Europe enormously (there is no Europe as we understand it without migration, invasion, hospitality) – although the dangers of welcoming guests might be illustrated by the fate of native Americans or that of the indigenous peoples of many formerly colonised nations. This reminds us that our current fascination with ourselves as magnanimous or less than magnanimous hosts ought to be tempered by a sense of ourselves as guests or visitors. Readers of Derrida tend to be fascinated by the impossible Law of hospitality – and it is of the nature of the Law to fascinate. We cannot live without it even if we cannot live with it. I hope this book has suggested that, with Derrida, we should also investigate at great length the pragmatic, empirical, material, contractual laws of hospitality – and that the feminine is not only another nickname for *différance*, but is also to be materialised.

Notes

1. Since I have made the case that naming is critical to hospitality I should like to note that: 'The name Wyandot (or Wendat) is Iroquoian for "people of the peninsula," a reference to a peninsula in southern Ontario east of Lake Huron where they originally lived. Their population was estimated at 20,000 in 1615 when first encountered by the French under Samuel de Champlain, who referred to them as Huron ('bristly-headed ruffian').' Bill Yenne, *The Encyclopedia of North American Indian Tribes: An Comprehensive Study of Tribes from the Abitibi to the Zuni* (London: Bison Books, 1986), p. 183. Thanks to Christopher Johnson for this reference. Bruce C. Johansen (ed.), *The Encyclopedia of Native American Economic History* (Westport, CT and London: Greenwood Press, 1999), dates the term 'Huron' from 1609, and suggests that it compares the men's hairstyles to the bristles on the forehead of a boar and is sometimes found racist by the Wyandot people (p. 264).
2. See my 'Hospitable Harems? A European Woman and Oriental Spaces in the Enlightenment', in *Extending Hospitality: Giving Space, Taking Time*, special issue of *Paragraph*, edited by M. Dikeç et al., 32:1 (2009), pp. 87–104, expanded in *Enlightenment Hospitality*, Chapter 5.
3. Since writing this sentence, Mark Robson has mentioned to me Dave Boothroyd's 'Of Ghostwriting and Possession: Translating "My Father", or *s'expliquer avec la mort*', in Joanne Morra, Mark Robson and Marquard Smith (eds), *The Limits of Death* (Manchester: Manchester University Press, 2000), pp. 198–219. Boothroyd, writing on death as his father is dying, quotes from 'Circumfession', finding a thought therein the most 'poignant and apposite' (p. 213) to this theme.

Bibliography

Works by Jacques Derrida

Adieu à Emmanuel Lévinas (Paris: Galilée, 1997)

'L'Animal que donc je suis (à suivre)', in Marie-Louise Mallet (ed.), *L'Animal autobiographique: Autour de Jacques Derrida* (Paris: Galilée, 1999)

Chaque fois unique, la fin du monde, ed. Pascale-Anne Brault and Michael Naas (Paris: Galilée, 2003)

Cosmopolites de tous les pays, encore un effort! (Paris: Galilée, 1997)

'Donner la mort', in Jean-Michel Rabaté and Michael Wetzel (eds), *L'Ethique du don: Jacques Derrida et la pensée du don*, (Paris: Transition, 1992)

Donner le temps. I, La fausse monnaie (Paris: Galilée, 1991)

L'Ecriture et la différence (Paris: Seuil, 1967)

Genèses, généalogies, genres et le génie: Les secrets de l'archive (Paris: Galilée, 2003)

Glas (Paris: Galilée, 1974)

H.C. pour la vie, c'est à dire (Paris: Galilée, 2002)

Mémoires pour Paul De Man (Paris: Galilée, 1988)

Le Monolinguisme de l'autre, ou, la prothèse d'origine (Paris: Galilée, 1996)

Points de suspension: Entretiens choisis et présentés par Elisabeth Weber (Paris: Galilée, 1992)

Politiques de l'amitié (Paris: Galilée, 1994)

Psyché: Inventions de l'autre (Paris: Galilée, 1987)

'Quand j'ai entendu l'expression *"délit d'hospitalité . . ."*', *Plein droit*, 34 (1997), pp. 3–8

'Responsabilité et hospitalité', in Mohammed Seffahi (ed.), *De l'hospitalité: Autour de Jacques Derrida* (Genouilleux: La passe du vent, 2001), pp. 131–49

Séminaire La bête et le souverain Volume I (2001–2002), ed. Michel Lisse, Marie-Louis Mallet and Ginette Michaud (Paris: Galilée, 2008)

Spectres de Marx: l'état de la dette, le travail du deuil et la nouvelle Internationale (Paris: Galilée, 1993)

Sur parole: Instantanés philosophiques (Saint-Etienne: Editions de l'Aube, 1999)

Ulysse gramophone: Deux mots pour Joyce (Paris: Galilée, 1987)

Bibliography

CO-AUTHORED WORKS

(with Geoffrey Bennington) *Jacques Derrida* (Paris: Seuil, 1991)
(with Anne Dufourmantelle) *De l'hospitalité: Anne Dufourmantelle invite Jacques Derrida à répondre* (Paris: Calmann-Lévy, 1997)
(with Marc Guillaume) *Marx en jeu* (Paris: Descartes et Cie, 1997)
(with Jürgen Habermas) *Le 'concept' du 11 septembre: Dialogues à New York (octobre–décembre 2001) avec Giovanna Borradori* (Paris: Galilée, 2004)
(with Elisabeth Roudinesco) 'Violences contre les animaux', in Jacques Derrida and Elisabeth Roudinesco, *De quoi demain . . . Dialogue* (Paris: Fayard and Galilée, 2001), pp. 105–27
(with Antoine Spire) *Au-delà des apparences* (Latresne: Le Bord de l'eau, 2002)
(with Michel Wieviorka) 'Accueil, éthique, droit et politique', in Mohammed Seffahi (ed.), *Autour de Jacques Derrida: De l'hospitalité* (Genouilleux: La passe du vent, 2001), pp. 179–95

Works by Jacques Derrida in translation

Acts of Literature/Jacques Derrida, ed. Derek Attridge (London and New York: Routledge, 1992)
Adieu to Emmanuel Levinas, translated by Pascale-Anne Brault and Michael Naas (Stanford: Stanford University Press, 1999)
'The Animal That Therefore I Am (More to Follow)', translated by David Wills, *Critical Inquiry*, 28 (2002), pp. 369–418
The Beast and the Sovereign, Volume 1, translated by Geoffrey Bennington (Chicago and London: Chicago University Press, 2009)
The Gift of Death, translated by David Wills (Chicago and London: University of Chicago Press, 1995)
Given Time. I, Counterfeit Money, translated by Peggy Kamuf (Chicago: Chicago University Press, 1992)
Glas, translated by John P. Leavey, Jr and Richard Rand (Lincoln and London: University of Nebraska Press, 1986)
'Hospitality, Justice and Responsibility: a Dialogue with Jacques Derrida', in Richard Kearney and Mark Dooley (eds), *Questioning Ethics: Contemporary Debates in Philosophy* (London and New York: Routledge, 1999), pp. 63–83
'Hostipitality', in Gil Anidjar (ed.), *Jacques Derrida: Acts of Religion* (New York and London: Routledge, 2002), pp. 356–420
Mémoires for Paul de Man, translated by Cecile Lindsay, Jonathan Culler and Eduardo Cadava (New York: Columbia University Press: 1986)
Monolingualism of the Other; or, The Prosthesis of the Origin, translated by Patrick Mensah (Stanford: Stanford University Press, 1998)

Negotiations. Interventions and Interviews 1971–2001, ed. Elizabeth Rottenberg (Stanford: Stanford University Press, 2002)

'A Number of Yes', translated by Brian Holmes, *Qui Parle*, 2:2 (1988), pp. 120–33

On Cosmopolitanism and Forgiveness, translated by Mark Dooley and Michael Hughes (London and New York: Routledge, 2001)

Points . . . Interviews, 1974–1994, ed. Elizabeth Weber, translated by Peggy Kamuf (Stanford: Stanford University Press, 1995)

Politics of Friendship, translated by George Collins (London and New York: Verso, 1997)

Specters of Marx: the State of the Debt, the Work of Mourning, and the New International, translated by Peggy Kamuf, with an introduction by Bernd Magnus and Stephen Cullenberg (New York and London: Routledge, 1994)

Spurs: Nietzsche's Styles. Eperons: Les Styles de Nietzsche, translated by Barbara Harlow (Chicago and London: Chicago University Press, 1979)

The Work of Mourning, ed. Pascale-Anne Brault and Michael Naas (Chicago: University of Chicago Press, 2001)

Writing and Difference, translated with an introduction and additional notes by Alan Bass (London: Routledge, 1990)

Co-authored works

(with Geoffrey Bennington) *Jacques Derrida*, translated by Geoffrey Bennington (Chicago and London: University of Chicago Press, 1993)

(with Anne Dufourmantelle) *Of Hospitality: Anne Dufourmantelle invites Jacques Derrida to Respond*, translated by Rachel Bowlby (Stanford: Stanford University Press, 2000)

(with Jürgen Habermas) *Philosophy in a Time of Terror: Dialogues with Jürgen Habermas and Jacques Derrida*, interviewed by Giovanna Borradori (Chicago and London: University of Chicago Press, 2003)

Works by Hélène Cixous

Le dernier Caravansérail (Odyssées) Programme, no pagination

Entre l'écriture (Paris: Des Femmes, 1986)

L'Exil de Joyce ou l'art de remplacement (Paris: Grasset, 1968)

'La Fugitive', *Etudes littérares*, 33:3 (2001), pp. 75–82

Le Jour où je n'étais pas là (Paris: Galilée, 2000)

Là (Paris: Gallimard, 1976)

'Mon Algériance', *Les Inrockuptibles*, 115, 20 August–2 September 1997, pp. 71–4

Messie (Paris: Des Femmes, 1996)

Or: les lettres de mon père (Paris: Des Femmes, 1997)

Osnabrück (Paris: Des Femmes, 1999)

'Pieds nus', in Leila Sebbar (ed.), *Une enfance algérienne* (Paris: Gallimard, 1997), pp. 57–66

Portrait de Jacques Derrida en Jeune Saint Juif (Paris: Galilée, 2001)

Rêve je te dis (Paris: Galilée, 2003)

Les Rêveries de la femme sauvage: Scènes primitives (Galilée: Paris, 2000)

'Le rire de la Méduse', *L'Arc*, 61 (1975), pp. 39–54

'La Venue à l'écriture', in *La Venue à l'écriture*, by Cixous, Madeleine Gagnon and Annie Leclerc (Paris: 10/18, 1977)

CO-AUTHORED WORKS

(with Catherine Clément) *La Jeune née* (Paris: 10/18, 1975)

(with Jacques Derrida) *Voiles* (Paris: Galilée, 1998)

Works by Hélène Cixous in translation

'Coming to Writing' and Other Essays, with an introductory essay by Susan Rubin Suleiman, ed. Deborah Jenson, translated by Sarah Cornell, Deborah Jenson, Ann Liddle and Susan Sellers (Cambridge, MA: Harvard University Press, 1991)

Dream I Tell You, translated by Beverley Bie Brahic (Edinburgh, Edinburgh University Press, 2006)

'The Laugh of the Medusa', translated by Keith Cohen and Paula Cohen, *Signs*, 1:4 (1976), pp. 875–93

Portrait of Jacques Derrida as a Young Jewish Saint, translated by Beverley Bie Brahic (New York: Columbia University Press, 2004)

Reading with Clarice Lispector, edited and translated by Verena Andermatt Conley (Minneapolis: University of Minnesota Press, 1990)

Readings: The Poetics of Blanchot, Joyce, Kafka, Kleist, Lispector, and Tsvetayava, edited and translated by Verena Andermatt Conley (Minneapolis: University of Minnesota Press, 1991)

Reveries of the Wild Woman: Primal Scenes, translated by Beverley Bie Brahic (Evanston: Northwestern University Press, 2006)

Stigmata: Escaping Texts (London and New York: Routledge, 1998)

The Writing Notebooks, edited and translated by Susan Sellers (New York and London: Continuum, 2004)

CO-AUTHORED WORKS

(with Catherine Clément) *The Newly Born Woman*, translated by Betsy Wing, foreword by Sandra Gilbert (Minneapolis: University of Minnesota Press; Theory and History of Literature Series, Vol. 24, 1986) (with Jacques Derrida) *Veils*, translated by Geoffrey Bennington (Stanford: Stanford University Press, 2001)

Works by Luce Irigaray

Amante marine (Paris: Minuit, 1980)
Le Corps à corps avec la mère (Montreal: Editions de la pleine lune, 1981)
Entre Orient et Occident: De la singularité à la communauté (Paris: Grasset, 1999)
Je, tu, nous. Pour une culture de la différence (Paris: Grasset, 1990)
Prières quotidiennes: Everyday Prayers, English translation by Luce Irigaray with Timothy Mathews (Paris/Nottingham: Maisonneuve and Larose/ University of Nottingham, 2004)
'La Transcendance de l'autre', in Bernard van Meenen (ed.), *Autour de l'idolâtrie: Figures actuelles de pouvoir et de domination* (Brussels: Publications des Facultés universitaires Saint Louis, 2003), pp. 43–55

Works by Luce Irigaray in translation

'Animal Compassion', in Peter Atterton and Matthew Calarco (eds), *Animal Philosophy* (London and New York: Continuum, 2004), pp. 195–201
Between East and West: From Singularity to Community, translated by Stephen Pluháček (New York: Columbia University Press, 2002)
'The Bodily Encounter with the Mother', in *The Irigaray Reader*, edited with an introduction by Margaret Whitford (Oxford: Basil Blackwell, 1991), pp. 34–46
Je, tu, nous. Toward a Culture of Difference, translated by Alison Martin (New York and London : Routledge, 1993)
Marine Lover. Of Friedrich Nietzsche, translated by Gillian C. Gill (New York: Columbia University Press, 1991)
'Questions to Emmanuel Levinas: On the Divinity of Love', in *The Irigaray Reader*, edited with an introduction by Margaret Whitford (Oxford: Basil Blackwell, 1991), pp. 178–89
Sharing the World (London and New York: Continuum, 2008)
Luce Irigaray: Teaching, edited by Luce Irigaray with Mary Green (London and New York: Continuum, 2008)
The Way of Love, translated by Heidi Bostic and Stephen Pluháček (London and New York: Continuum, 2002)
(Interview with Andrea Wheeler) 'About Being-two in an Architectural Perspective: An Interview with Luce Irigaray', *Journal of Romance Studies*, 4:2 (2004), pp. 91–107

Other Works

Adkins, Arthur W. H., '"Friendship" and "Self-Sufficiency" in Homer and Aristotle', *The Classical Quarterly*, 13:1 (1963), pp. 30–45

Ahmed, Sara, *Strange Encounters: Embodied Others in Post-Coloniality* (London and New York: Routledge, 2000)

Alloula, Malek, *Le Harem colonial, images d'un sous-érotisme* (essai illustré de photographies) (Paris: Séguier, 2001)

Alloula, Malek, *The Colonial Harem*, translated by Myrna Godzich and Wlad Godzich, Introduction by Barbara Harlow (Manchester: Manchester University Press, 1987)

Althusser, Louis, 'Idéologie et appareils idéologiques d'Etat', in *Positions* (Paris: Editions sociales, 1976), pp. 79–137

Althusser, Louis, 'Ideology and Ideological State Apparatuses', in *Lenin and Philosophy and Other Essays*, translated by Ben Brewster (London: New Left Books, 1971), pp. 121–73

Amara, F., with S. Zappi, *Ni Putes Ni Soumises* (Paris: La Découverte, 2004)

Andermatt Conley, Verena, *Hélène Cixous: Writing the Feminine* (Lincoln, NE: University of Nebraska Press, 1991)

Aristotle, *Eudemian Ethics*, in *The Complete Works of Aristotle*, The Revised Oxford Translation, ed. Jonathan Barnes, II (Princeton: Princeton University Press, 1984), pp. 1922–81

Aristotle, *Nicomachean Ethics*, translated by J. A. K. Thomson (revised by Hugh Tredennick) (Harmondsworth: Penguin, 1976)

Atterton, Peter and Matthew Calarco (eds), *Animal Philosophy* (London and New York: Continuum, 2004)

Badhwar, Neera Kapur (ed.), *Friendship: A Philosophical Reader* (Ithaca and London: Cornell University Press, 1993)

Barnett, Clive, 'Ways of Relating: Hospitality and the Acknowledgement of Otherness', *Progress in Human Geography*, 29:1 (2005), pp. 5–21

Barthes, Roland, *Mythologies* (Paris: Seuil, [1957] 1970)

Barthes, Roland, *Mythologies*, translated by Annette Lavers (London: Paladin, 1973)

Behdad, Ali, 'Nationalism and Immigration in the U.S.', *Diaspora*, 6:2 (1997), pp. 55–78

Belkaïd, Leyla, *Belles Algériennes de Geiser: costumes, parures et bijoux*, Introduction 'L'autre regard' by Malek Alloula (Paris: Marval, 2001)

Ben Jelloun, Tahar, *Eloge de l'amitié* (Dijon: Libris Editions, [1994] 1999)

Ben Jelloun, Tahar, *Hospitalité française: Racisme et immigration maghré-bine*, second edition (Paris: Seuil, 1997)

Ben Jelloun, Tahar, *French Hospitality: Racism and North African Immigrants*, translated by Barbara Bray (New York: Columbia University Press, [1984, 1987] 1999)

Bennington, Geoffrey, 'Derridabase', in Geoffrey Bennington and Jacques Derrida, *Jacques Derrida*, translated by Geoffrey Bennington (Chicago and London: University of Chicago Press, 1993)

Bennington, Geoffrey, *Dudding Des Noms de Rousseau* (Paris: Galilée, 1991)

Bennington, Geoffrey, *Interrupting Derrida* (London and New York: Routledge, 2000)

Benveniste, Emile, *Le Vocabulaire des institutions indo-européennes*, I (Paris: Minuit, 1969)

Benveniste, Emile, *Indo-European Language and Society*, translated by Elizabeth Palmer (London: Faber and Faber, 1973)

La Bible, translated and edited by André Chouraqui (Paris: Jean-Claude Lattès, 1992), Vol. 1 *Entête*

Bloom, Harold, *Poetry and Repression: Revisionism from Blake to Stevens* (New Haven and London: Yale University Press, 1976)

Blosser, Philip, and Marshell Carl Bradley (eds), *Friendship: Philosophic Reflections on a Perennial Concern* (Lanham, New York and Oxford: University Press of America, revised edition 1997)

Boothroyd, Dave, 'Of Ghostwriting and Possession: Translating "My Father", or *s'expliquer avec la mort*', in Joanne Morra, Mark Robson and Marquard Smith (eds), *The Limits of Death* (Manchester: Manchester University Press, 2000), pp. 198–219

Bourdieu, Pierre, and Jean-Claude Passeron, *The Inheritors: French Students and their Relation to Culture*, translated by Richard Nice (Chicago and London: Chicago University Press, 1979)

Bowlby, Rachel, 'Flight Reservations', *Oxford Literary Review*, 10 (1988), pp. 61–72

Brochier, J. J., *Camus, philosophe pour classes terminales* (Paris: Balland, 1979)

Brownmiller, Susan, *Against Our Will: Men, Women, and Rape* (London: Secker and Warburg, 1975)

Burke, Carolyn, Naomi Schor and Margaret Whitford (eds), *Engaging with Irigaray* (New York: Columbia University Press, 1994)

Cadava, Eduardo, Peter Connor and Jean-Luc Nancy (eds), *Who Comes After the Subject?* (New York: Routledge, 1991)

Camus, Albert, *L'Exil et le royaume* (Paris: Gallimard, 1957)

Camus, Albert, *Exile and the Kingdom*, translated by Justin O'Brien (Harmondsworth: Penguin, 1962)

Caputo, John D. (ed.), *Deconstruction in a Nutshell: A Conversation with Jacques Derrida* (New York: Fordham University Press, 1997)

Chanter, Tina, *Ethics of Eros: Irigaray's Rewriting of the Philosophers* (London and New York: Routledge, 1995)

Chardin, Jean, *Du bon usage du thé et des épices en Asie: Réponses à Monsieur Cabart de Villarmont*, ed. Ina Baghdiantz McCabe (Briare: L'inventaire, 2002)

Chardin, Jean, *Voyages en Perse*, ed. L. Langlès (Paris: Le Normant, 1811)

Charef, Mehdi, *Le Thé au harem d'Archi Ahmed* (Paris: Mercure de France, 1983)

Cicero, Marcus Tullius, *Laelius De Amicitia, On Friendship and the Dream of Scipio*, ed. and translated by J. G. F. Powell (Warminster: Aris and Phillips Ltd, 1990)

Coetzee, J. M., *Waiting for the Barbarians* (Harmondsworth: Penguin, [1980] 1982)

Cusset, François, *French Theory: Foucault, Derrida, Deleuze & Cie et les mutations de la vie intellectuelle aux Etats-Unis* (Paris: La Découverte, 2003)

Dayan-Herzbrun, Sonia and Etienne Tassin (eds), *Citoyennetés cosmopolitiques*, special issue of *Tumultes*, 24 (Paris: Kimé, 2005)

Delphy, Christine and Diana Leonard, *Familiar Exploitation: A New Analysis of Marriage in Contemporary Western Societies* (Cambridge: Polity Press, 1992)

De Man, Paul, *Allegories of Reading: Figural Language in Rousseau, Nietzsche, Rilke and Proust* (New Haven and London: Yale University Press, 1979)

Deutscher, Penelope, *A Politics of Impossible Difference: The Later Work of Luce Irigaray* (New York: Cornell University Press, 2002)

Deutscher, Penelope, *Yielding Gender: Feminism, Deconstruction and the History of Philosophy* (London and New York: Routledge, 1997)

Dikeç, Mustafa, 'Pera Peras Poros Longings for Spaces of Hospitality', *Cosmopolis*, special issue of *Theory, Culture and Society*, 19:1–2 (2002), pp. 227–47

Djebar, Assia, *Le Blanc de l'Algérie* (Paris: Albin Michel, 1995)

Dollimore, Jonathan, *Sexual Dissidence: Augustine to Wilde, Freud to Foucault* (Oxford: Clarendon Press, 1991)

Donaldson, Ian, *The Rapes of Lucretia: a Myth and its Transformations* (Oxford: Clarendon Press, 1982)

Dugas, Guy (ed.), *Algérie: Un rêve de fraternité* (Paris: Omnibus, 1997)

Duras, Marguerite, *L'Homme assis dans le couloir* (Paris: Minuit, 1980)

L'Etranger, ed. Rosie Pinhas-Delpuech, special issue of *JIM. Journal intime du Massif Central*, 8 (Editions du Bleu autour, 2004)

Extending Hospitality: Giving Space, Taking Time, special issue of *Paragraph*, 32:1 (2009), ed. Mustafa Dikeç, Nigel Clark and Clive Barnett.

Fallaize, Elizabeth, *French Women's Writing: Recent Fiction* (Basingstoke: Macmillan, 1993)

Fassin, Didier, Alain Morice and Catherine Quiminal (eds), *Les Lois de l'inhospitalité: Les politiques de l'immigration à l'épreuve des sans-papiers* (Paris: La Découverte, 1997)

Foucault, Michel, *Histoire de la sexualité. I, La Volonté de savoir* (Paris: Gallimard, 1976)

Bibliography

Foucault, Michel, *The History of Sexuality, Volume I: An Introduction*, translated by Robert Hurley (Harmondsworth: Penguin, 1978)

Friedman, Marilyn, 'Feminism and Modern Friendship: Dislocating the Community', in Neera Kapur Badhwar (ed.), *Friendship: A Philosophical Reader* (Ithaca and London: Cornell University Press, 1993), pp. 285–302

Friel, Brian, *Translations* (London and Boston: Faber and Faber, 1981)

Gauvin, Lise, Pierre L'Hérault and Alain Montandon (eds), *Le dire de l'hospitalité* (Clermont-Ferrand: Presses Universitaires Blaise Pascal, 2004)

Gilroy, Paul, *Between Camps: Race, Identity and Nationalism at the End of the Colour Line* (Harmondsworth: Allen Lane, 2000)

Gotman, Anne, *Le Sens de l'hospitalité: Essai sur les fondements sociaux de l'accueil de l'autre* (Paris: PUF, 2001)

Gotman, Anne (ed.), *Villes et hospitalité: Les municipalités et leurs 'étrangers'* (Paris: Editions de la Maison des Sciences de l'homme, 2004)

Grosz, Elizabeth, *Sexual Subversions: Three French Feminists* (Sydney: Allen and Unwin, 1989)

Guérin, Jeanyves, 'L'Autre comme hôte dans les derniers écrits algériens de Camus', in Lise Gauvin, Pierre L'Herault and Alain Montandon (eds), *Le dire de l'hospitalité* (Dijon: Presses Universitaires Blaise Pascal, 2004), pp. 145–56

Guyer, Sara, 'Albeit Eating: Towards an Ethics of Cannibalism', *Angelaki*, 2:1 (1995), pp. 63–80

Haddour, Azzedine, *Colonial Myths: History and Narrative* (Manchester: Manchester University Press, 2000)

Hallward, Peter, *Out of this World: Deleuze and the Philosophy of Creation* (London: Verso, 2006)

Hanrahan, Mairéad, '*Les Rêveries de la femme sauvage* ou le temps de l'hospitalité', *Expressions maghrébines*, special issue on Cixous, 2:2 (2003), pp. 55–70

Hanrahan, Mairéad, 'The Place of the Mother: Hélène Cixous's *Osnabrück*', *Paragraph*, 27:1 (2004), pp. 6–20

Haraway, Donna, *The Companion Species Manifesto: Dogs, People, and Significant Otherness* (Chicago: Prickly Paradigm Press, 2003)

Harrison, Nicholas, 'Learning From Experience: Hélène Cixous's "Pieds nus"', *Paragraph*, 27:1 (2004), pp. 21–32

Hiddlestone, Jane, 'Derrida, Autobiography and Postcoloniality', *French Cultural Studies*, 16:3 (2005), pp. 291–304

Hillis Miller, J., 'The Critic as Host', in Harold Bloom, Paul De Man, Jacques Derrida, Geoffrey H. Hartman, J. Hillis Miller, *Deconstruction and Criticism* (London and Henley: Routledge and Kegan Paul, 1979), pp. 217–53

Hobson, Marian, 'Derrida: Hostilities and Hostages (to Fortune)', *Paragraph*, 28:3 (2005), pp. 79–84

Bibliography

Hobson, Marian, *Jacques Derrida: Opening Lines* (London and New York: Routledge, 1998)

Hocqenghem, Guy, *La Beauté du métis* (Paris: Albin Michel, 1979)

Hodge, Joanna, 'Irigaray Reading Heidegger', in Carolyn Burke, Naomi Schor and Margaret Whitford (eds), *Engaging with Irigaray* (New York: Columbia University Press, 1994), pp. 191–209

Homer, *The Odyssey*, translated by A. T. Murray, revised by George E. Dimmock, (Cambridge, MA: Harvard University Press, 1998)

Homer, *The Odyssey*, translated by E. V. Rieu (Harmondsworth: Penguin, 1946)

Hulme, Peter, *Colonial Encounters: Europe and the Native Caribbean, 1492–1797* (London and New York: Methuen, 1986)

James, Ian, *Pierre Klossowski: The Persistence of a Name* (Oxford: Legenda, 2000)

Johansen, Bruce C., (ed.), *The Encyclopedia of Native American Economic History* (Westport, Connecticut and London: Greenwood Press, 1999)

Johnson, Christopher (ed.), *Thinking in Dialogue: The Role of the Interview in Post-War French Thought*, special issue of *Nottingham French Studies*, 42:1 (2003)

Jones, Ann Rosalind, 'Writing the Body: Towards an Understanding of l'Ecriture féminine', in Elaine Showalter (ed.), *The New Feminist Criticism* (London: Virago, 1986), pp. 369–71

Judy, Ronald A. T., *(Dis)forming the American Canon: African-Arabic Slave Narratives and the Vernacular* (Minnesota: University of Minnesota Press, 1993)

Kamuf, Peggy, *Signature Pieces: On the Institution of Authorship* (Ithaca and London: Cornell University Press, 1988)

Kamuf, Peggy, 'To Give Place: Semi-Approaches to Hélène Cixous', in Lynne Huffer (ed.), *Another Look, Another Woman: Retranslations of French Feminism*, special issue of *Yale French Studies*, 87 (1995), pp. 68–89

Kant, Immanuel, *Anthropology from a Pragmatic Point of View*, translated by M. J. Gregor (The Hague: Martinus Nijhof, 1974)

Kant, Immanuel, *Observations on the Feeling of the Beautiful and the Sublime*, translated by John T. Goldthwait (Berkeley and Los Angeles: University of California Press, 1960)

Kant, Immanuel, *Perpetual Peace and Other Essays*, translated by Ted Humphrey (Indianapolis: Hackett Publishing Company, 1983)

Kaplan, Caren, *Questions of Travel: Postmodern Discourses of Displacement* (Durham, NC and London: Duke University Press, 1996)

Kavanagh, Thomas, *Writing the Truth: Authority and Desire in Rousseau* (Berkeley: University of California Press, 1987)

Kearney, Richard, 'Aliens and Others: Between Girard and Derrida', *Cultural Values*, 3:3 (1999), pp. 251–62

Kenney, Anthony, *The Aristotelian Ethics: A Study of the Relationship between the* Eudemian *and* Nicomachean Ethics *of Aristotle* (Oxford: Oxford University Press, 1978)

Khatibi, Abdelkebir, *Amour Bilingue* (Paris: Fata Morgana, 1983)

Khatibi, Abdelkebir, *Love in Two Languages*, translated by Richard Howard (Minneapolis: University of Minnesota Press, 1990)

Klossowski, Pierre, *Les Lois de l'hospitalité, La Révocation de l'édit de Nantes, Roberte ce soir, Le Souffleur* (Paris: Gallimard, 1970)

Klossowski, Pierre, *Roberte Ce Soir and The Revocation of the Edict of Nantes*, translated by Austryn Wainhouse (London: Calder and Boyars, 1971)

Knight, Diana, *Barthes and Utopia: Space, Travel, Writing* (Oxford: Clarendon Press, 1997)

Kofman, Sarah, *Le Respect des femmes (Kant et Rousseau)* (Paris: Galilée, 1982)

Kristeva, Julia, *Etrangers à nous-mêmes* (Paris: Fayard, 1988)

Kristeva, Julia, *Strangers to Ourselves*, translated by Leon S. Roudiez (New York: Columbia University Press, 1991)

Kuzniar, Alice A., *Melancholia's Dog* (Chicago and London: University of Chicago Press, 2006)

Lane, Jeremy, 'Deleuze In and Out of this World', *Paragraph*, 30:2 (2007), pp. 109–16

Lane, Jeremy, '*La Femme adultère* d'Albert Camus', *Vives Lettres*, 13 (2002), pp. 187–203

Le Doeuff, Michèle, *Recherches sur l'imaginaire philosophique* (Paris: Payot, 1980)

Le Doeuff, Michèle, *The Philosophical Imaginary*, translated by Colin Gordon (Stanford: Stanford University Press, 1990)

Leclerc, Annie, *Parole de femme* (Paris: Grasset, 1974)

Lévinas, Emmanuel, *L'Au-delà du Verset: Lectures et discours talmudiques* (Paris: Minuit, 1982)

Lévinas, Emmanuel, *Autrement qu'être ou au-delà de l'essence* (The Hague: Martinus Nijhoff, 1978)

Levinas, Emmanuel, *Beyond the Verse: Talmudic Readings and Lectures*, translated by Gary D. Mole (London: Athlone, 1994)

Lévinas, Emmanuel, *Dieu, la mort et le temps* (Paris: Grasset, 1993)

Levinas, Emmanuel, *Difficult Freedom: Essays on Judaism*, translated by Séan Hand (Baltimore: Johns Hopkins University Press, 1990)

Levinas, Emmanuel, 'The Name of a Dog, Or Natural Rights', in Peter Atterton and Matthew Calarco (eds), *Animal Philosophy* (London and New York: Continuum, 2004), pp. 47–9

Levinas, Emmanuel, *Otherwise than Being or Beyond Essence*, translated by Alphonso Lingis (Pittsburgh: Duquesne University Press, 1998)

Lévinas, Emmanuel, *Totalité et infini: Essai sur l'extériorité* (The Hague: Martinus Nijhoff, [1971] 1980)

Levinas, Emmanuel, *Totality and Infinity: An Essay on Exteriority*, translated by Alphonso Lingis (Pittsburgh: Duquesne University Press, 1969)

Lispector, Clarice, *The Passion According to G.H.*, translated by Ronald Sousa (Minneapolis: University of Minnesota Press, 1988)

Lyndon Shanley, Mary, 'Marital Slavery and Friendship: John Stuart Mill's *The Subjection of Women*', in Neera Kapur Badhwar (ed.), *Friendship: A Philosophical Reader* (Ithaca and London: Cornell University Press, 1993), pp. 267–84

Macey, David, 'The Algerian with the Knife', *parallax*, 4:2 (1998), pp. 159–67

Magazine littéraire, mai 2006

Maley, Willy, 'Review of Jacques Derrida, *Monolingualism of the Other; or, The Prosthesis of Origin*, trans. Patrick Mensah (Stanford: Stanford University Press, 1998)', *Textual Practice*, 15:1 (Spring 2001), pp. 123–34

Marrati, Paulo, 'Le rêve et le danger: où se perd la différence sexuelle?', in Jean-Michel Rabaté and Michael Wetzel (eds), *L'Ethique du Don: Jacques Derrida et la pensée du don* (Paris: Transition, 1992), pp. 194–211

Massignon, Louis, *Parole donnée* (Paris: Seuil, 1983)

Meltzer, Françoise, *Hot Property: The Stakes and Claims of Literary Originality* (Chicago and London: University of Chicago Press, 1994)

Memmi, Albert, *The Colonizer and the Colonized*, translated by Howard Greenfield, introduced by Jean-Paul Sartre, new Introduction by Liam O'Dowd (London: Earthscan, 2003)

Memmi, Albert, *Portrait du Colonisé* (Paris: Gallimard, [1957] 1985)

Michaud, Ginette, '"Un acte d'hospitalité ne peut être que poétique": Seuils et délimitations de l'hospitalité derridienne', in Lise Gauvin, Pierre L'Hérault and Alain Montandon (eds), *Le dire de l'hospitalité* (Clermont-Ferrand: Presses Universitaires Blaise Pascal, 2004), pp. 33–60

Miller, William Ian, *The Anatomy of Disgust* (Cambridge, MA: Harvard University Press, 1997)

Montaigne, Michel de, *Essays*, translated by J. M. Cohen (Harmondsworth: Penguin, 1958)

Montaigne, Michel de, *Oeuvres complètes*, ed. Albert Thibaudet and Maurice Rat (Paris: Pléiade, 1962)

Naas, Michael, *Taking on the Tradition: Jacques Derrida and the Legacies of Deconstruction* (Stanford: Stanford University Press, 2003)

Nietzsche, *Ecce Homo* in *On the Genealogy of Morals and Ecce Homo*, edited and translated by W. Kaufmann (New York: Random House, 1969)

Ozouf, Mona, 'Fraternité', in François Furet, Mona Ozouf and Bronislaw Baczko (eds), *Dictionnaire critique de la Révolution française* (Paris: Flammarion, 1992), pp. 731–41

Ozouf, Mona, 'Fraternity', in François Furet and Mona Ozouf, *A Critical Dictionary of the French Revolution*, translated by Arthur Goldhammer

(Cambridge, MA and London: Harvard University Press, 1989), pp. 694–703

Pakaluk, M., 'The Egalitarianism of the *Eudemian Ethics*', *The Classical Quarterly*, New Series, 48:2 (1998), pp. 411–32

Patai, Daphne, 'Ethical Problems of Personal Narratives, or Who Should Eat the Last Piece of Cake', *International Journal of Oral History*, 8:1 (1987), pp. 5–27

Plato, *The Dialogues of Plato*, Vol. II, translated by Benjamin Jowett (London: Sphere, 1970)

Pooley, Timothy, *Chtimi: The Urban Vernaculars of Northern France* (Clevedon: Multilingual Matters, 1996)

Portevin, Catherine, 'Editorial', in *Les Lumières des idées pour demain*, Télérama hors série, Paris, 2006

Raynal, Abbé de, *Histoire philosophique et politique des deux Indes*, ed. Yves Benot (Paris: La Découverte, [1981] 2001)

Reece, Steve, *The Stranger's Welcome: Oral Theory and the Aesthetics of the Homeric Hospitality Scene* (Ann Arbor: University of Michigan Press, 1993)

Rice, Alison, 'Rêveries d'Algérie. Une terre originaire à perte de vue dans l'oeuvre d'Hélène Cixous', *Expressions maghrébines*, special issue on Cixous, 2:2 (2003), pp. 93–108

Rorty, Amélie Oksenberg (ed.), *Essays on Aristotle's Ethics* (Los Angeles: University of California Press, 1980)

Rosello, Mireille, 'Frapper aux portes invisibles avec des mots-valises: la *malgériance* d'Hélène Cixous', in Lise Gauvin, Pierre L'Herault and Alain Montandon (eds), *Le dire de l'hospitalité* (Dijon: Presses Universitaires Blaise Pascal, 2004), pp. 61–74

Rosello, Mireille, *Postcolonial Hospitality: The Immigrant as Guest* (Stanford: Stanford University Press, 2001)

Rossum Guyon, Françoise van, and Myriam Diaz-Diocaretz (eds), *Hélène Cixous, chemins d'une écriture* (Amsterdam: Rodopi, 1990)

Rousseau, Jean-Jacques, *Confessions*, translated by J. M. Cohen (Harmondsworth: Penguin, 1953)

Rousseau, J.-J., *Oeuvres complètes*, ed. Bernard Gagnebin and Marcel Raymond, 5 vols (Paris: Pléiade, 1959–95)

Sayad, Abdelmalek, *La double absence: Des illusions de l'émigré aux souffrances de l'immigré* (Paris: Seuil, 1999)

Scharfman, Ronnie, 'Narratives of Internal Exile: Cixous, Derrida and the Vichy Years in Algeria', in Anne Donadey and H. Adlai Murdoch (eds), *Postcolonial Theory and Francophone Literary Studies* (Gainesville: University Press of Florida, 2004)

Schérer, René, *Hospitalités* (Paris: Economica, 2004)

Schérer, René, *Zeus hospitalier: éloge de l'hospitalité* (Paris: La Table Ronde, [1993] 2005)

Sellers, Susan, *Hélène Cixous: Authorship. Autobiography and Love* (Cambridge: Polity and Blackwell, 1996)

Sellers, Susan (ed.), *The Hélène Cixous Reader* (New York: Routledge, 1994)

Shiach, Morag, *Hélène Cixous: A Politics of Writing* (London: Routledge, 1991)

Smith Pangle, Lorraine, *Aristotle and the Philosophy of Friendship* (Cambridge: Cambridge University Press, 2003)

Somerville, Margaret, *Body/Landscape Journals* (Melbourne: Spinifex Press, 1999)

Starobinski, Jean, 'Rousseau's Happy Days', *New Literary History*, 11 (1979), pp. 147–66

Still, Judith, 'A Feminine Economy: Some Preliminary Thoughts', in Helen Wilcox, Keith McWaters, Ann Thompson and Linda Williams (eds), *The Body and the Text: Hélène Cixous, Reading and Teaching* (Brighton: Harvester, 1990), pp. 49–60

Still, Judith, 'Acceptable Hospitality: from Rousseau's Levite to the Strangers in our Midst Today', *Journal of Romance Studies*, 3:2 (2003), pp. 1–14

Still, Judith, 'Can Woman Ever be Defined?', in Andrea Cady (ed.), *Women Teaching French: Five Papers on Language and Theory* (Loughborough: University of Loughborough European Research Centre, Studies in European Culture and Society 5, 1991), pp. 29–37

Still, Judith, 'Derrida: Guest and Host', *Paragraph*, 28:3 (2005), pp. 81–97

Still, Judith, *Enlightenment Hospitality: Cannibals, Harems and Adoption* (Oxford: Voltaire Foundation, 2011)

Still, Judith, 'Enlightenment Hospitality: The Case of Chardin', *French Studies*, 60:3, 2006, pp. 364–8

Still, Judith, *Feminine Economies: Thinking Against the Market in the Enlightenment and the Late Twentieth Century* (Manchester: Manchester University Press, 1997)

Still, Judith, 'France and the Paradigm of Hospitality', *Third Text*, 20 (2006), ed. Yoseva Loshitsky, pp. 703–10

Still, Judith, 'French {In}Hospitality: Cixous and *le francais au pluriel*', *Contemporary French Civilization*, 33:2 (2009), pp. 19–41

Still, Judith, 'Gendered Economies and Aneconomies: the Ambiguous Case of Barthes's "Incidents"', *Iichiko intercultural*, 11 (1999), pp. 43–64

Still, Judith, *Justice and Difference in the Works of Rousseau: 'Bienfaisance' and 'Pudeur'* (Cambridge: Cambridge University Press, 1993)

Still, Judith, 'Language as Hospitality: Revisiting Intertextuality via *Monolingualism of the Other*', *Paragraph*, 27:1 (2004), pp. 113–27

Still, Judith, 'Not Really Prostitution: The Political Economy of Sexual Tourism in Gide's *Si le grain ne meurt*', *French Studies*, 54 (2000), pp. 17–34

Still, Judith, 'When is a Technology not a Technology? When it's Women's Work', in *Tekhne, Technique Technologie*, special issue of *The Australian Journal of French Studies*, forthcoming

Still, Judith and Michael Worton, *Textuality and Sexuality* (Manchester: Manchester University Press, 1990)

Sullivan Kruger, Kathryn, *Weaving the Word. The Metaphorics of Weaving and Female Textual Production* (Selingsgrove: Susquehanna University Press London: Associated University Presses, 2001)

Tarr, Carrie, *Reframing Difference:* Beur *and* Banlieue *Film-Making in France* (Manchester and New York: Manchester University Press, 2005)

Thomson, A. J. P., *Deconstruction and Democracy: Derrida's 'Politics of Friendship'* (London and New York: Continuum, 2005)

Tregoning, William, 'It Feels Like Home: Hospitality in a Postcolonial Space', *Text Theory Critique*, 7 (2003), no pagination

Tzelepis, Elena and Athena Athanasiou (eds), *Rewriting Difference: Luce Irigaray and 'the Greeks'* (New York: SUNY Press, 2010)

Van der Cruysse, Dirk, *Chardin Le Persan* (Paris: Fayard, 1998)

Vasseleu, Cathryn, *Textures of Light: Vision and Touch in Irigaray, Levinas and Merleau-Ponty* (London and New York: Routledge, 1998)

Voltaire, *Dictionnaire philosophique*, ed. René Pomeau (Paris: Garnier-Flammarion, 1964)

Voltaire, *Zaïre, Le Fanatisme ou Mahomet le prophète, Nanine ou l'homme sans préjugé, Le Café ou l'écossaise*, ed. Jean Goldzink (Paris: Flammarion, 2004)

Wahnich, Sophie, *L'Impossible citoyen: L'Étranger dans le discours de la Révolution française* (Paris: Albin Michel, 1997)

Whitford, Margaret, 'Irigaray, Utopia, and the Death Drive', in Carolyn Burke, Naomi Schor and Margaret Whitford (eds), *Engaging with Irigaray* (New York: Columbia University Press, 1994), pp. 379–400

Whitford, Margaret, *Luce Irigaray: Philosophy in the Feminine* (London: Routledge, 1991)

Worton, Michael and Judith Still (eds), *Intertextuality: Theories and Practices* (Manchester: Manchester University Press, 1990)

Yenne, Bill, *The Encyclopedia of North American Indian Tribes: A Comprehensive Study of Tribes from the Abitibi to the Zuni* (London: Bison Books, 1986)

Index

Please note: this index does not include all names referenced in the book

Index

feminine economy, 133
as 'French feminist', 2, 47n,
  150–2, 177
on friendship, 104, 161–2
on Jewishness, 2, 25, 54, 145,
  162, 165, 166–7, 171, 185n
  194, 197
on maid Aïcha (Messaouda),
  162–4
mother, 160, 164, 171, 252n
name and 'identity', 25, 145,
  146, 150–3, 178n, 197, 215n
on reading, 36, 52, 53–4, 55, 84,
  107, 150, 159, 162
reception by Anglophone readers,
  2, 144, 181n
relation to cat, 232–8, 252–3n;
  see also Messie
writing, 23–7, 48n, 180–1n, 215,
  237, 250n, 259
writings, 181n; 'Coming
  to Writing' (La Venue à
  l'écriture), 25–6, 36n, 47n, 52,
  152; Le dernier Caravansérail
  (programme notes), 55–6, 81,
  199, 205, 215n, 222; Dream
  I Tell You (Rêve je te dis),
  48n, 120, 181n, 184n; Entre
  l'écriture, 24; L'Exil de Joyce,
  232; 'La Fugitive', 145–6; Le
  Jour où je n'étais pas là, 253n;
  'The Laugh of the Medusa'
  ('Le rire de la Méduse'), 24,
  151; Messie, 221, 234–8, 241,
  243, 250n, 252n, 253–4n; 'My
  Algeriance' ('Mon Algériance'
  and 'Pieds nus'), 152–3, 158,
  160–7, 178n, 180n, 183n; The
  Newly Born Woman (La jeune
  née), 24, 53–4, 107, 124, 151,
  223; Or, 221, 232–4, 262n;
  Osnabrück, 253n; Portrait
  of Jacques Derrida (Portrait
  de Jacques Derrida), 120,

156, 182n, 183n, 194, 197,
  215n; Reading with Clarice
  Lispector, 254n; Readings: The
  Poetics, 254n; Reveries of the
  Wild Woman (Les Rêveries
  de la femme sauvage), 120,
  152, 161–4, 168–70, 184–5n;
  'Savoir' in Veils (Voiles),
  159–60, 253n; Stigmata,
  178n, 252–3n; The Writing
  Notebooks, 181n
Cloots, Anacharsis, 30
Coetzee, J. M., 176, 178n, 185n
colonialism, 1, 3–4, 14, 29, 36,
  37–40, 42n, 45n, 54–5, 76, 77,
  103, 107, 115, 143–6, 151–86,
  187–8, 206, 210, 230, 259,
  262, 264
Colonna, Yvan, 201
Condorcet, 30, 202
Corsican hospitality, 29, 33, 201
cultural difference, 18–20, 23, 25,
  36, 39, 46–7n, 72n, 78–9, 133,
  144–5, 151, 157, 160, 181n,
  182n, 187–91, 197–218, 222,
  224, 256, 257, 259, 264

death, 32, 61, 64, 66, 67, 75, 78,
  95, 101–6, 113, 117–18, 119,
  138n, 151,168, 172, 174,
  185n, 224, 225, 229, 230, 238,
  243, 246, 257, 265, 267n
Debré, Jean-Louis, 32, 48n, 189
deconstruction, 1, 4, 42n, 43n, 80,
  85, 104, 125, 137n, 220, 230,
  232, 249n, 250n, 252n, 258
Deleuze, Gilles, 43n, 80, 90n
Demeter, 66
Derrida, Jacques
  on boundaries, 221–2, 249
  carno-phallogocentricism, 222,
    225, 230
  différance, 44n, 86, 106, 193,
    194, 250n, 261, 266, 267

285